WINTHROP PUBLISHERS, INC.

Cambridge, Massachusetts

SEARCH FOR ALTERNATIVES:
Public Policy And The
Study Of The Future

Franklin Tugwell

Pomona College

I want to express my appreciation to the students of my future studies seminars, who contributed a great deal, in their own manner, to shaping the contents of this book, and to Pomona College, where I have found flexibility, support and encouragement along the way. For assistance in preparing the manuscript I am indebted to Ruth Rice and Geraldine Jackson.

Cover by Donya Melanson

ACKNOWLEDGMENTS

John Platt, "What We Must Do," from *Science*, Vol. 166 (November 28, 1969), pp. 1115–1121. Copyright © 1969 by the American Association for the Advancement of Science. Reprinted by permission of the publisher and the author.

Bertrand de Jouvenel, "On the Nature of the Future." Excerpted from Chapter 1, "On the Nature of the Future" and Chapter 2, "A Need of Our Species" in *The Art of Conjecture* by Bertrand de Jouvenel, copyright © 1967 by Basic Books, Inc., Publishers, New York, and George Weidenfeld & Nicolson Ltd., London.

O. D. Duncan, "Social Forecasting: The State of the Art." From *The Public Interest* (Fall, 1969). Reprinted by permission of the publisher. Presented originally as a paper at the Proceedings of the Technical Forecasting Conference, held by the College of Business Administration, University of Texas, Austin, Texas, April, 1969.

Olaf Helmer and Nicholas Rescher, "On the Epistemology of the Inexact Sciences." Reprinted by permission of The Rand Corporation. From *Management Science* (1959).

Elise Boulding, "Futurology and the Imaging Capacity of the West," from *Human Futuristics*, edited by Magoroh Maruyama and James A. Dator, Social Science Research Institute, University of Hawaii, Honolulu. Reprinted by permission of the author.

Irene Taviss, "Futurology and the Study of Values." Reprinted from *International Social Science Journal*, Vol. XXI, No. 4, 1969, by permission of UNESCO.

Herman Kahn, "The Alternative World Futures Approach," from Morton Kaplan (ed.) *New Approaches to International Relations* (St. Martins, 1968). Reprinted by permission of the Hudson Institute.

Selwyn Enzer, "Delphi and Cross-Impact Techniques: An Effective Combination for Systematic Futures Analysis." From *Futures* (March, 1971). Reprinted by permission of the publisher, IPC Science and Technology Press, and the author.

Robert H. Ament, "Comparison of Delphi Forecasting Studies in 1964 and 1969," from *Futures* (March, 1970). Reprinted by permission of the publisher, IPC Science and Technology Press.

Arthur I. Waskow, "Looking Forward: 1999," from Robert Jungk and Johan Galtung (eds.) *Mankind 2000* (Allyn and Unwin, 1969). Reprinted by permission of the author.

Paul Ehrlich, "Eco-Catastrophe," from *Ramparts* (September, 1969). Copyright © 1969 by Paul R. Ehrlich. Reprinted by permission of the author.

Jay W. Forrester, "Counterintuitive Behavior of Social Systems." This paper appears in the book, *Toward Global Equilibrium: Collected Papers*, Dennis L. Meadows, ed. Copyright © 1972 by Wright-Allen Press, Cambridge, Mass., 02142.

Johan Galtung, "On the Future of the International System." From *Journal of Peace Research* (1967). Reprinted by permission of the publisher.

Daniel Bell, "Notes on the Post-Industrial Society." From "Notes on the Post-Industrial Society, Part I," by Daniel Bell in *The Public Interest*, No. 6 (Winter, 1967), © 1967 by National Affairs, Inc., and "Notes on the Post-Industrial Society, Part II," by Daniel Bell in *The Public Interest*, No. 7 (Spring, 1967), © 1967 by National Affairs, Inc.

Bertram Gross, "Friendly Fascism: A Model for America." From *Social Policy* (November-December, 1970). Reprinted by permission.

Donald N. Michael, "On Coping with Complexity: Urban Planning and Politics in 1976." Reprinted by permission of *Daedalus*, Journal of the American Academy of Arts and Sciences, Boston, Mass. Fall, 1968, *The Conscience of the City*.

Alvin Toffler, "The Coming Ad-Hocracy." From *Future Shock* by Alvin Toffler. Copyright © 1970 by Alvin Toffler. Reprinted by permission of Random House, Inc., and The Bodley Head, London.

58044

CONTENTS

INTRODUCTION

The world's greatest need is an appetite for the future . . . All healthy societies are ready to sacrifice the existential moment for their children's future and for children after these. The sense of the future is behind all good policies. Unless we have it, we can give nothing either wise or decent to the world.[1]

C. P. Snow

Anyone in touch with recent trends in the social sciences is aware of the startling growth of interest in the study of the future that has taken place in the last decade. Following the lead of prominent scholars in half a dozen countries, the formal study of the future has become an important trans-national intellectual phenomenon, replete with its own commissions, institutes, professional organizations, journals, and university courses. This development is all the more surprising because until recently the future has been treated, for practical purposes, as the special preserve of dreamers, doomsters and science fiction writers.

What are the reasons for this sudden growth of interest in the future? Part of it, as Daniel Bell has pointed out, is surely due to the magnetism of the year 2000, the coming millennial turning point.[2] Historically, the approach of symbolic dates of this kind has always stimulated speculation about the great tides of change in civilization and about possibilities the next great era might hold out. Certainly many of the forecasts of technological wonderlands made up of gleaming cities, push-button households and two-hour work days fit into this category.

But much more important, though related, is the emergence of a new orientation or attitude toward the future in our society generally. Increasingly social analysts are becoming aware that we face many profoundly difficult tasks in the immediate future if we are to secure a decent existence for our children and grandchildren. Writing in 1964, Kenneth Boulding pointed to an "invisible college" of people in many countries who had come to the conclusion that we stand precariously in the midst of a great transition in man's career—akin to the transition from pre-civilized to civilized society—but that construction of livable and enduring societies in the new age will require a commitment of energy and resources and a level of enlightenment beyond that which any era of the past has brought forth.[3] Today, the college of which

[1] Quoted in Louise Young, ed., *Population in Perspective* (New York: Oxford University Press, 1968), p. xi. From C. P. Snow, "What is the World's Greatest Need?" *New York Times Magazine* (April 2, 1961).

[2] "The Year 2000: Trajectory of an Idea," introduction to the special issue of *Daedalus* entitled *Toward the Year 2000: Work in Progress* (Summer, 1967), p. 640.

[3] *The Meaning of the Twentieth Century: The Great Transition* (New York: Harper and Row, 1964), pp. 191–3.

Boulding spoke is no longer invisible. It would be difficult to list the number of responsible social analysts who have joined its ranks and who agree with his assessment that "our precious little planet, this blue-green cradle of life with its rosy mantle, is in one of the most critical stages, perhaps the most critical stage, of its whole existence." Symbolic of this emerging consensus is the formation of the Club of Rome, an international group of leaders in government and business who have dedicated both time and money in an attempt to clarify and to call attention to what they have called the "predicament of mankind," fearing that the problems of population, war, race conflict, resource depletion and pollution, and political breakdown may overwhelm our civilization before we accurately assess their seriousness.[4]

As a result of the spreading recognition of this predicament, and of its relationship to the great transition in which we are involved, we live increasingly, and uneasily, in the shadow of the future; it has become a kind of brooding omnipresence in our lives. This has led many social analysts and policy-makers to press urgently for a much larger investment of energy and resources in clarifying the range of future alternatives open to us as a society and in specifying how we can best take advantage of the options we do have. A portion of recent work on the future has been a response to this call for action.

On a more practical level, the growth of futures studies in the last decade has been closely tied to the increasing commitment among social scientists to producing more operational knowledge in order to improve the quality of public policies. Experts in policy analysis have long understood that rational, goal-directed choices are possible only on the basis of some conceptions of the future, even if they are fuzzy or unrecognized, or both. At the same time, rapid transformative change combined with increasing density, complexity and interdependence have forced upon our institutions, private and public alike, the need to handle a constantly growing volume of difficult decisions, decisions which more and more involve, by necessity, long-range consequences. Perceiving these conditions, a growing clan of analysts has set to work to improve our ability to: 1) understand the predictive behavior of policy-makers and key institutions; 2) forecast what is foreseeable with care and elegance; 3) imagine what might be—that is, fashion images of plausible alternatives; and, finally, 4) help determine the strategic availability of the more desirable outcomes. Perhaps the most surprising fact about all of this is the degree of attention and support futures analysts have attracted in so short a time and in the face of considerable skepticism on the part of professional colleagues.

Whether their work is motivated by a generalized sense of unease and jeopardy or by a desire to take a direct hand in improving our institutional ability to deal with the future, most modern futurists share a common perspective which distinguishes them from the religious prophets and literary specu-

[4]The Club of Rome, formed in 1968, is best known for its sponsorship of the M.I.T. World Dynamics Project whose conclusions are reported in The Limits to Growth: A Report for the Club of Rome's Project on the Predicament of Mankind (New York: Universe Books, 1972).

lators who were the futurists of the past. The key to this perspective is its unyielding nondeterminism. Modern futurists view the future as a field of choice; they are concerned not so much with predicting what *will* be as with knowing what *might* be, and how this knowledge fits into the context of public policy in action. Thus the futurist perspective treats man as a being "in process," humanized by his capacity to contemplate and judge himself and choose his future, free only if he can build a world which allows him to develop his potentialities. It treats social institutions, especially political institutions, as creations by which groups of men organize their lives to shape their futures, and thus the means to build and sustain a decent world.

This collection brings together some of the best results of the decade's work in policy-oriented futures research, especially that which is broadly social, political and institutional in focus. Its object is to make available—to the student, the general reader, the policy-maker and the policy-adviser—a selection of readings that is both imaginative and sophisticated from the social science perspective and that contains representative work from many of the approaches that have been adopted by researchers in the field. The essays reflect a wide diversity in style and subject matter as well as differing political perspectives. Some are formal and "hard," with carefully sewn up logical arguments; others are quite literally "wild-eyed," methodologically imprecise but highly suggestive. Notorious military industrial technocrats, such as Herman Kahn, and some of their most cogent critics, such as Arthur Waskow, come together here because of their shared concern about the future and how to generate useful knowledge about it.

This diversity occurs throughout the futures research movement, in part because it has drawn people from a surprising variety of fields and professions. A recent survey of the academic background of individuals involved in futures research lists fifty-three fields, ranging from dance to chemical engineering.[5] This diversity also stems from the fact that futurists themselves have different perspectives on their own roles. Some are planners, immersed in particular problem areas; others are social critics, hoping to provide an early warning system for dangers to come; and still others are what might be called "synergists," seeking to stretch our social imagination, make new connections, and perhaps even show us how good things could be if we could only get "from here to there."[6]

Although it is rapidly becoming institutionalized, the study of the future is not a discipline in which the criteria for useful knowledge are narrowly defined by a commonly accepted paradigm nor, indeed, is it likely that it will soon become a discipline in the standard meaning of that term. This is because futures research is not concerned primarily with a form of behavior or a particular piece of the social world; rather, its specialty is a way of thinking that facilitates the linking of values, data, and theory to policy choices.

[5]John McHale, *Typological Survey of Futures Research in the United States*, Study sponsored by the Division of Mental Health Programs, National Institute of Mental Health, 1970, mimeo, 21.
[6]For further information on varieties of futurists and their orientations, see the Introduction to Alvin Toffler, ed., *The Futurists* (New York: Random House, 1972).

To be more explicit: rational, action-oriented choices, whatever the context, require a distinctive combination of intellectual tasks, especially if those choices are made consciously. A condensed description of these tasks includes the following:[7]

1) *Normative thinking.* The clarification and specification of values and goals. (What is good?)

2) *Scientific thinking.* The explanation of behavior, both static and dynamic, with predictive intent. (How do things work?)

3) *Futurist thinking.* The elaboration of possibilities and alternatives. (What is possible and what is probable?)

4) *Strategic thinking.* The specification of action paths or sets designed to attain desired outcomes at estimated cost. (How can I get what I want?)

Literally any policy decision can be broken down into these mental components, even though most decisions are made without conscious recognition that they involve assumptions and calculations under each of these categories. This is as true for major public policy decisions, such as imposing wage price controls or deploying a new weapon system, as it is for individual or personal decisions such as deciding where to spend a vacation or what job to take. Implicitly, and often simultaneously, such decisions require answers to the basic questions listed above. Problem-solving thinking of this kind is an art involving the quick and integrative assembly and recombination of different knowledge resources, each of which, while interrelated with the others, has distinctive characteristics of its own and draws upon slightly different skills. Futurist thinking, as indicated above, emphasizes the role of imagination and conjectural skill and relies more heavily on forms of "tacit knowledge" such as intuition. Its specialty is taking the building blocks provided by other forms of thinking and utilizing them to provide both greater variety and more structure to the field of the future as it appears to the policy-maker. Thus futures research should be viewed primarily as a kind of catalyst, facilitating the tying of analytical thought about values and human behavior to conscious policy choices, a necessary intermediary in the process of collective goal-seeking.

The central contention of the policy-oriented futurist, i.e., that any policy, especially one designed to cope with rapidly changing conditions, has the future unavoidably "bound into it," is extraordinarily compelling. And it strikes home at a time when we recognize that many of our most pressing problems are the long-term results of shortsighted policies or at least policies in which assumptions about the future went unexamined. It is this fact that has led policy-makers in the United States and elsewhere to invest many millions of dollars in futures research—something many of them would have laughed at a few years ago.

[7]A number of theorists have proposed models of the process of action-oriented choice which are similar to this and which have helped shape my own thinking. The most elaborate conceptualization is found throughout the work of Harold D. Lasswell, but can be sampled in condensed form in *The Future of Political Science* (New York: Atherton Press, 1963), pp. 1–2. See also John Friedmann, "Notes on Societal Action," *Journal of the American Institute of Planners* 35, No. 5 (September, 1969): 311–318; and Yehezkel Dror, *Policy Analysis: A Theoretic Framework and Some Basic Concepts* (Santa Monica: The Rand Corp., Memo p. 4156, July, 1969).

Because of this role the study of the future will probably continue to grow quickly as an important interdiscipline with a network of connections to the other disciplines and specialties concerned with policy and policy-making. From this position it can be expected to exert considerable reciprocal influence upon the established disciplines themselves, in part by demanding new kinds of scientific knowledge—knowledge that will be of greater use in improving public policies for the future. More important, it will also do so by calling forth conceptual frameworks more compatible with the futurist perspective than much of the theory which currently informs the social sciences.[8] Ultimately, perhaps the study of the future will take its place within a new metadiscipline having action-oriented individual and collective choice as its central concern—something akin to the unified Policy Sciences suggested several decades ago by Harold Lasswell, one of the first promoters of systematic futures research, and now experiencing a strong revival.[9]

Notwithstanding the wide range of approaches to futures research contained in this volume, there are several areas it does not attempt to cover. It does not deal extensively with the technical details of economic, technological or financial forecasting. There is more elaborate literature in these specialized areas which is widely available. Secondly, the collection does not deal with past or current science fiction or fantasy. Again, this is available in other anthologies. Finally, it does not attempt to survey the emerging genre of holistic or visionary "human futures" literature, integrated personal statements about mankind's predicament and how to go about resolving it, such as W. Warren Wagar's *Building the City of Man* or Aurelio Peccei's *The Chasm Ahead*. These are important contributions, both in themselves and because they affirm so strongly the constructive impulse in futurist work, but they should be read as a whole, not as excerpts. Other important areas have been omitted from this volume because of limitations of space.

The collection is divided into two parts, following an essay by John Platt expressing the critical need for future oriented studies and suggesting some guidelines for choosing research areas. The first part introduces the reader to the theoretical and methodological side of futures research, as indicated by the chapter titles. Its concern is how we can acquire useful knowledge about the future and how that knowledge fits into our analysis of public policy problems. The second part focuses upon the future of our institutions and policy systems themselves, our means of purposefully shaping the future to achieve our goals.

Judged in terms of its techniques and methods, futures research is really

---

[8]For examples of this "futurizing" process already underway, see: 1) Sociology—Wendell Bell and James A. Mau, eds., *The Sociology of the Future: Theory, Cases and Annotated Bibliography* (New York: Russell Sage Foundation, 1971); 2) Political Science—Harvey Perloff, ed., *The Future of the United States Government* (New York: George Braziller, 1971) and Albert Somit, ed., *Political Science and the Study of the Future* (New York: Dryden, 1973); 3) Anthropology—Magoroh Maruyama and James A. Dator, eds., *Cultural Futurology* Symposium (mimeo, 1970).

[9]See Harold D. Lasswell and Daniel Lerner, eds., *The Policy Sciences: Recent Developments in Scope and Methods* (Stanford: Stanford University Press, 1951), *passim.*; and Yehezkel Dror, *Public Policymaking Reexamined* (San Francisco: Chandler Publishing Co., 1968).

still in an experimental stage; therefore, many of the essays collected here are reports on work in progress rather than descriptions of perfected approaches. The first generation of futurists has opened the door to the possibility of structured, analytical thought about what lies ahead, but a great deal remains to be done, both in elaborating and adapting existing methods, such as the Delphi technique, and in devising new ones. In addition, the time is ripe for some evaluation of the impact and effectiveness of past efforts. Hundreds of large scale studies have been carried out in the last decade and these should provide ample material for a preliminary estimate of the strengths and weaknesses of various approaches. Also, the art of fitting futures research into decisional contexts in practical ways remains to be examined. Many forecast studies, such as those based on large scale interviewing exercises or on complex computer models, are very costly—too costly for all but the central problem areas of society. To a degree the results of these larger studies can inform policy analysis at more specialized levels—this has already happened in the case of studies described by Robert H. Ament in Chapter 5—but we need ways to bring the results of such efforts together and to make them more accessible, as well as shorthand techniques to help enrich and expand the futurist component of policy choices down to even local levels of society.

Assuming that we can improve our means of acquiring useful knowledge about the future and that we can find ways to fit this knowledge into policy thinking, there remains the question of whether all of this will have an impact, and if so, what kind. If it does, and if it is to be constructive, it must be the accomplishment of our institutions and policy systems—at the international, national and local levels. Our institutions and policy systems form the critical link between problem-oriented thinking and problem-solving action. But what of *their* future? Will we be equipped to utilize this and the many other helpful innovations coming from the policy-oriented social sciences in order to handle the tasks and responsibilities that crowd in upon us? What institutional alternatives are, in fact, open to us? In order to explore these questions and also to provide a sample of futurist thinking about the central problem area of our society, Part Two of this collection presents a selection of essays focusing upon institutional trends, possibilities and alternatives.

Writing five years ago, Harvard's Daniel Bell reported that he and his colleagues were "appalled by the fact that the Kennedy and Johnson Administrations had 'discovered' the problems of poverty, education, urban renewal and air pollution as if they were completely new."[10] What appalls many of us today is that in spite of this "discovery," and in spite of the well-intentioned commitment of considerable energy and resources, so little has been accomplished, and in many areas things have gotten worse rather than better. Problem-oriented "provider" bureaucracies have sprung up everywhere—we have reached the point where 18 percent of our work force is employed by local, state or national government—and large sums have been invested in research. Yet there is hardly a service system in our society that is not caught in serious trouble. This goes for the educational system, the medical system,

---

[10]"The Year 2000: Trajectory of an Idea," *op. cit.*, p. 48.

the legal-penal system, the transportation system, the welfare system, and the list goes on.

Evidently we are involved in a multidimensional management crisis in our society of entirely unforeseen dimensions. The cumulative result of our pursuit of the good life is that we are spinning out ahead of us a society that is becoming less manageable, relative to our needs, than the one we leave behind. It is tragic that just as we become self-consciously committed to knowing the future and shaping it to our ends, we find our means of collective action in such disarray. And because of this we find society suffused with a growing sense of uncertainty and aimlessness, a sense that the vitality and authority of our institutions is draining away. As Amitai Etzioni has so aptly put it, our society is "adrift," moving into the future increasingly unable to steer itself or set a course.[11]

Similar trends are evident at the international level as well. As interdependence and the need for cooperation have risen dramatically, the major nations have become even more firmly locked into a relationship in which each spends immense sums perfecting hypertrophied systems of mass destruction for which there could be no possible rational use outside of the context of long obsolete "rules of the game." As a result, our capacity to threaten the species life is well established and grows more secure daily. Indeed we have reached the point where a small covert organization—e.g., an extremist sect or the Mafia—or even an individual with considerable wealth, can produce biochemical destruction systems easily capable of setting off global disaster.[12]

If we are to work our way out of this multifold dilemma, we must begin to build forward rather than backward, shaping new ways of learning, choosing and doing that are based on the new principles of action that the post-industrial society is making available. There seems to be a growing consensus that the really catalytic development of the new era we are entering lies in the realm of information control and organization, and in the emergence of extremely efficient, rapid, and complex cybernetic systems—self-conscious learning-steering networks. Unlike the earlier agricultural and industrial revolutions, which involved the extension of man's physical power over nature through the harnessing of first animate and then inanimate energy sources,

---

[11]*The Active Society: A Theory of Societal and Political Progresses* (New York: The Free Press, 1968), p. 467. The theory of society presented in this volume is one of the most elaborate of those presented in a self-consciously futurist framework. Etzioni's work here builds upon the seminal contribution of Karl Deutsch in *The Nerves of Government: Models of Political Action and Control* (New York: The Free Press, 1966). Both of these should be read by anyone seeking to understand the cybernetic approach to social systems and political processes.

[12]Anthony Wiener made this point in an article adapted from remarks at a World Future Society luncheon in Washington, D.C. and subsequently published in *The Futurist* 3, No. 1 (February, 1969): 1. Consider also the statement by Robert S. McNamara when he was publicly describing the megadeath calculations of the Department of Defense for the future: in the early 1970's a counterforce Soviet strike against the United States would take a total of 122 megadeaths; a counter city strike, 149 megadeaths; an American retaliatory blow against the Soviet Union, 100 megadeaths. *New York Times*, Feb. 19, 1965, p. 10. This kind of public airing of casualty forecasts has become less common since then.

the current transition seems to involve an extension of man's mental power, his knowing and perceiving abilities.[13]

The essays of Part Two contain many insights into the possible effects of this new social technology as well as into the opportunities it brings us. Bell points to the rise of theoretical knowledge and its connection to planning, and he advocates, following the lead of others, the creation of a comprehensive national system of social indicators; Michael speaks of new modes of organizing the participation of ordinary citizens in highly sophisticated planning processes; Toffler describes the rise of new organizational forms which seek to do away with the rigidity of hierarchical "industrial era" forms. All, in their way, speak of new modes of handling problems that integrate learning and responsiveness with enhanced control and planning capabilities.

Although we are just beginning to perceive these new ways of doing things, we must quickly assess them to find out what they make possible, how they can be combined with existing institutions, and how they can be mis-used. Most important, we cannot do so retroactively and passively as in the past; i.e., we cannot expect to wait for new relationships to come into being and only then evaluate them. The old passive sequence of social learning (change-perception-adaptation) must, at least for some kinds of problems, be replaced by a new anticipatory one (perception-adaptation-change). Bertram Gross' sketch in Chapter 11 of one alternative future, what he calls "friendly fascism," is a convincing argument for this reorientation.

At this point a warning seems in order: as several observers have stressed, the futures research movement itself can take ill with the same institutional disease that afflicts the other more established sectors of society. It too can become ossified and narrow of perspective, facilitating not enlightened transformation of the whole society, but rather the success of particularistic factions in pursuit of private futures. The signs of this tendency are clear today. As is the case with much of the "advice establishment"—but which seems so much less justifiable here—only a tiny portion of people in the field are either female or nonwhite. Further, a vast majority of work in the field is to a significant degree dependent for funding and dissemination upon individuals and organizations capable (if not always so inclined) of imposing narrow perspectives of this kind. According to a recent survey, itself sponsored by the National Institute of Mental Health, the support profile for futures research is roughly as follows: Government, 50%; Corporate, 30%; Foundation, 10%; Academic, 10%.[14] This pattern is to be expected in view of the origins of much of futures research, and, to the degree that professional futurists continue to have wider, more holistic perspectives than regular bureaucrats and administrators, it is to be welcomed. But there is a danger that perspectives will gradually narrow as research topics focus in on individual problems. Clearly there is a need to provide some form of insulation from the institutional matrix of our society for a portion of futurist thinkers, as well as to provide indepen-

---

[13]See Boulding, Deutsch, Etzioni, all previously cited, for elaboration of the points in this paragraph.
[14]McHale, *op. cit.*, p. 27.

dent outlets for ideas to individuals and groups who are structurally excluded from legitimate channels.

In addition, and related to this, is the need for new forms of communication among all futurists, whatever their institutional links. Several years ago Bertrand de Jouvenel suggested the formation of a "surmising forum, where 'advanced' or 'forward-looking' opinions about what may be and what can be done will be put forward."[15] More recently Alvin Toffler has suggested the need for "imaginetic centers" and "social futures assemblies" to serve as means of assuring widespread and varied participation in the fashioning of proposals for change and images of alternative futures.[16] And in fact groups of futurists have begun to create such forums, centers and assemblies. Acting upon his own proposal, de Jouvenel and his wife, through the publication of the journal, *Analyse et Prévision,* have provided an exchange of this kind in France; futurist associations and research centers have also been formed in England, Germany, Italy, Denmark, Japan, Venezuela and many other countries. In the United States the World Future Society, publisher of *The Futurist,* as well as a number of smaller groups of individuals, have been trying to assure the rapid dissemination of ideas and research results.[17] Generally speaking, these channels have remained open to imaginative and nonconformist ideas and forecasts. Hopefully, they will stay this way and continue to multiply.

Pushing these proposals and activities just a bit further ahead and placing them in a computerized cybernetic context, it is easy to envision the emergence of national and transnational clusters of multimedia futurist networks— perhaps focusing upon different problem areas, such as education or transportation—capable of organizing the transfer, storage, retrieval, comparison and creation of ideas about the future with undreamed-of speed and agility. This would allow individual and group minds to interact with each other, and provide easy access to data sources and the results of other futures research projects. Such a development could open the future as a realm of thought and involvement to a large portion of society, providing an authentic and essential degree of participation in a new form of social dialogue. If, in turn, these clusters could themselves become associated, or interlinked even loosely, we might see the gradual emergence of a kind of techno-cybernetic collective imagination, able on short notice to generate a varied

[15]See Part Five, "Toward the Surmising Forum," in *The Art of Conjecture* (New York: Basic Books, 1967). Quote from p. 271.

[16]Chapter 20, "The Strategy of Social Futurism," in *Future Shock* (New York: Random House, 1970).

[17]Examples of these smaller groups are: the *Futures Information Network* (FIN) which has been organized by Michael Marien of the Educational Policy Research Center at Syracuse; the New World Mailing Service organized by Robert Theobald; and, for teachers of future studies, the *Future Studies Syllabus,* edited by Billy Rojas and H. Wentworth Eldredge of Alice Lloyd College and Dartmouth College, respectively. At the State University of New York at Binghamton a group of futurists are considering the creation of a computerized system "capable of accepting continuing inputs of data to maintain an up-to-date index of the current status of futures research programs." From McHale, *op. cit.,* p. 83.

landscape of images of the future for society and its parts that would be of immense value to our public institutions and policy systems at every level. Indeed, such a system and its linkage to collective choices would seem not just an ideal but a necessity if we are to acquire the kind of power over the future that is required if we are to survive and continue to develop.

For at the far edge of the future, at the logical end of the line of transformation upon which we currently move, is the advent of man's control over his own evolution itself—by choice, but also of necessity. This idea has been around a very long time, but now it is serious business; it is firmly on the agenda of the policy-oriented futurist. In fact, one of the most poignant debates that has been emerging among the ranks of futurists in recent years is, quite simply, whether man is really viable, whether we should keep him as he is or whether we should replace him, and, if so, by what. We are already involved in choosing man's genetic future—at least we have interrupted extensively the selective processes operating upon us in the past—and we are moving rapidly to the point where large scale intervention, very probably in coordination with population control policies, is becoming a plausible alternative.

As we attempt to find meaning in the great process of change and emergence which we have so recently become aware of—a process beginning with a boiling stew of chemicals and experienced now in the miraculously complex living world of which we are a part—it is tempting to agree with the proposition that complexity itself is linked to awareness and to self-control and that the three together are part of an anti-entropic evolution of energy forms that "wants" to continue onward in the universe. As John Platt has written:

If this property of complexity could somehow be transformed into visible brightness so that it would stand forth more clearly to our senses, the biological world would become a walking field of light compared to the physical world. The sun with its great eruptions would fade into a pale simplicity compared to a rose bush. An earthworm would be a beacon, a dog would be a city of light, and human beings would stand out like blazing suns of complexity, flashing bursts of meaning to each other through the dull night of the physical world between.[18]

Are we to tamper with such entities, even presume to give guidance to the process that produced them? This is a terrifying suggestion, but we must at least accept it as an emerging problem. If the next great threshold we face may be the threshold of transhumanity, we must try to see beyond it just as we try to cope with the current era of transition in which we find ourselves. For if we are to choose against it, or try to control it to promote our basic values, we must do so very soon. Unfortunately, it may be upon us before we have come to understand and manage the problems we inherit from the immediate past. And like most eras, it is probable that human societies will enter it at different times and at different rates and with different goals and objectives. Not one, but hundreds and perhaps thousands of altered forms of

[18]The Step to Man (New York: John Wiley & Sons, 1966) p. 151.

intelligent beings, Neo-men, may emerge upon our planet and any other planets we-they may populate. Indeed, it seems that long-range policy-oriented futures research ought already to be considering public policy problems that will emerge if we enter a multisapient world, in which new policy systems, based on knowledge garnered from new "social" sciences designed to understand and predict the behavior of multiple intelligent life forms, will be required.

All of this may seem far afield to the observer of our current public policy dilemmas. And it may be. Perhaps we have passed beyond the limits of our ability to cope with growing complexity, density and interdependence, and the immense social turbulence arising therefrom. We may even be on the verge of violent revolution or cataclysmic disasters such as the ones described by Forrester and Ehrlich in this volume; even worse, we may be at the start of a gradual downward spiral toward global decay, fragmentation, and purposeless conflict, punctuated by ineffectual interludes of authoritarianism. At least one source of optimism in the face of these possibilities is that we are beginning to acquire that "appetite for the future" that C. P. Snow has pointed to as so essential to our continued search for dignity, awareness and self-control.

1

Public Policy And The Study Of The Future: Setting An Agenda

IAT WE MUST DO
) john platt

There is only one crisis in the world. It is the crisis of transformation. The trouble is that it is now coming upon us as a storm of crisis problems from every direction. But if we look quantitatively at the course of our changes in this century, we can see immediately why the problems are building up so rapidly at this time, and we will see that it has now become urgent for us to mobilize all our intelligence to solve these problems if we are to keep from killing ourselves in the next few years.

The essence of the matter is that the human race is on a steeply rising "S-curve" of change. We are undergoing a great historical transition to new levels of technological power all over the world. We all know about these changes, but we do not often stop to realize how large they are in orders of magnitude, or how rapid and enormous compared to all previous changes in history. In the last century, we have increased our speeds of communication by a factor of 10^7; our speeds of travel by 10^2; our speeds of data handling by 10^6; our energy resources by 10^3; our power of weapons by 10^6; our ability to control diseases by something like 10^2; and our rate of population growth to 10^3 times what it was a few thousand years ago.

Could anyone suppose that human relations around the world would not be affected to their very roots by such changes? Within the last 25 years, the Western world has moved into an age of jet planes, missiles and satellites, nuclear power and nuclear terror. We have acquired computers and automation, a service and leisure economy, superhighways, superagriculture, supermedicine, mass higher education, universal TV, oral contraceptives, environmental pollution, and urban crises. The rest of the world is also moving rapidly and may catch up with all these powers and problems within a very short time. It is hardly surprising that young people under 30, who have grown up familiar with these things from childhood, have developed very different expectations and concerns from the older generation that grew up in another world.

What many people do not realize is that many of these technological changes are now approaching certain natural limits. The "S-curve" is beginning to level off. We may never have faster communications or more TV or larger weapons or a higher level of danger than we have now. This means that if we could learn how to manage these new powers and problems in the next few years without killing ourselves by our obsolete structures and behavior, we might be able to create new and more effective social structures that would last for many generations. We might be able to move into that new world of abundance and diversity and well-being for all mankind which technology has now made possible.

2

The trouble is that we may not survive these next few years. The human race today is like a rocket on a launching pad. We have been building up to this moment of takeoff for a long time, and if we can get safely through the takeoff period, we may fly on a new and exciting course for a long time to come. But at this moment, as the powerful new engines are fired, their thrust and roar shakes and stresses every part of the ship and may cause the whole thing to blow up before we can steer it on its way. Our problem today is to harness and direct these tremendous new forces through this dangerous transition period to the new world instead of to destruction. But unless we can do this, the rapidly increasing strains and crises of the next decade may kill us all. They will make the last 20 years look like a peaceful interlude.

The Next 10 Years

Several types of crisis may reach the point of explosion in the next 10 years: nuclear escalation, famine, participatory crises, racial crises, and what have been called the crises of administrative legitimacy. It is worth singling out two or three of these to see how imminent and dangerous they are, so that we can fully realize how very little time we have for preventing or controlling them.

Take the problem of nuclear war, for example. A few years ago, Leo Szilard estimated the "half-life" of the human race with respect to nuclear escalation as being between 10 and 20 years. His reasoning then is still valid now. As long as we continue to have no adequate stabilizing peace-keeping structures for the world, we continue to live under the daily threat not only of local wars but of nuclear escalation with overkill and megatonnage enough to destroy all life on earth. Every year or two there is a confrontation between nuclear powers—Korea, Laos, Berlin, Suez, Quemoy, Cuba, Vietnam, and the rest. MacArthur wanted to use nuclear weapons in Korea; and in the Cuban missile crisis, John Kennedy is said to have estimated the probability of a nuclear exchange as about 25 percent.

The danger is not so much that of the unexpected, such as a radar error or even a new nuclear dictator, as it is that our present systems will work exactly as planned!—from border testing, strategic gambles, threat and counterthreat, . . . up to that "second-strike capability" that is already aimed, armed, and triggered to wipe out hundreds of millions of people in a 3-hour duel!

What is the probability of this in the average incident? 10 percent? 5 percent? There is no average incident. But it is easy to see that five or ten more such confrontations in this game of "nuclear roulette" might indeed give us only a 50-50 chance of living until 1980 or 1990. This is a shorter life expectancy than people have ever had in the world before. All our medical increases in length of life are meaningless, as long as our nuclear lifetime is so short.

Many agricultural experts also think that within the next decade the great famines will begin, with deaths that may reach 100 million people in densely populated countries like India and China. Some contradict this, claiming that the remarkable new grains and new agricultural methods introduced in the last 3 years in Southeast Asia may now be able to keep the food supply ahead of population growth. But others think that the reeducation of farmers and consumers to use the new grains cannot proceed fast enough to make a difference.

But if famine does come, it is clear that it will be catastrophic. Besides the direct human suffering, it will further increase our international instabilities, with food riots, troops called out, governments falling, and international interventions that will change the whole political map of the world. It could make Vietnam look like a popgun.

In addition, the next decade is likely to see continued crises of legitimacy of all our overloaded administrations, from universities and unions to cities and national governments. Everywhere there is protest and refusal to accept the solutions handed down by some central elite. The student revolutions circle the globe. Suburbs protest as well as ghettos, Right as well as Left. There are many new sources of collision and protest, but it is clear that the general problem is in large part structural rather than political. Our traditional methods of election and management no longer give administrations the skill and capacity they need to handle their complex new burdens and decisions. They become swollen, unresponsive—and repudiated. Every day now some distinguished administrator is pressured out of office by protesting constituents.

In spite of the violence of some of these confrontations, this may seem like a trivial problem compared to war or famine—until we realize the dangerous effects of these instabilities on the stability of the whole system. In a nuclear crisis or in any of our other crises today, administrators or negotiators may often work out some basis of agreement between conflicting groups or nations, only to find themselves rejected by their people on one or both sides, who are then left with no mechanism except to escalate their battles further.

The Crisis of Crises

What finally makes all of our crises still more dangerous is that they are now coming on top of each other. Most administrations are able to endure or even enjoy an occasional crisis, with everyone working late together and getting a new sense of importance and unity. What they are not prepared to deal with are multiple crises, a crisis of crises all at one time. This is what happened in New York City in 1968 when the Ocean Hill-Brownsville teacher and race strike was combined with a police strike, on top of a garbage strike, on top of a longshoremen's strike, all within a few days of each other.

When something like this happens, the staffs get jumpy with smoke and coffee and alcohol, the mediators become exhausted, and the administrators find themselves running two crises behind. Every problem may escalate because those involved no longer have time to think straight. What would have happened in the Cuban missile crisis if the East Coast power blackout had occurred by accident that same day? Or if the "hot line" between Washington and Moscow had gone dead? There might have been hours of misinterpretation, and some fatally different decisions.

I think this multiplication of domestic and international crises today will shorten that short half-life. In the continued absence of better ways of heading off these multiple crises, our half-life may no longer be 10 or 20 years, but more like 5 to 10 years, or less. We may have even less than a 50-50 chance of living until 1980.

This statement may seem uncertain and excessively dramatic. But is there any scientist who would make a much more optimistic estimate after considering all the different sources of danger and how they are increasing? The shortness of the time is due to the exponential and multiplying character of our problems and not to what particular numbers or guesses we put in. Anyone who feels more hopeful about getting past the nightmares of the 1970's has only to look beyond them to the monsters of pollution and population rising up in the 1980's and 1990's. Whether we have 10 years or more like 20 or 30, unless we systematically find new large-scale solutions, we are in the gravest danger of destroying our society, our world, and ourselves in any of a number of different ways well before the end of this century. Many futurologists who have predicted what the world will be like in the year 2000 have neglected to tell us that.

Nevertheless the real reason for trying to make rational estimates of these deadlines is not because of their shock value but because they give us at least a rough idea of how much time we may have for finding and mounting some large-scale solutions. The time is short but, as we shall see, it is not too short to give us a chance that something can be done, if we begin immediately.

From this point, there is no place to go but up. Human predictions are always conditional. The future always depends on what we do and can be made worse or better by stupid or intelligent action. To change our earlier analogy, today we are like men coming out of a coal mine who suddenly begin to hear the rock rumbling, but who have also begun to see a little square of light at the end of the tunnel. Against this background, I am an optimist—in that I want to insist that there is a square of light and that it is worth trying to get to. I think what we must do is to start running as fast as possible toward that light, working to increase the probability of our survival through the next decade by some measurable amount.

For the light at the end of the tunnel is very bright indeed. If we can only devise new mechanisms to help us survive this round of terrible crises, we have a chance of moving into a new world of incredible potentialities for all mankind. But if we cannot get through this next decade, we may never reach it.

Task Forces for Social Research and Development

What can we do? I think that nothing less than the application of the full intelligence of our society is likely to be adequate. These problems will require the humane and constructive efforts of everyone involved. But I think they will also require something very similar to the mobilization of scientists for solving crisis problems in wartime. I believe we are going to need large numbers of scientists forming something like research teams or task forces for social research and development. We need full-time interdisciplinary teams combining men of different specialties, natural scientists, social scientists, doctors, engineers, teachers, lawyers, and many other trained and inventive minds, who can put together our stores of knowledge and powerful new ideas into improved technical methods, organizational designs, or "social inventions" that have a chance of being adopted soon enough and widely enough to be effective. Even a great mobilization of scientists may not be enough. There is no guarantee that these problems can be solved, or solved in time, no matter what we do. But for problems of this scale and urgency, this kind of focusing of our brains and knowledge may be the only chance we have.

Scientists, of course, are not the only ones who can make contributions. Millions of citizens, business and labor leaders, city and government officials, and workers in existing agencies, are already doing all they can to solve these problems. No scientific innovation will be effective without extensive advice and help from all these groups.

But it is the new science and technology that have made our problems so immense and intractable. Technology did not create human conflicts and inequities, but it has made them unendurable. And where science and technology have expanded the problems in this way, it may be only more scientific understanding and better technology that can carry us past them. The cure for the pollution of the rivers by detergents is the use of nonpolluting detergents. The cure for bad management designs is better management designs.

Also, in many of these areas, there are few people outside the research community who have the basic knowledge necessary for radically new solutions. In our great biological problems, it is the new ideas from cell biology and ecology that may be crucial. In our social-organizational problems, it may be the new theories of organization and management and behavior theory and game theory that offer the only hope. Scientific research and development groups of some kind may be the only effective mechanism by which many of these new ideas can be converted into practical invention and action.

The time scale on which such task forces would have to operate is very different from what is usual in science. In the past, most scientists have tended to work on something like a 30-year time scale, hoping that their careful studies would fit into some great intellectual synthesis that might be years away. Of course when they become politically concerned, they begin to work on something more like a 3-month time scale, collecting signatures or trying to persuade the government to start or stop some program.

But 30 years is too long, and 3 months is too short, to cope with the major crises that might destroy us in the next 10 years. Our urgent problems now are more like wartime problems, where we need to work as rapidly as is consistent with large-scale effectiveness. We need to think rather in terms of a 3-year time scale—or more broadly, a 1- to 5-year time scale. In World War II, the ten thousand scientists who were mobilized for war research knew they did not have 30 years, or even 10 years, to come up with answers. But they did have time for the new research, design, and construction that brought sonar and radar and atomic energy to operational effectiveness within 1 to 4 years. Today we need the same large-scale mobilization for innovation and action and the same sense of constructive urgency.

Priorities: A Crisis Intensity Chart

In any such enterprise, it is most important to be clear about which problems are the real priority problems. To get this straight, it is valuable to try to separate the different problem areas according to some measures of their magnitude and urgency. A possible classification of this kind is shown in Tables 1 and 2. In these tables, I have tried to rank a number of present or potential problems or crises, vertically, according to an estimate of their order of intensity or "seriousness," and horizontally, by a rough estimate of their time to reach climactic importance. Table 1 is such a classification for the United States for the next 1 to 5 years, the next 5 to 20 years, and the next 20 to 50 years. Table 2 is a similar classification for world problems and crises. [See pp. 8–11 below.]

The successive rows indicate something like order-of-magnitude differences in the intensity of the crises, as estimated by a rough product of the size of population that might be hurt or affected, multiplied by some estimated average effect in the disruption of their lives. Thus the first row corresponds to total or near-total annihilation; the second row, to great destruction or change affecting everybody; the third row, to a lower tension affecting a smaller part of the population or a smaller part of everyone's life, and so on.

Informed men might easily disagree about one row up or down in intensity, or one column left or right in the time scales, but these order-of-magnitude differences are already so great that it would be surprising to find much larger disagreements. Clearly, an important initial step in any serious problem study would be to refine such estimates.

In both tables, the one crisis that must be ranked at the top in total danger and imminence is, of course, the danger of large-scale or total annihilation

TABLE 1. Classification of problems and crises by estimated time and intensity (United States).

Grade	Estimated crisis intensity (number affected × degree of effect)	Estimated time to crisis*			
		1 to 5 years	5 to 20 years	20 to 50 years	
1.		Total annihilation	Nuclear or RCBW escalation	Nuclear or RCBW escalation	✝ (Solved or dead)
2.	10^8	Great destruction or change (physical, biological, or political)	(Too soon)	Participatory democracy	Political theory and economic structure
				Ecological balance	Population planning
					Patterns of living
					Education
					Communications
					Integrative philosophy
3.	10^7	Widespread almost unbearable tension	Administrative management	Pollution	?
			Slums	Poverty	
			Participatory democracy	Law and justice	
			Racial conflict		
4.	10^6	Large-scale distress	Transportation	Communications gap	?
			Neighborhood ugliness		
			Crime		
5.	10^5	Tension producing responsive change	Cancer and heart	Educational inadequacy	?
			Smoking and drugs		
			Artificial organs		
			Accidents		
			Sonic boom		

TABLE 1: (con't.)

Grade	Estimated crisis intensity (number affected X degree of effect)	Estimated time to crisis*		
		1 to 5 years	5 to 20 years	20 to 50 years
6.	Other problems—important, but adequately researched	Water supply Marine resources Privacy on computers Military R & D New educational methods Mental illness Fusion power	Military R & D	
7.	Exaggerated dangers and hopes	Mind control Heart transplants Definition of death	Sperm banks Freezing bodies Unemployment from automation	Eugenics
8.	Noncrisis problems being "overstudied"	Man in space Most basic science		

*If no major effort is made at anticipatory solution.

TABLE 2. Classification of problems and crises by estimated time and intensity (World).

Grade	Estimated crisis intensity (number affected × degree of effect)	Estimated time to crisis*		
		1 to 5 years	5 to 20 years	20 to 50 years
1.	10^{10}	Total annihilation	Nuclear or RCBW escalation	Nuclear or RCBW escalation	✝ (Solved or dead)
2.	10^9	Great destruction or change (physical, biological, or political)	(Too soon)	Famines Ecological balance Development failures Local wars Rich-poor gap	Economic structure and political theory Population and ecological balance Patterns of living Universal education Communications-integration Management of world Integrative philosophy
3.	10^8	Widespread almost unbearable tension	Administrative management Need for participation Group and racial conflict Poverty-rising expectations Environmental degradation	Poverty Pollution Racial wars Political rigidity Strong dictatorships	?
4.	10^7	Large-scale distress	Transportation Diseases Loss of old cultures	Housing Education Independence	?

TABLE 2 (con't.)

Grade	Estimated crisis intensity (number affected × degree of effect)	Estimated time to crisis*		
		1 to 5 years	5 to 20 years	20 to 50 years
5.	10^6 Tension producing responsive change	Regional organization Water supplies	of big powers Communications gap	
6.	Other problems—important, but adequately researched	Technical development design Intelligent monetary design	?	?
7.	Exaggerated dangers and hopes			Eugenics
8.	Noncrisis problems being "overstudied"	Man in space Most basic science		Melting of ice caps

*If no major effort is made at anticipatory solution.

by nuclear escalation or by radiological-chemical-biological-warfare (RCBW). This kind of crisis will continue through both the 1- to 5-year time period and the 5- to 20-year period as Crisis Number 1, unless and until we get a safer peace-keeping arrangement. But in the 20- to 50-year column, following the reasoning already given, I think we must simply put a big "✝" at this level, on the grounds that the peace-keeping stabilization problem will either be solved by that time or we will probably be dead.

At the second level, the 1- to 5-year period may not be a period of great destruction (except nuclear) in either the United States or the world. But the problems at this level are building up, and within the 5- to 20-year period, many scientists fear the destruction of our whole biological and ecological balance in the United States by mismanagement or pollution. Others fear political catastrophe within this period, as a result of participatory confrontations or backlash or even dictatorship, if our divisive social and structural problems are not solved before that time.

On a world scale in this period, famine and ecological catastrophe head the list of destructive problems. We will come back later to the items in the 20- to 50-year column.

The third level of crisis problems in the United States includes those that are already upon us: administrative management of communities and cities, slums, participatory democracy, and racial conflict. In the 5- to 20-year period, the problems of pollution and poverty or major failures of law and justice could escalate to this level of tension if they are not solved. The last column is left blank because secondary events and second-order effects will interfere seriously with any attempt to make longer-range predictions at these lower levels.

The items in the lower part of the tables are not intended to be exhaustive. Some are common headline problems which are included simply to show how they might rank quantitatively in this kind of comparison. Anyone concerned with any of them will find it a useful exercise to estimate for himself their order of seriousness, in terms of the number of people they actually affect and the average distress they cause. Transportation problems and neighborhood ugliness, for example, are listed as grade 4 problems in the United States because they depress the lives of tens of millions for 1 or 2 hours every day. Violent crime may affect a corresponding number every year or two. These evils are not negligible, and they are worth the efforts of enormous numbers of people to cure them and to keep them cured—but on the other hand, they will not destroy our society.

The grade 5 crises are those where the hue and cry has been raised and where responsive changes of some kind are already under way. Cancer goes here, along with problems like auto safety and an adequate water supply. This is not to say that we have solved the problem of cancer, but rather that good people are working on it and are making as much progress as we could expect from anyone. (At this level of social intensity, it should be kept in mind that there are also positive opportunities for research, such as the automation of clinical biochemistry or the invention of new channels of personal communication, which might affect the 20-year future as greatly as the new drugs and solid state devices of 20 years ago have begun to affect the present.)

Where the Scientists Are

Below grade 5, three less quantitative categories are listed, where the scientists begin to outnumber the problems. Grade 6 consists of problems that many people believe to be important but that are adequately researched at the present time. Military R & D belongs in this category. Our huge military establishment creates many social problems, both of national priority and international stability, but even in its own terms, war research, which engrosses hundreds of thousands of scientists and engineers, is being taken care of generously. Likewise, fusion power is being studied at the $100-million level, though even if we had it tomorrow, it would scarcely change our rates of application of nuclear energy in generating more electric power for the world.

Grade 7 contains the exaggerated problems which are being talked about or worked on out of all proportion to their true importance, such as heart transplants, which can never affect more than a few thousands of people out of the billions in the world. It is sad to note that the symposia on "social implications of science" at many national scientific meetings are often on the problems in grade 7.

In the last category, grade 8, are two subjects which I am sorry to say I must call "overstudied," at least with respect to the real crisis problems today. The Man in Space flights to the moon and back are the most beautiful technical achievements of man, but they are not urgent except for national display, and they absorb tens of thousands of our most ingenious technical brains.

And in the "overstudied" list I have begun to think we must now put most of our basic science. This is a hard conclusion, because all of science is so important in the long run and because it is still so small compared, say, to advertising or the tobacco industry. But basic scientific thinking is a scarce resource. In a national emergency, we would suddenly find that a host of our scientific problems could be postponed for several years in favor of more urgent research. Should not our total human emergency make the same claims? Long-range science is useless unless we survive to use it. Tens of thousands of our best trained minds may now be needed for something more important than "science as usual."

The arrows at level 2 in the tables are intended to indicate that problems may escalate to a higher level of crisis in the next time period if they are not solved. The arrows toward level 2 in the last columns of both tables show the escalation of all our problems upward to some general reconstruction in the 20- to 50- year time period, if we survive. Probably no human institution

will continue unchanged for another 50 years, because they will all be changed by the crises if they are not changed in advance to prevent them. There will surely be widespread rearrangements in all our ways of life everywhere, from our patterns of society to our whole philosophy of man. Will they be more humane, or less? Will the world come to resemble a diverse and open humanist democracy? Or Orwell's *1984*? Or a postnuclear desert with its scientists hanged? It is our acts of commitment and leadership in the next few months and years that will decide.

Mobilizing Scientists

It is a unique experience for us to have peacetime problems, or technical problems which are not industrial problems, on such a scale. We do not know quite where to start, and there is no mechanism yet for generating ideas systematically or paying teams to turn them into successful solutions.

But the comparison with wartime research and development may not be inappropriate. Perhaps the antisubmarine warfare work or the atomic energy project of the 1940's provide the closest parallels to what we must do in terms of the novelty, scale, and urgency of the problems, the initiative needed, and the kind of large success that has to be achieved. In the antisubmarine campaign, Blackett assembled a few scientists and other ingenious minds in his "back room," and within a few months they had worked out the "operations analysis" that made an order-of-magnitude difference in the success of the campaign. In the atomic energy work, scientists started off with extracurricular research, formed a central committee to channel their secret communications, and then studied the possible solutions for some time before they went to the government, for large-scale support for the great development laboratories and production plants.

Fortunately, work on our crisis problems today would not require secrecy. Our great problems today are all beginning to be world problems, and scientists from many countries would have important insights to contribute.

Probably the first step in crisis studies now should be the organization of intense technical discussion and education groups in every laboratory. Promising lines of interest could then lead to the setting up of part-time or full-time studies and teams and coordinating committees. Administrators and boards of directors might find active crisis research important to their own organizations in many cases. Several foundations and federal agencies already have in-house research and make outside grants in many of these crisis areas, and they would be important initial sources of support.

But the step that will probably be required in a short time is the creation of whole new centers, perhaps comparable to Los Alamos or the RAND Corporation, where interdisciplinary groups can be assembled to work full-time on solutions to these crisis problems. Many different kinds of centers will eventually be necessary, including research centers, development centers, training centers, and even production centers for new sociotechnical inventions. The problems of our time—the $100-billion food problem or the $100-billion arms control problem—are no smaller than World War II in scale and importance, and it would be absurd to think that a few academic research teams or a few agency laboratories could do the job.

Social Inventions

The thing that discourages many scientists—even social scientists—from thinking in these research-and-development terms is their failure to realize that there are such things as social inventions and that they can have large-scale effects in a surprisingly short time. A recent study with Karl Deutsch has examined some 40 of the great achievements in social science in this century, to see where they were made and by whom and how long they took to become effective. They include developments such as the following: Keynesian economics; Opinion polls and statistical sampling; Input-output economics; Operations analysis; Information theory and feedback theory; Theory of games and economic behavior; Operant conditioning and programmed learning; Planned programming and budgeting (PPB); Non-zero-sum game theory.

Many of these have made remarkable differences within just a few years in our ability to handle social problems or management problems. The opinion poll became a national necessity within a single election period. The theory of games, published in 1946, had become an important component of American strategic thinking by RAND and the Defense Department by 1953, in spite of the limitation of the theory at that time to zero-sum games, with their dangerous bluffing and "brinksmanship." Today, within less than a decade, the PPB management technique is sweeping through every large organization.

This list is particularly interesting because it shows how much can be done outside official government agencies when inventive men put their brains together. Most of the achievements were the work of teams of two or more men, almost all of them located in intellectual centers such as Princeton or the two Cambridges.

The list might be extended by adding commercial social inventions with rapid and widespread effects, like credit cards. And sociotechnical inventions, like computers and automation or like oral contraceptives, which were in widespread use within 10 years after they were developed. In addition, there are political innovations like the New Deal, which made great changes in our economic life within 4 years, and the pay-as-you-go income tax, which transformed federal taxing power within 2 years.

On the international scene, the Peace Corps, the "hot line," the Test-Ban Treaty, the Antarctic Treaty, and the Nonproliferation Treaty were all implemented within 2 to 10 years after their initial proposal. These are only small contributions, a tiny patch-work part of the basic international stabilization system that is needed, but they show that the time to adopt new structural designs may be surprisingly short. Our clichés about "social lag" are very misleading. Over half of the major social innovations since 1940 were adopted or had widespread social effects within less than 12 years—a time as short as, or shorter than, the average time for adoption for technological innovations. . . .

Future Satisfactions and Present Solutions

This is an enormous program. But there is nothing impossible about mounting and financing it, if we, as concerned men, go into it with commitment and leadership. Yes, there will be a need for money and power to overcome organizational difficulties and vested interests. But it is worth remembering that the only real source of power in the world is the gap between what is and what might be. Why else do men work and save and plan? If there is some future increase in human satisfaction that we can point to and realistically anticipate, men will be willing to pay something for it and invest in it in the hope of that return. In economics, they pay with money; in politics, with their votes and time and sometimes with their jail sentences and their lives.

Social change, peaceful or turbulent, is powered by "what might be." This means that for peaceful change, to get over some impossible barrier of unresponsiveness or complexity or group conflict, what is needed is an inventive man or group—a "social entrepreneur"—who can connect the pieces and show how to turn the advantage of "what might be" into some present advantage for every participating party. To get toll roads, when highways were hopeless, a legislative-corporation mechanism was invented that turned the future need into present profits for construction workers and bondholders and continuing profitability for the state and all the drivers.

This principle of broad-payoff anticipatory design has guided many successful social plans. Regular task forces using systems analysis to find payoffs over the barriers might give us such successful solutions much more often. The new world that could lie ahead, with its blocks and malfunctions removed, would be fantastically wealthy. It seems almost certain that there must be many systematic ways for intelligence to convert that large payoff into the profitable solution of our present problems.

The only possible conclusion is a call to action. Who will commit himself to this kind of search for more ingenious and fundamental solutions? Who will begin to assemble the research teams and the funds? Who will begin to create those full-time interdisciplinary centers that will be necessary for testing detailed designs and turning them into effective applications?

The task is clear. The task is huge. The time is horribly short. In the past, we have had science for intellectual pleasure, and science for the control of nature. We have had science for war. But today, the whole human experiment may hang on the question of how fast we now press the development of science for survival.

part one

ON KNOWING
THE FUTURE:
APPROACHES AND
INTERPRETATIONS

2

Prediction As A Form Of Knowledge

ON THE NATURE OF THE FUTURE
● *bertrand de jouvenel*

There is a difference between the nature of the past and that of the future. It should hardly be necessary to emphasize that I am referring here to the difference that is perceived by the mind of an active human being.

With regard to the past, man can exert his will only in vain; his liberty is void, his power nonexistent. I could say: "I want to be a former student of the Ecole Polytechnique"—but this is utterly absurd. The fact is that I did not go to the Ecole Polytechnique, and nothing can change this fact. . . .

But if the past is the domain of facts over which I have no power, it is also the domain of knowable facts. If I claim to be a graduate of the Ecole Polytechnique, evidence is easily assembled to prove me a liar. It is not always so easy to determine whether alleged facts are true or false, but we always consider that they are in principle verifiable. The impatience and irritation we feel when faced with conflicting testimony bearing on the same fact are signs of our deep conviction that this *factum* is knowable. And in such a situation we do not hesitate to say that one of the witnesses who presented testimony must have been lying or mistaken, even though we may not know which one was actually at fault.

Now let us suppose that I say: "I will go to Australia." Put into the past tense, my assertion would be a falsehood: it is not true that I have gone to Australia. But by using the future tense I have placed my assertion outside the domain of recorded, attested, and verifiable *facta;* I have projected my assertion beyond the domain of the true and the false, and this "beyond" constitutes another domain, where I can place images that do not correspond to any historical reality. An image of this kind is not a mere fantasy if I have the will and feel I have the capacity to bring about at some later time a state of affairs that corresponds to the image. The image represents a possibility because of my power to validate it in this way, and represents a *project* because of my will to do so. . . .

Now let us put ourselves in the position of someone who is waiting for me to visit him in Australia. For this Australian my arrival is a *futurum* attended by a measure of uncertainty until I actually come. If he attaches some definite probability to the event, the judgment by which he does so is a personal one. What he arrives at is a "subjective probability." Thus if two Australian friends of mine discuss this future event with one another, each may attach a very different degree of likelihood to the same *futurum*.

For man in his role as an active agent the future is a field of liberty and power, but for man in his role as a cognizant being the future is a field of uncertainty. It is a field of liberty because I am free to conceive that something which does not now exist will exist in the future; it is a field of power because I have some power to validate my conception (though, naturally, not all conceptions indiscriminately!). And indeed the future is our only field of power, for we can act only on the future. Our awareness of this capacity to act suggests the notion of "a domain in which one can act." . . .

. . . the only "useful knowledge" we have relates to the future. A man wishing to display his practical turn of mind readily says: "I am only interested in facts," although quite the opposite is the case. If his aim is to get to New York, the time at which a plane left yesterday is of small concern to him; what interests him is the takeoff time this evening (a *futurum*). Similarly, if he wants to see somebody in New York, the fact that this person was in his office yesterday hardly matters to him; what interests him is whether this person will be in his office tomorrow. Our man lives in a world of *futura* rather than a world of *facta*.

The real fact collector is at the opposite pole from the man of action. One erudite scholar might spend years establishing the facts about the assassination of Louis, duc d'Orléans, in 1407, while another might devote his time to tracing Napoleon's itinerary day by day. Here are *facta* that could have no effect on our judgments concerning the future and on our present decisions.

For this reason these *facta* do not concern our practical man. If he is interested in certain *facta*, it is only because he uses them in presuming a *futurum*. For example, he may be worried about the departure time of his plane. Tell him that this flight has left on time for a long succession of days, and he will be reassured. He regards these *facta* as a guarantee of the *futurum*, which is all that matters to him. Now let us suppose that this man contemplates buying a business that holds no interest for him except as an investment. If the accounts show that sales have increased steadily every year, he will derive from these figures a strong presumption that this steady increase will be maintained in future sales.

The case of the business concern differs from that of the airplane in two immediately apparent ways: first, a much larger stretch of time is considered; next, and more particularly, the investor counts on the continuance of the same change, whereas the traveler counts on a simple repetition of the same phenomenon.

In both cases, however, the only use of the known *facta* is as *raw material out of which the mind makes estimates of futura*. The unceasing transformation of *facta* into *futura* by summary processes in the mind is part of our daily life, and thus the undertaking of conscious and systematic forecasting is simply an attempt to effect improvements in a natural activity of the mind. . . .

Empirical psychologists represent the learning process as the progressive storing of procedures associated with favorable results. This is sufficient to explain why anthropological findings indicate that life in primitive societies is so largely ruled by custom. In a perilous world it is a fine achievement for a man if he lives to an uncommon old age, and having manifested their own prudence, the elders are now qualified to teach others the skills of prudence. What they inculcate are the well-tried procedures whose use should be continued. They pass on the recipes ("tradition" properly means "passing on") and recommend "routines"—the trodden paths.

Routines help to save us efforts of foresight: if I have an operational recipe, guaranteed to yield certain results, all I need do is follow the instructions faithfully. Who would be so foolish as to waste time trying out ways of cooking an egg or solving a quadratic equation? It is scarcely necessary to point out that the vast majority of our actions—at present, just as in the distant past—conform to recipes. Accordingly, it should not be difficult for us to imagine a society tied even more closely to recipes. At school, when we failed to do a sum, the teacher would say that we had not done it the right way, meaning the way we had been shown; similarly, we can assume that, in the past, failure and misfortune were readily attributed to departures from or breaches of the "right" practices.

Since we cannot live except in a social group, nothing matters more to us than our relations with other men, and nothing is more important to foresee than the way other men will behave. The more their conduct is governed by custom and conforms to routines, the easier it is to foresee. A social order based on custom provides the individual with optimal guarantees that his human environment is foreseeable. It is hardly surprising that the maintenance of a familiar social order has always been regarded as a Common Good whose preservation was essential.

Hence, aberrations of conduct were condemned, and change was feared and regarded as a corruption. The idea of the security afforded by the routine and familiar was so deeply ingrained that even extreme reformers appealed to this notion, saying they asked for no more than a return to the "good old ways." Thus, in calling for the redistribution of land holdings, Tiberius Sempronius Gracchus claimed, with some foundation, that his reform was designed to bring back a society of peasants who owned their own land and lived off their own crops. A rather fanciful theme dominated the long press campaign that helped to prepare the French Revolution: the advocacy of a return to the Frankish custom of the *champ de mars* or the *champ de mai*— assemblies of warriors at which decisions were taken concerning affairs of state. All this pseudoarcheology went to mobilize something that had never been, in the service of a leap into the unknown. And surely everyone knows that the Reformation, for all its radical innovations, was conceived and presented as a restoration of the practices of the early Church. The idea of "moving with the times" would have seemed abhorrent to the reformers, who wished, on the contrary, to "correct the abuses introduced over the centuries." The examples I have adduced are sufficiently striking and it seems unnecessary to cite any more. They all bear witness to the power of that which has already been seen, tried, and experienced. . . .

In fact, the more one thinks about man's efforts to introduce something known and steadfast—something reliable—into the shifting ground of the future, the more important these efforts appear to be. They may be interpreted as an offensive collectively waged on the future and designed to partly tame it. As a consequence, the future is known not through the guesswork of the mind, but through social efforts, more or less conscious, to cast "jetties" out from an established order and into the uncertainty ahead. The network of reciprocal commitments traps the future and moderates its mobility. All this tends to reduce the uncertainty. . . .

Our modern civilization has repudiated the sacredness of institutions and commitments, and therewith the means of achieving a known future. As we have loosened our guaranteed holds on the future, so have we facilitated change and made the future unknown. Clearly, we have far fewer certainties about the future of our civilization than the Chinese once had about the future of theirs. The great problem of our age is that we want things to change more rapidly, and at the same time we want to have a better knowledge of things to come. I do not say a reconciliation of these desires is impossible, but it does raise a problem.

SOCIAL FORECASTING: THE STATE OF THE ART

● o. d. duncan

A "state of the art" report on social forecasting should, in all honesty, be quite brief. Such an art, in the sense of a coherent body of precepts and practices, has not yet been developed. It would be misleading to claim that social forecasting is carried on in a continuous and concerted fashion as one could claim in regard to, say, economic or business forecasting. The contrast is readily verified by comparing the articles on (sociological) "Prediction" and "Prediction and Forecasting, Economic" in the *International Encyclopedia of the Social Sciences*. So prevalent is the latter activity, in fact, that the practice and performance of economic forecasters are now considered worthy of formal statistical analysis.

It is a banal observation that many kinds of social forecasting are routinely carried on in an implicit way. The very possibility of social organization rests on our ability to anticipate correctly, in a large proportion of instances, the behavior of others. Society, from this point of view, is an intricate reticulation of expectations and commitments concerning future actions and reactions. Thus, I have fairly little hesitation in forecasting that most of us will be reporting our incomes to the government in April 1970, just as we did in April 1969. Parents, at least some of them, save money now because they expect their children to be in college ten years hence. The round of social activity and the progress of the human life cycle are no doubt less strictly patterned and regular than some astronomical phenomena. But a social calendar is useful and is used for somewhat the same reasons as in an almanac.

The knowledge of the future that is a minimum requirement for organized social life has to do with commitments already undertaken or implied, or with intentions already expressed or assumed. There is legitimate concern with the fallibility of such expectations, that is, with the extent to which anticipations may be falsified by the operation of contingent factors. For some purposes, as for the calculation of insurance rates, the degree of fallibility may be expressed in terms of probabilities. Recurrent contingencies, despite their contribution to life's uncertainty in individual cases, may themselves have a kind of statistical pattern. In this event, the assumption of persistence of pattern may serve as an adequate basis for anticipating in the aggregate that which needs to be anticipated only on an aggregate basis.

Something quite different, of course, is conveyed by the more tantalizing connotation of social forecasting, which has to do with the anticipation of social *change*. Even in the case of social change, however, some kinds of gradual and progressive alterations of social arrangements are, under certain conditions, so monotonously repeated that a forecast of their continuation becomes routine. The expectation of continuous change then comes to be "built into" the social fabric; whole industries are predicted upon the assumption of more or less regular and expectable "growth." Such expectations may, of course, prove to be erroneous at one time or another. Indeed, perhaps the most interesting, severe, and significant challenge to put to any presumptuous discipline of social forecasting would be the demand that it anticipate the changes in the accustomed patterns of change.

Population Projections: A Parable

". . . fear skepticism far less than credulity."

—Bertrand de Jouvenel

There is one exception to the opening statement that an art of social forecasting has not yet been formulated. That exception is, indeed, instructive, for the production of demographic forecasts has gone on long enough for us to have materials with which to begin an inductive study of the behavior of forecasters. I do not tarry over the interesting "prehistory" of this subject, which is documented in various studies. Table 1 offers a compressed summary of the "reputable" or "scientific" population forecasts that have dominated our changing conceptions of the demographic future during most of this century.

The supposition that the curve of the future is implicit in the record of the past was, of course, most forthrightly acknowledged in the work of Pearl and associates with the logistic curve. Extrapolations to 1920 and beyond were based on a beautiful fit of the formula to decennial census counts for 1790 to 1910.

Among the attractive features of the logistic, as compared with other formulas that had been proposed, was its "rational" stipulation of an upper limit (approached asymptotically) to population growth.

Whelpton's introduction, in 1928, of the "component" method of forecasting marked a radical departure in technique from Pearl's logistic, and set the pattern for all subsequent official forecasting in this country. In simplest terms, the method requires the separate construction of future series of births, deaths, and migration balances which are then combined by demographic accounting formulas to secure both a projection of total population and its composition or makeup in terms of age, sex, color, and possibly other characteristics. Although in the initial presentation only one series of future populations was provided, it became customary in subsequent applications to prepare and publish several alternative projections, embodying a variety of assumptions concerning the future course of fertility, mortality, and migration. The exhibition of these alternatives was no doubt intended to reinforce the emphasis on the "empirical" character of the projections, as contrasted to the

TABLE 1. Projected Population, in Millions, of the United States, According to Selected Calculations: 1920–2000.*

Projection		1920	1930	1940	1950	1960	1970	1980	1990	2000
1. Pearl (logistic) (asymptote=197)		107	122	136	149	159	168	175	180	185
2. Whelpton		...	124	138	152	163	171	...	...	186
3. Thompson	High	...	...	133	147	160	174	187	...	...
and Whelpton	Low	...	...	132	137	138	135	128	...	...
4. Census	High	...	...	...	148	162	177	...	...	...
Whelpton	Medium	...	...	...	145	153	160	164	165	163
	Low	...	...	...	145	150	152	...	...	...
5. Census (Zitter	High	...	...	...	...	181	219	273	...	...
and Siegel)	Low	...	...	...	...	179	203	231	...	...
6. Census	High	...	...	...	...	...	209	250	300	361
(Siegel)	Low	...	...	...	...	...	205	228	256	282
(Observed)		106	123	132	151	171	...	...	...	...

*Sources: 1. Raymond Pearl, The Biology of Population Growth (New York: Knopf, 1925). 2. P. K. Whelpton, "Population in the United States, 1925–1975," American Journal of Sociology 34 (September, 1928): 253–270. 3. U. S. National Resources Committee, Population Statistics 1. National Data (Washington: Government Printing Office, 1937), estimates of future population prepared by Warren S. Thompson and P. K. Whelpton. 4. U. S. Bureau of the Census, Forecasts of the Population of the United States, 1945–1975, by P. K. Whelpton, assisted by Hope Tisdale Eldridge and Jacob S. Siegel (Washington: Government Printing Office, 1947). 5. U. S. Bureau of the Census, "Illustrative Projections of the Population of the United States, by Age and Sex, 1960 to 1980," by Meyer Zitter and Jacob S. Siegel, Current Population Reports, Series P-25, No. 187, November, 1958. 6. U. S. Bureau of the Census, "Projections of the Population of the United States, by Age, Sex, and Color to 1990, with Extensions of Population by Age and Sex to 2015," by Jacob S. Siegel, Current Population Reports, Series P-25, No. 381, December, 1967.

putative "rational" basis of the logistic. In any event, despite variation in terminology—figures on future population have been variously termed predictions, forecasts, projections, illustrative projections, calculations, or estimates—the "reputable" forecasters always stressed that their results were no more than a consistent deduction of the consequences of their assumptions. Nevertheless, in the discussions of the derivation of their assumptions, there was always implicit, and usually explicit, a quest for "reasonable" or "likely" anticipations of the future course of the vital rates.

Despite the completely different technique and somewhat variant philosophy underlying the first component projections as compared with the use of the logistic, the two techniques as initially applied yielded virtually indistinguishable forecasts for as long as seven decades ahead. The logistic curve, however, did imply a specific maximum population, while in 1928 Whelpton did not venture to project an upper limit on growth.

The 1930's and After

In the early 1930's, demographers began to contemplate seriously the possibility that population size would reach a maximum and then undergo a decline within the foreseeable future. The shift in mood is apparent from the fact that the projection made ten years earlier had, by 1937, come to look like a "high" alternative. The accompanying "low" alternative showed population numbers reaching a maximum by 1955 and beginning a decline thereafter. Discussion accompanying the numerical results, moreover, tended to suggest the credibility of incipient decline. Projections incorporating this feature were again issued in 1947, despite considerable upward revision of both "high" and "low" alternatives.

To speculate *ad hominem*, it seems that the prospect of incipient decline had gained a firm hold on the imagination of the demographer. Moreover, despite the general tendency to regard the prospective cessation of growth as a "pessimistic" outlook, it is clear that the pre-eminent American student of future population during the 1930's and 1940's, P. K. Whelpton, was persuaded of the desirability of an imminent stabilization of population size. In his 1947 report, Whelpton adduced arguments tending to show that the U. S. was not below its long run economic optimum population. He observed, moreover, that slackening of growth would be favorable to the interests of conservationists and that it might lead to improvement in the quality of the population.

Whereas by 1940 it was clear that the most reputable forecasts of the 1920's had erred on the high side, in 1950 it was plain that the demographic work of the depression and war period had issued in understatements of future population. The achievement of a new orientation was powerfully assisted by the stinging critique of the economist, J. S. Davis. He averred:

> For years demographers, biologists, economists, and other specialists have held the firm conviction that population "trends" are reliably predictable. Emphatically, *they are not.* . . .
>
> Two of the persistent errors in this field are: (1) the willingness of the specialists to attempt to comply with urgent requests for estimates or forecasts that cannot be reliably made—many such demands should be resisted; (2) the tendency of users of such estimates and forecasts to ignore the qualifications with which they are hedged. Three other errors have been important in the past three decades. One has been the tendency for those who make estimates based on assumptions to come to put faith in the results, ignoring their own awareness of the basic uncertainties. Another is the tendency to believe in a sort of trend magic; the very term "population trend" is deceptive and dangerous. A third has been a conservative bias in connection with future births, deaths, and net in-migration. . . .
>
> [T]here is now ample reason for rejecting, for the calculable future, the entrenched convictions that our population is approaching a peak from which a decline is more probable than even stability at that level. The grounds on which the former conviction was based have collapsed. No population peak of any size, at any date, is either in sight or safely predictable.

Although Davis's language was especially emphatic, his observations were not extreme by comparison with those of such critics as Dorn (1950), Hajnal (1955), and Glass (1967)—all of them eminent demographers, by the way.

The critics of demographic projections were clearly successful on one score. The assumption of a movement to a zero growth rate in the foreseeable future was eliminated in projections prepared in the 1950's and 1960's. Nothing the critics said, however, appeared to diminish the "willingness of the specialists" to accede to demands for frequently updated forecasts. Indeed, with the advent of the electronic computer it has become possible to calculate more elaborate projections as well as to experiment with new devices for deriving assumptions, notably the "cohort-fertility" approach used in the most recent Census Bureau projections.

The merit of this approach is not that it discloses the secret of what the future holds, but rather that it displays the mechanics of the projection in such a way as to make more evident exactly what is being assumed. The basis for calculating future births in these projections is the average number of children expected to be born to each cohort of women during its entire reproductive cycle, supplemented by an expected pattern of distribution of these births over the reproductive years. Thus the high pattern of fertility is taken to be one for which the mean number of births per woman completing the reproductive cycle is 3.35, while the low pattern calls for 2.45 children per woman. The latter figure, by the way, is not as low as the historic minimum of 2.3 reached by cohorts of women born between 1905 and 1915. Whereas the Whelpton projections had (implicitly) contemplated a further decline below that benchmark, the current projections make no allowance for such a decline. Apparently it is no longer interesting to contemplate even the hypothetical possibility that the American woman can breed at a mere replacement level. Accordingly, all alternative series in the official projections now show very substantial future growth with no cessation thereof in sight.

Prophets, Partisans, and Demographers

We are led, then, to certain observations on the behavior of demographic forecasters.

First, this species is in no way immune to the operation of social forces that distort the vision of other investigators. In particular, there is a strong element of the fad or social pressure operative here. It is magnified by the very fact of the high prestige and widespread acceptance of population projections. When the forecaster sees his results being adopted in many quarters and hears them coming back to him in the transmuted form of economic anticipations and the like, he can hardly resist the temptation to believe.

Second, sheer fascination with mechanics is the enemy of an imaginative approach. One cannot read Raymond Pearl without developing strong empathy for his purely esthetic response to the smooth symmetry of the logistic curve. For a demographer, the description of the procedures of a cohort-component projection has its own beauty—although in this case the outsider can less readily appreciate it.

Now, it should not be necessary to insist that there *is* real value in the work on population projections, entirely apart from their utility or disutility as the basis for forecasts. The logistic curve is, in fact, a most instructive model of growth, and equally so whether or not it applies in particular empirical instances. The component projection is, indeed, a useful way to convey insight into the mechanism of population change. One can see how, for example, future growth tends to be "built into" current age structure (itself the consequence of past growth) and thus capitalize on the resolution of the paradox that the crude birth rate may be rising while age-specific or cohort fertility is declining. Nevertheless, neither didactically illuminating models nor analytically incisive projection procedures are guarantees of forecasting accuracy. To the extent that the demographer has confused the two kinds of things, to that extent has he been mesmerized by his own devices.

Third, in person and collectively the demographer is not immune from the psychology of habit. Orientations useful for envisaging illuminating assumptions at one point persist into a period when they no longer have utility. While, in principle, the assumptions underlying a set of projections can be revised drastically at any time, there is a reluctance to give up that which has become familiar and comfortable through reiterations.

Davis's critique of the mentality of demographic forecasters could become pertinent again—*mutatis mutandis*—at any time. The upward curve of population cannot continue forever. When it breaks, will there be the same perplexity and equivocation on the part of the professionals that we witnessed in the late 1940's and early 1950's?

Apart from their reputation as prophets, demographers should be solicitous of their role as partisans of the open society. Just now, they are rendering a one-sided service. It is all to the good that they keep open the ugly possibility of "explosive" growth, with the nation moving rapidly toward the half billion mark shortly after the turn of the century. Should they not, at the same time, start now to state the demographic conditions under which a stationary state can be reached and chart for us some alternative time paths to that state, however unlikely (for the moment) such a prospect may seem? Before we shall bring a halt to population growth we must begin to believe that its cessation is a conceivable state of affairs. It can as easily be portrayed by demographic methods as can any situation of uninterrupted growth. If we keep always before us the alternatives of explosive growth and the transition to a stationary population, we will neither be bemused by the apparent inevitability of Pearl's logistic adjustment nor surprised by the unexpected change when it occurs, as it surely will.

Social Trends and Technological Influences

One of the few systematic and explicit statements of social forecasting appears in William F. Ogburn's study, *The Social Effects of Aviation* (chapters

3 and 4). The work as a whole is an effort to portray future progress in the technology of aviation, the probable uses and applications of this technology, and the impact of these upon a variety of social institutions and organizations. Among other things, Ogburn offered a "forecast of forecasting."

> The following study is a somewhat pioneer effort. . . . The ability to look ahead with some success is particularly important in a changing society. The best way to learn to do anything is to go ahead and try it. . . . What is needed is many social scientists working at the problem of forecasting the future as well as scientists writing histories of past events. With many social scientists working on the future, we should gradually accumulate a set of useful procedures. . . . In the course of time, with others working on forecasting, a tradition of usages will be built up, and we shall know better how to do it.

Perhaps to encourage the attitude of "getting one's feet wet," Ogburn began his discussion of forecasting with the observations that much forecasting is in fact carried on in planning and the conduct of everyday life and that rough approximations are useful for many practical purposes. There follows an exposition of "prediction by measurement," in which it is assumed that the problem is to extend into the future a time series established for the past. Extrapolation is stated to be more reliable in regard to the *trend* or general tendency of the series than in regard to the *fluctuations* around the trend, and to be more reliable, moreover, for the first few periods in the immediate future than for more distant periods. It is noted that "carrying curves forward is not an objective method even when it is done by means of a mathematical equation." Alternative mathematical formulas may provide about equally good fits to past data but yield widely differing extrapolations for future dates. In making an extrapolation, moreover, the forecaster will take into account the expected operation of limiting factors and other influences that may well cause the trend to bend up or down. In any event, extrapolations must rest on the assumption of the absence of major disturbing factors: "The logic of prediction is that the universe will be much like the universe of the past. If some greatly upsetting factor occurs, such as a war or a revolutionary invention, the conditions are so changed that extrapolation is hardly worth trying."

In discussing the problem of forecasting in the absence of statistical time series, Ogburn suggests that one proceed by imagining what such series would show if they did exist. Thus, the forecaster would first mentally estimate the past trend and then consider the prospect of its continuation. Warnings are given about the several kinds of bias that may easily distort thinking in this situation: "Try as we may to prevent wishful thinking, there is nothing so effective as plenty of data to correct it. But in cases of scarcity of data, one way of trying to reduce the error is to reduce the emotional element in thinking." In particular, Ogburn notes the danger of being too conservative, insofar as social pressures operate to discourage forecasters from making "wild" statements.

It is interesting that Ogburn was so clearly aware of the conservative bias in forecasting, for several of his own forecasts seem to have erred on the conservative side. His projection of air passenger traffic was seen to be too low within about five years of its publication. His discussion of the future of jet propulsion seems, at least in retrospect, to have been overly cautious. In another field, that of technological influences on the future of the family, Ogburn thought in 1955 that it would take "many years" for a physiological contraceptive to become widely used, and was unwilling to forecast that such a technique would become important within a quarter of a century even though he expected it to become so at some indefinite time in the future.

Turning from the abstract consideration of forecasting procedure to the substance of social forecasts, we recall that Ogburn laid emphasis on two closely related concepts: social trends and the social effects of inventions. The foundation for his use of these concepts was laid in the classic volume, *Social Change With Respect to Culture and Original Nature* (1922; new edition, 1950). This work develops thoroughly the thesis of cultural accumulation via invention, diffusion, and progressive augmentation of the culture base. It also gives the first exposition of the famous "cultural lag" concept, which provided a diagnosis of the social problems that arise when one part of culture—often, but not always, technology and scientific knowledge—changes in such a way as to require an adaptation by other parts of culture, but such adaptation is delayed or impeded by inertia and resistances.

Continuity in Change?

The specific application of the trend concept arose first in Ogburn's research on social correlates of the business cycle. Here, removal of the trend component from economic time series was undertaken as a preliminary step in the measurement of economic fluctuations; and the latter were then correlated with such social indicators as unemployment, immigration, strikes, marriages, births, deaths, suicides, and liquor consumption. There was no formal attempt to develop such correlations into forecasting models.

Trends themselves were the focus of interest in the several annual symposia on *Recent Social Changes* edited by Ogburn (published in *American Journal of Sociology*, 1928–35 and 1942) and in the monumental *Recent Social Trends* (President's Research Committee, 1933), of which Ogburn was research director. In initiating this work, he clearly had in mind the potential utility of trend studies for anticipating future problems. A statement written in 1928 was perhaps more prophetic than the author realized:

> The social sciences ought to render aid in these times of change and uncertainty. Unfortunately, as sciences, they are young. Indeed, their achievements in the exact measurement of the relationships of social

phenomena are meager, too much so for much reliable prediction. Nor do we know that the social sciences will ever attain the state of accurate prediction in the whole realm of sociology. But one generalization does stand out sharply in our social and historical studies. It is that there is a continuity in cultural change; one event grows out of another. An invention is a co-ordination of existing elements. Discoveries are based on previous knowledge. Miracles do not occur, and revolutions are few. The greater our knowledge, the rarer are unheralded changes. Indeed, sudden, dramatic, and complete changes are decidedly the exception. The principle of continuity in social change is very reassuring. Our various studies of statistical time series show a very important thing, namely, that the measured trend of events and phenomena is the best guide that we yet have for the prediction of the future. Knowledge is the antithesis of mystery and uncertainty. And the knowledge of what has occurred and of what is happening is the safest guide we have. With more complete statistics and with better measurement we shall attain fuller knowledge of what is happening to us and where we are going. Only with these shall we be in a position even to begin to speak of control.

Later statements reiterated the theme of continuity in change, and Ogburn actually went so far as to claim in 1957 as his "discovery" the principle "that social trends seldom change their direction quickly and sharply." Therefore, "the projection of a trend line into the future has some trustworthiness and tells us with some degree of probability what the future will be." A further implication is that planners and others concerned to influence future changes are generally well advised to note that "success is more likely to come to those who work for and with social trend than to those who work against it. . . . As the materials with which the architect works are stone and steel, brick and glass, the materials with which the statesman works are social trends."

The tie-in of social trends with the effects of invention arises from the observation that progressive technological changes are the basis of many persistent social changes. A number of different inventions may have convergent effects. This observation may partially explain the persistence of social trends, for if they are the product of many influences, each of them of relatively small import by itself, then a trend will not be readily altered by changing only one or two of these influences. Thus, Ogburn expected the advent of the helicopter to influence urban decentralization; but many other technological factors were seen as contributing to suburbanization.

In the effort either to catalog past effects of inventions or to anticipate future changes due to existing or anticipated technology, Ogburn recommended a sequence of inquiries. First, consider the uses of the invention and the immediate changes in individual habits or institutional practices that are required for these uses to be practical. These changes, more or less concurrent with the adoption of an invention, are termed primary influences.

There follow from them the derivative influences, coming into play via more or less lengthy chains of causation and often subject to considerable delay. While derivative effects are more numerous than primary influences, and second order derivative effects are more numerous still, the magnitude of the successive effects tends to be attenuated. Thus, the invention of the tin can may have contributed to the reduction of the labor of housekeeping, thereby facilitating women's emancipation from the home, and ultimately have led by this route to a reduction in the birth rate. But this particular influence on the birth rate, small as it must have been by comparison with the aggregate of other influences, would be difficult to demonstrate conclusively and could form no large part of the explanation of the decline in fertility.

Quite aside from its theoretical merit, therefore, the concept of derivative effects of inventions cannot be a powerful tool in forecasting. Although the book on aviation records a large number of past and potential effects of the technology, Ogburn conceded that few of them are due entirely to the airplane. By the same token, when reasoning from effect to cause, as in the attempt to infer or anticipate changes in the family, it is admitted that effects of technological change are but one source of past or potential changes in family life. Hence, an account of "Technology and the Future of the Family" (Ogburn and Nimkoff, 1955, chapter 12) "is not an attempt to describe the family of the future" but merely an effort to foresee the effects of inventions on the family. It is maintained, however, that there is an advantage in focusing on the technological factor. Whereas moral, religious, and ideological factors not primarily due to technology and science are difficult to project into the future, enough is known about recent and prospective inventions to make it worthwhile to conjecture their forthcoming effects: "For the next twenty to fifty years, probably most of the inventional influences that will change the family will come from inventions already in existence."

In summary, it is quite apparent that Ogburn envisaged a close working relationship between technological forecasting and social forecasting. Indeed, the former was seen as providing part of the basis of the latter. Technological forecasts would be examined for their bearing upon social trends so as to provide aid in the extrapolation of these trends. Since technological change was largely treated as an exogenous factor with respect to social change, it follows that Ogburn's scheme does not offer a major contribution to the art of technological forecasting proper. He was, however, not inattentive to the impact of social factors on technology. On the one hand he saw "demand" as an influence both on invention itself and on the adoption of inventions. On the other, he discussed various categories of social "resistances" to adoption. I think it is fair to say, however, that he did not actually contemplate a composite social-technological model in which technology becomes an endogenous variable subject to feedback from social factors which themselves responded earlier to technological changes, even though he would have freely conceded the possibility of such interactions.

Three Forecasts

I. THE IQ PARADOX

I wish now to mention three historically important social forecasts which may serve to illustrate the variety of possibilities and difficulties in this field. Perhaps these examples will show that forecasts may have considerable intellectual and social value quite apart from their accuracy as prognostications.

The first is the forecast of a decline in the intelligence of the general population which has been rather widely discussed for several decades, both in the United States and in Great Britain. The forecast was derived from the juxtaposition of several observations: that measured intelligence of both children and adults varies inversely with socioeconomic status; that the lower social strata generally have larger families than the higher; and that within strata, as well as in the population as a whole, children's intelligence test scores are inversely related to number of siblings. If the dull are outbreeding the gifted, the intelligence of future generations is expected to shift downward by comparison with the present generation, whether the transmission of intelligence between generations is genetic, environmental, or a combination of both. Lorimer and Osborn (1934), for example, presented one illustrative calculation on which an average decline of 0.9 IQ points per generation would be expected. They cited another estimate by the psychologist Lentz (1927) of a change of 4.4 points in median IQ's in two successive generations. Whereas the former calculation was derived only from class differences in IQ scores, the latter takes account of variations among individual families according to size.

How seriously such a forecast might be taken was illustrated by the discussion of Robert C. Cook (1951), who restated it quite bluntly: "Competent scholars who have had the patience to separate the grains of verified fact from the mountainous chaff of mere opinion and faulty methodology are agreed that today's differential birth rate makes a decline in intelligence inevitable." Cook went on to argue at some length that a perceptible drop in average IQ would bring a complex modern industrial civilization to the brink of disaster: "Each new technological development in our society demands more intelligence, rather than less." Indeed, he went so far as to contemplate the very "destruction of modern technological culture requiring a high level of ability to operate its complex machinery."

It should be noted that the projection of a declining trend in intelligence was not based on the actual observation of such a trend over some period in the past. Instead, the projection was a derivation or inference. Actually, there was not the degree of unanimity of qualified opinion concerning this inference that Cook implied. Some competent psychologists and geneticists expressed strong disagreement while others supported it with equal vehemence. By the early 1950's, there was, moreover, an accumulation of considerable evidence showing an actual *increase* in measured intelligence in both the British and American populations. Tuddenham (1948) calculated, for example, that the median test score for World War II enlisted soldiers was distinctly superior to those of World War I, even after adjusting for the change in educational level. The monumental inquiry of the Scottish Mental Survey Committee (1949) found an increase of about two IQ points in the average score of the population of eleven-year olds as of 1947 by comparison with the same age group in 1932. In these and other studies reporting similar results, the investigators were careful to note that the observed increase could well be due to environmental improvements. In this case a rise in average test scores might occur concurrently with an actual deterioration of the genetic basis of intelligence, with the environmental effect masking the genetic effect.

The true explanation, though anticipated in some of the discussion in the early 1950's, was not actually established for another decade. I quote the summary of their study by Higgins, Reed, and Reed (1962):

> This is a study of 1,016 families in which IQ values for both parents and one or more of their children were available. It is the first *large* sample with IQ data for both parents and offspring. IQ values were also at hand for the unmarried or the nonreproducing siblings of the parents. The inclusion of these siblings allowed us to resolve the old paradox presented by the failure of the general intelligence level to decline in accord with the large negative correlation ($-.30$) between intelligence and the number of children in the family.
>
> The explanation of the paradox is that when the single or non-reproductive siblings of the parents are included the negative correlation disappears. The higher reproductive rate of those in the lower IQ groups who are parents is offset by the larger proportion of their siblings who never marry or who fail to reproduce when married. Thus, the IQ level of the whole population should remain relatively static from one generation to the next, or at least not drop rapidly.

Independent confirmation of these results was shortly reported by Bajema (1963).

There is, of course, more to be learned about the intricate mechanisms that give rise to these several kinds of findings. The utility of the original forecast was perhaps in lending a sense of urgency to the scientific quest and in stimulating investigators to exercise their imagination in seeking a resolution of the paradox.

The vision of a "nation of congenital morons" that Cook had conjured up on the basis of the forecasted dysgenic trend may perhaps be regarded as an example of a "developmental construct," as that notion was presented by Lasswell (1941). Lasswell urged social scientists to "consider alternative versions of the future, making explicit those expectations about the future that are so often buried in the realm of hunch." A "picture of the probable," not a "dogmatic forecast," will "stimulate the individual specialist to clarify for himself his expectations about the future, as a guide to the timing of scientific work," for it is "rational for the scientist to give priority to problems connected with the survival of democratic society."

II. THE GARRISON STATE

Where Cook and others perceived a threat to survival in the prospect of an erosion of the supply of mental ability, Lasswell foresaw a movement toward a world of "garrison states." This construct was presented as "frankly imaginative though disciplined by careful consideration of the past." Emphasis was placed on a configuration of developments and their synthesis into a "total" picture of the future, as contrasted with the "itemistic" analysis of particular trends. Thus, a comprehensive portrayal of the garrison state subsumes a number of specific forecasts, and it is difficult to do justice to the construct in a brief summary. By the same token, some of these forecasts can be seen— nearly three decades after the fact—to have been wide of the mark, or at least premature, while others appear to have been inspired by remarkable prescience.

Present-day critics of the "military-industrial complex" will surely not wish to argue that Lasswell erred in anticipating the emerging "supremacy of the specialist on violence, the soldier" and in foreseeing that the military elite would come to cultivate expertness in the skills of civilian management. Thus, the studies in military sociology of the last few years may be seen as a response to Lasswell's insistence that "we need more adequate data . . . about the trends in the skill pattern of dominant elite groups in different parts of the world."

Lacking essential qualifications for the task, I do not feel it would be appropriate for me to attempt a point-by-point assessment of Lasswell's forecast. The interested reader will wish to consult the author's own restatement and defense of it, written two decades later, as well as the critical remarks of Samuel P. Huntington, who concludes that such "images of increasing military power in the United States were . . . at best only partially true." One difficulty in any assessment is that the original forecast was offered in the context of a discussion of "world politics" and the ramifications of the development toward the garrison state were seen as subject to considerable variation from one nation to another. Thus, Lasswell's "development construct" is in some ways like a Weberian "ideal type," which cannot as such be verified or disproved but can only be used with greater or lesser success for heuristic purposes.

I do wish to comment on one aspect of the fate of Lasswell's forecast. In teaching a course in social change for undergraduates, I have found it difficult to get them interested in Lasswell's argument. If I read their attitude correctly, it is along the lines of "What else is new?" I suppose that if one lives in a garrison state from infancy to adulthood, the forecast that such a thing will come to pass is not very newsworthy. This diagnosis of the undergraduate reaction may be relevant to the theme of cohort analysis alluded to later in this paper.

III. CLASS STRATIFICATION

Like the two forecasts already described, Sibley's forecast of the future emergence of social classes in America was not a mere trend extrapolation. For one thing, he did not, writing in 1942, have actual measurements of social stratification at hand. Hence, he had first to infer what the past trend had been. He then engaged in some analysis of the forces producing that trend, estimated their probable strength in the foreseeable future, and issued his forecast on the basis of their estimated impact on the trend. The forecast, moreover, was not unconditional; instead, he was concerned to point out a mechanism that might be brought into play to counteract the projected trend and thus to falsify the forecast. Although the student of social stratification today has much more information to go on than did Sibley, there has hardly been any improvement on the general strategy of his procedure.

Summarized in his own words, the argument went as follows:

> Not universal equality nor near-equality of status but a high rate of vertical mobility has been the most important demographic basis of this nation's tradition of classlessness. The long-existing favorable balance of vertical circulation of individuals in American society, i.e., the excess of upward over downward moves, has diminished and seems likely to be further reduced. Development of class consciousness will be likely to occur unless our social institutions are so readjusted as to produce a large amount of compensating up-and-down movement of individuals. The educational system, which is the chief American institution explicitly conceived as a mechanism for facilitating the ascent of talented individuals, must become more highly selective of individual merit if the loss of certain dwindling sources of upward mobility is to be offset.

Three factors were identified as having created in the past a net balance of upward over downward mobility. First, technological progress and economic growth continuously reduced the proportion of jobs requiring low degrees of skill applied to physical production while increasing the proportion demanding educational qualifications and the exercise of intellectual skills. Thus the proportion of white collar workers had grown continuously at the expense of the proportion of manual and farm workers. As to the future, Sibley was concerned that technological unemployment might come to assume large proportions, and that the economic stagnation of the 1930's might return upon the close of World War II. Hence, it was regarded as quite uncertain that this past source of mobility would continue to work in the same way.

Second, the tide of immigration during the latter part of the 19th and the early part of the 20th centuries was shown to have been a powerful factor in vertical circulation, inasmuch as most immigrants, being unskilled, entered the occupational structure at the bottom, inducing an upward shift on the part of native workers. But this flow of immigrants was checked by World War I and subsequently limited by statutes. Sibley did not foresee a resumption of this influence on upward mobility.

Third, the differential birth rate prevailing during the historical period with which Sibley was concerned tended to create a "vacuum" at the top of the occupational structure, thus inducing upward movement from the more prolific lower strata. Although Sibley was not in a position actually to show a reduction in the intensity of fertility differentials, he reasoned on the basis of European experience that such a reduction might well occur in America. (In fact, this subforecast was borne out by fertility statistics from the 1950 and 1960 censuses.) In short:

> The last three decades have seen one of the three sources of the move-
> ment, namely immigration, choked off, once for the duration of a war
> and later seemingly permanently. Another source, differential fertility,
> may conceivably be drying up. The future of the third source, tech-
> nological progress, depends upon the not-yet-demonstrated ability of
> the nation's leaders to readjust political-economic institutions so as to
> produce a genuine "economy of plenty."

But even if these factors should work toward an increase in rigidity of the social structure, it was possible that their effects might be offset by the improvement of the mechanism of social selection on the basis of ability. For if the less able offspring of high status families were exposed to fair competition with the more able offspring of low status families, compensating streams of upward and downward movement would ensue in such a way as to maintain the rate of vertical circulation. Sibley did not venture a forecast of whether this would occur. Instead, he contented himself with showing that existing inequality in educational opportunity was sufficiently great that its rectification could well have the effect under consideration. Specifically, he demonstrated that boys whose fathers had high occupational status had much better chances of continuing their education than boys of the same measured ability levels from less advantaged occupational backgrounds. Hence "it is evident that the American educational system is far from being as effective as it might be in counteracting tendencies toward social stratification." In conclusion:

> If we propose to preserve the American faith in freedom from social-
> class barriers to individual achievement, some institutional changes
> must be planned and effectuated in order to offset the previously dis-
> cussed diminution of the favorable balance of vertical circulation. Edu-
> cational institutions appear to offer the most promising field for such

changes. If the changes are made well enough and quickly enough, they may forestall the onset of an acute case of class conflict and indefinitely postpone the death of a leading American ideal. If not, our social arteries are likely to become sclerotic.

A complete evaluation of Sibley's forecast would require too great a digression into problems of concept and measurement in the analysis of stratification trends; I have fully discussed these issues elsewhere. One can, however, state that Sibley's forecast of increasing rigidification and declining rate of vertical circulation has not—at least, not yet—been borne out by events. Indeed, it appears from Natalie Rogoff's research that Sibley was also in error in supposing that there had been such a trend in the decades immediately preceding the time of his study.

One can also comment briefly on the component parts of Sibley's forecast. First, contrary to his guarded or even pessimistic outlook (which was shared by many at the time), rapid economic growth did persist after World War II, and changes in the occupational structure favorable to upward movement continued. Second, although immigration operated in about the way that Sibley expected, the role previously played by immigration has been assumed, for the last two or three decades, by an accelerated movement off farms. Inasmuch as that movement is now nearly spent, Sibley's conjecture becomes relevant once more. Third, although Sibley's anticipation of diminished fertility differentials was correct, this was the least important element in his forecast, and the least adequately analyzed one. As to the impact of the educational system, it is difficult to say exactly what has happened. One thing is clear: the impact of social class origins on educational opportunity is still clearly visible. The most recent data on the relative roles of personal ability and parental socioeconomic status in educational attainment (U. S. Department of HEW, 1969) look very much like the data for the late 1920's that Sibley studied. On the other hand, it is also clear that the educational system introduces much variation into occupational achievement that is independent of family background and thus, on balance, is a force inducing openness rather than rigidification of the stratification structure. Combining this observation with the strong suspicion that schooling has come to have a larger role in occupational selection in recent decades than in the past (Blau and Duncan, 1967), we surmise that the educational system has indeed functioned as a "counteracting tendency," though not exactly in the way that Sibley anticipated it might. At the same time, it should be emphasized that the diagnosis offered by Sibley still holds good: the educational system has a long way to go in becoming as effective as it might be in effecting equality of opportunity.

A significant point about all three of the forecasts just described—declining intelligence, the garrison state, and rigidification of the social structure—as well as the forecasts of population decline summarized earlier, is that they do not become uninteresting or irrelevant just because they are wholly or partially inaccurate for the period immediately following their formulation.

The tendencies that might issue in the realization of any of these prospects remain latent even if held in check by other tendencies whose influence is preponderant for the moment. If so, what really matters is not whether the forecasts in question are "right" or "wrong," but rather that they focus concern where it should be focused. I am told that the slogan for the 1970 census will be, "We need to know where we are so we will know where we are going." One might well reverse the proposition: *we need to know where we may be going in order to understand where we are.*

Futurism

I shall not attempt a comprehensive review or evaluation of the mushrooming intellectual and social movement that is conveniently labeled "futurism," but some casual observations are offered on the basis of a limited sampling of its literature.

First, there is much excitement about the purported novelty of these efforts. As befits the subject matter, the futurist spends little time looking backward in order to establish the credentials of his intellectual ancestors. There is clearly an urgent need for good historical work on the development of futurist ideas; one suspects it would be easy to establish a filiation to the 18th and 19th century concepts of "progress." An interesting beginning of such historical work is the late Arthur M. Schlesinger's essay on "Casting the National Horoscope" (1947). He sampled a "rich and abundant literature of conjecture" dating from colonial times, which he noted has been neglected by historians. I find it salutary that Schlesinger juxtaposed the modern work of "scientific" demographic forecasters with the popular 19th century prophecies of the Millennium.

Second, one has the strong suspicion that much of the futurist literature, when it touches on specifically sociological issues—as distinct from technological change—is really not much more than a rhetorical stance for discussing *present* social problems. As such, it is a perfectly legitimate and time-honored device. Schlesinger records, for example, that much of the controversy between North and South in the period preceding the Civil War was conducted in terms of "secular prophecy." One need not, therefore, impute to all futurist writing a serious intent to forecast. The "scenario" (as it sometimes is now called) may only be an exceptionally dramatic way of presenting an issue that is ready to be confronted now.

One way to see this is to observe how modifications of purported long-term forecasts occur within short periods of time. One member of the Commission on the Year 2000 learned how events can catch up with forecasts. In a 1967 article, Daniel P. Moynihan wrote:

> These notes were originally written in February 1966, at a time when the continuity of American government seemed almost a fact of nature. Now, in the early summer of 1967, one learns that the approval of only two state legislatures is required in order for a national constitutional

convention to be convened. . . . the possibility that a convention will meet and will go on to draft profoundly important innovations is altogether real. Nothing is fixed.

The author of this instructive confession leaves us wondering whether he came to realize that the perceptive analysis written in 1966 was really about 1966 and not about 2000.

Third, to judge from fragmentary and secondary accounts, the futurist methods of foreseeing are not so very different from those that Ogburn prescribed in more prosaic language some time ago. (See, for example, the summary of Burnham Beckwith's *The Next 500 Years* in the October 1968 issue of *The Futurist.*) There is the same emphasis on continuity of trends and on trend extrapolation as the basic method of forecast, and the same treatment of technology as the exogenous prime mover of social change. We need not assume that there is a direct derivation of futurist forecasting techniques from Ogburn's work on social change; common social and intellectual influences may account for the resemblance between them.

Fourth, it would be a mistake to exaggerate the extent to which futurist inquiry is in fact governed by explicit and communicable methods. The title of Daniel Bell's essay, "Twelve Modes of Prediction" (1965), may arouse the prospective reader's anticipation of reading a balanced assessment of forecasting techniques. But the author quickly tells us that he will "not be concerned with relevant methodological tests of adequacy." Indeed, he concedes at the outset that the work of developing a logical classification of approaches and a specification of their appropriateness for different kinds of problems remains to be done. What he has given us, therefore, is a kind of sampling of conceptual schemes current in political sociology, the exposition of which is enlivened by occasional remarks about the problems involved in trying "to anticipate certain likely occurrences. . . ."

In the work of the Commission on the Year 2000 (1967) relatively little attention has been given thus far to problems of method. The Commission has provided us, instead, with an interesting collection of wise essays on various social problems, some of which are explicitly oriented toward the future while many of them are really about the urgent problems of the present, as I had occasion to note above. There was evidently little disposition to respond to the challenge of one of the Commission's members, Fred Iklé, who observed, "Unless we have some way of gauging the quality of predictions, all our efforts to forecast, conjecture about, or anticipate the future must remain essentially dilettante." Iklé's own paper is valuable for the observation that much social "prediction" is used primarily for entertainment, while another large category concerns prognostications without predictive validity that merely resolve a current indecision. The forecasts which are to be taken seriously are those that include an evaluation of alternative courses of action. Forecasts may be in error, in the sense that they do not serve our purposes, when they omit the statement of such alternatives. Another type of error, distinct from the mere failure to anticipate what comes to pass, is that of miscalculating what values will prevail over the forecast period. Thus Iklé seems to be arguing that an otherwise self-fulfilling prophecy could come to be self-defeating, given a shift in values.

De Jouvenel

In a number of ways, Bertrand de Jouvenel's book, *The Art of Conjecture* (1967), contrasts favorably with the progress report of the Commission on the Year 2000. The latter is a symposium, many contributions to which were obviously prepared in haste and under the control of no sufficiently forceful guiding conception of the collective task, whereas de Jouvenel's book is the work of a single mind, a disciplined and witty one. There is no dilettante toying with futuristic "scenarios," but rather a humane exposition of what modern social science looks like if one tries to assay its capabilities for formulating forecasts. A moderately well-read professional social scientist will find little here that is "new"—certainly not a presentation of a novel formula for foreseeing. (Any literate reader not acquainted with the social science literature might well find de Jouvenel's book a congenial introduction thereto.) What is innovative is the consistency with which each of the classic problems of epistemology and method in the social sciences is expounded from the standpoint of its bearing upon the problem of making forecasts—or "conjectures," as de Jouvenel prefers to call them. The work is written so lucidly that it is deceptive in its simplicity; one does well to read it closely. For instance, Auguste Comte's mischievous confusion of scientific prediction and historical forecasting is dealt with in less than two pages. If one has previously read Popper on this point, de Jouvenel's treatment seems deft and incisive. If one had not encountered the distinction before, perhaps it would seem to be dealing with a minor issue.

There is no possibility of summarizing de Jouvenel's book. The only sensible course is to recommend that it be read. A reading may leave one both more skeptical of the possibility of making forecasts accurate and more convinced of the necessity for attempting them.

Social Reporting

A commonplace remark in the futurist literature is that improvement in the art of forecasting requires a great expansion in the quantity, comprehensiveness, and reliability of social measurements. The statement seems to enjoy the status of an axiom, although it begs the question of what the relationship really is between the past and future observations in a time series.

The emphasis on improved social measurement found in futurist writing is convergent with a variety of proposals recently put forth concerning needed work on "social accounting," "social indicators," or "social reporting." One focus of this discussion is the "Full Opportunity Act of 1969," a bill introduced in the 91st Congress by Senator Walter F. Mondale and closely similar to a bill first introduced by him in the 90th Congress (see *Congressional Record,* vol. 115, no. 9, January 15, 1969). This legislation would provide for a Council of Social Advisors to gather information and statistics, appraise government programs and activities, conduct studies, and develop priorities for programs designed to implement a full opportunity policy. The Council would assist the President in the preparation of an annual social report.

A possible prototype of such a report was issued at the end of President Johnson's term of office by the staff of the U.S. Department of Health, Education, and Welfare (1969), whose work was assisted by an Advisory Panel on Social Indicators comprising more than 40 social scientists.[1]

The work of the Panel on Social Indicators was partly preceded by and partly overlapped that of three other groups. A collaborative volume on *Social Indicators* (edited by Raymond Bauer, 1966), was issued by a committee of the American Academy of Arts and Sciences on behalf of the National Aeronautics and Space Administration. A symposium on "Social goals and Indicators," edited by Bertram Gross for the American Academy of Political and Social Science (1967), may be seen as a further exploration of issues raised in the Bauer volume as well as an argument on behalf of the Mondale bill. Somewhat more academic in tone is the Russell Sage Foundation symposium on *Indicators of Social Change* (1968), in which the emphasis is on "concepts and measurements."

Without summarizing the scope of these several reports I think it is fair to state that the linkage of social reporting, as it is now being discussed, with social forecasting is largely implicit. Certainly, none of these collaborative projects has made a self-conscious effort to develop forecasting strategies or new techniques of projection and the like. Instead, the thrust of the discussion is the expression of dissatisfaction with current and past efforts at social measurement on two counts: (1) an insufficiency of data and (2) a failure to rationalize data collection systems in terms of relevance to the actual performance of American society with respect to its widely acknowledged social goals. Most of the participants in these symposia are prepared to admit that our problem is at least as much that we do not know just what we *ought* to be measuring (and, therefore, how we ought to go about measuring) as that we are failing to accumulate the kinds of information we do know how to collect. For all the number of words that have gone into the discussion of what "social accounting" might be or what "social indicators" really are for, there is clearly an uneasy feeling that we do not, in fact, have sufficient warrant for proposing these as valid analogies to economic accounting and economic indicators.

Even if it is not axiomatic that the study of past trends is the key to forecasting the future, it does give one pause to reflect that a demand for social

[1]A summary of this report and two articles about it appeared in *The Public Interest,* no. 15, 1969.

forecasting is forthcoming in the absence of a clear consensus as to what it is that should be forecast. If we do not know what measurements to make on the present state of American society, or how to make them, for what variables are we to offer forecasts of future magnitudes?

The predicament has been somewhat exaggerated here for sake of emphasis. There is, to be sure, no reason to believe that any reasonable proposal for social accounts will result in discarding our well-developed system of demographic bookkeeping or certain of our more reputable series of social statistics. Projections of these magnitudes will continue to be the backbone of attempts at forecasting for the foreseeable future (a forecast of forecasting!). Moreover, one would have to question the wisdom of putting the matter of forecasting in a position of top priority in the effort to institutionalize a periodic social report. As I have argued earlier, many forecasts may serve primarily to signal issues requiring attention now. A social report will, of necessity, contain many future-oriented interpretations.

Social Forecasting: What Next?

In this report on social forecasting—which is too long, as the apology goes, because of insufficient time to write a short report—I have not resisted the temptation to be critical of fellow social scientists and skeptical of their ability to foretell. It is hoped that the picture is not one-sided. One of the participants in discussions of the Commission on the Year 2000 observed, "In reading an old document, *Recent Social Trends,* which dates from the 1930's, I was first struck by the excellence in methodology and then by the similarity between its projections and those of today." *Recent Social Trends* was not, of course, an enterprise primarily oriented to forecasting. Its intention was, as President Hoover phrased it, "to help all of us to see where social stresses are occurring and where major efforts should be undertaken to deal with them constructively." As I have just said, any good social report will contain many future-oriented interpretations, and this holds for the volume in question. Perhaps it was precisely at the points where the attention to forecasting became most self-conscious—as in the discussion of future population—that the investigators' statements about the future became least useful.

I have tried to show that useful forecasts issue from good analysis, and that to be useful they need not be "correct." The forecasts of declining population or explosive population growth, of the emergence of garrison states, of declining intelligence, and of increasing social rigidification that were reviewed above remain pertinent even if "wrong." If anyone had the illusion that prudent conduct depends on *knowing* what will happen in regard to such matters as these, it is time for him to remedy deficiencies in his education.

One answer to our question, "What next?" is, therefore, "More of the same." Social science at its best can produce good analysis; and the results of good analysis can almost always be given an orientation toward the future.

But good is not good enough. In concluding I want to suggest two points of departure for future analyses that may well be fruitful in producing formal forecasts as well as productive of better analysis.

The Idea of "Cohort"

The first is the notion of cohort, which has been exploited with exceedingly instructive results in demography but has only lately been systematically considered as a strategic approach to the analysis of social change (e.g., by Norman Ryder). A cohort is the aggregate of all persons who experience an event defining their membership at approximately the same time; the "birth cohort" of persons born in a given year or in a five year period is the prototypical example. The metabolism of a society involves the replacement of each cohort by its successor *pari passu* with the passage of time, while each cohort proceeds through a sequence of ages. This obvious statement acquires significance when coupled with three others, also obvious; first, that the inclinations and response tendencies of human beings alter with age; second, that experiences leave more or less lasting impressions; and third, that persons alive at one time have different experiences from those living at a different time. The possibility arises of treating the collective life history of a cohort as a biography, attending to the features that distinguish it as well as to the structural outlines it shares with any other such biography.

The use to which we can put these truisms depends upon the knowledge we have of the causal connections between events occurring at different junctures of the life cycle. He who would forecast what ideas will be attractive twenty years hence might be well advised to investigate what is happening now in the nursery schools. To be sure, we know all too little about what carries over from childhood to early adulthood, and how. But there is a strong suspicion abroad that current problems of communication are complicated by the fact that some cohorts grew up listening to radio while younger ones had TV for a nursemaid.

Some social change has as prerequisite a kind of "intercohort forgetting." Rapid progress in the computer field seems to require the participation of the young, who have never learned the now obsolete techniques of information processing. Science moves because the apprentice investigator never has to learn all the false theories his master has disproved, and therefore has a mind uncluttered with irrelevance. The case is different with politics and war, except as these acquire the orientation of the sciences, for in these fields leadership devolves not to the young and imaginative but to the old and experienced. Hence the generals are proverbially fighting the last war before this one, and the politicians act on the assumption that the power alignments prevailing in their youth remain in force.

The projection of a social trend will be quite a different matter according as one of two situations pertains: (a) a set of dispositions is firmly established in youth and remains relatively fixed thereafter, or (b) people in the several segments of the life cycle are about equally susceptible to change. In the former category might be placed various habits and qualifications. For example, the eradication of illiteracy or cigaret smoking from a population is probably best approached by means of the education of youth; the passage of time and the succession of cohorts, if such education is successful, will accomplish the desired result in due course. (The example may be faulty if more effective techniques of adult education can be brought to bear upon the situation.) Cases approximating the conditions assumed for this example require analysis and forecasting procedures that take advantage of inter- and intracohort comparisons.

Even if all age groups are in some sense equally exposed to the impact of current social changes, they are likely to be differentially responsive thereto. Such response differentials will set up a pattern of age-grading that has a potentiality for inducing intercohort (mis-called "intergenerational") conflict or erecting communications barriers. Most accounts of the socialization process focus on the socialization of the young by the old. The diffusion of norms and ideas in the reverse direction merits closer study, for to the extent that this can happen, the pace of social change may be accelerated.

If we reckon the central or "adult" portion of the life cycle as comprising the fifty years from ages 15 to 64, it is obvious that in a half century there is a complete turnover in the adult population of any society. In forecasting for any date in the future we are implicitly describing the future of at least some people who have not yet experienced adult life. In forecasting for a date more than fifty years hence, all our statements apply to persons who have not yet reached maturity. The self-conscious adoption of a cohort perspective may prevent the forecaster from being more presumptuous than he should.

The Ecological Approach

My treatment of the other promising approach I wanted to mention must be equally cursory. It is the notion of analyzing social change and formulating forecasts in an ecological framework. At least a nominal commitment to this strategy is much more widespread today than it was a decade ago when I first joined in a manifesto on its behalf. Incidentally, in regard to forecasts about the diffusion of ideas, I should like to call attention to the successful forecast by the literary critic, Kenneth Burke, back in 1937: "Among the sciences, there is one little fellow named Ecology, and in time we shall pay him more attention."

The idea of ecology is being literally forced upon us, not only by the explosive growth of human numbers, but also by a multifaceted expansion of the human niche in the planetary ecosystem, which involves (in addition to sheer numerical increase) and acceleration in technological capability; a much deeper penetration of the environment, or intervention in the flows of materials and energy through the ecosystem; and an increasing complexity and elaboration of systems of human social organization. In consequence, one is unable meaningfully to discuss many "social trends" or "technological trends" in isolation, much less to extrapolate them in a blind fashion. The analytical or projection model must take account of the interactions of population, environment, technology, and social organization. Once the possibility of far-reaching ramifications of these interactions is seen, the analyst is constrained to question the compatibility of apparently distinct trends, when they are extrapolated even a short distance ahead. For what period into the future can one project the increasing population size and the increasing ratio of automobiles to people in the Los Angeles metropolitan area without having to entertain the possibility that this population will suffocate itself?

Many have commented on the ecological dilemma of mankind in the present age; for example, John McHale writes: "Without touching upon the more familiar problems of war, hunger and human disease, even a cursory glance at our ecosystem is sobering. It should be apparent to all, that we now live in such close community, and within such delicate 'life' margins, that all our actions are now cast on a planetary scale and that our gross ecological errors may reverberate for centuries."

The theme is carried forward in the most audacious proposal I have yet seen for a venture in social forecasting, Clifford Humphrey's suggested project to produce the Century Report, "a comprehensive outline of the ensuing ecological crisis, its expected symptoms and possible implications for our values, aspirations and social institutions." Apart from his diagnosis of "ecological crisis," the challenging aspect of Humphrey's proposal is his argument that neither the use of historical precedents as analogies nor the extrapolation of trends representing technological "progress" or economic "growth" is adequate to the forecasts that need to be made. The crisis in the making is one for which our standard techniques will not serve much longer.

A final "forecast of forecasting," therefore, might go as follows: As ingredients of our forecasts we will, with increasing methodological sophistication, continue to prepare projections, trend extrapolations, model simulations, and developmental constructs so as to provide as broad an array as may be useful of the logically possible pathways to hypothetical futures. In issuing responsible *forecasts* on the basis of such materials, however, we will self-consciously include several components:

1. a delineation of the trends or developments as projected, extrapolated, or constructed;
2. an assessment of mutual facilitation or incompatibility of the several trends as projected;
3. an estimate of the ecological ramifications of the trends, if realized;
4. an appraisal of the potential social feedbacks upon the trends and their ecological ramifications; and
5. a conspectus of the apparent range of alternatives that are open: X *can happen* if . . . , but Y *may* happen unless . . .

There will be no pretense that we can gradually move toward the perfection of methods of anticipating what will actually occur, for such perfectibility is not logically possible, esthetically appealing, or morally inspiring. What we may hope to improve, if not perfect, is our sense of responsibility for making known the implications of our knowledge.

References

Bajema, Carl Jay. "Estimation of the Direction and Intensity of Natural Selection in Relation to Human Intelligence by Means of the Intrinsic Rate of Natural Increase," *Eugenics Quarterly* 10: 175–187.

Bauer, Raymond A., ed. *Social Indicators* (Cambridge, Mass.: M.I.T. Press, 1966).

Bell, Daniel. "Twelve Modes of Prediction," in Julius Gould (ed.), *Penguin Survey of the Social Sciences 1965* (Baltimore: Penguin Books).

Bell, Daniel. "The Study of the Future," *The Public Interest*, no. 1, pp. 119–130.

Blau, Peter M., and Otis Dudley Duncan, *The American Occupational Structure* (New York: John Wiley & Sons, 1967).

Burke, Kenneth. *Attitudes toward History*, Vol. I (New York: New Republic, 1937).

Commission on the Year 2000. "Toward the Year 2000: Work in Progress," *Daedalus* (Proceedings of the American Academy of Arts and Sciences) 96: 639–994.

Cook, Robert C. *Human Fertility: The Modern Dilemma* (New York: William Sloan Associates, 1951).

Davis, Joseph S. "Our Changed Population Outlook and Its Significance," *American Economic Review* 42: 304–325.

De Jouvenel, Bertrand. *The Art of Conjecture* (New York: Basic Books, 1967).

Dorn, Harold F. "Pitfalls in Population Forecasts and Projections," *Journal of the American Statistical Association* 45: 311–334.

Duncan, Otis Dudley. "Is the Intelligence of the General Population Declining?" *American Sociological Review* 17: 401–407.

Duncan, Otis Dudley. "From Social System to Ecosystem," *Sociological Inquiry* 31: 140–149. Reprinted in P. Meadows and E. H. Mizruchi, eds., *Urbanism, Urbanization, and Change* (Reading, Mass.: Addison-Wesley Publishing Co., 1969).

Duncan, Otis Dudley. "Social Organization and the Ecosystem," in R.E.L. Faris, ed., *Handbook of Modern Sociology* (Chicago: Rand McNally, 1964).

Duncan, Otis Dudley. "The Trend of Occupational Mobility in the United States," *American Sociological Review* 30: 491–498.

Duncan, Otis Dudley. "Methodological Issues in the Analysis of Social Stratification," in N.J. Smelser and S.M. Lipset, eds., *Social Structure and Mobility in Economic Development* (Chicago: Aldine Publishing Co., 1966).

Duncan, Otis Dudley. "Social Stratification and Mobility: Problems in the Measurement of Trend," in Eleanor Bernert Sheldon and Wilbert E. Moore, eds., *Indicators of Social Change* (New York: Russell Sage Foundation, 1968).

Duncan, Otis Dudley, and Leo F. Schnore. "Cultural, Behavioral, and Ecological Perspectives in the Study of Social Organization," *American Journal of Sociology* 65: 132–146.

Glass, D. V. "Demographic Prediction (The Third Royal Society Nuffield Lecture)," *Proceedings of the Royal Society*, Ser. B., 168: 119–139.

Gross, Bertram N., ed., *Social Intelligence for America's Future* (Boston: Allyn & Bacon, 1969). (Reprinted from vols. 371 and 373, *The Annals of the American Academy of Political and Social Science*, 1967.)

Hajnal, John. "The Prospects for Population Forecasts," *Journal of the American Statistical Association* 50: 309–322.

Hempel, Carl G. "The Function of General Laws in History," in Patrick Gardiner, ed., *Theories of History* (Glencoe, Ill.: Free Press, 1959).

Hempel, Carl G., and P. Oppenheim. "The Logic of Explanation," *Philosophy of Science* 15: 135–175.

Higgins, J. V., Elizabeth W. Reed, and S. C. Reed. "Intelligence and Family Size: A Paradox Resolved," *Eugenics Quarterly* 9: 84–90.

Humphrey, Clifford C. "The Anthropologist and Contemporary Society: A Call for Ethical Action," paper presented at the 22nd Annual Northwest Anthropological Conference, Victoria, B.C., April 3–5, 1969.

Huntington, Samuel P. "Civil-Military Relations," *International Encyclopedia of the Social Sciences* 2: 487–495.

Jackson, Elton F., and Harry J. Crockett, Jr. "Occupation Mobility in the United States: A Point Estimate and Trend Comparison," *American Sociological Review* 29: 5–15.

Janowitz, Morris. *The Military in the Political Development of New Nations* (Chicago: University of Chicago Press, 1964).

Kaplan, Abraham. *The Conduct of Inquiry: Methodology for Behavioral Science* (San Francisco: Chandler Publishing Co., 1964).

Lasswell, Harold D. "The Garrison State." *American Journal of Sociology* 46: 455–468.

Lasswell, Harold D. "The Garrison-state Hypothesis Today," in Samuel P. Huntington, ed., *Changing Patterns of Military Politics* (New York: Free Press, 1962).

Lentz, Theodore, Jr. "Relation of I.Q. to Size of Family," *Journal of Educational Psychology* 18: 486–496.

Lorimer, Frank, and Frederick Osborn. *Dynamics of Population* (New York: Macmillan, 1934).

McHale, John. "The Future of the Future," *Architectural Design*, February 1967, pp. 65–66.

Moore, Wilbert E. "Predicting Discontinuities in Social Change," *American Sociological Review* 29: 331–338.

Moynihan, Daniel P. "The Relationship of Federal to Local Authorities," *Daedalus* (*Proceedings of the American Academy of Arts and Sciences*) 96: 801–808.

Ogburn, William F. *Social Change: With Respect to Culture and Original Nature* (New York: B. W. Huebsch, 1922).

Ogburn, William F. *The Social Effects of Aviation* (Boston: Houghton Mifflin, 1946).

Ogburn, William F. *On Culture and Social Change* (Chicago: University of Chicago Press, 1964).

Ogburn, William F., and M. F. Nimkoff. *Technology and the Changing Family* (Boston: Houghton Mifflin, 1955).

Popper, Karl R. "Prediction and Prophecy in the Social Sciences," in Patrick Gardiner, ed., *Theories of History* (Glencoe, Ill.: Free Press, 1959).

Popper, Karl R. *The Open Society and Its Enemies* (Princeton: Princeton University Press, 1950).

President's Research Committee on Social Trends. *Recent Trends in the United States* (New York: McGraw-Hill, 1933).

Rescher, Nicholas. "On Prediction and Explanation," *British Journal for the Philosophy of Science* 8: 281–290.

Rogoff, Natalie. *Recent Trends in Occupational Mobility* (Glencoe, Ill.: Free Press, 1953).

Ryder, Norman B. "The Cohort as a Concept in the Study of Social Change," *American Sociological Review* 30: 843–861.

Schlesinger, Arthur M. "Casting the National Horoscope," *Proceedings of the American Antiquarian Society* 55: 53–94.

Schnore, Leo F. "The Myth of Human Ecology," *Sociological Inquiry* 31: 128–139.

Schuessler, Karl F. "Prediction," *International Encyclopedia of the Social Sciences* 12: 418–423.

Scottish Mental Survey Committee. *The Trend of Scottish Intelligence* (London: University of London Press, 1949).

Sheffler, Israel. "Explanation, Prediction, and Abstraction," in A. Danto and S. Morgenbesser, eds., *Philosophy of Science* (New York: Meridian Books, 1960).

Sheldon, Eleanor Bernet, and Wilbert E. Moore, eds., *Indicators of Social Change* (New York: Russell Sage Foundation, 1968).

Sibley, Elbridge. "Some Demographic Clues to Stratification," *American Sociological Review* 7: 322–330; reprinted in R. Bendix and S. M. Lipset, eds., *Class, Status and Power* (Glencoe, Ill.: Free Press, 1953).

Spengler, Joseph J. "Population Prediction in Nineteenth Century America," *American Sociological Review* 1: 905–921.

Tuddenham, R. D. "Soldier Intelligence in World Wars I and II," *American Psychologist* 3: 54–56.

U.S. Department of Health, Education, and Welfare. *Toward a Social Report* (Washington: Government Printing Office, 1969).

Winthrop, Henry. "The Sociologist and the Study of the Future," *American Sociologist* 3: 136–145.

Zarnowitz, Victor. "Prediction and Forecasting, Economic," *International Encyclopedia of the Social Sciences* 12: 425–437.

Zarnowitz, Victor. "The New ASA-NBER Survey of Forecasts by Economic Statisticians," *American Statistician* 23: 12–16.

ON THE EPISTEMOLOGY OF THE INEXACT SCIENCES

● *olaf helmer and nicholas rescher*

1. The Mythology of Exactness

It is a fiction of long standing that there are two classes of sciences, the exact and the inexact, and that the social sciences by and large are members of the second class—unless and until, like experimental psychology or some parts of economics, they mature to the point where admission to the first class may be granted.

This widely prevalent attitude seems to us fundamentally mistaken; for it finds a difference in principle where there is only one of degree, and it imputes to the so-called exact sciences a procedural rigor which is rarely present in fact. For the sake of a fuller discussion of these points, let us clarify at the very outset the terms "science," "exact science," and "inexact science," as they are intended here.

For an enterprise to be characterized as *scientific* it must have as its purpose the explanation and prediction of phenomena within its subject-matter domain and it must provide such explanation and prediction in a reasoned, and therefore intersubjective, fashion. We speak of an exact science if this reasoning process is formalized in the sense that the terms used are exactly defined and reasoning takes place by formal logico-mathematical derivation of the hypothesis (the statement of the fact to be explained or predicted) from the evidence (the body of knowledge accepted by virtue of being highly confirmed by observation). That an exact science frequently uses mathematical notation and concerns itself about attributes which lend themselves to exact measurement, we regard as incidental rather than defining characteristics. The same point applies to the precision, or exactness, of the predictions of which the science may be capable. While precise predictions are indeed to be preferred to vague ones, a discipline which provides predictions of a less precise character, but makes them correctly and in a systematic and reasoned way, must be classified as a science.

In an inexact science, conversely, reasoning is informal; in particular, some of the terminology may, without actually impeding communication, exhibit some inherent vagueness, and reasoning may at least in part rely on reference to intuitively perceived facts or implications. Again, an inexact science rarely uses mathematical notation or employs attributes capable of exact measurement, and as a rule does not make its predictions with great precision and exactitude.

Using the terms as elucidated here—and we believe that this corresponds closely to accepted usage—purely descriptive surveys or summaries, such as the part of history that is mere chronology or, say, purely descriptive botany or geography, are not called *sciences*. History proper, on the other hand, which seeks to explain historical transactions and to establish historical judgments having some degree of generality, is a science; it is in fact largely coincident with political science, except that its practitioners focus their interest on the past while the political scientists' main concern is the present and the future.

As for *exactness*, this qualification, far from being attributable to all of the so-called natural sciences, applies only to a small section of them, in particular to certain subfields of physics, in some of which exactness has even been put to the ultimate test of formal axiomatization. In other branches of physics, such as parts of aerodynamics and of the physics of extreme temperatures, exact procedures are still intermingled with unformalized expertise. Indeed the latter becomes more dominant as we move away from the precise and usually highly abstract core of an exact discipline and towards its applications to the complexities of the real world. Both architecture and medicine are cases in point. Aside from the respective activities of building structures and healing people, both have a theoretical content—that is, they are predictive and explanatory ("this bridge will not collapse, or has not collapsed, because . . ."; "this patient will exhibit, or has exhibited, such and such symptoms because . . . "). They must therefore properly be called sciences, but they are largely inexact since they rely heavily on informal reasoning processes.

If in addition to these examples we remember the essentially in-between status of such fields as economics and psychology, both of which show abundant evidence of exact derivations as well as reliance on intuitive judgment (exhibiting intermittent use of mathematical symbolism and of measurable attributes and an occasional ability to predict with precision) it should be obvious that there is at present no clear-cut dichotomy between exact and inexact sciences, and, in particular, that inexactness is not a prerogative of the social sciences.

However, leaving aside their present comparative status, it still might be possible to hold the view that there exists an epistemological difference in principle between the social sciences on the one hand and the natural or physical sciences on the other, in the sense that the latter, though not necessarily quite exact as yet, will gradually achieve ultimate exactness, while the former, due to the intangible nature of their subject-matter and the imperfection in principle of their observational data, must of necessity remain inexact. Such a view would be based upon false premises, viz., a wholly misguided application of the exactness vs. inexactness distinction. Indeed, the artificial discrimination between the physical sciences with their (at least in principle) precise terms, exact derivations and reliable predictions as opposed to the vague terms, intuitive insights and virtual unpredictability in the social sciences has retarded the development of the latter immeasurably.

The reason for this defeatist point of view regarding the social sciences may be traceable to a basic misunderstanding of the nature of scientific endeavor.

What matters is not whether or to what extent inexactitudes in procedures and predictive capability can eventually be removed; rather it is *objectivity*, i.e., the intersubjectivity of findings independent of any one person's intuitive judgment, which distinguishes science from intuitive guesswork however brilliant. This has nothing to do with the intuitive spark which may be the origin of a new discovery; pure mathematics, whose formal exactness is beyond question, needs that as much as any science. But once a new fact or a new idea has been conjectured, no matter on how intuitive a foundation, it must be capable of objective test and confirmation by anyone. And it is this crucial standard of scientific objectivity rather than any purported criterion of exactitude to which the social sciences must conform.

In rejecting precision of form or method as well as degree of predictability as basic discriminants between the social and the physical sciences it thus remains to be seen whether there might not in fact be a fundamental epistemological difference between them with regard to their ability to live up to the same rigorous standard of objectivity. Our belief is that there is essentially no such difference, in other words, that the social sciences cannot be separated from the physical on methodological grounds. We hope to convince the reader of the validity of our position by offering, in what follows, at least some indications as to how the foundations for a uniform epistemology of all of the inexact sciences might be laid—be they social sciences or "as yet" inexact physical sciences.

Our goal is more modest than that of presenting a comprehensive epistemology of the inexact sciences. We merely wish to outline an epistemological attitude toward them that we would like to see adopted more widely. Since epistemology is concerned with the role of evidence in the attainment of scientific laws and with the scientific procedures implied by that role, we need to re-examine the status of such things as laws, evidence, confirmation, prediction and explanation, with special reference to the case of inexact sciences.

2. Historical Laws

Let us first take a brief look at historical science in order to obtain some illustrative examples of the form of laws in the social sciences and of the function they perform. An *historical law* may be regarded as a well-confirmed statement concerning the actions of an organized group of men under certain restrictive conditions (such group actions being intended to include those of systems composed conjointly of men and nonhuman instrumentalities under their physical control). Examples of such laws are: "A census takes place in the U. S. in every decade year", "Heretics were persecuted in 17th century Spain", "In the sea fights of sailing vessels in the period 1653–1803, large formations were too cumbersome for effectual control as single units." Such statements share two features of particular epistemological importance and interest: they are *law-like,* and *loose.* These points require elaboration.

To consider law-likeness, let us take for example the statement about the cumbersomeness of large sailing fleets in sea fights. On first view, this statement might seem to be a mere descriptive list of characteristics of certain particular engagements: a shorthand version of a long conjunction of statements about large-scale engagements during the century and a half from Texel (1653) to Trafalgar (1803). This view is incorrect, however, because the statement in question is more than an assertion regarding characteristics of certain actual engagements. Unlike mere descriptions, it can serve to explain developments in cases to which it makes no reference. Furthermore, the statement has counterfactual force. It asserts that in literally any large-scale fleet action fought under the conditions in question (sailing vessels of certain types, with particular modes of armament, and with contemporaneous communications methods) effectual control of a great battle line is hopeless. It is claimed, for example, that had Villeneuve issued from Cadiz some days earlier or later he would all the same have encountered difficulty in the management of the great allied battle fleet of over thirty sail of the line, and Nelson's stratagem of dividing his force into two virtually independent units under prearranged plans would have facilitated effective management equally well as at Trafalgar.

The statement in question is thus no mere descriptive summary of particular events; it functions on the more general plane of law-like statements, specifically, in that it can serve as a basis for explanation, and that it can exert counterfactual force. To be sure, the individual descriptive statements which are known and relevant do provide a part of the appropriate evidence for the historical generalization. But the content of the statement itself lies beyond the sphere of mere description, and in taking this wider role historical laws become marked as genuine law-like statements.

The second important characteristic of historical laws lies in their being "loose." It has been said already that historical laws are (explicitly or obliquely) conditional in their logical form. However, the nature of these conditions is such that they can often not be spelled out fully and completely. For instance, the statement about sailing fleet tactics has (among others) an implicit or tacit condition relating to the state of naval ordnance in the 18th century. In elaborating such conditions, the historian delineates what is typical of the place and period. The full implications of such reference may be vast and inexhaustible; for instance, in our example, ordnance ramifies *via* metalworking technology into metallurgy, mining, etc. Thus the conditions which are operative in the formulation of an historical law may only be indicated in a general way and are not necessarily (indeed in most cases cannot be expected to be) exhaustively articulated. This characteristic of such laws is here designated as *looseness*.

It is this looseness of its laws which typifies history as an inexact science in the sense in which we have used the term: in a domain whose laws are not fully and precisely articulated there exists a limit to exactitude in terminology and reasoning. In such a sphere, mathematical precision must not be expected. To say this implies no pejorative intent whatever, for the looseness of historical laws is clearly recognized as being due, not to slipshod formulation of otherwise precise facts, but to the fundamental complexities inherent in the conceptual apparatus of the domain.

A consequence of the looseness of historical laws is that they are, not universal, but merely quasi-general in that they admit exceptions. Since the conditions delimiting the area of application of the law are often not exhaustively articulated, a supposed violation of the law may be explicable by showing that a legitimate (but as yet unformulated) precondition of the law's applicability is not fulfilled in the case under consideration. The laws may be taken to contain a tacit caveat of the "usually" or "other things being equal" type. An historical law is thus not strictly universal in that it must be taken as applicable to all cases falling within the scope of its explicitly formulated conditions; rather it may be thought to formulate relationships which obtain generally, or better, as a rule.[1]

Such a "law" we will term a quasi-law. In order for the law to be valid, it is not necessary that no apparent exceptions occur, it is only necessary that, if an apparent exception should occur, an adequate explanation be forthcoming, an explanation demonstrating the exceptional characteristic of the case in hand by establishing the violation of an appropriate (if hitherto unformulated) condition of the law's applicability.[2]

For example, the historical law that in the pre-revolutionary French navy only persons of noble birth were commissioned is not without apparent exceptions, since in particular the regulation was waived in the case of the great Jean Bart, son of a humble fisherman, who attained great distinction in the naval service. We may legitimately speak here of an apparent exception; for instead of abandoning this universal law in view of the cited counter-example, it is more expedient to maintain the law but to interpret it as being endowed with certain tacit amendments which, fully spelled out, would read somewhat as follows: "In the pre-revolutionary French navy as a rule only persons of noble birth were commissioned, that is, unless the regulation was explicitly

---

[1]This point has been made by various writers on historical method. Charles Frankel, for example, puts it as follows in his lucid article on "Explanation and Interpretation in History": "It is frequently misleading to take statements such as 'Power corrupts, and absolute power corrupts absolutely,' when historians use them, as attempts to give an exact statement of a universal law. . . . But such remarks may be taken as statements of strategy, rules to which it is best to conform in the absence of very strong countervailing considerations." (Philosophy of Science, vol. 24, 1957, p. 142.)

[2]In his book The Analysis of Matter (London, 1927), Bertrand Russell writes "Our pre-scientific general beliefs are hardly ever without exceptions; in science, a law with exceptions can only be tolerated as a makeshift" (p. 191). We regard this as true only in some of the physical sciences. A far juster view was that of Alfred Marshall (Principles of Economics, 1892): "The laws of economics are to be compared with the law of the tides, rather than with the simple and exact law of gravitation. For the actions of men are so various and uncertain, that the best statement of tendencies, which we can make in a science of human conduct, must needs be inexact and faulty."

waived or an oversight or fraud occurred or some other similarly exceptional condition obtained." While it may be objected that such a formulation is vague—and indeed it is—it cannot be said that the law is now so loose as to be vacuous; for the intuitive intent is clear, and its looseness is far from permitting the law's retention in the face of just any counter example.[3] Specifically, if a reliable source brings to light one counter-instance for which there is no tenable explanation whatsoever to give it exempt status, an historian may still wish to retain the law in the definite expectation that some such explanation eventually be forthcoming; but should he be confronted with a succession or series of unexplained exceptions to the law, he would no doubt soon feel compelled to abandon the law itself.

We thus have the indisputable fact that in a generally loose context, that of history being typical of the inexact sciences, it would be hopeless to try to erect a theoretical structure which is logically, perhaps even esthetically, on a plane with our idealistic image of an exact theory. Yet, if we consider the situation, not from the standpoint of the wishful dreamer of neat and tidy theory construction, but from that of the pragmatist in pursuit of a better understanding of the world through reasoned methods of explanation and prediction, then we have good reason to take heart at the sight even of quasi-laws, and we should realize that the seemingly thin line between vagueness and vacuity is solid enough to distinguish fact from fiction reasonably well in practical applications.

3. Quasi-Laws in the Physical Sciences

We have chosen to illustrate the nature of limited generalizations (quasi-laws) by means of the graphic example of historical laws. Use of this example from a social-science context must not, however, be construed as implying that quasi-laws do not occur in the natural, indeed even the physical sciences. In many parts of modern physics, formalized theories based wholly on universal principles are (at least presently) unavailable, and use of limited generalizations is commonplace, particularly so in applied physics and engineering.

Writers on the methodology of the physical sciences often bear in mind a somewhat antiquated and much idealized image of physics as a very complete and thoroughly exact discipline in which it is never necessary to rely upon limited generalizations or expert opinion. But physical science today is very far from meeting this ideal. Indeed some branches of the social sciences are in better shape as regards the generality of their laws than various departments of physics, such as the theory of turbulence phenomena, high-velocity aerodynamics, or the physics of extreme temperatures. Throughout applied physics in particular, when we move (say in engineering applications) from the realm of idealized abstraction ("perfect" gases, "homogeneous" media, etc.)

---

[3]Michael Scriven, in a paper shortly to be published, speaks of historical generalizations as having a "selective immunity to counter-examples."

to the complexities of the real world, reliance upon generalizations which are, in effect, quasi-laws becomes pronounced. (Engineering practice in general is based on "rules of thumb" to an extent undreamed of in current theories of scientific method.)

Thus no warrant whatever exists for using the presence of quasi-laws in the social sciences as validating a methodological separation between them on the one hand and the physical sciences on the other. A realistic assessment of physical science methods shows that quasi-laws are here operative too, and importantly so.

With this in mind, let us now turn to a closer examination of the role played by laws—or quasi-laws—in prediction and explanation.

4. Explanation and Prediction

A somewhat simplified characterization of scientific explanation—but one which none-the-less has a wide range of applicability, particularly in the physical sciences—is that explanation consists in the *logical derivation* of the statement to be explained from a complex of factual statements and well-established general laws. One would, for example, explain the freezing of a lake by adducing (1) the fact that the temperature fell below 32°F and (2) the law that water freezes at 32°F. These statements, taken together, yield the statement to be explained deductively.[4]

This deductive model of explanation, while adequate for many important types of explanations encountered in the sciences, cannot without at least some emendation be accepted as applying to all explanations. For one thing there are probabilistic explanations, which can be based upon statistical (rather than strictly universal) laws. ("I did not win the Irish Sweepstakes because the chances were overwhelmingly against my doing so.") And then there are what we have been referring to as quasi-laws, occurring in the inexact sciences, which because of their escape clauses cannot serve as the basis of strict *derivation,* and yet can carry explanatory force. (For example, the quasi-law quoted earlier surely explains—in the accepted sense of the word—why the French fleet which supported Washington's Yorktown campaign was commanded by a nobleman (namely, the Comte de Grasse).)

The uncertainty of conclusions based on quasi-laws is not due to the same reason as that of conclusions based on statistical laws. For a statistical law asserts the presence of some characteristics in a certain (presumably high) percentage of cases, whereas a quasi-law asserts it in all cases for which an exceptional status (in some ill-defined but clearly understood sense) cannot be claimed.

We note for the moment, however, that the schema of explanation when

---

[4]For a full discussion of this matter, see C. G. Hempel and P. Oppenheim, "Studies in the Logic of Explanation," *Philosophy of Science* 15 (1948): 135–175.

either type of non-universal law is involved is the same, and in fact identical with what it would be were the law universal; and an explanation is regarded as satisfactory if, while short of logically *entailing* the hypothesis, it succeeds in making the statement to be explained highly *credible* in the sense of providing convincing evidence for it. (We shall return to a discussion of the concept of evidence below.)

With regard to prediction as opposed to explanation, analyses of scientific reasoning often emphasize the similarities between the two, holding that they are identical from a logical standpoint, inasmuch as each is an instance of the use of evidence to establish an hypothesis, and the major point of difference between them is held to be that the hypothesis of a prediction or of an explanation concerns respectively the future or the past. This view, however, does not do justice to several differences between prediction and explanation which are of particular importance for our present purposes.[5]

First of all, there are such things as *unreasoned* predictions—predictions made without any articulation of justifying argument. The validation of such predictions lies not in their being supported by plausible arguments, but may, for example, reside in proving sound *ex post facto* through a record of successes on the part of the predictor or predicting mechanism.

It is clear that such predictions have no analogue in explanations; only reasoned predictions, based upon the application of established theoretical principles, are akin to explanations. However, even here there is an important point of difference.

By the very meaning of the term, an explanation must *establish* its conclusion, showing that there is a strong warrant why the fact to be explained— rather than some possible alternative—obtains. On the other hand, the conclusion of a (reasoned) prediction need not be well established in this sense; it suffices that it be rendered *more tenable than comparable alternatives.* Here then is an important distinction in logical strength between explanations and predictions: An explanation, though it need not logically rule out alternatives altogether, must beyond reasonable doubt establish its hypothesis as *more credible than its negation.* Of a prediction, on the other hand, we need to require only that it establish its hypothesis simply as *more credible than any comparable alternative.* Of course predictions may, as in astronomy, be as firmly based in fact and as tightly articulated in reasoning as any explanation. But this is not a general requirement to which predictions *must* conform. A doctor's prognosis, for example, does not have astronomical certitude, yet practical considerations render it immensely useful as a guide in our conduct because it is far superior to reliance on guesswork or on pure chance alone as a decision-making device.

[5]On the contrast between prediction and explanation see further I. Scheffler, "Explanation, Prediction, and Abstraction," *British Journal for the Philosophy of Science* 7 (1957): 293–309, and N. Rescher, "On Prediction and Explanation," *British Journal for the Philosophy of Science* 8 (1958): 281–290.

Generally speaking, in any field in which our ability to forecast with precision is very limited, our actions of necessity are guided by only slight differences in the probability which we attach to possible future alternative states of the world, and consequently we must permit predictions to be based upon far weaker evidence than explanations. This is especially true of a science such as history, or rather its predictive counterpart—political science. Here, in the absence of powerful theoretic delimitations which narrow down the immense variety of future possibilities to some manageable handful, the *a priori* likelihood of any particular state of affairs is minute, and we can thus tolerate considerable weakness in our predictive tools without rendering them useless. Consider, for example, the quasi-law that in a U.S. off-year election the opposition party is apt to gain. This is certainly not a general law, nor is it intended to be a summary of statistics. It has implicit qualifications of the "ceteris paribus" type, but it does claim to characterize the course of events "as a rule" and it generates an expectation of the explainability of deviations. On this basis, an historical (or political) law of this sort can provide a valid, though limited, foundation for sound predictions.

The epistemological asymmetry between explanation and prediction has not, it seems to us, been adequately recognized and taken into account in discussion of scientific method. For one thing, such recognition would lead to a better understanding of the promise of possibly unorthodox items of methodological equipment, such as quasi-laws, for the purposes of prediction in the inexact sciences. But more generally it would open the way of explicit consideration of a *specific methodology of prediction*—a matter which seems to have been neglected to date by the philosophers of science. As long as one believes that explanation and prediction are strict methodological counterparts, it is reasonable to press further with solely the explanatory problems of a discipline, in the expectation that only the tools thus forged will then be usable for predictive purposes. But once this belief is rejected, the problem of a specifically predictive method arises, and it becomes pertinent to investigate the possibilities of predictive procedures autonomous of those used for explanation.

Before discussing such possibilities in greater detail, it is imperative, in order to avoid various misunderstandings, that we give a brief clarification of the meaning of probability and of some associated concepts.

5. Probability

From the viewpoint of the philosophy of science the theory of probability occupies a peculiar position. To the extent that it deals with relations among propositions it is part of semantics and thus of pure logic. To the extent that it deals with credibility, rational beliefs, and personal expectations, it is part of empirical pragmatics and thus a social science. (The view, not held by us, that probability theory properly belongs entirely in the second field rather than the first is sometimes referred to as *psychologism*.)[6] Even for the logical part of the theory, the foundations are not yet established very firmly, and only with regard to applications to the simplest forms of one-place predicate languages has real progress been made to date.[7] Because of this, some vagueness must still be accepted even in discussing the purely logical aspects of probability; that is, unless we were content to confine ourselves to the aforementioned simplest case, which we are not, since the linguistic demands of the inexact sciences transcend these limits of simplicity even more frequently than do those of the exact sciences.

It is convenient to distinguish three probability concepts, namely *relative frequency, degree of confirmation*, and *personal* (or *subjective*) *probability*. Of these, the first is an objective, empirically ascertainable property of classes of physical objects or physical events; the second is also purely objective, namely a logical relation between sentences; the third is a measure of a person's confidence that some given statement is true, and is thus an essentially subjective matter. Let us briefly consider each of these three probability concepts.

RELATIVE FREQUENCY

Relative frequency requires the statement of a reference class (of objects or events), also called the population. If the class is finite it is simply the ratio of the number of elements having some property or trait divided by the total number of elements in the class. Thus we speak of the relative frequency of males in the present U. S. population, or of rainy days in Los Angeles in the first half of this century.[8] Sometimes the notion of relative frequency is extended to classes of either indefinite or infinite size. For example, we may speak of the relative frequency of male births in the U. S. over an extended period, without precisely specifying that period; or we may speak of the relative frequency "in the long run" of Heads in tosses with a particular coin, where the sequence of tosses is of indefinite length, and may even be idealized into an infinite sequence (in which case the "relative frequency" is the limit of the relative frequencies of the finite subsequences). In a situation like this, it is even customary to ascribe this probability, that is, the relative frequency of Heads in the long run, as a property to the coin itself (in particular, a "fair coin" is one for which this probability is ½). But it is best to interpret such a statement merely as a paraphrase for the longer statement that in a long

[6]An incisive critique of psychologism is given in chapter II of R. Carnap's book, *Logical Foundations of Probability* (Chicago, 1950).

[7]See R. Carnap's massive study of the *Logical Foundations of Probability* (Chicago, 1950), and various studies cited by him in the extensive Bibliography, in particular those of Helmer, Hempel, and Oppenheim.

[8]It is a technical refinement into which we need not here enter that in applications it is common to use, instead of the relative frequency proper, some statistical *estimate* thereof.

sequence of possible tosses with this coin (but not so long as to alter the physical characteristics of the coin) the relative frequency of Heads will be such and such.

DEGREE OF CONFIRMATION

The degree of confirmation is a logical relation between two sentences, the hypothesis H and the evidence E. The degree of confirmation of H on the basis of E is intended to be a measure of the credibility rationally imparted to the truth of H by the assumed truth of E. Precise definitions have thus far been suggested only for the one-place predicate calculus. In the simplest case, where E has the form of a statistical record of n observations, to the effect that exactly m out of n objects examined had a property P, and where the hypothesis H ascribes this property P to an as yet unexamined object, then the degree of confirmation of H on the basis of E, or $dc(H, E)$, is defined to be either the observed relative frequency m/n or else a quantity very close to it (and having the same limit as n gets large) which may differ somewhat from m/n due to technical requirements of elegance of the formalism. It is irrelevant for our present purposes which particular definition we adopt, but to fix the idea let us assume simply that in the above case $dc(H,E) = m/n$.

If E does not have the simple form of a statistic or H does not just affirm another like instance, then some plausible extension of the definition of 'dc' is required; this may lead to cases where no single number can reasonably be specified but where the evidence merely warrants a narrowing down of the probability of H to several possible numbers or an interval of numbers. For instance, if H is the hypothesis that a certain Irish plumber will vote Democratic in the next presidential election, and the evidence E amounts solely to saying that 70 percent of the Irish vote Democratic and 20 percent of the plumbers do; then all that one might reasonably assert is that the required probability lies somewhere between .2 and .7.

Ambiguities of this kind can, of course, be removed by *fiat* (and in fact this has been the path followed in the formalisms proposed to date by Carnap). That is to say, one can transfer the ambiguity from the object language to the meta-language, by stating the matter as follows: There are several ways in which 'dc' can be defined, but under each particular definition the degree of confirmation is a single-valued function.

No matter which of these two alternatives is chosen, at least the situation can still be resolved, as long as we are dealing with one-place predicates only. As soon as we move into a subject-matter where adequate discourse requires multi-place predicates or predicates of several logical levels, no formal proposals for an extended definition of 'dc' are as yet available, and we have to rely largely on trained intuition as to how a numerical measure of the "credibility rationally imparted to H by E" should be estimated in specific cases.

Since it is not the purpose of this article to deal at length with the foundations of probability theory, while on the other hand the use of some notion of degree of confirmation in the vague sense introduced here seems to us unavoidable, we shall largely have to ignore the technical problems pointed out above. For practical purposes this means, not that we shall maintain the fiction of a well-defined formula being available which permits computation of $dc(H,E)$ for all H and E, but rather that we shall assume that, in specific cases arising in situations of interest, reasonable and knowledgeable persons, when confronted with the question of ascertaining a value of $dc(H,E)$, will find this definitely, if vaguely, meaningful and will arrive at estimates of the value that will not be too widely disparate. This leads us to the next probabilistic concept we must discuss.

PERSONAL PROBABILITY

Personal, or subjective probability is a measure of a person's confidence in, or subjective conviction of, the truth of some hypothesis. With Savage[9] it is measured behavioristically in terms of the person's betting behavior. If a person thinks that H is just about as likely as its negation $\sim H$, then if he were placed in a situation where he had to make an even bet on either H or $\sim H$, he would presumably be indifferent to this choice. Similarly, if he thought H to be twice as likely as $\sim H$, he would have no preference as to which side to take in a 1:2 bet on $H: \sim H$. Generalizing this idea, we shall say that the person attaches the personal probability p to the hypothesis H if he is found to be indifferent between the choice of receiving, say, one dollar if H turns out to be true or receiving $\frac{p}{1-p}$ dollars if H turns out to be false (his "personal expectation" in either case being p dollars).[10]

We shall call a person "rational" if (1) his preferences (especially with regard to betting options) are mutually consistent or at least, when inconsistencies are brought to his attention, he is willing to correct them; (2) his personal probabilities are reasonably stable over time, provided he receives no new relevant evidence; (3) his personal probabilities are affected (in the right direction) by new relevant evidence; and (4) in simple cases where the evidence E at his disposal is known, and E and H are such that $dc(H,E)$ is defined, his personal probability regarding H is in reasonable agreement with the latter; in particular, he is indifferent as to which side to take in a bet which to his knowledge is a "fair" bet.

A (predictive) "expert" in some subject-matter is a person who is *rational* in the sense discussed, who has a large background knowledge E in that field,

---

[9]L. J. Savage, *The Foundations of Statistics* (New York, 1952).
[10]There are certain well-known difficulties connected with this behavioristic approach, which we will ignore here. We will merely mention that, in experimental situations designed to elicit personal probabilities, care must be taken that the stakes involved are in a range where the utility of money is effectively linear and the utility (or disutility) of gambling is negligible.

and whose predictions (actual or implicit in his personal probabilities) with regard to hypotheses H in that field show a record of comparative successes in the long run. This is very much of a relative concept, as it depends on the predictive performance of which the average non-expert in the field would be capable. (In a temperate climate, a lay predictor can establish an excellent record by always forecasting good weather, but this would not support a claim to meteorological expertise.) We will return to a more detailed consideration of predictive expertise below.

With regard to the relationship between degree of confirmation and personal probability, it may be said that $dc(H,E)$ is intended to be a conceptual reconstruction of the personal probability which an entirely rational person would assign to H, given that his entire relevant information is E. In practice this relation can be applied in both directions: In simple cases where we have a generally acceptable definition of "dc" we may judge a person's rationality by the conformity of his personal probabilities—or of his betting behavior—with computable (or, if his information E is uncertain, estimable) dc-values. Conversely, once a person has been established as rational and possibly even an expert in a field, we may use his personal probabilities as estimates, on our part, of the degrees of confirmation which should be assigned given hypotheses.

We shall make use of these probability concepts below, primarily in connection with the use of expert judgment for predictive purposes. But we must first consider the use of evidence in prediction, beginning with some examples to illustrate the problems arising in the predictive use of probabilistic evidence.

6. Some Examples of the Use of Evidence in Prediction

The simplest use of evidence occurs when there is a direct reference to prior instances. Will my car start on this cold morning? Its record of successful starting on previous cold mornings is around 50 percent. I would be unduly hopeful or pessimistic in assigning as personal probability of its starting today a number significantly different from ½. This use of a record of past instances as a basis for probability assignments with regard to future events is a common, and generally justified, inductive procedure (and of course is the basis on which the definition of degree of confirmation is constructed). However, under some circumstances it is a very poor way indeed of marshalling evidence.

Consider the case of Smith, who has been riding the bus to work for a year, the fare having been 10¢. One morning he is required to pay 15¢. Smith may wonder if his return fare that evening will be 10¢. It is highly unlikely—despite the great preponderance of 10¢ rides in Smith's sample. For Smith well knows that public transportation fares do change, and not by whim but by adoption of a new fare structure. In the light of this item of *background information*, it is unreasonable for Smith to base his personal probability directly on the cumulative record of past instances.

This illustrates the need for the use of background knowledge as indirect evidence, in the sense of furnishing other than direct instance confirmation. This need is encountered constantly in the use of evidence, and it constitutes one of the prime obstacles to a more sophisticated definition of degree of confirmation than has hitherto been achieved. Consider another example. Will my new neighbor move away again within five years? He is a carpenter (the average carpenter moves once every 10 years) and a bachelor (the average bachelor moves once every 3 years). I can assess the likelihood of my neighbor's moving within the next five years relative to either the reference class of carpenters or that of bachelors. Which one I should choose, or what weight I should give to each, must depend strongly on my background information as to the relative relevance of occupation versus marital status as a determining factor in changes of domicile.

Such reference-class problems arise even with statistical information of the simplest kind. Consider a sample of 100 objects drawn at random from a population, with the following outcome as regards possession of the properties P and Q:

	has Q	has not Q
has P	1	9
has not P	89	1

Given this information, what is the probability that another object drawn from the population, which is known to have the property P, will also have the property Q? Should we use a value around 0.1 (since only 1 of 10 observed P's is a Q) or a value around 0.9 (since altogether 90 percent of the observed sample has the property Q)? Here again, an expedient use of the statistical evidence before us must rely on background information, if any, regarding the revelance of P-ness to Q-ness. If we know that most Texans are rich and most barbers poor, and are given as only item of information specifically about a man by the name of Jones that he is a Texan barber, we would do well to assign a low probability to the statement that Jones is rich, precisely because occupation is known to us to be more relevant to financial status than is location.

7. The Role of Expertise in Prediction

The implication of the examples we have been discussing is that a knowledge about past instances or about statistical samples—while indeed providing valuable information—is not the sole and sometimes not even the main form of evidence in support of rational assignments of probability values. In fact the evidential use of such *prima facie* evidence must be tempered by reference to background information, which frequently may be intuitive in character and have the form of a vague recognition of underlying regularities, such as analogies, correlations, or other conformities whose formal rendering would require the use of predicates of a logical level higher than the first.

The consideration of such underlying regularities is of special importance for the inexact sciences, particularly the social sciences (but not exclusively)[11] because in this sphere we are constantly faced with situations in which statistical information matters less than knowledge of regularities in the behavior of people or in the character of institutions, such as traditions and customary practices, fashions and mores, national attitudes and climates of opinion, institutional rules and regulations, group aspirations, and so on. For instance, in assessing the chances of a Republican presidential victory in 1960, a knowledge of the record of past election successes matters less than an insight into current trends and tendencies; or in answering a question as to the likelihood, say, of U. S. recognition of Communist China by 1960, it is hard to point to any relevant statistical evidence, yet there exists a host of relatively undigested but highly relevant background information.

This non-explicitness of background knowledge, which nonetheless may be significant or even predominantly important, is typical of the inexact sciences, as is the uncertainty as to the evidential weight to be accorded various pieces of *prima facie* information in view of indirect evidence provided by underlying regularities. Hence the great importance which must be attached to experts and to expertise in these fields. For the expert has at his ready disposal a large store of (mostly inarticulated) background knowledge and a refined sensitivity to its relevance, through the intuitive application of which he is often able to produce trustworthy personal probabilities regarding hypotheses in his area of expertness.

The important place of expert judgment for predictions in the inexact sciences is further indicated by the prominence of quasi-laws among the explanatory instrumentalities of this domain. Since the conditions of applicability of such generalizations are neither fully nor even explicitly formulable, their use in specific circumstances presupposes the exercise of sound judgment as to their applicability to the case in hand. The informed expert, with his resources of background knowledge and his cultivated sense of the relevance and bearing of generalities in particular cases, is best able to carry out the application of quasi-laws necessary for reasoned prediction in this field.

8. The Problem of the Predictive Use of Evidence in an Inexact Context

In summary, the foregoing illustrations of the predictive use of evidence may be said to indicate that we are frequently confronted with what must be considered as a problematical, and far from ideal, epistemological situation. For the examples we have been considering show that in assessing the probability

---

[11]Use of background information, to temper the application of statistical information, is just as operative in the physical sciences, e.g., in engineering, so that no difference in principle is involved here.

of an hypothesis *H*—typically a description of some future event—we are in many instances required to rely not merely upon some specific and explicit evidence *E*, but also on a vast body of potentially relevant background knowledge *K*, which is in general not only vague in its extent (and therefore indefinite in content) but also deficient in explicit articulation. In many practical applications, particularly in the inexact sciences, not even that part of *K* which is suitably relevant to *H* can be assumed to be explicitly articulated, or even articulable. One is unable to set down in sentential form everything that would have to be included in a full characterization of one's knowledge about a familiar room; and the same applies equally, if not more so, to a political expert's attempt to state all he knows that might be relevant to a question such as, for example, that of U. S. recognition of Communist China.

These considerations point up a deficiency for present purposes in the usual degree-of-confirmation concept quite apart from those already mentioned. For such an indefinite *K*, we cannot expect $dc(H, E \& K)$ to be determinable or even defined. This suggests, as a first step, the desirability of introducing a concept $dc_K(H,E)$—the "degree of confirmation of *H* on *E* in view of *K*"— which is defined to be equal to $dc(H,E \& K)$ whenever it is possible to articulate *K* fully within the same language in which *H* and *E* are stated. But how is such a quantity to be determined when *K* is not fully formulated? Furthermore in addition to the difficulty involved in formulating it completely, *K* almost invariably contains probability statements (both of an objective, or *dc*-, type, and of the indirect form "So-and-so attaches to *H* the personal probability *p*"). To date, there is no hint of any suggestion as to how '$dc(H,X)$' might be formally defined when *X* contains statements of this kind.

Faced with this situation—which is surely not likely to be resolved in the near future—we must either for the present renounce all claims to systematized prediction in the inexact sciences, or, as indicated earlier, turn to unorthodox methods which are based upon judicious and systematic reliance on expert judgment. One such course, to which we previously alluded, may possibly help us out of the present perplexity. Let *A* be an expert and *K(A)* his relevant background knowledge. Then *A*'s personal probability, $pp_A(H,E)$, may be taken as an estimate on our part of $dc_{K(A)}(H,E)$. Thus the device of using the personal probabilities of experts, extracted by appropriately devised techniques of interrogation, can serve as a means of measuring quantities of the *dc*-type even in cases where there is no hope of application of the formal degree-of-confirmation concepts.

It might seem that in resorting to this device we conjure up a host of new problems, because—to all appearances—we are throwing objectivity to the winds. Of course, since we insist upon remaining within our own definition of scientific activity, we do not propose to forego objectivity. However, before attempting to analyze the possibility of salvaging objectivity in this situation, it may be well to look at a few examples illuminating the application of expertise in the sense just described.

9. The Intrinsic Use of Experts for Prediction

A source of characteristic examples of the predictive use of expert judgment is provided by the field of diagnostics, especially medical diagnostics.[12] A patient, let us assume, exhibits a pattern of symptoms such that it is virtually certain that he has either ailment A or ailment B, with respective probabilities of .4 and .6, where these probabilities derive from the statistical record of past cases. Thus the entire body of explicit symptomatic evidence is (by hypothesis) such as to indicate a margin in favor of the prediction that the patient suffers from disease B rather than A, and thus may respond positively to a corresponding course of treatment. But it is quite possible that an examining physician, taking into consideration not only the explicit indicators that constitute the "symptoms" (e.g., temperature, blood pressure, etc.) but also an entire host of otherwise inarticulated background knowledge with regard to this particular patient, the circumstances of the case, etc., may arrive at a diagnosis of disease A rather than B. Thus the use of background information, in a way that is not systematized but depends entirely on the exercise of informal expert judgment, may appropriately lead to predictive conclusions in the face of *prima facie* evidence which points in the opposite direction.

Quite similar in its conceptual structure to the foregoing medical example are various other cases of predictive expertise in the economic sphere. The advice of an expert investment counsellor, for example, may exhibit essentially the same subtle employment of non-articulate background knowledge that characterized the prediction of the diagnostician.

Again, in such essentially sociological predictions of public reactions as are involved in the advertising and marketing of commercial products, the same predictive role of expert judgment comes into play. When the production of a motion picture is completed, a decision must be made regarding the number of prints to be made. There are economic reasons for an accurate prediction of the need: if too few prints are ready to meet the immediate demand, film rental income will be lost; on the other hand, the prints are costly, and an over-supply leads to considerable excess expenditure. Here again, as in the medical or economic examples, certain limited predictions can be based wholly on the record of past statistics in analogous instances. The presence of certain actors in the cast, the topic, theme and setting of the film, perhaps even its reception by preview audiences, may suggest a probability distribution for its demand. However, the major studios involved in motion-picture production are not content to rely on these explicit indicators alone. Aware of the potential influence of a whole host of subtle intangibles (e.g., so-called "audience appeal," timeliness with respect to current events, existence of competitive offerings), all of which are susceptible of explicit statistical treat-

---

[12]An extensive and useful discussion of medical prediction is contained in P. E. Mehl's book on *Clinical vs. Statistical Prediction* (Minneapolis, 1954).

ment only with the greatest difficulty if at all, they prudently rely on the forecasts of professional experts in the field, who have exhibited a demonstrated ability to supplement the various explicit elements by appropriate use of their capacities for an intuitive appraisal of the many intangible factors which critically affect the final outcome.

Other examples drawn from the applied sciences, engineering, industry, politics, etc.,will easily suggest themselves. What they have in common is the reliance, in part or wholly, on an expert, who here functions in an intrinsic rather than extrinsic role. By *extrinsic expertise* we mean the kind of inventiveness, based on factual knowledge and the perception of previously unnoticed relationships, that goes into the hypothesizing of new laws and the construction of new theories; it is, in other words, the successful activity of the scientist qua scientist. *Intrinsic expertise*, by contrast, is not invoked until after an hypothesis has been formulated and its probability, in the sense of degree of confirmation, is to be estimated. The expert, when performing intrinsically, thus functions within a theory rather than on the theory-constructing level.

10. The Role of Prediction as an Aid to Decision-Making

The decisions which professional decision-makers—governmental administrators, company presidents, military commanders, etc.—are called upon to make inevitably turn on the question of future developments, since their directives as to present actions are invariably conceived with a view to future results. Thus a reliance upon predictive ability is nowhere more overt and more pronounced than in the area of policy formation, and decision-making in general.

For this reason, decision-makers surround themselves by staffs of expert advisers, whose special knowledge and expertise must generally cover a wide field. Some advising experts may have a great store of factual knowledge, and can thus serve as walking reference books. Others may excel through their diagnostic or otherwise predictive abilities. Others may have a special analytical capacity to recognize the structure of the problems in hand, thus aiding in the proper utilization of the contributions of the other two types of experts (e.g., operations analysts, management consultants, etc.). The availability of such expertise constitutes for the decision-maker a promise of increased predictive ability essential to the more effective discharge of his own responsibilities. Thus the ultimate function of expert advice is almost always to make a predictive contribution.

While the dependence of the decision-makers upon expert advisers is particularly pronounced in social-science contexts, for instance, in the formulation of economic and political policies, such dependence upon expertise ought by no means to be taken to contradistinguish the social from the physical sciences. In certain engineering applications, particularly of relatively underdeveloped branches of physics (such as the applied physics of extremes of temperature or velocity) the reliance upon "know-how" and expert judgment is just as pronounced as it is in the applications of political science to foreign-policy formation. The use of experts for prediction does *not* constitute a line of demarcation between the social and the physical sciences, but rather between the exact and the inexact sciences.

Although we have held that the primary functions of expert advisers to decision-makers is to serve as "predictors," we by no means intend to suggest that they act as fortune tellers, trying to foresee specific occurrences for which the limited intellectual vision of the non-expert is insufficient. For the decision-supporting uses of predictive expertise, there is in general no necessity for an anticipation of particular future occurrences. It suffices that the expert be able to sketch out adequately the general directions of future developments, to anticipate—as we have already suggested—some of the major critical junctures ("branch points") on which the course of these developments will hinge, and to make contingency predictions with regard to the alternatives associated with them.

While the value of scientific prediction for sound decision-making is beyond question, it can hardly be claimed that the inexact sciences have the situation regarding the use of predictive expertise well in hand. Quite to the contrary, it is our strong feeling that significant improvements are possible in the predictive instruments available to the decision-maker. These improvements are contingent on the development of methods for the more effective predictive use of expert judgment. In the final section we shall give consideration to some of the problems involved in this highly important, but hitherto largely unexplored area.

11. Justification of the Intrinsic Use of Expertise

We come back to the problem of preserving objectivity in the face of reliance upon expertise. Can we accept the utilization of intrinsic expert judgment within the framework of an inductive procedure without laying ourselves open to the charge of abandoning objective scientific methods and substituting rank subjectivity?

To see that explicit use of expert judgment is not incompatible with scientific objectivity, let us look once more at the medical-diagnosis example of the preceding section. Consider the situation in which a diagnostician has advised that a patient be treated for ailment A (involving, say, a major surgical operation) rather than B (which might merely call for a special diet). Our willingness, in this case, to put our trust in the expert's judgment surely would not be condemned as an overly subjective attitude. The reasons why our reliance on the expert is objectively justified are not difficult to see. For one thing, the selection of appropriate experts is not a matter of mere personal preference but is a procedure governed by objective criteria (about which more will be said in the ensuing section). But most importantly, the past diagnostic performance record makes the diagnostician an objectively reliable indicator (of diseases), in the same sense as one of any two highly correlated physical characteristics is an indictor of the other. ("If most hot pieces of iron are red, and vice versa, and if this piece of iron is red then it is probably hot.")

Even if the expert's explicit record of past performance is unknown, reliance upon his predictions may be objectively justified on the basis of general background knowledge as to his reputation as an expert. The objective reliability of experts' pronouncements may also be strongly suggested by the fact that they often exhibit a high degree of agreement with one another, which—at least if we have reason to assume the pronouncements to be independent—precludes subjective whim.

Epistemologically speaking, the use of an expert as an objective indicator—as illustrated by the example of the diagnostician—amounts to considering the expert's predictive pronouncement as an integral, intrinsic part of the subject matter, and treating his reliability as a part of the theory about the subject matter. Our information about the expert is conjoined to our other knowledge about the field, and we proceed with the application of precisely the same inductive methods which we would apply in cases where no use of expertise is made. Our "data" are supplemented by the expert's personal probability valuations and by his judgments of relevance (which, by the way, could be derived from suitable personal probability statements), and our "theory" is supplemented by information regarding the performance of experts.

In this manner the incorporation of expert judgment into the structure of our investigation is made subject to the same safeguards which are used to assure objectivity in other scientific investigations. The use of expertise is therefore no retreat from objectivity or reversion to a reliance on subjective taste.

12. Criteria for the Selection of Predictive Experts

The first and most obvious criterion of expertise is of course knowledge. We resort to an "expert" precisely because we expect his information and the body of experience at his disposal to constitute an assurance that he will be able to select the needed items of background information, determine the character and extent of their relevance, and apply these insights to the formulation of the required personal probability judgments.

However, the expert's knowledge is not enough; he must be able to bring it to bear effectively on the predictive problem in hand; and this not every expert is able to do. It becomes necessary also to place some check upon his predictive efficacy and to take a critical look at his past record of predictive performance.

The simplest way in which to score an expert's performance is in terms of "reliability": his *degree of reliability* is the relative frequency of cases in which, when confronted with several alternative hypotheses, he ascribed to the eventually correct alternative among them a greater personal probability than to the others.

This measure, while useful, must yet be taken with a grain of salt, for there are circumstances where even a layman's degree of reliability, as defined above, can be very close to 1. For instance, in a region of very constant weather, a layman can prognosticate the weather quite successfully by always predicting the same weather for the next day as for the current one. Similarly, a quack who hands out bread pills and reassures his patients of recovery "in due time" may prove right more often than not and yet have no legitimate claim to being classified as a medical expert. Thus what matters is not so much an expert's absolute degree of reliability but his relative degree of reliability, that is, his reliability as compared to that of the average person. But even this may not be enough. In the case of the medical diagnostician discussed earlier, the layman may have no information that might give him a clue as to which of diseases A and B is the more probable, while anyone with a certain amount of rudimentary medical knowledge may know that disease A generally occurs much more frequently than disease B; yet his prediction of A rather than B on this basis alone would not qualify him as a reliable diagnostician. Thus a more subtle assessment of the qualifications of an expert may require his comparison with the average person having some degree of general background knowledge in his field of specialization. One method of scoring experts somewhat more subtly than just by their reliability is in terms of their "accuracy": the *degree of accuracy* of an expert's predictions is the correlation between his personal probabilities p and his correctness in the class of those hypotheses to which he ascribed the probability p. Thus of a highly accurate predictor we expect that of those hypotheses to which he ascribes, say a probability of 70%, approximately 70% will eventually turn out to be confirmed. Accuracy in this sense, by the way, does not guarantee reliability,[13] but accuracy in addition to reliability may be sufficient to distinguish the real expert from the specious one.

13. The Dependence of Predictive Performance on Subject Matter

Not only are some experts better predictors than others, but subject matter fields differ from one another in the extent to which they admit of expertise. This circumstance is of course in some instances due to the fact that the scientific theory of the field in question is relatively undeveloped. The geology of the moon or the meteorology of Mars is less amenable to prediction than their mundane counterparts, although no greater characteristic complexity is

[13]For instance, suppose experts A and B each gave 100 responses, assigning probabilities .2, .4, .6, .8 to what in fact were the correct alternatives among 100 choices of H and ~H, as follows:

p	A	B
.2	10	0
.4	20	0
.6	30	60
.8	40	40

Then A is perfectly *accurate* (e.g., exactly 60 percent, or 30, of the 20 + 30, or 50, cases to which he assigned .6 were correct), but he is only 70 percent *reliable*; B, on the other hand, is 100% reliable, but his accuracy is quite faulty (e.g., 100 percent, rather than 60 percent, of the 60 cases to which he assigned .6 were correct).

inherent in these fields. In other cases, however, predictive expertise is limited despite a high degree of cultivation of a field, because the significant phenomena hinge upon factors that are not particularly amenable to prediction.

In domains in which the flux of events is subject to gradual transitions and constant regularities (say, astronomy), a high degree of predictive expertise is possible. In those fields, however, in which the processes of transition admit of sharp jolts and discontinuities, which can in turn be the effects of so complex and intricate causal processes as to be "chance" occurrences for all practical purposes, predictive expertise is inherently less feasible. The assassination of a political leader can altogether change the policies of a nation, particularly when such a nation does not have a highly developed complex of institutions that ensure gradualness of its policy changes. Clearly no expert on a particular country can be expected to have the data requisite for a prediction of assassinations; that is, his relevant information is virtually certain not to include the precisely detailed knowledge of the state of mind of various key figures that might give him any basis whatsoever for assigning a numerical value as his personal probability to the event in question. This situation is quite analogous to that of predicting the outcome of a particular toss of a coin; only the precise dynamic details of the toss's initial conditions might provide a basis for computing a probability other than ½ for the outcome, and these details again are almost certainly unavailable. We may here legitimately speak of "chance occurrences," in the sense that not even an expert, unless he has the most unusual information at his disposal, is in a better position than the layman to make a reliable prediction.

In the inexact sciences, particularly in the social sciences, the critical causal importance of such chance events makes predictive expertise in an absolute sense difficult and sometimes impossible, and it is this, rather than the quality of his theoretical machinery, which puts the social scientist in a poor competitive position relative, say, to the astronomer.

However, when the expert is unable to make precise predictions, due to the influence of chance factors, we can expect him to indicate the major contingencies on which future developments will hinge. Even though the expert cannot predict the specific course of future events in an unstable country, he should be able to specify the major "branch points" of future contingencies, and to provide personal probabilities conditionally with respect to these. Thus, for example, while it would be unreasonable to expect an expert on the American economy to predict with precision the duration of a particular phase of an economic cycle (e.g., a recession), it is entirely plausible to ask him to specify the major potential "turning points" in the cycle (e.g., increased steel production at a certain juncture), and to indicate the probable courses of development ensuing upon each of the specified alternatives.

Such differences in predictability among diverse subject-matter fields lead to important consequences for the proper utilization of experts. One obvious implication is that it may clearly be more profitable to concentrate limited resources of predictive expertise on those portions of a broader domain which are inherently more amenable to prediction. For example in a study of long-range political developments in a particular geographic area, it might in some cases be preferable to focus on demographic developments rather than the evolution of programs and platforms of political parties.

However, the most important consideration is that even in subject-matter fields in which the possibility of prediction is very limited the exercise of expertise, instead of being applied to the determination of *absolute* personal probabilities with respect to certain hypotheses, ought rather more profitably be concentrated on the identification of the relevant branch-points and the associated problems of the *relative* personal probabilities for the hypothesis in question, i.e., relative with regard to the alternatives arising at these branch-points.

Even in predictively very "difficult" fields—such as the question of the future foreign policy of an "unstable" country—the major branch-points of future contingencies are frequently few enough for actual enumeration, and although outright prediction cannot be expected, relative predictions hinging upon these principal alternative contingencies can in many instances serve the same purposes for which absolute predictions are ordinarily employed. For example, it would be possible for a neighboring state, in formulating its own policy toward this country, to plan not for "the" (one and only) probable course of developments but to design several policies, one for each of the major contingencies, or perhaps even a single policy which could deal effectively with all the alternatives.

14. Predictive Consensus Techniques

The predictive use of an expert takes place within a rationale which, on the basis of our earlier discussion, can be characterized as follows: We wish to investigate the predictive hypothesis H; with the expert's assistance, we fix upon the major items of the body of explicit evidence E which is relevant to this hypothesis; we then use the expert's personal probability valuation $pp(H,E)$ as *our* estimate of the degree of confirmation of H on the basis of E, i.e., as our estimated value of $dc(H,E)$.

This straightforward procedure, however, is no longer adequate in those cases in which *several* experts are available. For here we have not the single value $pp(H,E)$ of only one expert, but an entire series of values, one for each of the experts: $pp_1(H,E)$, $pp_2(H,E)$, etc. The problem arises: How is the best joint use of these various expert valuations to be made?[14]

Many possible procedures for effecting a combination among such diverse probability estimates are available. One possibility, and no doubt the simplest, is to select one "favored" expert, and to accept his sole judgment. We might, for example, compare the past predictive performance of the various experts, and select that one whose record has been the most successful.

Another simple procedure is to pool the various expert valuations into an

[14]Compare A. Kaplan, A. L. Skogstad, M. A. Girshick, "The Prediction of Social and Technological Events," *Public Opinion Quarterly*, Spring, 1950.

average of some sort, possibly the median, or a mean weighted so as to reflect past predictive success.

Again, the several experts might be made to act as a single group, pooling their knowledge in round-table discussion, if possible eliminating discrepancies in debate, and the group might then—on the basis of its corporate knowledge—be asked to arrive at one generally agreeable corporate "personal" probability as its consensus, which would now serve as our dc-estimate. (One weakness in this otherwise very plausible-sounding procedure is that the consensus valuation might unduly reflect the views of the most respected member of the group, or of the most persuasive.)

One variant of this consensus procedure is to require that the experts, after pooling their knowledge in discussion, and perhaps after debating the issues, set down their separate "second-guess" personal probabilities, revising their initial independent valuations in the light of the group work. These separate values are then combined by some sort of averaging process to provide our dc-estimate. The advantage of such a combination of independent values over the use of a single generally acceptable group value is that it tends to diminish the influence of the most vociferous or influential group member. Incidentally, in any consensus method of this kind in which separate expert valuations are combined, we can introduce the refinement of weighting an expert's judgment so as to reflect his past performance.

Another consensus procedure, sometimes called the "Delphi Technique," eliminates committee activity altogether, thus further reducing the influence of certain psychological factors, such as specious persuasion, the unwillingness to abandon publicly expressed opinions, and the bandwagon effect of majority opinion. This technique replaces direct debate by a carefully designed program of sequential individual interrogations (best conducted by questionnaires) interspersed with information and opinion feedback derived by computed consensus from the earlier parts of the program. Some of the questions directed to the respondents may, for instance, inquire into the "reasons" for previously expressed opinions, and a collection of such reasons may then be presented to each respondent in the group, together with an invitation to reconsider and possibly revise his earlier estimates. Both the inquiry into the reasons and subsequent feedback of the reasons adduced by others may serve to stimulate the experts into taking into due account considerations they might through inadvertence have neglected, and to give due weight to factors they were inclined to dismiss as unimportant on first thought.

We have done no more here than to indicate some examples from the spectrum of alternative consensus methods. Clearly there can be no universally "best" method. The efficacy of such methods is very obviously dependent upon the nature of the particular subject-matter, and may even hinge upon the idiosyncrasies and personalities of the specific experts (e.g., on their ability to work as a group, etc.). Indeed this question of the relative effectiveness of the various predictive consensus techniques is almost entirely an open problem for empirical research, and it is strongly to be hoped that more experimental investigation will be undertaken in this important field. . . .

Our starting point has been the distinction between the "exact" and the "inexact" areas of science. It is our contention that this distinction is far more important and fundamental from the standpoint of a correct view of scientific method than is the case with superficially more pronounced distinctions based on subject-matter diversities, especially that between the social and the physical sciences. Some branches of the social sciences (e.g., certain parts of demography), which are usually characterized by the presence of a formalized mathematical theory, are methodologically analogous to the exact parts of physics. By contrast, the applied, inexact branches of physical science—for instance, certain areas of engineering under "extreme" conditions—are in many basic respects markedly similar to the social sciences.

This applies both to methods of explanation and to methods of prediction. Partly because of the absence of mathematically formalized theories, explanations throughout the area of inexact sciences—within the physical and the social science settings alike—are apt to be given by means of the restricted generalizations we have called quasi-laws. The presence of such less-than-universal principles in the inexact sciences creates an asymmetry between the methods of explanation and those of prediction in these fields. This suggests the desirability of developing the specifically predictive instrumentalities of these fields, for once the common belief in the identity of predictive and explanatory scientific procedures is seen to be incorrect, it is clearly appropriate to consider the nature and potentialities of predictive procedures distinct from those used for explanation. As for predictions in the inexact sciences (physical as well as social), these can be pragmatically acceptable (that is, as a basis for actions) when based on methodologically even less sophisticated grounds than are explanations, such as expert judgment, for example.

These general considerations regarding the methodology of the inexact sciences hold particularly intriguing implications for the possibility of methodological innovation in the social sciences. Here the possible existence of methods which are unorthodox in the present state of social-science practices merits the closest examination. This is particularly true with respect to the pragmatic applications of the social sciences (e.g., in support of decision-making), in which the predictive element is preponderant over the explanatory.

One consideration of this sort revolves about the general question of the utilization of expertise. We have stressed the importance in the social sciences of limited generalizations (quasi-laws), which cannot necessarily be used in a simple and mechanical way, but whose very application requires the exercise of expert judgment. And more generally, when interested in prediction in this field (especially for decision-making purposes), we are dependent upon the experts' personal probability valuations for our guidance. A systematic investigation of the effective use of experts represents a means by which new and powerful instruments for the investigation of social-science problems might be forged. . . .

3

Imagination And Values In The Study Of The Future

FUTUROLOGY AND THE IMAGING CAPACITY OF THE WEST

● *elise boulding*

The Theory of the Image of the Future

With professional futurists crowding to the microphone to announce the out-lines of the future, it is of some interest to examine today's futurology in the light of the work of one of the first post World War Two futurologists, Fred Polak. When he sat down at his desk in the Hague to write *The Image of the Future*[1] in 1951, he felt driven by a sense of extreme urgency to point out to his colleagues in the West that their visioning capacity was becoming seriously impaired. Many great European thinkers had suffered, gone underground or died, and he himself emerged from years of continuous hiding as a Jew in the Netherlands determined to show that young men could still dream dreams.

At a time when the next meal was the major preoccupation of most Euro-peans, he was calling people to look to the far horizon, to imagine the totally other. He saw the Spenglerian gloom which was settling on Europe as essen-tially a disease of the imagination, and became totally preoccupied with the self-fulfilling qualities of expectations of disaster.

His book was written as a documentation of the role of images of the future in the development of western civilization, tracing inputs from Sumerian, Hellenic and Judeo-Christian sources. Then having shown how the heights of the Renaissance, the Enlightenment and the early industrial era had been achieved through continuous daring breaches of time, he turned angrily to the present and held up the mirror to moment-ridden, mid-century man, clinging desperately to today for fear of what tomorrow would bring.

He was angry because he saw his contemporaries failing to exercise a capacity which they still had but might soon lose through disuse. Failure to work with the imagination to create other and better futures would lead to endless projections of present trends and a petty unfolding of technological possibilities which would in the end leave man crippled.

Fred Polak's concept of the image of the future and its dynamic shaping action on the social present, deals with a rather different dimension of man's imaging capacity than does most current futurism. Social planning, blue-printing, and the technological fix are not what Polak had in mind. Social prediction based on extrapolation of existing trends or predicted break-throughs are not what he meant either.

[1]References to Fred Polak's *Image of the Future* (1961) are to the original, unabridged translation, but the wording is taken from the abridged edition published in 1972.

In Polak's view, the "ideal type" of the image of the future has both eschatological and utopian elements. The eschatological, or transcendant, is the element which enables the visionary to breach the bonds of the cultural present and mentally encompass the possibility of a totally other type of society, not dependent on what human beings are currently capable of realizing. The totally other is, of course, in fact not conceivable by man, but this term (an exact translation of the Dutch) is used without modification because it emphasizes the notion of discontinuity as a key aspect of dynamic social change. Kenneth Boulding's discussion of "Expecting the Unexpected" (1966), points up the dilemma underlying the concept of discontinuity. (See also Peter Drucker, *The Age of Discontinuity*, 1968.) It is clear, however, that a society with an eschatological outlook, one which conceives the possibility, even the desirability, of drastic social change, is very different from the society that seeks familiar tomorrows.

The second element in the ideal-type image of the future is the humanistic utopian, or immanent, element which designates men as the co-partners in the shaping of The Other in the Here-And-Now. Polak suggests that the Judaic image of the future was an ideal embodiment of these twin elements. The Judaic conception of the Covenant, a unique bonding between man and the supernatural, held man responsible for creating the new Zion out of the dusty materials of the planet earth. Paradise was to be nowhere but here. But man had instructions, and he had to listen carefully to get them right. If he didn't listen, the deal was off—the covenant broken. It was the character of the instructions that set a handful of nomads apart from their fellow tribes in Syriac-Palestine.

This delicately balanced conception of the relationship between transcendance and immanence, man and the supernatural, has never lasted for long, though it has reappeared from time to time in the history of the West. The pendulum has swung back and forth. Either God was taking care of everything and man had but to go along with it (St. Augustine), or everything was up to man and he'd better get with it (Comte). Furthermore, societies have alternated between optimistic and pessimistic views of the nature of reality and man. Four modes of imaging the future emerge from various combinations of attitudes to the Kantian categories of Seinmüssen and Seinsollen:

1. *Essence optimism combined with influence optimism:* The world is good and man can make it even better.
2. *Essence optimism combined with influence pessimism:* The world is good but it goes of itself and man cannot alter the course of events.
3. *Essence pessimism combined with influence optimism:* The world is bad but man can make it better.
4. *Essence pessimism combined with influence pessimism:* The world is bad and there isn't a damn thing man can do about it.

Influence optimism can be further divided into direct and indirect influence optimism, depending on whether man is perceived as running the show or acting in partnership with the supernatural. Clearly, a society suffering from both essence and influence pessimism is not generating any dynamic images of the future, and the social paralysis engendered by the lack of positive images of the future will lead to the death of that society, according to Polak. The most dynamic society is the one with both essence and influence optimism, and if the image has eschatological elements with a sense of the possibilities of breakthrough to a totally new order, this adds to the dynamism. These eschatological elements always present a danger to any society, however, in that there is a tendency to spiritualize the other reality and come to think of it as realizable only in heaven, or in an after-life, and not in this world. This is what happened to Christianity. The ever-deferred parousia, conceived as imminent in Jesus' time, was finally thought to be not for this world at all.

Out of the turbulence of the Middle Ages, when conflicting modes of viewing the future were doing battle with each other both inside and outside the church, came the great surges of influence optimism that characterized the Renaissance. From that time on the utopian and eschatological were increasingly separated as the church retreated in the face of increasing confidence in man's capacity to shape his own destiny, with the aid of science. In the end only the pentecostal and adventist sects kept intact the concept of "the peaceable kingdom" as coming on earth, and the rest of the Christian church settled for a spiritualized kingdom within man or located at a comfortable remove in outer space.

Two sets of discoveries released the pent-up energy of the Middle Ages for utopian construction of possible future societies: scientific discoveries that opened up the possibilities of using nature as a tool to shape the environment, and voyagers' discoveries of exotically other cultural patterns which revealed that human society was highly malleable. The sixteen, seventeen and eighteen hundreds produced a heady array of "futures." These ranged from classical-style platonic utopias such as Bacon's *New Atlantis*, which drew on a prevision of future scientific and technological developments to outline a kind of universal communism, through romantic, satirical and rollicking utopias which combined sharp critique of the times with glimpses of an upside-down, right-side-up society—Rousseau, Rabelais, Defoe, Swift, Fenelon, Holberg[2] and on to the socialist utopias of Owen, Saint-Simon and Fourier.[3] This is the point at which social scientists got into the utopia-writing business,

---

[2] Rousseau, *Confessions*; Rabelais, *L'Abbaye de Theleme*; Defoe, "Essays of Projects"; Swift, *Gulliver's Travels*; Fenelon, *Les Aventures de Telemaque*; Holberg, *The Underground Journey of Nicholas Klim*.

[3] Owen, *Signs of the Times, or the Approach of the Millennium*, and *Book of the New Moral World*; Saint-Simon, *De la Réorganisation de la Société Européenne*; Fourier, *The Social Destiny of Man, Theory of the Four Movements*, and *The Passions of the Human Soul*.

and Comte and Marx each constructed utopian future societies based on "natural law," though Marx vehemently attacked the concept of utopism itself.

Utopian writing about the future interacted with social experimentation and the more popular imagination to create social innovations in every sphere from the economic (the trade union movement, profit-sharing, social security, scientific management) through the political (parliamentary democracy, universal suffrage) to the social (universal education, child welfare practices, women's "emancipation," New Towns, social planning). As Polak says, most features of social design in contemporary western society were first figments of a utopia-writer's imagination.

Somewhere in the eighteen hundreds, however, something began happening to the "other space" and the "other time" of utopian fantasy. It began in Germany, home of the universalistic utopians Lessing (1730) and Kant (1795) in such works as Fichte's *Geschlossene Handelsstaat* (1800), which designs a specific future for a specific country—Germany. From this time on nationalism and an orientation toward the immediate future begin eroding the creative imaging powers of the utopist. The sense that man can breach time and create the totally other is gone.

It is Polak's contention that the capacity to image the future is a core capacity in any culture that is manifested in every aspect of that culture. Therefore the decline in the ability to envision totally other "realities," the compressing of the mental perceptions of time and space into the here and now, will be revealed not only in the literature of an era, but also in its art, architecture, poetry and music, in its science and philosophy, and in its religion. Polak in fact documents this decline in imaging capacity in science, philosophy and religion in the twentieth century. The predominantly Orwellian tone of twentieth century science fiction is presented as the most damaging evidence of all concerning the diseased futurism of the present. Prometheus is re-bound, tied up in knots by his own science and technology and fear of the future he had thought to master. What went wrong?

The cultural lag in ability to generate new visions appropriate to the complex knowledge structure of a hyper-industrialized society has been examined at length in contemporary social science literature. The rate of change itself is usually seen as the culprit. Whether or not the human imagination can adapt itself to reconceptualizing reality as fast as reality changes in this century of exponential growth curves is a subject for debate. An element usually left out of the debate, however, is the disappearance of the eschatological sense of a totally other order of reality. The divorce of utopia from eschatology which characterized the enlightenment appeared as a liberation of human thought at the time, but Polak points out that the utopian and eschatological modes are symbiotic and either without the other goes into decline. Once the eschatological otherness of utopian images of the future was weeded out, utopias themselves came to be conceived as more and more static images of a boring, end-state of man. The true utopia is not static, however, but historically relative.

> It carries within itself the seeds of its own elimination through progress in time. The vision which it holds up of the best conceivable future at any given time, is by definition a vision subject to change, and utopias do change both in form and content with the course of history (1961:I, 442).

Our weakened capacity to image the future may therefore not be due to the rates of social change (which we probably adapt to more effectively than we think), but to a general cultural loss of a sense of transcendance. Whether such a culture trait, once lost, can be reconstituted again is a question. Polak takes the position that it has not been lost, only weakened, and that awareness of its weakening can lead to new insights concerning the importance of "otherness" and a rejuvenation of the capacity for imaginative construction of The Other.

Contemporary Futurism

No general cultural survey of contemporary images of the future will be attempted here, but only a brief examination of relatively specialized developments in futurism in the last decades.[4] Within social science futurism has taken various forms, including social planning in specialized and general systems-type planning, the development of special techniques for inventing new futures such as brainstorming, and the development of a variety of conceptual tools for predicting the future à la Kahn and Wiener, Helmer, etc. Straddling the social and engineering sciences are the evolutionary nucleators such as Mead, Platt and Doxiades. The ecological futurists range from Ward and Boulding, who offer a space-ship earth vision of the future, through social geographers and ecologists to whole-earth romanticists and pre-Raphaelite Aquarians. Finally there are the revolutionary futurists, some political, some non-political, some militant, some gentle, and all dedicated to a completely new society for man—and there are the science fiction writers. Each of these will be briefly discussed.

SOCIAL PLANNERS

Born in the womb of the socialist utopia, centralized government planning for total societies first caught the world's imagination in the 1920's when Lenin announced the first of a series of Five Year Plans which were to build the socialist New World by stages in the Soviet Union. Many socialist planning principles have now been accepted in the world at large. The accompanying problems caused by the tendency of plans to bog down because of the large

[4]Every reader is bound to feel that *his* favorite futurists have been left out, but a high degree of selectivity is unavoidable in a short paper. Polak's *Prognostics*, published by Elsevier, deals more fully with the topic.

number of uncontrolled variables at work, have also had to be accepted. Competing economic and political interests loom large among the uncontrolled variables, whether the economy is socialist or capitalist. Regional and urban planning in the U. S. has been forced into continual ad hoc deviations from plans that may have had little merit in the first place, with end results that no one will take responsibility, such as the urban renewal fiascos that leave the poor more ill-housed than before. The disillusionment with social planning is most complete among those who have the greatest concern with reconstructing society, to the point where planning bureaucracies are viewed as instruments for the deliberate exploitation of minority groups by the New Left.

To the liberals still committed to planning, the push has been toward total systems planning, in order to gain control of more variables. Boguslaw (1965) calls these total system designers the New Utopians. They have identified the human element as the source of failure in previous planning, and seek to design mechanical systems that minimize the scope of human action within those systems. He points out the paradox of this Skinnerian Walden II-type development:

> It is perhaps a significant commentary on contemporary psychological and social science that its efforts often appear directed toward making men less than human through the perfecting of behavioral control techniques, while contemporary physical science seems to be moving in the direction of increasing the number of possible machine responses to environmental stimuli (1965:18).

Optimists think that they see a general trend toward the humanization of planning. Toffler (1970:400–05), for example, predicts the death of present econocentric technocratic planning, to be replaced by public and private planning which places the highest value on human welfare. Since planning has always been clothed in the rhetoric of human welfare, one could say "plus ça change, plus c'est la même chose."

Even while the significance of the surrender of critical human decision-making in sophisticated systems planning is being hammered home by social philosophers, the practice of elaborate systems planning goes on apace. The weapons system approach developed within the Department of Defense is the prototype, and is rapidly spreading to the civilian sector, particularly in the area of urban planning (Schon, 1967). A spurious sense of control is achieved by establishing a logically complete program to accomplish specified objectives, and then ruling out any possible feedback from the environment concerning changed parameters of the situation. Some New Town planning is done this way too.

Development economists engage in a kind of modified systems planning when they go into a non-industrialized society and draw up a blueprint for industrialization. If people in a given society don't happen to behave the way the economic model used in planning calls for, so much the worse for them.

The golden era of development planning initiated by Tinbergen is grinding to a reluctant standstill with Myrdal's pessimistic discovery that people do not in fact behave as plans call for (Myrdal, 1968).

Some systems engineering is, quite properly, trying to design people back into the systems. An example of this is the proposal to train people for "Societal Engineering" (Lewis and Pinkau, 1968). The key concept here is long-lived societal systems which "are people-oriented, structured arrangements of processes and elements responding to a real need (or needs) of the society" (Lewis and Pinkau, 1968:111).

System design approaches, however, even when they explicitly try to provide for feedback and changing values, rule out radical long-term changes by their very need for tidying up the variables. Short of an explicitly evolutionary approach (Maruyama's (1968) deviation-amplifying feedback systems) systems planning tends to narrow down alternatives and shorten time horizons. At its worst it threatens man with an oppressive and frozen anti-utopia. At its best, it can only move man toward a well-understood and thoroughly probed alternative structure which lies well within the grasp of the contemporary mind.

BRAINSTORMING

For those who are concerned with generating radically different possibilities for the future, the technique of brainstorming (Osborn, 1963; Gordon, 1961) has been developed which is designed to jog people loose from their customary mental ruts and help them imagine wildly different "somethings." Problem solving groups are given a series of exercises which free the mind for totally unexpected solutions. Since the technique is frequently used for such elevated purposes as coming up with a new name for a deodorant, its future-creating potential has not been very evident. Corporations do hire "blue-sky" thinkers to dream up remote possibilities, but according to the report of at least one such tame visionary, the job is very bad for the imagination! Toffler, who is very concerned about warding off "Future Shock" (the title of his latest book) by dreaming up alternative futures before they arrive, proposes the establishment in every community of " 'imaginetic centers' devoted to technically assisted brainstorming" (1970:410). He would create a profession of imagineers to work with technical specialists, to make sure that all permutations and combinations of given sets of relationships are examined.

One significant limitation upon brainstorming is the point made by Barnett that "the expectation of change always envisages limits upon its operations. Change is expected only between certain minimal and maximal boundaries" (1953:57). Barnett cites the example of the Samoans, who set a high value on innovation in design, but the range of total variation is so narrow that the untrained western eye has difficulty in detecting between one design and another, whether in textiles, songs or dances. Whether the range is wide or narrow, the cultural limits are firmly set. In short, the proverbial man from Mars might not be very impressed with the alternative futures dreamed up by the wildest of blue-sky imagineers. While this kind of limitation operates on all human fantasying, it operates much more strongly in a technique-oriented setting such as brainstorming than it does for the lone fantasist.

PROFESSIONAL FUTURISTS

The difference between the professional futurist and the planner is that the former specializes in the delineation of alternative futures from which, presumably, the planner may choose. Waskow (1970) divides them into the technocrats, the humanists and the participatory futurists. European technocratic futurists include Bertrand de Jouvenel (1967) who has directed the Ford Foundation-sponsored Futuribles project at the Société d'Etudes et de Documentation Economique Industrielles et Sociales in Paris since the fifties; Denis Gabor (1963), University of London physicist, and Fritz Baade (1962), development economist of Kiel University. In the U. S., think factory specialists Olaf Helmer (1966), developer of the Delphi technique for long-range forecasting, and Herman Kahn (1967), writer of scenarios of the future, are leading examples. So is Charles Osgood (Report, 1966) using the computer at the University of Illinois to develop future contingency models. A variety of efforts in this direction were coordinated by Daniel Bell in his capacity as chairman of the American Academy of Arts and Sciences Commission on the Year 2000. The new Institute for the Study of the Future at Middletown, Connecticut, which Bell helped to establish, carries out research on the social technology of forecasting. The World Future Society and its journal, *The Futurist*, have provided a very useful communications network for this group of futurists, but also extends its net more widely and reports on the whole gamut of future-oriented work in the U. S.

The technocratic futurists operate largely within the frame of reference of the present national and international distribution of power and resources, and on the assumption of continuation of present trends of technological development and scientific breakthroughs. It is therefore perhaps not surprising that the future which they project is being vigorously rejected by an increasing number of younger scholars and activists.

Hampden-Turner (1970:305–6) outlines some objections to the forecasting approach:

> . . . The projection of present trends into the future represents a vote of temporary approval for such trends. Yet the trends themselves are the consequence of thousands of individual human decisions . . . the decision not to change direction (is) a decision. By concentrating upon the technical and material aspects of the trends, the impression is fostered that these things "are," like stars and planets around us, so

that "realistic" men must humbly subordinate their minds to these physical "facts . . ."

But these projections of existing trends are quite *unlike* the physical universe of dead objects. They are *cultural, political* and *social* choices. Men have the capacity to rebel against any trend at any time, in any place, by deciding to stop it, or alter its direction, or persuade others to do so . . . the shared expectation that the trend whose direction you oppose will *not* be continued in the future may be politically essential to any success in halting or redirecting it.

The obverse is also true. The acceptance of a trend which is implicit in projecting it into the future, the gathering together of technical statistics, scholarly opinions, and humanistic concerns about what this trend will mean by the year 2000, has the *inevitable effect of strengthening that trend and making it more certain to occur.* Much of the efforts of these scholars would be wasted if by the year 1975 a major social rebellion against certain trends were to succeed.

Typical of an even more serious type of criticism is Waskow's (1970:138) observation about the technocrats:

For them "planning" was clearly a way of helping those who now hold power to know what they must do in order to keep holding power thirty or fifty years hence. What must they change, where should they beat a strategic retreat, what new organizations and technologies should they invent, when can they hold the line?

To the extent that these criticisms imply intentional malevolence, they are unfair. In fact, the memorandum written by Lawrence K. Frank to Hudson Hoagland (Bell, 1967:647), then president of the American Academy, which led to the establishment of the Commission on the Year 2000, raises questions very similar to those of the above criticisms:

If we are to maintain a free social order in the face of the discontent and anxiety (we) will probably provoke, we must attempt the. Promethean task of renewing our traditional culture and reorienting our social order as a deliberately planned process . . .

But if Polak's theory has validity at all, it has validity in relation to the work of these futurists; they are indeed reenforcing the possibilities for one kind of future.

The second group of futurists, the ones Waskow calls the humanists, are worried about precisely this aspect of current social-technological trends. Polak himself belongs in this category, and so does Robert Jungk, the Austrian-born futurist who founded the Institut für Zukunftsfragen in Vienna in 1965 and sowed the seeds in Europe and North America of an idea to internationalize the effort to work for better futures which became Mankind 2000.

Incorporated as an international foundation in 1966 with Jungk as Honorary President, Polak as Treasurer, and the English Quaker Kenneth Lee as Chairman, this group has held international congresses in Oslo and Tokyo and worked in a variety of ways to further the following aims:

A. To ensure that the future of mankind be person-centered and democratically determined. To this end, to encourage personal involvement and choice in defining and realizing the future course of events, on the understanding that failure to participate is, in effect, to abdicate responsibility and to choose by default, unless such responsibility is intentionally delegated.

B. To promote a comprehensive (total systems) approach to the problems and possibilities of the near future, in the context of futures research and planning, having as a time-horizon the end of the present century. To this end, to encourage inter-communication and cooperation between culture, disciplines, and people generally.[5]

The humanists are an older generation of futurists who have observed the seamy side of central planning in eastern Europe and fear a similar sacrifice of human values to planning in western Europe and the U. S. The disillusionment which the many failures of the much-looked-to socialist planning aroused in both the socialist countries themselves and among their admirers in the West cannot be overestimated in relation to imaging the future. The buoyant optimism of the twenties about possible new futures cannot be evoked again, particularly in the face of the difficulties which creative new variants of socialist planning in countries such as Czechoslovakia have met.

The humanist futurists seek to protect the common man's future by involving him in planning it himself, and in helping men generally to think creatively about longer time spans. The idea of a travelling exhibit of possible futures has been a feature of the Mankind 2000 project from the beginning. Perhaps even more important, these humanists come out of a cultural milieu in which the perfume of the empty eschatological vase (to misquote Renan) still lingers, and their forecasting is tinged with a visionary quality of otherness not to be found in their younger colleagues.

The participatory futurists (among whom Waskow counts himself) are equally distressed by what they consider to be the authoritarianism of the technocrats and the fuzziness of the humanists. They are committed to what Waskow calls creative disorder, and act on their chosen visions of possible futures by building chunks of that future from the bottom up (without permission from the authorities). Johan Galtung (with Jungk and Polak a major moving force in Mankind 2000) is the apostle of creative disorder in Europe,

---

[5]From a July, 1969, mimeographed report from the Secretariat of Mankind 2000 in London, England. Since 1971 the headquarters of Mankind 2000 is located in Rome.

as Waskow is in the U. S. Galtung is a rather unique "chunk of the future" in himself, in that he takes the world to be his home in a way that very few twentieth century scholars have achieved. Also his own images of the future take account of the entirely new order of social innovations taking place in the Peoples Republic of China, thus giving his futurism different dimensions and broader perspectives than most contemporary futurism. The increasingly action-oriented younger generation of scholars who find themselves naturally at home in this group already find both Galtung and Waskow too conservative. Not all "movement" people qualify as participatory futurists, but to the extent that their community-building experiments are based on larger visions, they are indeed futurists. Neither are they professionals in the conventional sense, but they will breed professionals!

Certain fears about professional futurism shared by the humanists and the participatory futurists are reflected in the Postscript to the published proceedings of the first Mankind 2000 Conference in Oslo (Jungk and Galtung, 1969:368). Pointing out that four-fifths of the work done in the new specialty of futurism is financed either by governments, military establishments or large corporations, they warn against futurist expertise becoming a monopoly of power groups within nations, and of rich nations in the international community. Internationalization and democratization of future research is urgently needed.

> The onesided use of "technological forecasting" . . . can lead us straight into new forms of totalitarianism. If we tamper with the time ahead of us, as we have already done with the space around us, in an egocentric, power-directed, narrow-minded spirit, if we spoil the future as we have spoiled our environment, then we are in for an epoch of despotism and desperation—a tyranny of a new modernistic type, which like all tyrannies, will loudly proclaim its virtue and benevolence.
>
> This must not happen. The future belongs to all of us . . .

Differences and mutual criticisms aside, all three types of futurists have one strong trait in common: they are interested in realizable futures with a turn-of-the-century time-horizon. Regardless of the differences in their prognostic styles, they have all been caught up in the twentieth century version of that chiliastic enthusiasm which swept Europe in the decades preceding the year 1000. None of these futurists would admit to millennialist thinking, but the basic cultural undercurrent is a powerful one, and probably therapeutic. I detect in the writings of all these futurists a note of unscientific enthusiasm for a time when things will be better than they are now, which may act as an antidote to the time neurosis and fear of the future which Polak diagnosed twenty years ago. As we near the year 2000, this long-forgotten cultural heritage of millennialism may penetrate a three-centuries-old shell of rationalism and infuse a new quality of otherness into future-thinking.

THE SOCIAL EVOLUTIONARIES

When Margaret Mead (1964:322) called for purposeful attention to social evolution in 1964, she put into words what an increasing number of gifted and future-oriented thinkers were feeling:

> If we can create living networks of the diversely gifted and the diversely trained whose concern it is to safeguard our present heritage and to learn from and teach those who will be the carriers of this heritage, we shall automatically focus our inventiveness on the very center of the evolutionary process.

Rather than being committed to any particular image of the future, these evolutionists are committed to a kind of high-level brainstorming—a mutating of new conceptions of social forms, structures and ideologies, in order that selections may be made from a far wider range of alternative possibilities than are conventionally considered.

These living evolutionary networks are bound to be as diverse as the nucleating minds which form their various centers. Many of them overlap. A list of the people who have joined architect-planner Constantinos Doxiades' famous yacht cruises into Tomorrowland would be a fairly dazzling network. The scholars whom Ralph Tyler has brought to the center for Advanced Study in the Behavioral Sciences in Palo Alto in the last sixteen years have spun off a number of new networks as a result of nucleating power of "the Palo Alto experience." Hutchins' Center for the Study of Democratic Institutions is intended to perform this same nucleating function. John Platt, the physicist-social philosopher and Buckminster Fuller and John McHale of World Design Science Decade, World Resources Inventory fame, are each nucleating groups of people committed to designing alternative world structures that will make life humane and enjoyable for every kind of social group. So is Marshall McLuhan, although he operates in a different dimension than most futurists.

Such nucleating individuals tend to think at a very fast pace and be tremendously optimistic. Most of them are not young, but they are extraordinarily at home in the midst of accelerating change, as if to demonstrate that there are no inherent problems for humans in the need to adjust to exponential growth rates. Nothing smaller than a world will do for the Richard Meiers (1965) of the twentieth century to think in and about. The 700 million megalopolis on the Bay of Bengal planned for the middle of the next century is for them a perfectly "natural" conception. To optimists like John Platt (no date, p. 5) the present situation represents a temporary lock-in for society, and we need only move through a period of inertia to get to a significant choice point, when we can start using the systems design capability we now have. With our . . .

knowledge of feedback stabilization, cybernetic goal-seeking, and hierarchical decision-systems . . . of the biological and psychological bases
of individual and group behavior . . . and our new abundance, it is
possible to make new designs . . . for the benefit of the whole society
. . . designs that will satisfy both urban and farm, suburb and central
city, workers and intellectuals, managers and consumers, blacks and
whites, males and females—designs that can permit and encourage
pluralism and diversity of tastes and life styles, with abundance for
every group.

He feels that utopias are definitely realizable because they "will be enormously profitable for everybody, in economic as well as human terms" and
that they can be demonstrably profitable "for every individual or group
involved in the (social) change." The sheer audacity of suggesting the imminent possibility of pay-as-you-go utopias in the midst of today's welter of
social problems gives Platt's image of the future that prophetic touch of
"otherness" which is characteristic of the evolutionists. Their images are not
precise, but they give a sense of movement, of direction.

ECOLOGICAL FUTURISM

Since ecology deals with metastable systems in the ecosphere, it seems a
contradiction in terms to link ecology and futurism. Until earth's time-clock
runs down, however, there is a good deal to happen yet on what Ward
(1966) and Boulding (1966) have both called space-ship earth. Boulding's
image of the future (as extracted from his *Meaning of the 20th Century,* 1964)
pictures an earth with a stable closed-cycle technology. Since biological
processes are much more efficient than mechanical processes, the technology
of the future will probably be based on biological processes. Evolution within
this closed-cycle spaceship requires the careful spending of capital to build
complex social forms and according to the laws of entropy should result
in a gradual diminution of the evolutionary potential of the system. There
are, however, anti-entropic processes at work. One relates to knowledge and
learning and consists of "the capacity of his images—that is, the knowledge
present in his mind—to grow by a kind of internal breeder reaction: the
imagination (1964:141)." The other, even more anti-entropic capacity is *agape.*
"It always builds up, it never tears down, and it does not merely establish
small islands of order in society at the cost of disorder elsewhere (1964:146)."
For evolutionary potential, *agape* clearly wins hands down. The imaged
future, then, is one in which men have learned to economize their geological
capital by relying as far as possible on biological rather than mechanical
systems for energy and work, and live in a society structured in such a way
that man's capacity to learn and to love is maximized, in turn creating ever
higher-level institutions and relationships. New mutations may well be in the

direction of man's capacity for spiritual experience. That is about as specific as an ecological image of the future can get. It also brings back the eschatological element missing in the "man-as-the-measure-of-all things" utopia, and draws on the great Catholic biologist-mystic Teilhard de Chardin's vision of the noosphere (1959).

Boulding is hardly a typical ecologist, but many of the writings of members of the Society for Human Ecology, and of the environmentalists who are increasingly weaving their own scientific specialty into a larger social fabric in their public speaking and writing, often evoke this sense of man's moving toward higher things. The promise of release from the wheels, gears and smells of mechanical technology seems to have a very liberating effect on the imagination!

The ecological perspective moves along an imperceptible continuum from scientific ecology through a fairly robust back-to-the-land whole earth romanticism (*Whole Earth Catalog*, 1970) to a pre-Raphaelite fantasy-world Aquarianism (*Aquarian Oracle*, 1970). The image of the future eventually turns into a blurry fantasy about a return to a golden age in the past, much as in the romantic nineteenth century utopias of Hudson (1906) and Morris (1891). The intellectual and spiritual vigor of the best of the ecological visions of the future, however, gives the lie to economists and Chamber of Commerce types who maintain that industrialization must proceed apace and that a zero-growth rate economy would mean stagnation and social decay.

THE REVOLUTIONARY FUTURISTS: POLITICAL, SOCIAL AND LITERARY

1. Political: Violent Liberation Movements. Liberation movements from all continents have in common an overriding preoccupation with tactical strategy, a vivid sense of the enemy, and a burning conviction that they are building a new world. An apocalyptic sense that oppression has reached an intensity which can only represent the death throes of an inwardly rotten world imperialist structure gives an immediacy to the revolutionary image of the future which is lacking in more sedate sectors of society. But the need of the guerilla to act, to seize every momentary advantage in case this is *the* moment (in his millennialist frame of mind every moment could be the moment) also gives a child's picture-book quality to his images of the future. An attempt to analyze the images of the future which appear in *Tricontinental*, the monthly publication of the Organization of the Solidarity of the Peoples of Africa, Asia and Latin America (OSPAAL) brings this out very clearly. Every guerilla and liberation movement carried out anywhere in the world (even occasionally North America) is reported on here, but the content does not vary very much from country to country. A recently reprinted 1948 Appeal for Patriotic Emulation from Ho Chi Minh gives the flavor of most of the writing (*Tricontinental*, 1969:17):

Each Vietnamese, old or young, boy or girl, rich or poor, must become
a fighter struggling in a front which is either military or economic,
political or cultural,
To realize the slogan:
Nation-wide Resistance.
Thus we realize:
The whole people will have enough to eat and dress.
The whole people will know how to read and write.
The whole army will have enough food and armament to kill the invaders.
The whole nation will be entirely unified and independent.
Thus we realize:
Independence for the nation.
Freedom for the people.
Happiness for the people.

This is a poignantly modest image of the future; hardly a greedy, power-grasping one. This image of a future in which people shall have work, food, knowledge, dignity and joy is the same image held by the militant minority movements in the U. S. (red, black, brown, female), and the fact that violence seems the only road to this simple, basic vision for increasing numbers of people on all continents speaks for itself. Can our futurists tell us how to fit the evolutionary potential of *agape* into this scene?

The striking feature of the image is its ordinariness, for all the millennialist fervor with which it is held. It involves no technological breakthroughs, asks nothing that is not easily realizable in strictly non-political terms. The revolutionary lives with very narrow time horizons. The quality of otherness in his visions lies mainly in his refusal to accept existing political constraints as real. In this sense, he would indeed make a breach in time in the best utopian tradition.

2. Political: Non-Violent Liberation Movements. Political thinking and *agape* are hard to marry, and most people who try to effect the union in their own lives or in the movements they work in wind up being those very well-meaning, fuzzy-minded humanitarian liberals everyone despises these days. The next significant social mutation will be the one which enables skills of political and economic organization and the capacity to love to be maximized in the same person. (This is what Charles Hampden-Turner (1970) has written his book, *Radical Man*, to help bring about.) A century of relatively ineffective Euro-North American peace and humanitarian movements gives no evidence to date that this combination is as yet workable. (Some observers feel that this mutation is taking place in China. Examining the evidence for this would require a separate paper.)

A. J. Muste, a life-long political activist Christian and pacifist and organizer in the labor movement as well as the peace movement, gives a clue to the possibility of such a social mutation in the West. The combination of political insight and *agape* which he embodies was such that in the turbulent last years of his life, when violence was becoming the order of the day in hitherto non-violent civil rights movements, he was still in the mainstream of the action. Consulted by everyone, present at everything, he was able to move through the maelstrom of violence and respond at another level. But images of the future were almost incidental to a life of action.

Martin Luther King was developing an image of the future which people could respond to, but he did not have enough time, and much of the non-violent thrust of his image of the future has been lost since his death—a sad parallel with Gandhi.

David Harris, leader of the non-violent branch of the Draft Resistance, on his last tour with his wife Joan Baez before entering jail seemed to realize the need of the movement for a positive image of the future. He is one of the few in recent times who has tried to spell out the details of alternative social structures for a non-violent world. His main contributions in this direction still lie in the future. I have left out a whole generation in between A. J. Muste and David Harris. That is my generation—currently caught in a life-and-death struggle between images of the future based on *agape* and on the sword. In the clash between vagueness and fury, my generation does not come off well.

I note that this attempt to delineate images of the future from the peace movement has produced nothing more than a few individual biographies. This would seem to indicate that powerful images of the future of this genre have yet to be formed.

3. Non-Political: International Organizations. The international movement for a peaceful integrated world, reflected in the rapid proliferation of non-governmental associations which are creating international networks based on every kind of human interest, has moved both forward and backward in the last fifty years. It has moved forward in the sense that where there were 202 international organizations in 1905, there were 1,897 in 1965. From one point of view, the noosphere appears to be meshing more tightly. But only recently is there an awareness that these organizations are almost entirely Euro-North American in conception, ideology, and ways of working. The third-world components of international organizations are beginning angrily to let their international leaders know that they must change drastically if they are to represent the international community and not the West. This is equally true of peace organizations, church organizations, and cultural, civic, and professional organizations. While international secretariats are beginning to respond to this pressure, and more international headquarters are now to be found in Africa, Asia and Latin America year by year, it will be a long time before any international organization can honestly call itself representative of the world community, quite apart from the issue of China's participation in such activities. This means that one cannot accurately speak of "world" images of the future emerging from these organizations. The images of the future so far generated by the NGO's are western images. Until the transition to a more reality-based internationalism has been effected, one cannot look for guiding images from this sector of world publics.

4. *Non-Political: The Now People and Their Images of the Future.* The familist-oriented communes reported in the monthly, *Modern Utopian*, the new Dionysians for whom Norman O. Brown speaks so eloquently in *Love's Body* (1966), and the self-actualizers that Maslow (1954, 1968) wrote of, all protest mechanistic images of the present or the future which are based on manipulation of things instead of on openness to the unique creative qualities of the individual human being. The Now orientation is a reaction against "jam yesterday, jam tomorrow, but never jam today." While they are not explicitly in the "future-creating" business, to the extent that the Now people live in communes or interact in groups of any kind, they are developing working models in the present of a desired future society. Some of them would deny the validity of thinking for others or designing social structures, but some of them are in the communitarian tradition of trying out models of society for mankind. Toffler's suggestion that intentional communities should experiment with new super-industrial forms rather than "back-to" agrarianism (1970:414) is in fact now happening in a few groups that are designing new types of instrumentation and intermediate-type technology for developing countries instead of making candles or milking cows. Transforming the toy industry has been the goal of several communes!

The present flowering of communes in the U. S. is an indication of the same social vigor which stimulated the numerous utopian communities of a hundred years ago, described by Charles Nordhoff (1965, 1875). There is more than a touch of transcendence in many of these utopian communes, ranging from identifiably Christian to exotic cultic features. Even the far-left rationalist weathermen communes have their own eschatological style à la Marx. Many of these groups belong to the "participatory futurists" mentioned earlier. To the extent that they are acting out a part of a larger vision for society, they are indeed participatory futurists. To the extent that they are retreating into a private Now, they do not belong in that category.

It is difficult to make generalizations about the Now people, individually or in groups, because the scene is so rapidly changing. Communes form, break up and re-form and the average life-expectancy of a commune is probably a few weeks. In general, these groups can be ranged on a continuum from private escapism to model-building for the future. The model-builders are most certainly in the minority.

5. *Science Fiction.* No discussion of revolutionary futurists is complete without science fiction being included. The great majority of science fiction writers, like professional futurists, make projections based on the present.

Galactic bureaucracies with fantastic physical and social technologies (including ESP) and cowboy-mentality citizens are projected by the majority of science fiction writers—an all-too-convincing image of the future looked at from today's world!

Whether they are written as social criticism, as just plain yarns, or as images of a naively hoped for future, the cumulative impact of the majority of science fiction is precisely toward self-justifying expectations of galactic bureaucracy!

There are gifted minds in science fiction which do play with alternative futures, and imaginatively construct other worlds in the tradition of the Enlightenment at its liveliest. The sheer feat of constructing a totally other kind of society, with different basic values and totally other institutional patterns for dealing with what we think of as the economic, social, political and cultural-religious aspects of life in groups, is very liberating to the social imagination of the reader. Hence books like Frank Herbert's *Dune* (1965) leave one with a feeling of reverence for the evolutionary and adaptive capacity of human beings in the face of grimly limited resources even though the features of such a society are only remotely relevant for proximate human futures. A book such as Ursula LeGuin's *Left Hand of Darkness*, imaging a society whose members are without permanent bi-sexual attributes, opens up possible human futures which leave behind today's kinds of sex-role patterns. Science fiction fans will know who the creative future-inventors are among science fiction writers. No attempt is made to survey them here.[6]

The science-fiction tradition of picturing men as evolving into a higher, more spiritual order of beings, which Olaf Stapledon contributed to so brilliantly earlier in the century, has for its contemporary model Arthur Clarke's *Childhood's End* (1953). Polak mistrusts this tradition, which represents an abdication of human effort in hope of being rescued by a higher spiritual being or by a chance mutation, but it is a durable human trait to hope for rescue from "outside." Since Polak has also recognized the importance of the eschatological element, we must conclude that science fiction would not be doing its job if it did not give glimpses of a totally other future state of the human race.

The Frames of Reference of Futurism

The social planners and systems designers, the brainstormers and the technocratic futurists all operate within a cultural frame of reference well sum-

[6]Hampden-Turner (1970:340) cites research in the performance of different categories of people on Terman's Concept Mastery Test, which measures ". . . verbal intelligence, breadth of knowledge and interest, the capacity to deal with ideas at an abstract level, to associate meanings, think divergently via analogies, and to converge logically." Creative writers are far out ahead, and engineers, military officers and independent inventors (Edison types?) at the bottom. It is attractive to contemplate what might ensue if we turned over government policy-making to our most creative science fiction writers!

marized in Kahn and Wiener's (1967:7) list of Thirteen Basic, Long-Term Multifold Trends which involve a world-wide extension of western socio-economic and political developments coupled with a nostalgic revival of the Golden Age of Greece in the twenty-first century. This is the "Standard World" that Kahn writes about. The projections allow for Canonical Variations on the Standard World in terms of the degree of political and economic success of the communist world. In general, they picture a Sorokian twenty-first century West abandoning its achievement orientation and returning to a sensate Hellenism based on a high-level technology, some reduction in world-leadership roles of the U. S., and unspecified development of China and the communist world, and a somehow minimally organized and industrialized world with no one getting in anyone else's way. The most far-out changes they expect, apart from the usual technological projections of innovations in communication, transportation, human physiologic capacity-extension and general productivity, are things like the extension of life expectancy well beyond 150 years, possible modification of the human species, and interstellar travel.

They have left an escape hatch by allowing for the "psychologically upsetting impact of new techniques, ideas, philosophies and the like (1970:24)." Three concepts missing from their projections are:

1. The possibility of a totally other path to decent physical levels of living by-passing the western sequence of technological developments, developing in China or elsewhere in the third world, and this path being followed by the rest of the third world.
2. The simultaneous not-so-remote possibility that the West will choke on its industrial effluence and become China's (or country x's) pupil in a different order of technologies.
3. Spiritual breakthroughs in developing the human capacity to love which will lead to totally different cultural values and socio-economic patterns.

Points (1) and (2) are not meant to imply an idealization of China as the deus ex machina, but rather the likelihood that there will be a major shift in the locus of cultural innovation on the planet, following in a line of such major shifts in the past (hardly reflected in the world history books studied by Americans or Europeans). China is the most likely candidate for new leadership because of her protective isolation from western developments for a quarter of a century. On point (3), I do not wish to make any predictions on where love could make a breakthrough!

The professional futurists are too tied to present spatial distributions of social, economic and political resources, and too wedded to thirty-year projections based on an artificial isolation of a Hellenic-European stream of history from the total stream of history, to be able to conceive of the breaches in time and space that history in its planet-wide dimensions should lead us to expect. Their man-computer symbiosis allows for no sense of the totally other, transcendant or otherwise. The paradoxical thought arises that it may be precisely the most professionalized of the professional futurists who will be in for the most violent "future shock."

The humanist, participatory, evolutionist, ecological and revolutionary futurists all have some kind of intellectual and moral commitment to thinking in a wider frame of reference than the western one. Whether they succeed, is another matter. At the least, they extend the range of conceivable futures portrayed for modern man because of their commitment of exploring a radically different set of social possibilities than those indicated by present trends. That same commitment to otherness reintroduces the note of transcendance which is missing in much professional futurism. This does not mean a return to earlier prevailing Christian conceptions, in all likelihood, but a different sense of the relationship of man and nature to other orders of reality.

Polak's critique of the future-imaging capacity of contemporary man shares with much of professional futurism the tendency to think of the West as an isolatable compartment on the planet. The scope of his own ideas, however, goes beyond any such compartmentalization. If we review the humanist-to-revolutionary futurists in the light of his most urgent concerns about that imaging capacity, we can see some interesting developments:

1. The time horizon. It is both foreshortened and extended, in that participatory futurists are both creating "chunks of the future" now, and they are visualizing social orders that will not come into being for a long time. Guerilla movements have a very narrow time horizon, yet they are acting for a socially distant future. The Now people are similarly split. The evolutionary nucleators and the ecologists operate with very distant time horizons indeed, as they attempt to visualize very long-term planetary processes, but they also have considerable concern about how to deal with the immediate present.

2. The spatial sense. Increasingly futurists are thinking in planetary (and inter-planetary) terms, though their conceptualizations are often inadequate to the scale on which they are attempting to think.

3. Otherness. Openness to the possibility of radically different types of social structures is very widespread, but only in some militant political groups is there a doctrinaire futurism intent on a specific future pattern. Many militant groups are as open to possible futures as the evolutionary nucleators—if only because they don't have much time to think about it.

4. Transcendance. The possibility of transcending presently conceived human limitations is very widely accepted among futurists. Whether achieving this transcendance with the aid of computer technology or through a new perception of the non-physical world represents an ultimately significant distinction in terms of the power to transcend is not clear. Either form of transcendance has a significant impact on man's images of the future.

5. *Optimism.* There are signs that the creative minority which generates images of the future in the West are climbing out of the pessimism concerning the nature of reality and the human capacity generated by two world wars and a prolonged cold war. The discovery that the Colossus Technology has feet of clay has encouraged creative thinking about alternatives among people who until recently felt oppressed and paralyzed by technology-based life styles. Furthermore, the cultural heritage of millennialism leads to a widespread feeling of hope that rounding the bend of this last thousand-year cycle will usher in a new and better era for man.

Perhaps it will.

Bibliography

Aquarian Oracle 1 (No. 1). Los Angeles, California, 1970.

Baade, Fritz. The Race to the Year 2000. Translated from the German by Ernst Pawel. Garden City, New York: Doubleday, 1962.

Barnett H. G. Innovation: The Basis of Cultural Change. New York: McGraw-Hill, 1953.

Bell, Daniel. "The Year 2000—The Trajectory of an Idea." *Daedalus* 96 (Summer, 1967): 639–651.

Boguslaw, Robert. The New Utopians: A Study of System Design and Social Change. Englewood Cliffs, N. J.: Prentice-Hall, 1965.

Boulding, Kenneth E. The Meaning of the 20th Century: The Great Transition. New York: Harper and Row, 1964.

———. "Expecting the Unexpected: The Uncertain Future of Knowledge and Technology." In *Prospective Changes in Society by 1980 Including Some Implications for Education,* edited by Edgar L. Morphet and Charles O. Ryan, pp. 199–215. Reports Prepared for the First Area Conference Designing Education for the Future, Denver, Colorado.

Brown, Norman O. Love's Body. New York: Random House, 1966.

Clarke, Arthur. Childhood's End. New York: Ballantine, 1953.

De Jouvenel, Bertrand. The Art of Conjecture. New York: Basic Books, 1967.

Drucker, Peter F. The Age of Discontinuity. New York: Harper and Row, 1968.

Gabor, Dennis. Inventing the Future. New York: Alfred A. Knopf, 1964.

Gordon, William J. J. Synectics. New York: Collier Books, 1961.

Hampden-Turner, Charles. Radical Man. Cambridge, Mass.: Schenkman, 1970.

Helmer, Olaf. Social Technology. New York: Basic Books, 1966.

Herbert, Frank. Dune. New York: Ace Paperback Books, 1965.

Hudson, William Henry. Crystal Age. New York: Dutton, 1922.

Jungk, Robert and Galtung, Johan, eds. Mankind 2000. Oslo: Universitetsforlaget; London: Allen and Unwin, 1969.

Kahn, Herman and Wiener, Anthony J. The Year 2000. New York: Macmillan, 1967.

LeGuin, Ursula. Left Hand of Darkness. New York: Ace Publishing Company, 1971.

Lewis, Frederick J., Jr., and Pinkau, Irene. "Societal Engineering: A New Career for Societal Systems." *Engineering Education* (October, 1968): 111–114.

McHale, John. *The Future of the Future.* New York: George Braziller, 1969.

Maruyama, Magorah. "The Second Cybernetics-Deviation-Amplifying Mutual Casual Processes." In *Modern Systems Research for the Behavioral Scientist,* edited by Walter Buckley, pp. 304–313. Chicago: Aldine Publishing Company, 1968.

Maslow, Abraham. *Motivation and Personality.* New York: Harper and Row, 1954.

———. *Toward a Psychology of Being.* 2nd. ed. New York: Van Nostrand Reinhold, 1968.

Mead, Margaret. *Continuities in Cultural Evolution.* New Haven: Yale University Press, 1964.

Meier, Richard. *Developmental Planning.* New York: McGraw-Hill, 1965.

Morris, William. *News from Nowhere.* Boston: Roberts, 1890.

Myrdal, Gunnar. *Asian Drama: An Inquiry into the Poverty of Nations.* 3 vols. New York: Random House, Pantheon, 1968.

Nordhoff, Charles. *Communistic Societies of the United States.* New York: Schocken Books, 1965.

Osborn, Alex. *Applied Imagination.* 3rd ed. New York: Charles Scribner's Sons, 1963.

Platt, John. "How Men Can Shape Their Future." Mimeo. Distributed by the World Future Society.

Polak, Fred L. *The Image of the Future.* Translated from the Dutch by E. Boulding. New York: Oceana Publications, 1961 (See the condensation by E. Boulding published by George Braziller in 1971).

"Report of Developments Since the Conference of Overseas Sponsors Held in London in November, 1965." *Mankind 2000,* London: Preparatory International Secretariat, 1966. (Charles Osgood's Project PLATO is noted in the above report; a further report appears in "Involving the Public in Futures," *Futures,* September, 1968.)

Schon, Donald A. *Technology and Change.* New York: Delta Books, Dell, 1967.

Toffler, Alvin. *Future Shock.* New York: Random House, 1970.

Tricontinental. Ho Chi Minh, "Appeal to the Entire People to Wage the Resistance War." *Tricontinental* 44, 4 (November, 1969): 16–28.

Ward, Barbara. *Spaceship Earth.* New York: Columbia University Press, 1966.

Wascow, Arthur I. *Running Riot.* New York: Herder and Herder, 1970.

Whole Earth Catalog: Access to Tools. Menlo Park, California: Portola Institute, 1970.

FUTUROLOGY AND THE STUDY OF VALUES

 *irene taviss*

The motivations which underlie the study of the future are no different from those which support most scientific and social scientific research: understanding and control. Nevertheless, the interest in the future would seem to be especially related to control—that is, to the attempt to plan and to set policy so that the best possible course of action might be chosen among the possibilities which the future offers. This link between futurology and social action makes an inquiry into values particularly important.

The policy-oriented futurologist must ask what values can or should serve as guide-lines to action. But this question immediately raises a second, and equally thorny, question: how to evaluate the future desirability of a given state of affairs. Even if the values underlying current actions could be neatly specified, would these values still be operative in the future? As Ikle has noted, " 'guiding predictions' are incomplete unless they evaluate the desirability of the predicted aspects of alternative futures. If we assume that this desirability is to be determined by our future rather than our present preferences . . . then we have to predict our values *before* we can meaningfully predict our future. Or rather, since values will be affected by the future state of the world, we may face what mathematicians call a problem of iteration: We have to shift from evaluation to prediction and back to evaluation".[1] This shifting of time perspectives makes the study of values a peculiarly difficult one for the policy-oriented futurologist.

But even in the absence of a concern for policy, the very attempt to study or understand the future cannot be meaningfully undertaken without taking value change into account. For "as long as the structure of society is simple and static, established valuations will last for a very long time, but if society changes this will immediately be reflected in the changing valuations. Re-valuations and re-definitions of the situation will necessarily accompany the changed structure of society. A new social order cannot exist without these re-valuations and re-definitions, as it is through them alone that individuals will act in a new way and respond to new stimuli. Thus the valuation process is not simply an epiphenomenon . . . but an aspect of social change . . . ."[2] The future will be different from the present in part because the values that guide social action will have changed.

[1] Fred Charles Iklé, "Can Social Predictions Be Evaluated?" *Daedalus* 96 (Summer, 1967): 747.
[2] Karl Mannheim, *Diagnosis Of Our Time* (New York: Oxford University Press, 1944), p. 20.

A cogent example of the way in which changes in values "could make our current predictions for the year 2000 look badly out of focus" is given by Ikle. "A few decades ago," he recalls, "the view prevailed that demographic 'stagnation' was bad; yet today many people favor a stable, or nearly stable population. Economic stagnation, on the other hand, is still felt to be bad. Perhaps in the year 2000, more of us will favor John Stuart Mill's 'stationary state', not only in the demographic sphere but also in much of the economic sphere (though not in culture). If this happens, economic growth will be smaller than we now project on the basis of the current trade-off between more goods and more leisure. By the same token, people will care less about economic growth. Thus, our predictions regarding economic growth will not only be rather inaccurate, but they will describe what, by the year 2000, will be quite an uninteresting feature."[3]

This intimate relationship between value change and other aspects of social change calls into question the validity of the whole enterprise of futurology unless some means can be devised to integrate value forecasting into the methodology of the futurologists. To determine the nature of contemporary values and those of the recent past, the researcher has at his disposal a battery of standard techniques: survey research, observation of behaviour, analysis of choice behaviour (including expenditures of time and money), and content analysis of the arts, the mass media, laws, folklore, and various other public documents.[4] But such techniques are not applicable to the study of future values.

What methods can be used to predict value change? If one starts with the premise that value change occurs in response to changed social conditions, and if changes in social conditions can be forecast, then one can attempt to predict the value changes that are likely to result. Most analysts who attempt to determine the nature of future values use some variant of this approach. However, the two variants which have been employed suffer from conceptual inadequacies, while a third variant—which is nascent in the writings of those social critics who decry the lags between social change and value change— has not been put to the test.

In the first of its variants, the application of this method takes the form of an exercise in logical deduction, without the use of any model of the process of value change. That is, a deterministic and one-to-one correspondence between structural change and value change is assumed. Thus, Kahn and Wiener sketch a continuum of attitudes toward work which run from work as "interruption" to work as "mission" and then predict that in the year 2000, Americans will increasingly shift towards the "interference" end of the continuum. At this time, they argue, "the man whose missionary zeal for work

[3]Ikle, op. cit., p. 750.
[4]See Robin M. Williams, Jr., "Individual and Group Values," Annals of the American Academy of Political and Social Science 371 (May, 1967): 20–37.

takes priority over all other values will be looked on as an unfortunate, perhaps even a harmful and destructive neurotic. Even those who find in work a 'vocation' are likely to be thought of as selfish, excessively narrow, or compulsive."[5] These predictions appear to be based on the assumption that the amount of time devoted to work will decrease significantly by the year 2000 and therefore the values traditionally associated with work will undergo a similar decline. Yet the persistence of traditional values despite the fact that they may be inappropriate to changed social conditions argues against this easy equation, which fails to take into account the time lags in the process of social change. The consensus of most students of American society appears to be that the work-oriented values, though declining, are unlikely to undergo such radical change within the next thirty years. Such evidence as may be gleaned from studies of retired people and of workers on reduced work-weeks points to the persistent hold of the work ethic. Many retired people cannot abandon the Protestant ethic and feel that they are no longer socially useful once they have stopped working; and many workers who have gained free time engage in moonlighting or in frantically paced activities.[6] Thus, the attempt to extrapolate value change directly from structural changes is likely to produce conclusions that do not accord with social realities.

A second variant of the attempt to forecast value change in response to projected social changes utilizes a model of the modes of value change. Rescher's work on value change, representative of this approach, employs a typology of "modes of upgrading" and corresponding "modes of downgrading" of existing values. Whether a particular value is likely to be upgraded or downgraded in the face of social change is determined by means of a cost-benefit analysis.[7] On this basis, Rescher predicts, for example, that nationalistic values will be downgraded because the cost of maintaining them will be too high, while social accountability will be upgraded and self-advancement downgraded as automation, "socioeconomic rigidity," and the size and complexity of the social system are extended. This approach is appealing because of its attempt to link specific social changes with specific value changes via a set of assumptions about the factors that strengthen or weaken adherence to values. But it is severely flawed by inconsistencies which become apparent when the model is applied. Thus, "devaluation of privacy" is noted as a possible consequence of the population explosion and urban crowding, while in

[5]Herman Kahn and Anthony J. Wiener, *The Year 2000* (New York: Macmillan, 1967), p. 209.
[6]See, for example, Erwin O. Smigel, "The Problem of Leisure Time in an Industrial Society," *Computer Technology—Concepts for Management* (New York: Industrial Relations Counselors, Inc., 1965, Industrial Relations Monograph No. 25), pp. 101–20; and Donald N. Michael, "Free Time—The New Imperative In Our Society," in *Automation, Education, and Human Values*, ed. William W. Brickman and Stanley Lehrer (New York: School & Society Books, 1966), pp. 293–303.
[7]Nicholas Rescher, "What is Value Change?" in *Values and the Future*, ed. Kurt Baier and Nicholas Rescher (New York: The Free Press, 1969), pp. 68–109.

response to the "onset of the 'Big Brother' State," a "probable upgrading of democratic values" is predicted "(in face of obvious threats thereto, demanding greater investment)."[8] It is unclear why threats to a value lead to downgrading in the case of privacy and to upgrading in the case of democratic values. Perhaps the underlying assumption is that democratic values are much more important than privacy in American society and would thus be maintained despite the costs involved. But this explanation would not account for the "upgrading of beauty (natural and artistic)" which is also seen as accompanying the population explosion and urban crowding. Presumably this value too would be threatened, and few analysts would rank it as being especially salient in American society. Moreover there is a deficiency in the model if the strength of adherence to a particular value today becomes the central determinant of the strength of adherence to this value in the changed social situation of the future. The simplest type of value change is precisely that in which values which were earlier of central importance become downgraded and vice versa.

Another method of attempting to predict value changes could be devised which would be less subject to the flaws of the two variants just outlined. This method would take into account the phenomenon of "cultural lag" and would also not impute values to future generations on the basis of current values. The procedure here would be to examine the current inconsistencies between social requirements and traditional value patterns and to note those values which appear to be in need of change. Speculation could then proceed as to the direction of change and the rapidity with which such change is likely to occur. A central problem would be to determine whether the conditions for the institutionalization of the new values exist or are likely to be forthcoming.

[8]*Ibid.*, p. 99–100.

4

The Alternative Futures Approach

THE ALTERNATIVE WORLD FUTURES APPROACH

● *herman kahn*

"Alternative World Futures" may seem an awkward, even an offensive phrase, since it implies an abstract, perhaps a naive, approach to the tangled reality of contemporary international affairs and to their potential developments. Yet we have found no better term to describe a tool which we believe to be a modest but useful contribution to the objectives of policy research. Those objectives may be described as follows:

1. To stimulate and stretch the imagination.
2. To clarify, define, name, expound, and argue major issues.
3. To design and study alternative policy "packages" and contexts.
4. To create propaedeutic and heuristic expositions, methodologies, paradigms and frameworks. (We use these rather pedantic words reluctantly, but they seem to be the best available to describe our objectives.) By "propaedeutic" we mean pertaining to introductory instruction, although there is no suggestion of the oversimplified. Because creative integration of ideas must ultimately take place in a single mind, even a very sophisticated and knowledgeable policy-maker, analyst, long-range planner (or member of an interdisciplinary study group) must absorb many ideas from unfamiliar fields. Hence, propaedeutic techniques are indispensable. By "heuristic" we refer to that which serves to discover, or to stimulate investigation, or to methods of demonstration that lead an investigator to probe further. While heuristic techniques are not necessarily scholarly or rigorous, their value need not be belabored. Rather than define "methodology" for our present purposes, let us merely suggest that our notion of it will emerge from this paper. "Paradigm," a structured set of propositions, is discussed more fully below.
5. To improve intellectual communication and cooperation, particularly by the use of historical analogies, scenarios, metaphors, analytic models, precise concepts, and suitable language.
6. To increase the ability to identify new patterns and crises and understand their significance.[1]

[1]The reader may be puzzled by not finding three of the more conventional objectives of policy research: (1) To furnish specific knowledge and generate and document conclusions, recommendations, and suggestions. (2) To clarify currently realistic policy choices, with emphasis on those that retain flexibility for a broad range of contingencies. (3) To improve the "administrative" ability of decision-makers and their staffs to react appropriately to the new and unfamiliar.

While these objectives are clearly important, they are not the primary objectives of the Hudson Institute study of Alternative World Futures.

This paper outlines some of the basic techniques, issues, themes, and variables used in the Hudson Institute project on Alternative World Futures. The project in turn is a small segment of an attempt to fulfill the above objectives for decision-makers, planners, and analysts. It is not an attempt to provide a systematic account of current and likely developments in international relations, though this effort is to some degree inevitably implicit in such work. It is not only a mixture of research and exposition, but contains some research in exposition. It is perhaps more accurately "presearch" than "research." To the extent that it succeeds, the Alternative World Futures approach is, among other things, a kind of high-level "college outline" of international relations for the nonexpert in international relations, as well as a reasonably systematic account, of possible interest to the expert, of some basic factors and tendencies in the current international situation.

Some General Comments

The decision-maker who must deal with international affairs, inaugurating long-range programs or establishing other policies that will have consequences in the distant future, has the problem of coping imaginatively and realistically with future situations he can only dimly perceive. The analyst, in trying to develop a context for "serious" studies, may wish to range more widely and peer even further into the future. Historians usually are reluctant to study even the contemporary period because perspective is lacking, but the future obviously is harder yet to interpret, and any kind of perspective even more difficult to achieve.

The decision-maker or planner, though knowing his own inadequacy and the probable inadequacy of his advisors, must nevertheless make decisions and plans *now* which will seriously affect the success or failure of those who follow him, and which will even influence those who see the future differently or seek different future objectives. Since he can neither plan for, nor think of, everything, the planner presumably should try to look at a relevant range of possibilities, remembering the importance of examining possibilities which seem relatively unlikely but which would have very desirable—or catastrophic—consequences if they occurred. Indeed, the enhanced importance of *unlikely* events is a novel and most significant element in our age of technology; and to plan prudently means increasingly to extend the boundaries of plausibility. Prediction about future possibilities depends upon an understanding of the present and past, and it also involves the making of imaginative and analytical leaps as well as extrapolations. Again the analyst, being less responsible for immediate decisions than the government official, but more responsible for "stretching the imagination," should, on occasion, be more willing to consider seriously the unlikely and the bizarre, or spend more energy in re-examining and reinterpreting the old and familiar.

To appraise the future is, at the simplest level, difficult because important aspects of the future are not only unknown but unthought of. Even those aspects of the future which are relatively accessible to the imagination—more or less simple projections of present trends—may still be ignored because an individual's view of the future is necessarily conditioned by emotional and intellectual biases. In addition, the future is uncertain in a statistical or probabilistic sense. There are many possibilities, and while one can attempt to pick the "winner" of the "race," unless this choice is overwhelmingly probable it is more prudent to describe the probability distribution over the potential winners. Even then a planner is most unlikely to do as competent a job as an amateur, much less a professional, racecourse handicapper or stock or commodity speculator. The military-political analyst is not only unlikely to be less "skillful" than the handicapper or speculator, he has less reliable or objective criteria available for making and checking predictions. Not only have such criteria not been devised, they are not likely to be.

Yet the modern policy-maker or analyst cannot evade these problems. Many aspects of aid programs, alliance arrangements, weapons systems, and military-political strategies tend, in the common phrase, to be "cast in concrete" for years to come by present decisions, and the planner must begin now to develop concepts and doctrine for systems, programs and policies which will address the challenges he expects to face in the decade of the 1970's and even the 1980's. Systems, programs and policies should, of course, be made as flexible as possible, and be designed to enable future decision-makers to "muddle through." Yet the problem is that unless such a "muddling through" capability is thoughtfully designed—that is, unless the range of possibilities in various challenges, requirements, and opportunities is adequately foreseen—the decisions made now are likely to prove to have many undesirably inflexible consequences. One must explicitly arrange to have a sort of "lobby for the future" or else some of the claims of the future are likely to be neglected.

Nor do ordinary standards of care and prudence suffice for those responsible for such decisions or even such studies. U.S. political and military decision-makers—and analysts—not only carry the burden of American national security, but their work may greatly affect the future of the world. They can and should be held to higher standards of responsible examination and thought than any ordinary man in ordinary times; they are not likely to be excused responsibility in case of disaster on grounds that the outbreak or conditions of a crisis cannot easily—or even "reasonably"—be foreseen. The problem, however, is not entirely hopeless. While it may be impossible to predict the future in detail, it is possible to speculate usefully on many aspects of the future and even predict some. And even moderate care and prudence—hedging—can have spectacularly useful results should the unlikely occur.

To predict trends, government and industry most often refer the problem to one or more "experts." But experts typically do not offer systematic explanations of the bases of their predictions. Experience also suggests strongly that they tend: (1) to be immersed in the past—and even more in the current—

professionally relevant details of the situation being projected; (2) to know the details of how professionally relevant similar situations have developed or are developing; (3) to have worked out for themselves a few useful rules of thumb in regard to the historical processes of interest to them (although these may not always be clearly stated); and (4) to have imaginatively or prosaically fused these elements of thought into some kind of (at least implicit) picture of the future. In general this is no doubt one of the most convincing approaches to social and political prediction. However, it is usually more adaptable to a smaller scale of prediction than world or other gross trends: for the grasp of empirical detail which forms half of the presumptive cases for the method is seldom sufficient to take account of events on truly extensive or long-term scales. There is also the danger of professional bias, or parochialism. Beneath the texture of such informed intuition there may be a selective professional distortion of the reception of data, the formulation of the problem, and the structuring of intuitions.

No matter how badly overall studies—as opposed to the specialist's predictions—are needed, the problems in doing them successfully are immense. Moreover, until recently there was relatively little motivation to do them. Until World War II it was virtually axiomatic in academic life and scholarship that serious knowledge about any area was obtained only by a lifetime of highly specialized research. The breadth of the area to be studied would depend upon the individual and the field, but there were pressures on a researcher not to attempt a wide field of scholarship. There were good reasons for this, the most obvious being that any attempt to go beyond intensive specialization involved the risk of falling behind in the initial specialty, risking superficiality there as well as failing to achieve more than superficiality in other areas.[2]

An even more important inhibition against broad studies has resulted from

[2]Perhaps one of the clearest and most persuasive statements of the desirability of specialization and of the avoidance of large overall projects was given by Max Weber in a talk, "Science As a Vocation," at Munich University in 1918. Among other things, he said:
    . . . science has entered a phase of specialization previously unknown and that this will forever remain the case. Not only externally, but inwardly, matters stand at a point where the individual can acquire the sure consciousness of achieving something truly perfect in the field of science only in case he is a strict specialist.
    All work that overlaps neighboring fields, such as we occasionally undertake and which the sociologists must necessarily undertake again and again, is burdened with the resigned realization that at best one provides the specialist with useful questions upon which he would not so easily hit from his own specialized point of view. One's own work must inevitably remain highly imperfect. Only by strict specialization can the scientific worker become fully conscious, for once and perhaps never again in his lifetime, that he has achieved something that will endure. A really definitive and good accomplishment is today always a specialized accomplishment. And whoever lacks the capacity to put on blinders, so to speak, and to come up to the idea that the fate of his soul depends upon whether or not he makes the correct conjecture at this passage of this manuscript, may as well stay away from science. . . . For nothing is worthy of man as man unless he can pursue it with passionate devotion.

the circumstances that until recently there has been almost no scholarly market for integrated, overall work unless the author is a recognized "authority"—or an elder statesman.There has not even been a nonscholarly market except for authors with a facility for dramatizing and popularizing this kind of work. Today, though, such "grandiose" studies are becoming more fashionable; we may soon suffer from the problem of too much demand and a subsequent vulgarization.

Almost all who have attempted such broad research agree that the danger of superficiality is great even when these generalizing or synthesizing efforts are carried out with high seriousness. But, just as detailed and specialized research is worth doing even if it often proves to be of narrow or sharply limited relevance, general treatments may also be worthwhile, even if they begin in superficialities.

Extensive, "shallow" studies, in order to be useful, must often meet higher standards than intensive and narrow research. The risk of total "failure" is much less in the narrow study, since even a routine level of competence can usually guarantee some usefulness for the product—if it is sufficiently specialized. But the broad contextual study normally must be done unusually well if it is to have any usefulness at all; however, when it is done well, it is likely to be of correspondingly unusual value.

The task of creating a usable context for an overall study is probably best done iteratively. Once an overall context has been set forth for discussion, generalizations can be corrected and most of the superficiality removed. Ordinarily it is at just this point that the interdisciplinary approach can yield important and unusual dividends. Eventually the corrected context may be made into a usable and respectable framework or "paradigm," in the sense of the word employed by Robert K. Merton (see below).

This study of "Alternative World Futures" obviously is an attempt to overcome some of the obstacles that stand in the way of broad, syncretic studies. Hudson Institute has, since its formation in 1961, attempted to do exactly this kind of work in a planned and organized manner. Since 1961 we have accumulated nearly one hundred man-years of experience in some of the problems which are involved, and we believe that we have obtained modest but useful outputs from systematic, interdisciplinary examination of the possibilities of the future. We are encouraged to expect additional successes in carrying out the study by making use of the synthesis and integration of very diverse specialities and areas of knowledge, and the cooperation of a varied group of researchers and specialists. This essay represents the first in what we expect to be a series of efforts to explicate some of the possible political and military problems and contexts of the future.[3]

[3]For other approaches see such books as:
    Arthur C. Clarke, Profiles of the Future (New York: Harper and Row, 1962).
    Dennis Gabor, Inventing the Future (New York: Alfred A. Knopf, 1964).
    Fritze Baade, The Race to the Year 2000 (New York: Doubleday and Company, 1962).
    Bertrand de Jouvenel, ed. Futuribles (Droz Library, Geneva, Switzerland, 1962).

The Best Tools Versus Policy Research Methodologies

In dealing with the problems of national security and international order, there are no adequate substitutes for such "tools" as relevant and accurate knowledge, experience, perception, judgment, insight and intuition. Yet though substitutes may be inadequate, decision-makers may nonetheless have to make use of substitutes. In some, perhaps in most, of the subjects of greatest concern to decision-makers, relevant knowledge, experience, perception, judgment, insight and intuition may be wholly or partially lacking. People may also have the mistaken belief that they possess these qualities when they do not, or they may believe that they have them in a greater degree than they in fact do.

On particular aspects of various problems there will, of course, be people who do have the qualities we have listed, and to the extent that the decision-maker can identify these people and the limits of their capabilities, he will wish to use them. But even then, for most issues that arise, for an advisor's judgments to be valuable to decision-makers and analysts it is necessary that he be able to convey explicitly and "usably" how he arrives at his conclusions. In some cases it may be more useful to the decision-maker to have erroneous counsel which nevertheless can be explicated, and therefore corrected and effectively made use of in conjunction with other conclusions and assumptions, than flat declaratory statements which may be correct in their context but which must stand or fall on their apparent merits. If one does not know how flashes of intuition fit into a chain of reasoning, in general one does not know how to make use of them, particularly under changing conditions, assumptions, or criteria—even if one has faith in the intuitions. An unquestioning faith is hard for a responsible policy-maker to achieve in dealing with great issues. In the absence of such faith, it does little good for a decision-maker to be provided with information which is in a form he cannot use. Occasionally, and usually with respect to a narrow topic, a study, rather than claiming to supplement the judgment of the decision-maker, may claim with some justice to define a policy which is as reasonable as can be obtained in an imperfect world, and the study group will argue that the best thing a decision-maker can do is simply to accept the conclusions of the study. But such situations are rare. Normally the results of policy research studies are quite inconclusive, since the techniques are so limited and the assumptions and criteria so uncertain. In these circumstances it is almost worthless to give only results. One must explain how the results depend upon assumptions,

Technological Trends and National Policy, National Resources Committee (June, 1937).

Alfred M. Low, *The Future* (New York: International Publishing, 1925).

Nigel Calder, ed., *The World in 1984*, Vols. 1 & 2 (Baltimore: Penguin Books, 1965).

Sir George Thomson, *The Foreseeable Future* (New York: The Viking Press, 1955).

Arnold B. Barach, et al., *1975 and the Changes to Come* (New York: Harper and Row, 1962).

values, and calculational techniques, and even more important, how decision-makers can use these results in formulating their own policies within their own assumptions, values, and calculational techniques.

The kind of policy research we are concerned with here, then, emphasizes attempts to derive substitutes for "relevant knowledge, experience, judgment, perception, insight and intuition." It tends to rely heavily on such things as empirical research and analysis, and simple theory; metaphors and historical analogues; analytic models (involving an analyzable description of systems, devising alternative policies, and explicating criteria, objectives, or values); propaedeutic and heuristic methodologies and paradigms; scenarios, gaming and other use of "arbitrary" specifications and stimulation.

EMPIRICAL RESEARCH AND ANALYSIS AND SIMPLE THEORY

The first, and in some ways the most important tools of the decision-maker are empirical research and analysis, and simple theory. These make up the simple attempt to examine carefully the realities of some relevant aspect of the world, and to draw immediate and direct conclusions from the examination. It is startling how often this produces unexpected information, at least in the study of rapidly changing or isolated portions of the world, since many issues or questions have for one reason or another—bureaucratic, geographical, technical, or intellectual—not been properly examined. Any careful examination may disclose facts or even central issues that are very different from what commonly is expected or asserted.

Thus, in the early 1950's, an almost trivial examination of the actual condition of strategic forces indicated that they were surprisingly vulnerable to attack "out of the blue" (and, indeed, according to Mr. McNamara's 1963 testimony, Soviet forces are—in the mid-sixties—still vulnerable). Or, in the late 1950's and early 1960's, there was a common assumption that NATO forces could not match "Soviet hordes," but this assumption actually represented a serious underestimation of NATO capability. The facts disclosed that NATO had more men under arms than the Soviets did (i.e., the problem lay more in utilizing manpower efficiently than in matching "Soviet hordes"). Similarly, many people today worry about a large-scale Chinese attack on South Vietnam with millions of soldiers, yet the most cursory examination of the logistics involved indicates that there would be sharp restrictions on any Chinese offensive against a U.S.-supported South Vietnam.

It is often possible to supplement empirical research and analysis with very simple theory which indicates trends or possibilities. Such theory is rarely rigorous but it may be stimulating or illuminating. Some simple ideas that could constitute simple theory are:

1. The friend of an enemy is often an enemy.
2. The ally of an enemy is almost invariably an enemy.

3. The enemy of an enemy is often a friend, and is almost invariably at least an *ad hoc* ally on many issues.
4. If the basis for an alliance changes, the alliance itself may soon be strained unless it too changes to fit the new conditions.
5. A violent left wing revolution is likely to parallel the experience of the French, the English, or the Russian revolutions in many of its phases, rather than the U.S. experience.
6. A hostile but submerged and suppressed emotion may easily emerge when conditions allow it to.

We will not discuss these political aphorisms or theories in any detail here, but such simple ideas can, when applied, be very stimulating, particularly when others are not applying them. There are similar ideas in the strategic field, for example:

1. If one's offensive weapons are vulnerable, there may be serious instabilities in deterrence.
2. If one's civilians are vulnerable, deterrence is likely to become a two-way street.
3. When deterrence becomes a two-way street, strategic guarantees are likely to be considered less reliable.
4. Permanent conditions are more important than results that ensue from temporary defeats and wartime disorganization, so one should not be misled by such early postwar conditions.
5. Since technological secrets are rarely kept for more than five or ten years, it is not likely that major nations will be more than ten or fifteen years behind the United States and the Soviet Union.
6. And so on.

While all the above seem trivially obvious today, four years ago it would have taken a bold and perceptive observer to advance them.

Closely related to research on the current situation is the derivation of simple theories from such research. Such research on historical situations or on various current aspects of a culture or society often generates simple generalizations which, in effect, summarize the descriptive data that has been supplied by such research. For our purposes we will be very much interested in the dominant characteristics of various cultures and on the impact of one culture on another culture, particularly of a dominant culture (such as the West in the industrial age) on various other cultures. The kind of theory which comes out of such study is often difficult to apply rigorously. Sometimes, as indicated in the next section, such theories are best used as metaphors rather than as strict tools for analysis; but they are more than metaphors since they are likely to be better grounded, to have more valid or useful structural analogies with the explicit situation being studied. It may be just as much a disservice to ignore the insights and extrapolations that such theorizing and generalizing can generate, as to abuse them by taking them too literally or misinterpreting them.

Many studies of historical or current situations obviously can be seriously misleading if applied to a specific situation of interest today, since many or all of the conditions that apply to the example may not apply to the specific situation. Often the most that can be argued is that the historical analogy should be used metaphorically rather than analytically; that while there is no particular reason to assume that the two situations are similar as far as prediction goes, it is still useful to refer to the analogy simply because it enhances communication. If one is using such an analogy as a metaphor then there is no theory of historical inevitability or prediction being assumed or argued, but simply a facilitation of communication through the use of a vivid, rich, or concrete example. One can also argue that certain insights or perceptions hold true for new situations without arguing that the fact that they were true in old situations makes them in itself any more likely to be valid in the new situation. For example, in conjecturing about difficulties that the Soviets may have with any future foreign "Communist" or "pro-Communist" leaders, it is useful to be able to say, "He might play the role of a Tito—or a Mao—or a Sukarno—or a Castro—or an Ulbricht—or a Nkrumah—etc." There obviously are many other important roles they could play that have not yet occurred, and for which we do not have names. Thus, in many cases the range of discussion is unfortunately restricted to minor variations on that which has already occurred. One of the major tasks of this kind of research—or "presearch"— is to identify new possibilities and to give them names (perhaps by using scenarios or artificially specified contexts as described below).

The list below not only illustrates a range of phenomena covered in the use of metaphors, scenarios, and historical analogues but includes some of the most important ones for Hudson studies (a careful consideration of the list would reveal a good deal about some of our major preoccupations).[4] If space were available it would be worthwhile to give detailed descriptions of almost every one of the metaphors and their historical analogies, since if the richness of the metaphor is increased and shared with the reader, later communication is greatly improved.

A. 1945–1965 (The two postwar decades)

1. The "indefensible" enclave (Berlin-Goa)

[4]In particular it should be clear that we are as interested, in this book, in what can go wrong as in what may go well, and almost every item in the list illustrates an important way in which history can paraphrase itself more or less unpleasantly. This is in some ways a reasonable bias, but the list probably gives an exaggerated picture. Unfortunately, for many of the "constructive" things we will consider here (or which are considered elsewhere) we do not have simple metaphors or historical analogues. This is one of the things which makes their serious discussion and study difficult. But this last gap in our language can in part be filled by specially written scenarios and contexts.

2. The extensive limited conventional war or police operation with neighboring sanctuaries (Korea-Vietnam-Angola-Algeria)
3. The counterinsurgency war (Malaya-Indochina-Philippines-Algeria-Venezuela-Bolivia)
4. The problem of the restive satellites (East Germany-Hungary-Poland-Rumania-Czechoslovakia)
5. The problem of Communist (and democratic) heresy and revisionism
6. The problem of a coalition being taken over by a radical party—from salami tactics to coup (Czechoslovakia in 1948; Cuba sometime in 1959 or 1960)
7. Aggression by a risk-taking irredentist power (China-Egypt-Indonesia)

B. 1930–1940 (The prewar decade)[5]

1. Rapallo
2. Revisionism (against "unfair" postwar treaties)
3. Reichstag Fire
4. Munich
5. Hacha
6. Rotterdam
7. Pearl Harbor
8. Russo-German Pact
9. Catastrophic economic depression
10. Chauvinistic or Messianic fanaticism (in relatively developed nations)
11. "War is unthinkable" syndrome
12. Loss of nerve by *status quo* nations

C. 1815–1914, "Barbarian" invasions, progressive revolutions and *Ancien régime* morale, or the rise and fall of almost any culture (civilization), empire or movement.

D. *Lex talionis*

---

[5]A relevant discussion of items 2–7 and 11–12 can be found in my *On Thermonuclear War* (Princeton, New Jersey: Princeton University Press, 1960), pp. 319–416, 524–531 (items 2–7) and 150–157, 163–165 (items 9–10).

Very briefly, "Rapallo" illustrates the prospect of two "outlawed" nations pooling their strength (say, China and a frustrated West Germany) and thus developing new strengths which would have been impossible in isolation. (It could also refer simply to a Soviet-West German agreement on broad matters.) Revisionism (against "unfair" postwar treaties) illustrates the difficulty of maintaining a united front against a nation if all members of the united front do not have the same stake in maintaining that front. (This may be of particular importance with regard to Germany and Japan in the next decade or so.) Some members of the winning coalition which defeated the Axis in 1945 seem to wish to keep the defeated countries in a condition that may imply to them that "until you win a war you are second class." Other members of the coalition of victors are more sympathetic with the internal and external problems that Germans and Japanese have, and are more or less willing eventually to accept them as full members of the international community. The Reichstag Fire reminds us that it is possible deliberately to stage or exploit a provocative event so as to justify extreme actions which otherwise would be implausible. Hacha, President of Czechoslovakia after Munich, was the victim of one of the most dramatic and forceful instances of political-military blackmail in history. (A comparable example might be found in the situation in which Hitler's representatives negotiated with the government of Denmark for a peaceful occupation of Denmark while Nazi bombers circled overhead.) Rotterdam demonstrates that civilized nations as well as Mongols can (even more today

For the modern man who, even though he may be highly educated, may be relatively ignorant of history, the chief source of historical analogies and inspiration for metaphors and scenarios is likely to be the events of the last four decades. The period includes the depression, the rise of fanatic and chauvinistic movements in such relatively developed nations as Japan, Italy, and Germany and their subsequent almost hysterically aggressive careers, the demonstration of weakness by the seemingly strong and powerful *status quo* nations and the various events of World War II and of the cold war. This brief span of modern history is rich in the kind of problems many believe can arise again. Some, of course, argue that we are too preoccupied with these particular problems; having once experienced a "Munich," we may be overly fearful of any negotiations with or concessions to an opponent. Having experienced Pearl Harbor, Americans may be overly preoccupied with the danger of surprise attack. The author would argue that these judgments may, in a sense, be both correct and irrelevant. Such dangers as appeasement and surprise attack require a relatively high standard of prudence in a government. While popular or even professional discussion may overestimate these dangers, the government, in terms of actual preparations, has tended to underestimate them.

But while the last four decades supply a rich store of historical examples of problems which could recur, it is no complete catalogue of possibilities. Yet it is startlingly difficult for most people, even analysts and decision-makers, to discuss seriously problems for which they cannot find analogies in these last four decades. . . .

ANALYTICAL MODELS

The next important methodological technique is the use of various types of analytical models. The first difficulty with models is that they require a description of the systems to be analyzed which is complete enough to include all of the relevant characteristics. The classical example of how abstract and simple such a description can be is the mass point of astronomy and physics. All that one needs to know if one wishes to predict an astronomical body's motion is its total mass and the location of its center of gravity. All other details such as shape, color, texture, composition, etc., are irrelevant. But such simplicity is rarely found in the kind of study considered here.

The second difficulty with models is that the description must be phrased

---

than before) deliberately create examples of the use of terror in the hope of persuading others not to resist. The Russo-German Pact illustrates the very surprising changes in the short-run *status quo* that can result from seemingly improbable realignments—changes which affect major calculations of war or peace and other vital issues. The last two items in the list indicate that the "War is Unthinkable" syndrome, and a potential loss of nerve by *status quo* nations, is no novelty but has occurred over and over again in history—most recently just before World War II. The other items on the list are either discussed in the text or are more or less self-evident.

in such a way that the analysis can, at least conceptually, be carried through. Generally this means either quantitative description or at least a fairly explicit detailing of the various components so that a chain of logical reasoning can be conducted.

One must also explicate for the model the various policies that are to be tested. Here there is often room, or need, for creativity. One often can invent new and very advantageous policy programs; one can then set forth a model which emphasizes the unfavorable aspects of the preferred policy and favors an alternative policy and still show that the recommended policy is superior; or one can provide a break-even analysis describing what assumptions or parameters one must have, or believe will obtain, in order to justify the recommended policy.[6] But often, if unfavorable assumptions and simplifications are used, the values or advantages of the recommended policy are not so overwhelming that its preference can still be demonstrated.

In addition to the interaction of policy and model, there are questions as to the criteria, objectives or values to be used in judging alternative policies. Again it often proves very difficult to explicate all the relevant criteria, objectives or values, and the result, often enough, particularly in the simple cost-effectiveness type of analysis, is an analysis of only that part of the problem which is easily subjected to analysis, leaving it up to the "judgment" of the decision-maker to take account of the "imponderables." If this kind of analysis is done well, it may be possible for the decision-maker freely to use his judgment and modify the analysis correspondingly. But to do the analysis well is not easy, and normally the final "meta-analysis" comes down to a simplistic intuition or an expression of bias rather than a careful synthesis and balancing of the analysis with more subtle qualitative considerations.

Thus, in the problems we are considering here, the role of analytical models of the cost-effectiveness type is limited. It often is impossible to include all the important relevant aspects of a system in the model, or to devise a suitable range of alternative policies, or to explicate criteria, objectives or values in such a way that the analysis can be carried through. This does not mean that it is unimportant to do those parts of such an analysis as can be done with a model, particularly if they are done in such a way that the decision-maker can combine the results sensibly with his own judgments.

It often happens that one cannot set forth an analytical model with all the properties that are needed in order for it to be directly useful to policy research. Such models can often, though, be used metaphorically—that is, the analyst can concede that there is no necessary analogy between the findings resulting from his analytical studies of models and the real world, yet his study of analytical models may well enable him to define and deepen concepts and issues and thus enable him to develop a language in which

---

[6]See discussion RAND Report RM-1829-1, *Techniques of System Analysis*, by Herman Kahn and Irwin Mann, pp. 142 to 148; and *On Thermonuclear War*, pp. 119 to 126, for discussion on choosing a preferred system.

the problem can better be discussed—in particular, important elementary issues and principles can often be discussed more clearly and intensively than if the examples were taken from the real world. One can then also use the model, if he desires, in a metaphoric fashion. Much of the current study of game theory is useful in this way (and usually only in this way). Other simple models or theories can be equally useful. Trouble can ensue if the lesson learned from such models is blindly applied to more complicated and real problems. But it is better to take the risk of misuse than to forego the attempt to develop a clear understanding of some issues or parts of the problem (e.g., it is difficult to discuss what role rationality may play in deterrence and war unless one first has some idea of what is or is not rational conduct).

PROPAEDEUTIC AND HEURISTIC METHODOLOGIES AND PARADIGMS

We have already used these terms (if apologetically). In defining propaedeutic and heuristic, we noted that the concepts they express are so basic to the method and purpose of this paper, and to much policy research in general, that they deserve and need names; similarly for the concept of the paradigm.

For our purpose, a paradigm is an explicitly structured set of questions, assumptions, typologies, concepts, outlines, classifications, descriptions, definitions, etc., that attempts to provide for a problem or issue frameworks, patterns of relationships, and some relevant approaches or points of view. We may think of it as between a metaphor and a model, but more rigorous, more careful, more complex, more relevant than a metaphor, without attempting to be as complete or rigorous as an analytical model. However, a paradigm attempts to be as much of a model as is possible, given the limitations of information and analytical capabilities.[7]

Most of the "Alternative World Futures" project can be thought of as the development of an early version of a paradigm for the examination of key international developments in the next decade or two. We hope by the use of such paradigms to put a floor—so to speak—under the discussion: to create a secular upward trend in the level of speculation, conjecture, exposition, and analysis.

The terms propaedeutic and heuristic are, however, more relevant to this essay than "paradigms." In looking at problems as complex as the ones discussed here, one is automatically involved in interdisciplinary research. Today, "interdisciplinary research" tends to be regarded with some disillusionment and skepticism, if not with hostility. The reason for this is that such research is primarily workable when the questions at issue have been clearly and well formulated. If, for example, the only question is, "How do we answer the

[7]The functions of paradigms in sociology are well analyzed and demonstrated by Robert K. Merton in his *Social Theory and Social Structure* (New York: The Free Press, 1949, rev. ed. 1956); see especially pp. 12–16.

following question?" and if there is relevant knowledge available, the problem is simply to bring this knowledge to bear, and an interdisciplinary committee of "equals" will succeed. More often, though, the problems require creative integration and synthesis, the answering of the question, "What is the question?" (i.e., "What kinds of knowledge are needed? What are the issues?"). In this kind of interdisciplinary research, integration and synthesis are widely held to be possible only, in Clyde Kluckhohn's phrase, "within a single skull." Much information must be absorbed by that one mind, accurately and rapidly. The problem is then to cram a great deal of relevant "interdisciplining" into one skull.

Similarly, in the complex decision-making problems we are addressing, the decision-maker requires access to a large number of different skills, even though his own background, and even the major issues, may be relatively specialized. Thus there is a great need for the organization and presentation of material which is propaedeutic and heuristic, and much policy research is occupied with the development, explication and exposition of methodologies and paradigms of this kind.

Let us digress for a moment on the reasons for this. Before World War II senior political leaders often relied heavily on congressional investigators, free-lance journalists, and newspaper columnists for counsel. These were almost the only people who were spending full time on national problems as a whole, and they then had a sense of perspective and a breadth of information otherwise unavailable. Others were doing specific jobs and tended to have relatively narrow and parochial points of view. To some degree the columnist and the congressional investigator have today been replaced by the research institute. These organizations are also trying to grasp the problem as a whole. We sometimes observe that at Hudson Institute more than half the staff spends more than half its time implicitly playing such roles as President of the United States, Secretary of State, Secretary of Defense, or Secretary General of the U.N. It is difficult to play President unless there are many propaedeutic and heuristic paradigms and other special pedagogical materials available. It is of great importance to have, in effect, simple "college" (or better, "postgraduate") outlines[8] directed to the needs of these people. Such

[8]The term "college outline" is a good one, even though it has an unfortunate connotation, stemming from the poor character of many such outlines and the frequent misuse of such outlines by college students who have neglected their work. Such literature often is, but need not be, misleading, mistaken, or inadequate to its purposes. It is usually designed to give the student just the information he needs for his immediate purposes (which might be passing a test, reviewing his previous studies, or quickly obtaining a basic grasp of a subject); presumably different outlines would be appropriate for each of these purposes. Because of its limited objectives it is often simplified. Despite this simplification a college outline may provide a valuable review in outline even for the expert, conveying a comprehensive perspective of the structure of a subject. This simplification is not necessarily a vice but can be, in some circumstances, a virtue if it does not result in a treatment inadequate to the task. The student's objective in our analogy is to be replaced

literature needs to be produced to order; it is not likely to be produced accidentally. By "literature" we include methodologies for analysis and design. For example, we would hope that almost any competent political scientist or policy planner reading Hudson Institute reports would get a good many simple, yet not unsophisticated, ideas of how international relations, technology, strategy and other large issues should influence his specialized considerations. He may even be able to acquire some complex, sophisticated and subtle nuances from these reports which he might otherwise have missed.

Of course, experts in particular fields are likely to feel some annoyance, if not anger, at how complicated ideas must be used in seemingly simplistic ways in interdisciplinary research for planning and policy purposes. But this is a classical problem: nonexpert usages often seem to experts to caricature, vulgarize, or satirize their stock-in-trade. And experts are almost always annoyed by intruders who have an *ad hoc* competence in their fields while lacking the depth and background that the expert feels are essential. Though we sympathize with this feeling, it seems clear that the necessities of planning are overriding. We believe it to be an observable fact that planning requires that at least some participants step outside their specialties.[9]

The kind of work that has to be done on problems of national security and international order requires the integration of a large number of different disciplines, and almost anything that can help in achieving this should be encouraged. Nonspecialists must maintain reasonable standards of depth and thoroughness, but these standards should not be self-defeating or so high as unnecessarily to prevent an important job from being done. In any case,

---

by the specialized needs of the researcher, planner, or decision-maker, but the principle is the same.

[9] A personal note may help to clarify some of the resistance that is felt toward people who work outside their own specialities. I was trained as an applied mathematician and physicist, and occasionally I have explained certain ideas in either applied mathematics or physics to people trained in other fields. Later, I have heard these explanations used by these people in their own lectures or briefings. I usually had no specific objection to what they said, but felt slightly frustrated and annoyed. When a speaker on a platform discusses a subject, there should be an iceberg effect—he should be giving only about ⅛ of what he knows. But these speakers were inverse icebergs. They were telling approximately ⅞ or more of what they knew about that particular subject. Even though the speaker often apologized for lecturing outside his field, I still felt, quite unreasonably, that some degree of fraud was being perpetrated on the audience. For one thing, I knew that at that point the speaker could not answer "deep" questions. There was the not-uncommon feeling that anyone who speaks publicly or writes on a subject *ought* to be able to answer such questions, whether or not they are asked, and even though, strictly speaking, they would be irrelevant to the point he was making. But it was also that I could not help being annoyed at the subtle differences in style—almost like having the wrong accent, or wearing the wrong clothes—by which the nonexpert gives himself away even when he is making correct statements.

Such reactions are both to be expected and suppressed (or sublimated). They should not be permitted to interfere with work that needs to be done.

interdisciplinary workers must almost necessarily rely on secondary sources, or on the advice of experts whom they have difficulty evaluating, though this problem can be much alleviated by a suitable playing of experts against one another.[10]

"Teams" of experts or staffs cannot avoid the problem of the nonexpert. At some point a plan or solution must be achieved within a single mind and communicated to other minds. However much the result is the product of collaborative efforts, it is clear that the *result* cannot require more than one mind to understand it. Thus, one or more specialists must step outside their fields, one or more nonspecialists must perform, and subsequently receive and comprehend, the final integration of specialties. Both the seriousness of this problem and the somewhat unreasonable irritation we have referred to will be much reduced if a better set of shared concepts and common vocabulary as well as special propaedeutic devices are developed.

Probably the most important heuristic technique and the most dangerous as well (i.e., the one most subject to abuse) is to make explicit some shared agreement and then without expending a great deal of time and resources (perhaps because it is not practical to do so) to proceed on the basis of this shared agreement.

Scholars are often very uncomfortable at this procedure. Among other things, such a procedure could easily succeed in spreading more widely, confirming, or even canonizing whatever errors actually exist as a result of the biases and errors of current assumptions. This possibility is particularly likely if the discussion is restricted to some narrow group with a more or less similar professional, institutional, or other common perspective—shared assumptions which arise out of a narrow group perspective are particularly likely to reflect narrow, invalid, or poorly interpreted experiences and analyses —and are likely to have these biases and emphases reinforced if the assumptions are explicated but not challenged. Fortunately even if the discussion takes place in a narrow and relatively homogeneous group the very act of explication is likely to increase the probability that the assumptions will be challenged or limited more carefully. In any case, in the policy-research, policy-making fields, one must deal with issues on the basis of whatever data and theories are available. Where scholarly data and rigorous theories are not available—or are misleading—then shared perceptions or shared rules of thumb are all that one has. To ignore these is to condemn oneself to ineffectiveness and futility—to decision by default and inaction or to unnecessarily abstract and misleading judgments. While explicating widely held assumptions and theories may seem to be giving them too great a validity, the various dangers are probably decreased, not increased. As already suggested, uncovering and discussing shared understandings and then making explicit conclusions is especially desirable to establish limits and cautions on the

[10]See Herman Kahn and Irwin Mann, *Ten Common Pitfalls* (Santa Monica: The RAND Corporation), pp. 49–52.

process; such limits could not, or would not, be recognized in the absence of such explicit consideration of both assumptions and consequences.

Such explication is particularly important if there has been, or seems to have been, a basic change in the situation and the official rhetoric has not caught up with the change. In this case, many people know, more or less unconsciously, that the official rhetoric does not really express their actual positions so they try to trim their conclusion to make up for the bias in the official rhetoric. They are often shocked to find, when the new position is explicated, that it is often a rather widely held view rather than an idiosyncratic and special perception of the individual concerned.

Furthermore, it is just because these new perceptions are not part of the official rhetoric, but nevertheless widely held, that they go unexamined and excessive interpretations or suggestions are based on them. Once the new position is explicated, people often see that they have pushed the new idea too far and the reason why others do not agree with them is not that they do not share the new point of view but that these others are simply not willing to push it so far. Thus, whether the new view is right or wrong, explicating it can be helpful by making clear the disparity between the lagging official rhetoric and the widely held new idea and thus cause both positions to be more closely examined.

SCENARIOS, GAMING, AND OTHER USE OF "ARBITRARY" SPECIFICATION AND STIMULATION

One of the most important aspects of the postwar international arena is the emphasis on deterrence. This often has meant that military programs were supposed to work without a single failure; thus there can be no realistic testing or straining of the system without having one failure too many, or risking such a catastrophe. However, deterrence does seem to work remarkably well in the sense that almost everybody judges that if both sides are competent, central wars, or even very intense crises, are relatively unlikely to arise between the Soviet Union and the United States in, say, the next decade or two. And yet the weapons exist and might be used. Even those who think that thermonuclear war is unlikely in the next hundred years; even those who believe that the invention and procurement of thousands of nuclear weapons in the middle of the twentieth century has effectively abolished, or will lead peacefully and inevitably to the abolishment of, all-out war cannot be certain. They still have need to examine the circumstances in which these weapons might be used or, possibly more important, the ways in which their existence or threat of their use might influence subwar events in an important way. One of the most important problems in this examination arises from the inherent implausibility—whether justified or deceptive—of the kinds of events which are being studied. One basic objective, therefore, is somehow to find and examine the most plausible examples of the most important cases that tend to be overlooked by the standard methods of studying these problems.

Two now common semianalytical approaches to this problem are the "scenario" and the "war (or peace) game." These are methodological devices which have become more and more common wherever efforts have been made to generate relatively plausible contexts in which the requirements of future weapons, command and control systems, war-fighting strategies, and arms control agreements may be tested or at least evaluated or discussed. While the kinds of scenarios and gaming that we will be discussing in this essay have in fact been most useful in the deterrence-crisis-nuclear-war context suggested above, they also seem to be useful, though perhaps to a lesser degree, for a much larger range of contexts—in fact, for the study of international relations generally.

Such scenarios attempt to describe in more or less detail some hypothetical sequence of events. They can emphasize different aspects of "future history." Some scenarios may explore and emphasize an element of a larger problem such as a crisis or other event which could lead to war, the process of "escalation" of a small war or local violence into a larger war, the spread or contraction of a limited war, the fighting of a war, the termination of the war, or the subsequent peace. The focus of the scenario can be military events and activities, the internal dynamics of various countries, bargaining among enemies, or inter-Allied relations, and so on. The scenario is particularly suited to dealing with several aspects of a problem more or less simultaneously. By the use of a relatively extensive scenario, the analyst may be able to get a "feel" for events and for the branching points dependent upon critical choices. These branches can then be explored more or less systematically.

Some of the advantages of the scenario as an aid to thinking are:

1. They serve almost all of the objectives of policy research by calling attention, sometimes dramatically and persuasively, to the larger range of possibilities that must be considered. They are one of the most effective tools in lessening the "carry-over" thinking that is likely even when it is clear to all that 1975 cannot be the same as 1945 or even 1960. Thus scenarios are one way to force oneself and others to plunge into the unfamiliar and rapidly changing world of the present and the future by dramatizing and illustrating the possibilities they focus on. (They may do little or nothing for the possibilities they do not focus on.)
2. They force the analyst to deal with details and dynamics which he might easily avoid treating if he restricted himself to abstract considerations. Typically, no particular set of the many possible sets of details and dynamics seems specially worth treating, so none are treated, even though a detailed investigation of even a few arbitrarily chosen cases could be most helpful. We will discuss this particular problem below.
3. They help to illuminate the interaction of psychological, social, political, and military factors, including the influence of individual political personalities upon what otherwise might be an abstract analysis, and they do so in a form which permits the comprehension of many interacting elements at once.
4. They can illustrate forcefully, sometimes in oversimplified fashion, certain

principles or questions which would be ignored or lost if one insisted on taking examples only from the complex and controversial real world.

5. They may also be used to consider alternative possible outcomes of certain real past and present crises, such as Suez, Lebanon, Laos, or Berlin.

6. They can be used as artificial "case histories" and "historical anecdotes" either to make up to some degree for the paucity of actual examples as discussed earlier, or as "existence theorems" or examples to test or demonstrate the technical feasibility or plausibility of some possible sequence of events.

However, even if used as an existence theorem, specific scenarios, war games or other artificial devices normally cannot and should not be used to "prove" anything. They are literary and pedagogical tools rather than instruments of rigorous analysis, are useful to stimulate, illustrate and teach, to provide both preciseness and richness to communication, and to check details. A Hudson Institute report, *On Escalation: Metaphors and Scenarios*,[11] indicates some ways in which scenarios and metaphors can systematically be used in analyzing and explicating the issues that arise in considering escalation and crises. In the Alternative World Futures project we are considering even more complex, diffused, and less well formulated issues. As a result these "artificial" tools may eventually prove even more important for these issues than in the study of escalation.

The use of scenarios has been criticized as being both "paranoid" and "schizophrenic." In the first case, the criticism is sometimes that only the paranoid personality, unjustifiably distrustful and suspicious, could conceive of the kind of plots and hostilities that characterize many scenarios. This criticism seems largely misguided. The analyst is, of course, interested in ingenious or unpleasant means others might contrive to injure or to destroy his country; he is also interested in what they might not do. To the extent that the criticism of paranoia is justified, it pertains more to the implausibility of a particular scenario than to the methodology in itself.

A second criticism may be more to the point. It is that scenarios may be so divorced from reality as to be not only useless but misleading, and therefore dangerous. However, one must remember that the scenario ought not to be used as a predictive device. The analyst is dealing with the unknown and to some degree unknowable future. In many specific cases it is hard to see how critics can be so certain there is a sure divorce from a reality which does not yet exist and may yet surprise them. Imagination has always been one of the principal means for dealing in various ways with the future, and the scenario is simply one of many devices useful in stimulating and disciplining the imagination. To the extent that particular scenarios genuinely are divorced from reality, this seems more a fault of particular scenarios than of the methodology. . . .

[11](New York: Frederick A. Praeger, 1965).

Themes for Alternative Future Worlds

We list below twenty-one themes which suggest where important aspects of the next decade or two might lie. The ordering is for convenience of exposition and has no other significance, nor does the number twenty-one have any special significance. It seems to be a convenient number to use, being large enough to allow much specificity in the categories and yet small enough to be reasonably manageable.

Classical Themes:
1. Containment and Confrontation (Chi – χ)
2. Communism on the March (Kappa – κ)
3. Other Manifestations of Soviet Power (Sigma – σ)
4. Mostly Peaceful and Prosperous (Gamma – γ)
5. Détente—Many Structural Stresses (Delta – δ)
6. Extensive Multipolarity (Mu – μ)

A New and Old Theme:
7. Challenges from Europe (Eta – η)

New Political Themes:
8. Challenges from Japan (Iota – ι)
9. Challenges from China (Psi – ψ)
10. Challenges from Latin America (Lambda – λ)
11. Challenges from other Underdeveloped Nations (Omega – ω)
12. New Super Powers (Upsilon – υ)
13. Major Realignments (Rho – ρ)
14. Erosion or Resurgence of the West (Epsilon – ε)
15. Typical Phases or Patterns (Phi – φ)

New Technological Themes:
16. Technological Challenges and Opportunities (Tau – τ)

Medium and Long-Run Prospects:
17. Gallois-Millis-Khrushchev Non-war (Nu – ν)
18. Other Relatively Successful "Arms Control" (Alpha – α)
19. Post-Nuclear-Use International Systems (Pi – π)
20. Other Basic Change in International System (Beta – β)
21. Other Themes (Omicron – o)

The themes are grouped in five categories for convenient discussion. We will, however, only make some preliminary comments on each theme in this report.

Each theme is identified with a Greek letter since, rather than refer to "Containment and Confrontation Worlds," it is often more convenient to speak of "Chi Worlds." Thus when discussing various forms of "Containment and Confrontation Worlds," they may be labeled Chi-1, Chi-2, and Chi-3. And various subclassifications can also be labeled (such as Chi-1.1, Chi-1.2). While this system may be a slight burden for the reader (and tend at times to a certain deadliness in the discussion), it seems to provide useful increase in the ability to systematize discussion, especially since one use of this report is as a "text" for Hudson Institute Seminar-Courses. We hope the reader will not only tolerate this terminology but even come to find it useful.[12]

However, we will use it so little in this paper that even the allergic reader should not be too alienated—at least not for this cause alone.

There is clearly an implicit framework and emphasis built into the selection of the twenty-one themes, a framework and emphasis which we judge appropriate to the plausible problems of international relations from 1965 to 1975 and perhaps beyond. On the other hand, this framework and emphasis is not so restrictive that it forecloses discussion of any particular issue of importance. Thus while other researchers might impart a different view of the current international situation and its likely developments, they could still use the suggested framework for much or all of their discussion without doing violence to it (although possibly adding overlooked themes).

The twenty-one themes that will be described below are a first step toward the construction of a systematic group of Alternative World Futures (AWF's). Any particular world future is likely to have several specific elaborations of the themes synthesized into some coherent picture of the relevant aspects of the world as a whole—or the themes can be studied in isolation. Not only is it possible to meld consistent themes together, it often also is possible to meld inconsistent ones in a way that creates "worlds" with tensions, or with

---

[12]The reader may find the following mnemonics useful (though it is not necessary to memorize the identification in order to read this report):

Alpha	Arms Control
Beta	Basic Change
Gamma	Grand Design
Delta	Détente
Epsilon	Erosion or Resurgence of the West
Zeta	
Eta	Europe
Theta	
Iota	Japan
Kappa	Communism (on the March)
Lambda	Latin America
Mu	Multipolar or Multinuclear
Nu	Non-war (or New Non-war)
Xi	
Omicron	Other Themes
Pi	Post-Nuclear-Use
Rho	Realignment
Sigma	(Other) Soviet (Challenges)
Tau	Technology
Upsilon	Upside Down (Rise of New Power)
Phi	Phases or Patterns
Chi	Containment and Confrontation
Psi	Sino (China)
Omega	Other Underdeveloped Areas

plausible internal conflicts or contradictions. We will, in what follows, usually discuss the themes separately (leaving to the later report on contexts and examples the discussion of the packages), thus losing in this report much of the richness of "reality" but eliminating also the arbitrariness and specialization associated with any particular correlation of specific themes. Some of the most interesting work which the Institute hopes to do will involve such systematic exploration of combinations of themes and of how such combinations may change considerations.

We have labeled the first six themes "classical AWF's"—classical in the sense that much of the discussion of the last twenty years has been preoccupied with these themes. Thus almost all policy-makers and decision-makers are familiar, to some degree, with the possibilities listed. One of our major arguments is that the next ten to twenty years are likely to see the introduction of relatively new themes. While we think of the world in the next decade or so as having a reasonable probability of relative calm, its calmness in part will be the calmness of gestation and preliminary evolution for new structures and tendencies. To some great degree, then, the last fifteen themes are likely to be at least as interesting as the first six—indeed for our purposes more interesting.

1. CHI (CONTAINMENT AND CONFRONTATION) THEMES

These are cold and near-hot cold wars. They are likely to consist substantially in retrogression to the conditions of 1948, 1950, or 1953. Thus they usually assume relatively tight alliance structures, and usually a bi-polar world with both sides pressed against each other, perhaps in "eyeball-to-eyeball" confrontations.

2. KAPPA (COMMUNISM ON THE MARCH) THEMES

The nightmare of the late forties and early fifties. The unity and morale of the Communist bloc are restored. The Communists are strong, aggressive, rapidly increasing in power, while the Western bloc is disunited, weak, demoralized, and everywhere on the defensive or in retreat.

3. SIGMA (OTHER SOVIET) THEMES

Even if the Soviets were no longer leaders of a world-wide revolutionary movement or of a major bloc of Communist states, they would still be one of the great world powers and we would be much concerned with their military and foreign policies. In Sigma Worlds we study: (a) a decline of Soviet power which could include internal disunity and weakness in the Soviet Union or simply a relative withdrawal of the Soviets from international affairs and influence, either because of a Russian "neo-isolationism" or because of an inability of the Soviet to project effectively their internal power externally. In any case, the Soviets of this projection lose their morale and vigor, experience disintegration, or otherwise tend to slide back or turn inwards; (b) a nationalistic Soviet Union which exploits Communist ideology when convenient but is essentially an assertive power with nationalist motivations. Such a U.S.S.R. might have territorial ambitions, or pan-Slav tendencies in policy, or follow economically or politically aggressive policies without conventional territorial ambitions but in order to limit or destroy the power of competitive nations; (c) etc.

4. GAMMA (MOSTLY PEACEFUL AND PROSPEROUS GRAND DESIGN) THEMES

These, in effect, are worlds in which the major constructive and positive international objectives of the U.S. government have been achieved. They ordinarily are worlds in which conflict among nations is channeled by legal and open means, much as is economic competition in an orderly but free marketplace. Such conflict provides useful social functions, stimulating and directing various kinds of changes and "natural" developments, but without violence. This world contains no "enemies"—at most only opponents or competitors. The threat of war or of escalation to violent levels of conflict has either disappeared or is under firm control.

5. DELTA (DETENTE—MANY STRUCTURAL STRESSES) THEMES

Something between a relatively "violent" Gamma World and an unusually "serene" Chi-Mu (see below) combination, often with much sound but little fury. Conflict may be nascent and potential—i.e., many inter- and intra-bloc crises and strains may exist which could escalate, but they seem to be under practical and effective control, even if this control is not always explicitly recognized in the public rhetoric. Thus, in contrast with the entente Gamma Worlds or hostile Chi Worlds, these are détente worlds. Conflicts still exist but there is a large measure of agreement on what to disagree about and how to handle conflicts. There is tacit acknowledgment of various nations' vital and traditional areas of interest, and implicit agreement on behavior in the low-level escalations which inevitably occur (or are caused). Because rules or conventions have been established, there is a widespread expectation that conflicts, at least in the foreseeable future, will not escalate to large-scale warfare. There may also be some effort to develop the entente conditions of the Gamma Worlds.

6. MU (EXTENSIVE MULTIPOLARITY) THEMES

This kind of world could involve the restoration of something like the old-fashioned Great Power nation-state system, possibly with an extensive diffusion of nuclear weapons. In all Mu Worlds there is at least a partial erosion or breakdown of bipolarity as the dominating form of the international structure, either because of the increasing strength, vigor and assertiveness of powers other than the Soviet Union and the United States, or because of an inability of the Soviet Union and the United States to utilize the strength they possess. Such conditions are usually, but not necessarily, at least initially associated with Delta Worlds.

7. ETA (CHALLENGES FROM EUROPE) THEMES

For more than 500 years Europe has been the great center of the modern world's civilization. For some 300 years Europe actually dominated the world. There are those who believe that after World War II Europe went into the same kind of irreversible decline as did the Egyptians, Assyrians, Persians, Classical Greeks, Romans, various Chinese dynasties, and even the Renaissance Italians, sixteenth-century Spanish and Portuguese, seventeenth-century Dutch, and eighteenth-century and nineteenth-century British. All eventually declined in power; so, it is assumed, has Europe as a whole declined—there is ample precedent for such decline. But even if this estimate were accurate, Europe could still be the breeding ground—an occasion and cause—of important international crises and other developments. But there is another possibility; particularly and most obviously because there has been a sustained and spectacular economic growth rate in Europe in the last decade, and an increasing political and military assertiveness, but for other reasons as well, Europeans are occupying more and more the center of the international stage, and as creators and major actors rather than as puppets or pawns. The belief of so many that the mantle of Europe was about to be inherited by the Soviets, the Americans, or the "new nations" is no longer so widely held—and thus many new (and old) issues are raised (and discussed in other papers in the Alternative World Futures project).

8. IOTA (CHALLENGES FROM JAPAN) THEMES

We turn now to the new political themes. Japan plays a very special role in our consideration of such future possibilities. It is possibly the most achievement-oriented of all modern societies; it is cohesive; it is technologically adept; it is in many ways the natural leader of Asia and the "non-white" peoples—though for various reasons, most rising out of its aggressive and provocative history in the second quarter of the twentieth century, it has not achieved this leadership. But it may turn out that Japan will become, as the last two Japanese Premiers have been fond of claiming, one of the three pillars of the modern democratic world—the other two, of course, being Europe and the United States. Or it may be that Japan will find a more assertive and independent role to play—either within or outside the framework of world affairs that exists today. In any case, any serious study of future possibilities must pay attention to the various roles which Japan can undertake.

9. PSI (CHALLENGES FROM CHINA) THEMES

China, of course, is the great contemporary bugaboo. It has replaced Genghis Khan and the Mongols, Tamerlane, the Turks, the yellow (Japanese) peril, even the Soviet menace, in much popular literature and thinking. The degree to which this is justified, the various ways these forebodings could materialize, obviously are important elements in any study of future possibilities. But the range is very wide and the full range should be considered.

10. LAMBDA (CHALLENGES FROM LATIN AMERICA) THEMES

For the last two centuries, Latin America has been culturally isolated from modern Europe, a world backwater—indeed, sometimes referred to as "a backwater of a backwater" (the Iberian Peninsula). But soon it, too, seems likely to claim a certain share of the center of the international stage both as a creator and an actor, as well as providing occasions for conflicts and competitions by others. Indeed, Latin America could, by the end of the twentieth century, prove to be one of the great new forces. By the year 2000 it is expected to have a population surpassing that of North America by perhaps 2 to 1, and a GNP which, while not comparable with that of North America in the year 2000, could be comparable to the U.S. GNP of today.

11. OMEGA (CHALLENGES FROM OTHER UNDERDEVELOPED NATIONS) THEMES

The important major areas here, of course, are Black Africa, the Arab League, the "Southern Tier" bordering the Soviet Union (Turkey, Iran, Afghanistan, Pakistan), India, Southeast Asia (including Indonesia and the Philippines), and perhaps Eastern Europe (including Yugoslavia and Greece) and the economically backward areas of Western Europe (Spain, Portugal, southern Italy and Ireland). All of these areas are either undergoing rapid change or experiencing serious frustration because they are not changing. All have their typical instabilities; all can present their typical challenges to the world.

Many will feel that we display a lack of focus and judgment in placing all these areas together in the single class of Omega themes, but we would judge, though experience may prove us wrong, that the emphasis is about right (i.e., from our point of view China and Latin America seem worth special attention; all of the other underdeveloped areas together are about equally important to these two).

12. UPSILON (NEW SUPER POWERS) THEMES

Hardest of all the possible worlds for an American or Russian to consider undoubtedly is one in which America and Russia are succeeded in world pre-eminence by another great power or by several new great powers. There are no obvious candidates for this new role or roles, nor (in the short run) is the transitional process easy to imagine. Yet it would perhaps have been no easier for a nineteenth-century Englishman to imagine the decline of British world power,[13] though in Russia and America there were plausible candidates for succession. Consider, though, a West European or all-European union which mobilized the material and intellectual resources of the continent to an aggressive political and military mission. Consider, too, that this kind of challenge might come at a time when the United States and the Soviet Union were undergoing a failure of nerve, or a disillusionment in their political ambitions, or an emotional withdrawal from world involvement, or even internal crises or failures that undermined their ability to carry on great power international policies. Or consider the possibility of a major part of Asia's finding inspired leadership and challenging the existing world powers by means of a political or revolutionary strategy that undercut their technological superiority. Even though this Upsilon World is the least easy to imagine, it is, in the long run, the most certain: Soviet and American primacy in the world is, on the evidence of history, certain to be transitory, and the interesting questions are really how long the primacy will endure and the process by which it will be ended.

13. RHO (MAJOR REALIGNMENTS) THEMES

One of the startling things about the twenty postwar years is the degree to which alliance relationships have been stable. However, the kind of flexible, rapid and even bewildering changes of partners that characterized the diplomacy of Europe and the world generally in the five centuries before World War I may in the future be to some degree restored. While it is unlikely that·alliance policies will be as flexible as during the Concert of Europe era, some important changes may occur in the current structure. Thus Rho Worlds envisage situations in which there not only has been a change in the classical bipolar structure, but actual realignment of the broken components or the new actors. Such realignments can be important and dramatic, and despite recent trends are common in history.

14. EPSILON (EROSION OR RESURGENCE OF THE WEST) THEMES

The world today presents a rather perplexing and paradoxical aspect. Everywhere many of the central ideals and concepts (dignity of individual man, progress, consent of the governed, technology, science, etc.) associated with Western Europe are more or less accepted, or paid lip service to (and from this point of view, Marxism and other current socialisms are all Western heresies, belonging, in large degree, to the Western tradition). In addition the

[13]But see the de Tocqueville quotation below for such a prediction.

physical prosperity of that part of the world made up of Western Europe and its direct progeny is at a peak, both relatively and absolutely (and it is interesting to note that most of the countries which are now modernizing most rapidly and successfully are the ones that tend to be closest in culture to Western Europe, i.e., Eastern Europe, Greece, southern Italy, Spain, Portugal, Ireland, and Latin America).

Yet Western Europe and even to some degree Western civilization is in a state of retreat or at least withdrawal. Much of this withdrawal is clearly voluntary and in part reflects a change in the concept of the national interest, the internal morale of the countries concerned—both colonizer and colony—and/or a change in moral or other standards. In part it is clearly a retreat forced by the development of forces that were themselves initially created, at least in part, by Western European precept and example and in part by a disillusionment with Western European ideals (resulting from the excesses of World Wars I and II even more than the excesses of colonialism). Nevertheless it is clear that the balance of physical power, technology, science, and probably even morale lies with Western Europe and the United States. (And to some degree the other areas of the world are likely to accept the Western nations at their own evaluation—thus, if these nations, as a group, achieve high morale the third world is likely to grant them great respect; when they have a low morale the third world, and others, will indeed be contemptuous of them.) It is not in the least inconceivable that the West may experience a renaissance of political assertiveness as well as of internal morale.

It is also quite possible that despite its material vigor the retreat of the West will continue, that there will be a further erosion of morale which may be followed by a decline in strength and dynamism. For example, if the Nazis had taken over Europe there would have been an abrupt repudiation of some important (but not all) Western ideals and values, even though physically Western Europe might have experienced an enormous increase in power. More likely than a revival of totalitarianism in its Hitlerian form seem developments along the line suggested by such authors as Spengler, Orwell, Huxley, Sorokin, and others. Or such a decline would take the form, which many see as common in history, of a weakening of the moral fiber of a society as a result of its very success. This might mean that these societies would no longer be capable of the kind of efforts necessary to compete with vigorous, enterprising, and dynamic "new" societies.

15. PHI (TYPICAL PHASES OR PATTERNS) THEMES

There are, of course, many cyclical theories or semi-cyclical theories of history. In our own country the names of Toynbee, Quigley, Sorokin and Spengler are usually associated with such ideas, though earlier centuries also had their theorists of rise and fall. Some of these, such as Toynbee's hypothesis of social "Challenge and Response," seem at least partially valid, describing a typical pattern of events even if failing to give a completely plausible explanation of this pattern. Many such theories can be used to supply a useful language, such as Sorokin's "Idealistic, Ideational and Sensate Cultures," without the use of this language necessarily implying any acceptance of the theoretical implications of Sorokin's analysis. One must also consider such patterns as are provided by variations in business cycles or in the recovery of nations which have been temporarily submerged as a result of defeats in war, etc.

16. TAU (TECHNOLOGICAL OPPORTUNITIES AND CHALLENGES) THEMES

To some degree these opportunities and challenges can be studied in isolation and we have so considered them in separate papers, but eventually our major interest will be studying how technology can affect the various worlds and be affected by these contexts.

17. NU (GALLOIS-MILLIS-KHRUSHCHEV NON-WAR) THEMES

These describe a particular type of arms control world in which the possibility of eruption to all-out wars or the large-scale use of thermonuclear weapons against a major power simply is not plausible—either actually or potentially —yet the world remains basically multipolar and mostly unorganized by any international sovereignty or explicit international institution, though these institutions may have important roles in certain Nu Worlds.

18. ALPHA (OTHER SUCCESSFUL "ARMS CONTROL") THEMES

In addition to the world described above there are other ways in which the use and control of nuclear threats and force could be more or less successfully controlled. Included is some greater legal ordering of the current relative disorder and anarchy of the world—the many different kinds of developments in the area of explicit international law and international legal arrangements generally as well as the implicit customs and expectations of a nation. We will also consider the newer aspects of arms control—ways by which access to, and the use of, violence might be controlled by agreement, conventions, and widely shared expectations. (These areas are also included, to some degree, in the Beta Worlds discussed below.) Finally, arms control practices and institutions might be built up on variations of the *lex talionis* rule.

19. PI (POST-NUCLEAR-USE INTERNATIONAL SYSTEMS) THEMES

If there is a third use of nuclear weapons (the first two having been at Hiroshima and Nagasaki) it is likely to be an important turning point of history. There is, first of all, the prospect of a new world system emerging from a war which destroys the old system—possibly a new system of one or several dictatorships, autocracies or technocracies established by the surviving nations; possibly a supranational authority established by the surviving political authorities or institutions (not necessarily nation-states) or by the participants in the war themselves; possibly a system closer to feudalism, a multiplicity of those regional powers or "city-states" which survive the destruction or discrediting of national governments; possibly, if the war had been really severe and extensive, something approaching world anarchy—a world of robber barons and isolated communities.

There is also the possibility of a less momentous use of nuclear weapons, but one in which the psychological impact and the expectations and images that are created have a profound effect on international relations. Some argue that this is one of the most important types of world to be considered, since if thermonuclear war (or some lesser use of nuclear weapons) really is likely or even a serious possibility, the shock of such war or use would plausibly make new political beginnings or radical international reforms a real possibility; it might prove important to have made some intellectual preparations that might provide useful guidance in such a crisis.

20. BETA (OTHER BASIC CHANGES IN INTERNATIONAL SYSTEM) THEMES

Other kinds of changes that could be associated with, or be independent of, the Alpha and Nu Worlds could also occur—in particular there could be some basic change in the nation-state system that has dominated international relations for the past three or four hundred years. While many consider our nation-state system to be the natural and inevitable way of organizing the existing world, during most of recorded history it would have been thought of as an unlikely and transitory system, and this judgment may yet turn out to be correct before the twentieth century is over. Such changes need not take the simple form of a constitutional or confederal world state. Many other structures are possible, some of which are discussed in this report.

21. OMICRON (OTHER) THEMES

This is clearly a catchall category which includes some international themes that could arise from internal changes in the United States or Europe other than those that have already been suggested in other categories. For example, one might imagine the United States developing by the end of the century into a high-consumption, leisure-oriented society, in which the European tradition of the gentleman of leisure would be to some extent re-established —that is, individuals would emphasize acquiring and using different kinds of skills, few of which were related to their normal vocations. (Thus if one asked somebody in this situation what he was or did, he would be likely to reply that he was a skier, a diver, an artist or a poet rather than a manager, lawyer or computer programmer.) Such a U.S. is compatible with a "smug, self-satisfied" neo-isolationism, a crusading interventionism, an attitude of objective observer and/or active participant in the international scene, or with a frightened, or blasé, selfish nationalism jealously guarding or aggrandizing U.S. wealth—but all with overtones which reflect the emphasis on high consumption and leisure.

There are other possibilities, too. For example, we have considered elsewhere the rise of a near-"Orwellian" 1984 state through the continued heavy involvement of the United States in a large number of foreign areas and the consequent effects on people of this kind of medium-level but dramatic and "institutionalized" war. Such a situation might also lead to a revival of what might be thought of as the "Roman virtues," or to a kind of garrison state. Another scenario suggests a neo-isolationist withdrawal by the United States from international affairs, perhaps followed by an abrupt and dangerous return. All these and many other possibilities need consideration.

Caveats on the Propaedeutic and Heuristic Material Presented in this Report

It is clear that without generalizing it is impossible either to organize data or to present it effectively. Yet any generalization is almost certain to be false if pressed too far. In this report we are attempting to deal with extremely complex subjects, and the generalizations we will find useful will often, comparatively speaking, be less justified and reasonable than is normal in scholarly work. Thus our emphasis on the propaedeutic and heuristic—our attempt to deal with subjects with sufficient sophistication to give those skilled in areas other than international relations, sociology, anthropology, and technology, the background they may need for synthesis or integration of disciplines. We do not, of course, claim in this short essay to supply more than some contexts that can structure a beginning of studies of these problems. It is important for the reader, however, to be very conscious of the relative superficiality and inaccuracy of some of our generalizations. In this respect another kind of example may be useful.

Consider the four sets of curves which are shown in Figure 1. Assume that the first two curves (Set A) describe respectively the distribution of heights among men and women. The two curves indicate, as they should, that there are some men who are shorter than some women, yet we would be willing to characterize the relationship between the two curves of Set A as indicating that "men are taller than women" and few would argue, despite the overlap, that this was an inaccurate statement. (However, if we are manufacturing clothes for the two groups, it would be important to note the overlap or somebody will be very badly or inappropriately fitted.)

We can still make the same statement even if the situation is as illustrated by Set B, and the overlap between the two curves is larger than in Set A. But under these circumstances the generalization that "men are taller than women" might be less useful and less interesting—depending on the circum-

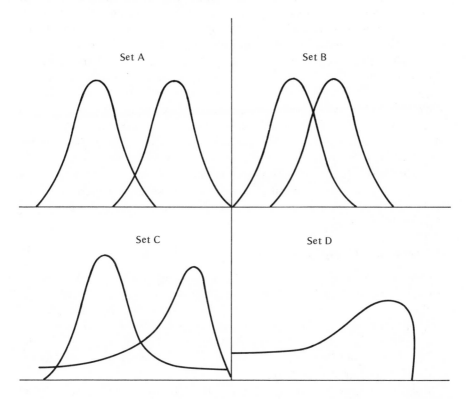

Set A   Set B

Set C   Set D

stances—and we would also be slightly less willing to make it; but under some circumstances it would be a useful observation and we might feel willing to make the generalization. We might be willing to make the generalization that "men are taller than women" even if (as illustrated by Set C) some men were shorter than the shortest women or even if some women were taller than the tallest man.

Or consider, for another example, the curve in Set D, which could (but does not) indicate the distribution of blond hair color, from light to dark, among Germans. We sometimes say that Germans are blond, but the curve indicates that the majority of Germans are brunet. Yet Germany does have more blonds than most European countries, though not as many as does Scandinavia. Even among the Scandinavians, who are usually thought of as blond, it turns out that by any strict definition, blonds are still in a minority —probably less than half the population.[14] Yet a good many people seen on the streets of Stockholm or Copenhagen are blond. If we were contrasting Germans with French or Italians or Spaniards, we might still be willing to say

[14]If reliable statistics exist, I would be grateful for the reference.

that Germans are blond, or we might tend to qualify the statement and say "relatively blond," and this might be an interesting piece of information. However, if the situation was as in Set D of Figure 1, but reversed, we should have no hesitation in making the generalization, "Germans are blond"—even though almost half were not blond. (We do hesitate to make such statements, of course, but for reasons that are sociopolitical and emotional rather than statistical.)

We will find it convenient to make exactly these kinds of sweeping generalizations in the material which follows, and we will warn the reader when we feel a warning is of special importance; but we do not wish to clog the presentation with caveats and qualifications, so we will rewarn the reader only when we believe it is specially important to remind or alert him to the possibility that a generalization is subject to misuse or is being pushed to the limit. We will leave warnings out elsewhere, though we understand there is danger in so doing.

The Method of Classes of Variables

We are attempting to examine, look at, and discuss the future. We are not, of course, trying to pick the winner of a horse race, only to describe most of the important horses that are running—important perhaps because the probability of winning is high or because the payoff for winning is so spectacular, or for an appropriate combination of probability and intrinsic importance. We would also like to give some "feel" or orientation as to the reasonable odds on various horses.

In trying to examine the variables which might affect important issues of the future or even determine them to some degree, we find it convenient to divide them into six categories as indicated below:[15]

1. **Relatively Stable:** Climate, gross topography, language, religion, "national character, institutions and style," many frontiers, etc.
2. **Slowly (Exponentially or Linearly?) Changing:** Natural resources, demography, capital resources, skill and training, technology, GNP, welfare policies, etc.
3. **"Predictable":** Typical scenarios, prime movers, overriding problems, etc.
4. **Constrained:** More political changes, alliances, business activity, defense budget, morale, military posture, military skill, etc.
5. **Accidental:** Some outcomes of war or revolution, many natural calamities, some kinds of personalities, some kinds of foreign pressures and intervention, some kinds of other events.
6. **Incalculable:** Excessively complex or sensitive or involving unknown or unanalyzed mechanisms of causes in an important way.

[15]For a somewhat different scheme see "Twelve Modes of Prediction" by Daniel Bell in *Daedalus* (summer, 1965), Vol. 3, No. 3 of the Proceedings of the American Academy of Arts and Sciences.

To the extent that one feels the future is more or less predictable, one tends to emphasize the importance of the first categories—particularly the first four. To the extent that one feels the future is unpredictable, one tends to emphasize the latter categories—particularly the fifth and sixth. We, of course, will adopt the position that many important aspects of the future are predictable—particularly if "other things are equal"—that many important aspects are not, and that the effect of the predictable things may be quite different from what we think because of the effects of the unpredictable variables—yet that it still may be worthwhile to try to "predict" that which can be predicted, or at least to describe the possibilities and turning points. Indeed, it is the purpose of policy to plan for that which is more or less predictable and hedge against that which is uncertain, both to be able to exploit favorable events and to guard against the consequences of unfavorable ones.

The first class of variables, the Relatively Stable, are by definition slow to change, though they may change faster than is usually believed. Thus the climate of an area can certainly change within a matter of centuries, perhaps even within decades. Topography also can change. In fact, some soil specialists have argued that it has usually taken about a thousand years for a typical civilization to wear out the fertility of the soil.[16] There now exist relatively efficient possibilities for deliberate topographical engineering, so this rate might in the future be slowed down indefinitely, or even speeded up for specific purposes. Language is also always evolving and, in particular, may become "corrupted." In any case there is an enormous difference in the speaking style of Americans today and pre-World War I. Similarly, religion, or at least its social content and influence, may change quite rapidly, though the forms tend to change slowly. But the change can still be revolutionary even though the form is not explicitly affected to a great degree.

. . . National character, institutions and style change remarkedly slowly even in the modern world, and . . . in many areas one can often see traits today that are directly traceable to characteristics formed a hundred or even a thousand years earlier. Frontiers too seem today remarkable stable. Latin America has several simmering disputes, but none that seem likely to boil; Western Europe (except for the German frontiers) looks remarkably stable, and so on. The crucial point about these relatively stable variables, however, is that while they can indeed change, for many of our predictions, particularly those dealing with a decade or so ahead, the change in these variables is likely to be small or negligible. This is so obvious that we often do not realize that we are assuming they are constant when we are making predictions. So we need not only to make the point that this is a reasonable assumption, but also that it is an assumption that could be wrong.

[16]See, for example, *Topsoil and Civilization* by T. Dale and V. G. Carter (University of Oklahoma Press, 1955).

The second class of variables, the Slowly (Exponentially or Linearly?) Changing, are the kind most usually studied when one is "predicting." One can often do amazingly well on these variables, at least in the short or medium run, and occasionally even in the long run. While these variables change, the change tends both to be slow and proportional to what already exists, so that if one knows what the variable is and the rate of change, extrapolation is possible. If the rate of change is more or less a constant percentage (or if one can meaningfully use an average rate), we call this an exponential variable—and it is then, of course, quite predictable. Such variables are national resources, demographic composition of the population, capital resources, skilled training, technological capability, gross national product; and to a lesser extent many welfare and tax policies, tend to change in this way. (At least in many modern societies there seems to be a built-in tendency for many such welfare and tax policies, once started, to be extended—for example, the income tax. When this was first introduced into the United States some fifty years ago, the tax rate was about 1 percent with very generous allowances, and it was considered onerous. We have seen it rise in recent

FIGURE 2: WORLD ENERGY CONSUMPTION.

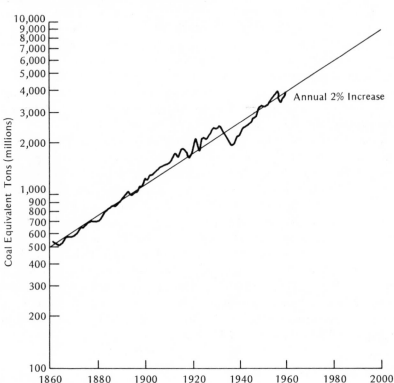

(From World Population and Resources) PEP [Political & Economic Planning], London, 1955.)

years to 94 percent in some brackets, though the maximum has now dropped to 78 percent.) It is reasonable in a democracy that this kind of increase should occur, even overshoot, and then drop back, but the rate of increase may be quite as predictable as with some of the other variables. Other of these variables have relatively constant or characteristic rates and thus allow for relatively precise predictions—at least as long as the basic structural relations do not change. Typical variables of interest to us are given on the next ten charts, which have been selected to show the large range of variables which seem to obey simple constant, exponential, or at least predictable growth curves—at least within a reasonable range of values. The curves also indicate that there must often eventually be a "topping out" or exhaustion phenomenon.

As described later, such simple extrapolations, in the form of "envelope curves" may turn out to be startlingly accurate, often more accurate than more complicated and seemingly more sophisticated predictions done by experts, and there are good reasons why this should be expected.

A good example of a prediction based on the first two classes of variables

FIGURE 3: GROWTH OF SHORT-HAUL CARRIER CHANNELS.

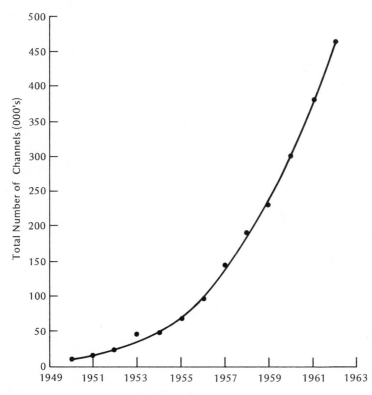

(From Bell Labs. Record, July–Aug., 1963.)

is de Tocqueville's famous anticipation (in 1835) of the cold war and bipolar world.[17]

> There are at the present time two great nations in the world, which started from different points, but seem to tend towards the same end. I allude to the Russians and the Americans. Both of them have grown up unnoticed; and while the attention of mankind was directed elsewhere, they have suddenly placed themselves in the front rank among the nations, and the world learned their existence and their greatness at almost the same time.
>
> All other nations seem to have nearly reached their natural limits, and they have only to maintain their power; but these are still in the act of growth. All the others have stopped, or continue to advance with ex-

FIGURE 4: GROSS NATIONAL PRODUCT AND RESEARCH DEVELOPMENT.

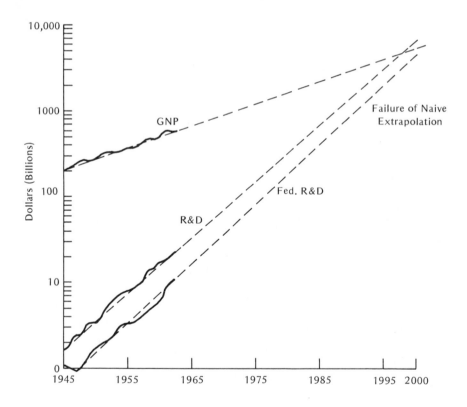

(*From* International Science & Technology, *Dec., 1963.*)

[17]*Democracy in America*, translated by Henry Reeve (New York: Schocken Books, 1959), pp. 521–522.

treme difficulty; these alone are proceeding with ease and celerity along a path to which no limit can be perceived. The American struggles against the obstacles that nature opposes to him; the adversaries of the Russian are men. The former combats the wilderness and savage life; the latter, civilization with all its arms. The conquests of the American are therefore gained by the plowshare; those of the Russian by the sword. The Anglo-American relies upon personal interest to accomplish his ends and gives free scope to the unguided strength and common sense of the people; the Russian centers all the authority of society in a single arm. The principal instrument of the former is freedom; of the latter, servitude. Their starting-point is different and their courses are not the same; yet each of them seems marked out by the will of Heaven to sway the destinies of half the globe.

Next are what we call "predictable" variables. These are of special significance not because they are necessarily the most important but because

FIGURE 5: CORPORATION OFFICIALS WITH SCIENCE OR ENGINEERING DEGREES OR EQUIVALENT EXPERIENCE.

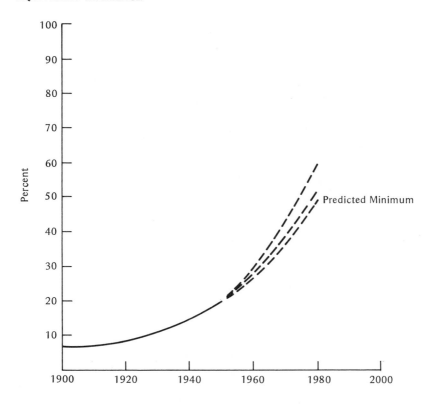

(From J. R. Killian [MIT], Electronic News, Dec. 7, 1964.)

they are reasonably predictable and usually overlooked so that competent policy research can play an important role in dealing with them—i.e., this is an area in which one can often "do something," even if nothing often is done unless attention is directed, perhaps by a policy research organization, to the issue. Naturally we will concentrate, to an extent, on this category of variables.

But what do we mean by "predictable"? For one thing, we can discuss situations in which certain variables can be described by typical scenarios or sequences. We need not claim that the described pattern will inevitably be followed, simply that it may be followed and the possibility should be allowed for.

Thus, any of the "simple" theories given earlier are examples of rather good "predictive rules" that are often suggestive of what may happen, although none of them are inevitable. We can rephrase them to show how they can be used to raise questions:

FIGURE 6: PHYSICS DOCTORATES GRANTED ANNUALLY.

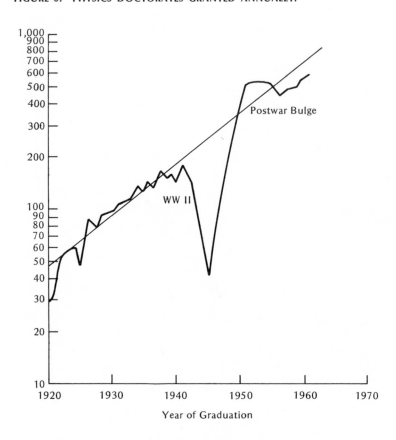

Year of Graduation

(From Physics Today.)

POLITICAL RULES

The friend of an enemy is . . .
The ally of an enemy is . . .
The enemy of an enemy is . . .
If the basis for an alliance changes . . .
A submerged hostile emotion may emerge when . . .

ECONOMIC RULES

Since bourgeoisation accompanies a creative industrialization . . .
If an economic trend is anticipated . . .

STRATEGIC RULES

If one's offensive weapons are vulnerable . . .
If one's civilians are vulnerable . . .

FIGURE 7: UNIT SALES OF COMPUTERS AND EDP'S.

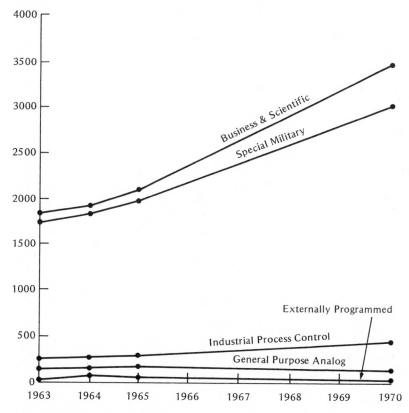

(From Industrial Res., June, 1964.)

When deterrence becomes a two-way street . . .

"Permanent" conditions are more important than defeats and wartime disorganization, so . . .

Since technological secrets are rarely kept more than five or ten years . . .

A most important example of a simple prediction which is often underestimated (or overestimated) is that decision-makers die and others take their place. Thus as of the end of 1968, consider the ages of the following statesmen:

Bustamante	84
Chiang Kai-shek	82
Salazar	79
de Gaulle	78
Franco	76
Tito	76
Ho Chi Minh	76
Jomo Kenyatta	75
Mao Tse-tung	75
Ulbricht	75

The typical underestimation of the significance of this factor is to ignore the fact that these decision-makers will be replaced. The typical overestimation

FIGURE 8: PRODUCTIVITY OF FARM LABOR.

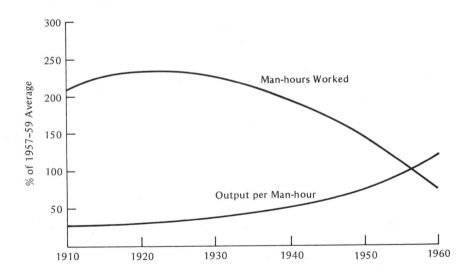

(*From* International Science Technology, *Dec., 1963.*)

comes in believing that such changes will necessarily produce immediate and dramatic differences. They sometimes do, but more usually they mean, at most, the start or acceleration of a developing or continuing process.

An important example of a typical scenario or prototype is discussed by Crane Brinton in his book, *Anatomy of Revolution*,[18] discussing one possible sequence for a progressive revolution:

1. *Ancien régime* morale, etc.
2. The rule of the moderates
3. The revolt of the extremists
4. The appeal to the conservatives
5. The accession of the extremists
6. Reigns of terror and virtue
7. Thermidor
8. Long-term changes

FIGURE 9: NUCLEAR POWER.

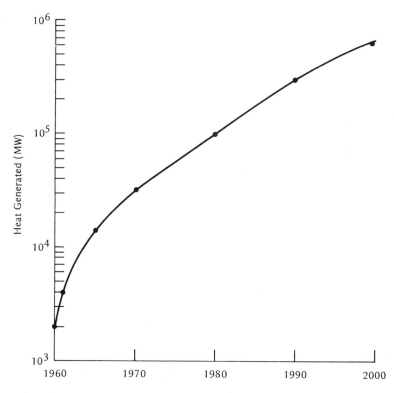

(*From* Nucleonics.)

[18](New York: Vintage Books, 1960).

It is startling how useful the above categories are in discussing the possibilities for a progressive revolution.

Another important example of a "predictable" effect occurs when a single dominating variable is crucially important—when there is what can be called a prime mover. Examples of prime movers might include the well known Japanese desire for prestige and status; the role the ownership of the means of production plays in Marxian theory; the pervading (and oppressive) influence of the United States on Latin American radical movements and their search for self-definition; some of the effects of modernization on traditional societies; the so-called "Americanization" that occurs in a high-consumption twentieth-century society; and so on. Similarly, if there is some overriding problem, such as defense from an imminent threat (early NATO), or dealing with a near-universal war guilt (postwar Germany), or internal war against a well-entrenched government (almost any postwar subversive movement), and so on, then typically there are only a small number of solutions possible and one of these will be identified and used, producing many similarities or

FIGURE 10: CREEP LIMIT AUSTENITIC STEELS.

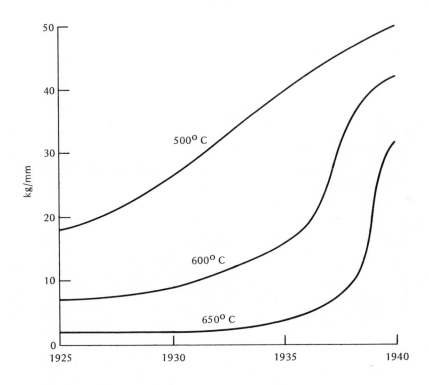

(From H. Thirring. Energy for Man, Harper & Row, New York, 1962.)

analogies to historical events. This does not mean that there are no special or specific characteristics that are important, but only that there are some aspects in many situations which are relatively general and which can be identified.

The fourth group of variables are called "constrained," since although they are to some extent predictable, they depend more on details than do the generalizations mentioned above. Factors such as political changes, alliances, business activity, defense budget, morale, military posture, military skill, etc., operate within reasonably precise and usually known constraints— at least within reasonable limits. Barring a revolution, a government can be just so radical or conservative. Under modern conditions the defense budget can be as low as 1 percent of GNP or as high as 50 percent, most likely oscillating between 5 percent and 15 percent, and so on. There are only a limited number or range of possibilities and they can be strong or weak, good or bad, high or low, etc.

The fifth category of factors is the accidental ones. In many cases the out-

FIGURE 11: ROCKET THRUST (PLOTTED ACCORDING TO YEAR OF INITIATION).

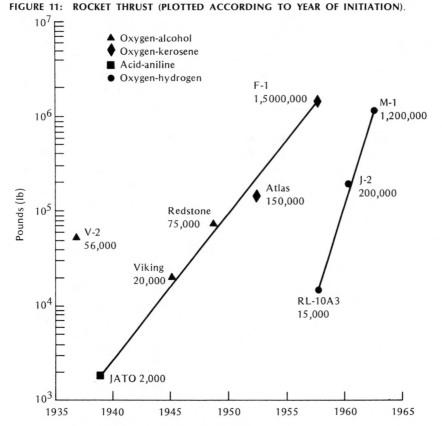

(*From* International Science & Technology, *Dec., 1962.*)

come of a war or revolution seems almost probabilistic. For example, the Germans *might* have won World War I in a few weeks just as Schlieffen had hoped, and the whole history of our times would then have been different. In particular, the disillusionment experienced by—and with—Europe's society in the interwar years might not have occurred, and such commonplace beliefs as that "war is unthinkable," "war never pays," and "war does not decide anything," would quite possibly never have become commonplace. Indeed, war, in the 1920's and 1930's, might have been seen as advantageous and useful. Similarly, Hitler came very close to winning World War II. One can argue that if Mussolini had never attacked Greece, or if the Yugoslavs had not resisted Hitler's attack, or if the 1941 winter in the Soviet Union had not been so severe, Hitler might have won at least the war against Russia. (Most members of the general staffs of the British, French, German, American and Russian armies seemed to have felt that Hitler had the war "won" at the end of the first summer campaign in Russia.)

If Germany had won either of these two wars, de Tocqueville's famous prediction most likely would not have become true in our day. Yet the old factors which de Tocqueville had identified did operate in the way he had expected, coming to fruition in 1945. Predictable and relatively analyzable factors can be very important so long as they are not interfered with by what we here call accidental events.

Finally, it is, of course, important to note that even if there were no accidents or intrinsic uncertainties, in the probabilistic sense all events still could not necessarily be predicted. Even without getting into the free will argument we note that human societies are complicated beyond the power of scientific generalization. The atomic nucleus or the genetic code are both much less complicated than social and historical action and interaction; both are only now beginning to be understood. We may still be in the nineteenth or much earlier centuries with regard to any "science" of public policy. Thus while we may not be prevented from breeding cattle or discovering and using radium, we do need to be heavily empirical and intuitive about many or most policy issues.

5

The Delphi Technique And The Cross-Impact Matrix

DELPHI AND CROSS-IMPACT TECHNIQUES: AN EFFECTIVE COMBINATION FOR SYSTEMATIC FUTURES ANALYSIS

 selwyn enzer

In but a few decades our time has been alternatively called the atomic age, the space age, and the age of automation. Perhaps it may be more accurate to call our time simply the age of change. For indeed we are experiencing many major changes in our society. Progress in science and technology has produced changes which have already affected our planet markedly, and progress in biogenetic engineering may soon lead to changes in man himself. However, these changes are also evident in our concepts of society and social order. As a result, the coming decades may be called the age of improving the quality of life and the age of technological assessment.

An awareness of the need for social control over aspects of change in our society is evidenced in many government programmes. However, moving from problem awareness to effective control or corrective action requires a level of technological and sociological understanding which can promote appropriate decisions. Decisions concerning society typically involve long time-lags between action and reaction. They also involve data, and considerations which are highly subjective—subjective in the sense that they do not obey any known specifiable laws and must, therefore, be evaluated judgmentally.

Of course, any decision, regardless of the type of data on which it is presumed to rest, involves judgment—typically value judgments regarding effectiveness, cost, and risk. And, in spite of widespread use of systematic planning techniques, complex problems—particularly social problems—still defy meaningful analysis. This leads to difficulties in anticipating prospective changes sufficiently far into the future to improve long-range decisions and avoid either premature obsolescence or unexpected difficulties.

The combination of long-term programmes and the rapid pace of change has shaken the confidence of many decision-makers who are too frequently confronted with programmes that are out-dated before they are completed. NASA's Dyna Soar and the US Air Force's Manned Orbital Laboratory programmes are two examples of this problem. Numerous less-publicised examples of this type can be found in many aspects of our society, including our every-day lives.

On the other hand, premature obsolescence may be less significant than many of the technologically-caused problems we face today, because accompanying our propensity for change has been a marked increase in the magnitude of changes we have produced. Major changes can produce secondary effects which can be highly important in their own right. Moreover, when they are coupled with the secondary effects of other programmes, they can produce changes of still greater magnitude. And, since our ability to anticipate prospective developments for single programmes is limited, we experience even greater difficulties in effectively anticipating the interrelated consequences of many actions.

Futures research is directed toward the goal of providing greater insight into prospective developments and their interactions in a dynamic society. This research is not a passive or merely intellectual exercise; that is, it is not premised on the assumption that the future is inevitable and that the business of the forecaster is simply to describe it as it will be. On the contrary, futures research assumes a multiplicity of possible futures and the necessity of choosing among them. For this reason, such research is intimately tied to the present in that it attempts to provide today's decision-makers not only with an improved ability to anticipate likely occurrences, but to evaluate how their actions can change the outcomes.

The elements of a futures analysis are very similiar to those of a systems analysis and are relatively insensitive to the specific issues being addressed. Generally involved are the steps outlined in Table 1. The initial step is concerned with defining the problem in as clear and concise a manner as possible, understanding the dynamics of the functions involved, and establishing the nature of the information needed to enable the decision-maker to act most effectively. Failure to understand and organise these aspects may often be the cause of an ineffective analysis.

Subsequently the analysis is concerned with forecasting the developments relevant to the issue. Initially non-intervention on the part of the decision-maker is assumed. It should be emphasised that 'non-intervention' here means

TABLE 1: Elements of Futures Analysis

Issue-oriented information
  Objectives
  Scope (relevant domain, time period)
  Factors influencing the issue (values, motivations)
  Information needs (indicators, measures of effectiveness, credibility)
  Current status
Prospective developments
  Major events
  Event-oriented information (likelihood, time-period, importance, desirability)
  Event interactions
Potential actions
  Alternatives
  Anticipated effect on events
Alternative futures
  Potential outcomes (likelihood, time period)
  Assessment of outcomes (indicators, measures of effectiveness, credibility)
  Most important alternatives and actions

---

no change from current behaviour, that is, maintenance of the *status quo*. The third step explicitly addresses the actions that reflect alternatives which the decision-maker controls and the possible effects of choosing those alternatives on the outcomes that might otherwise be expected.

The final step consists of the identification and assessment of the potential futures, and the determination of those outcomes which are most important for the decision-maker to address. This is not to be interpreted in terms of the best or most desirable outcome, but rather by a combination of probability and desirability (or undesirability). These 'most important' outcomes, including the possible actions they embody, are intended to provide the framework for more rigorous operations analyses before any specific recommendations are made.

The following paragraphs discuss an approach to that portion of futures analyses concerned with anticipating likely developments and alternative actions. Two experimental techniques being used for systematically assessing expert judgment in evaluating future-oriented issues—the Delphi technique and cross-impact analysis—are described and shown to be highly effective when used in conjunction with each other. As will be seen, the use of these techniques in this manner requires that the information derived from the Delphi process be in the format required for cross-impact analysis.

Prospective Developments

Only if the decision-maker understands the likely consequences of inaction can he determine the need for action on his part. This requires understanding at least the major developments (or events) that may occur in the time period of interest, relevant to the issues being considered.

Developments or events as referred to here denote specific items which may occur in the future. They are 'specific' in the sense that their occurrence or non-occurrence can be rigorously determined. In this context, scientific breakthroughs, political or social actions, and trends are all admissible. However, each must be specified so that occurrence or non-occurrence can be rigorously determined on a yes-or-no basis. This can be quite difficult when the quantitative indicator of an event can change by relatively small values. For example, an event can be that by some time in the future the population will be K people or more. Introducing such events on a specific yes/no basis implies that a population of K has a given level of importance, whereas a population of $K - 1$ is of a different level of importance. Clearly, when K is very large, this difference is trivial.

Identification and definition of prospective developments alone is inadequate; the likelihood of occurrence of these developments as a function of time also must be determined. And it must at least be recognized that the likelihood of occurrence of any one event typically depends upon the occurrence or non-occurrence of other future events which precede the event in question.

A futures analysis attempts to evaluate the prospects reflected in combinations of potential events, considering all of their possible sequences and alternative actions for the time period of interest. Clearly, many futures are possible. And, when many events are included, the likelihood of a single combination in any one sequence is typically very slight. Therefore, a futures analysis is apt to be more concerned with identifying populations of similar outcomes and determining what the relative desirability of these populations is and how amenable they are to changes in the face of possible action programmes.

To satisfy these needs, forecasts must be obtained in a manner that permits analysis not only of changes in likelihoods of individual events, but also of alternative permutations and combinations. Efficiency in this procedure is highly important. Since an extremely large number of possibilities may be derived from an array of events including alternative actions, data compaction is practically a necessity. Consequently, the nature of the forecasted data is dictated more by the informational processing technique than by the issue being studied.

The Delphi and cross-impact techniques can be highly effective in dealing with this problem in futures research. These techniques are discussed in the following pages. First, cross-impact analysis is described. This is followed by a discussion of the nature of the information to be forecasted and a description of the Delphi technique, which is recommended for obtaining this information. Finally, an experiment using these techniques is described and discussed, whose aims, structure and results were presented in the previous issue of *Futures*.[1]

Cross-Impact Analysis

Cross-impact analysis[2] is an experimental tool that attempts to evaluate average likelihoods of occurrence for each event in a set of inter-related events, considering all possible sequences and occurrences or non-occurrences among the events in the set. "Inter-relations among events" refers to the increase or decrease in the likelihood of occurrence of a subsequent event produced by the occurrence or non-occurrence of all predecessor events in the set.

To perform a cross-impact analysis, a specific set of events and probabilistic data must be obtained. This consists of the relevant events believed to be important to the issues in the time period being investigated; estimates of their initial (or individual) likelihoods of occurrence; and a quantitative description of the effect of the occurrence (or non-occurrence) of one event on the likelihood of occurrence of each of the others in the set.

All important events which are coupled (a term explained below), which are relevant to the issue or issues being evaluated, and whose outcome is uncertain (as opposed to those that almost certainly will or will not occur) should be included in the set to be analysed. Practical computational con-

[1]Selwyn Enzer, "A Case Study Using Forecasting as a Decision-making Aid," *Futures* 2, No. 4 (December, 1970).

[2]T. J. Gordon and H. Hayward, "Initial Experiments With the Cross-impact Matrix Method of Forecasting," *Futures* 1, No. 2 (December, 1968).

straints often necessitate limiting the number of events that can be handled. These constraints include both subjective input requirements and computer capacity.

"Coupling of events" refers to the manner in which the occurrence or non-occurrence of one event affects the likelihood of a subsequent event. Three types of coupling are possible: 1. totally uncoupled, 2. coupled, and 3. totally included. Figure 1 illustrates each of these types.

Events which are *totally uncoupled*, are those whose occurrence or non-occurrence has no effect on the likelihood of occurrence of the others in the set. These should not be included in a cross-impact matrix. For a simple example of uncoupled events, consider the issue of the future economic state of some country. Event A may refer to the discovery of a mineral deposit in that country, and event B to the size of the fishing harvest at some time in the future. Events A and B may be regarded as uncoupled since the occurrence of A appears to have no impact on the likelihood of occurrence of B, and *vice versa.*

In actual analyses, uncoupled events are of relatively little importance, since the events which are both important and relevant to a particular issue are rarely uncoupled from all of the other events in the set.

Coupled events also can be illustrated using the same example. Consider event A to refer to the size of agricultural harvests, and event B to be the development of low-cost electric power at some time in the future. It may be

FIGURE 1: RELATIONSHIPS AMONG EVENTS

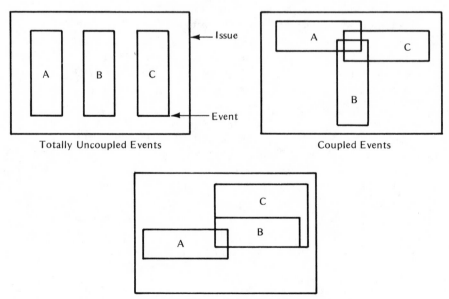

Totally Uncoupled Events

Coupled Events

Totally Included Events

argued that event B could lead to an economical source of water for irrigation through de-salination and thereby strongly enhance the likelihood of an increased harvest. Important coupled events should always be included in a cross-impact analysis.

Totally included events can be illustrated by expanding the previous example. This expansion consists of including as an explicit event, event C, the development of a means of obtaining low-cost water for irrigation. If C is the result of B, the impact of event B on A may now be considered fully contained in C. And, while the occurrence of B may increase the likelihood of occurrence of C, it would be incorrect to note both B and C as having directly enhancing impacts on A. Totally included events may be included in a cross-impact analysis, but care must be taken to avoid estimating their impacts more than once.

Performing a cross-impact analysis of the totally uncoupled type requires estimates of initial individual likelihoods of occurrence and of the cross-impact factors among the events in the set. In providing the initial probability estimates, the forecaster considers an environment which might have normally evolved from present circumstances. He then develops the cross-impact factors by assessing the inter-relationships among the events in terms of whether the occurrence of each event increases or decreases the likelihood of occurrence of each of the other events, and if so, to what degree. These inter-relationships are evaluated to determine the 'final' likelihoods of occurrence of each event in the set. These final probabilities represent the average likelihood of occurrence of each event considering the accumulated impacts of all of the occurrences of the other events in the set, but restricted to interactions among pairs of events only.

The analysis can be performed with no preferred sequence of occurrence among the events, that is, in a random order, which is used only in the absence of information which could fix the sequence. Conditional sequences, such as one in which event A must come after B, or A is to be included in the set only after B and then only if B is deemed to occur (or not occur), are also permitted. The final probabilities reflect the effects that a specified or random sequence and the cross-impact factors have on the likelihood of occurrence of the other events in the set.

The major advantages of the cross-impact technique are its ability to account for interactions among many events systematically; to organise data describing a large number of possible outcomes so that a *relatively* small number of inputs are sufficient; to test the sensitivity of average outcomes to changes in initial likelihoods of occurrence or in sequence, or both; and to provide logical retraceability, in that a change in probability (initial to final) can be reviewed and the reasons why the change occurred can be ascertained, at least generally.

The major weaknesses of the cross-impact technique (as originally conceived) are that it does not account for the effect of non-occurrence of events, a situation which leads to ambiguity in defining the initial likelihoods of occurrence; the definition of the cross-impact factors is not specific; the mathematical transform and analytic procedure has no logical justification; the relative likelihood of individual sequences of events cannot be directly assessed; and only the interactions among event-pairs are considered.

Forecast Requirements (Delphi Technique)

The literature on major social issues always abounds with anticipated developments. These are typically the result of individual or group analyses or foresight, and they are generally reviewed by decision-makers in attempting to steer an appropriate course into the future. However, group opinion regarding likely future developments is often more important to decisions which represent or affect social actions or anticipations.

The common vehicles for obtaining these opinions include conferences, elections, and polling. And these are likely to continue to be the prime vehicles for obtaining such judgments. However, there are other techniques which systematically elicit judgments that appear to be capable of improving group insight into likely occurrences. The Delphi technique is an attractive, although still experimental, method of overcoming some of the difficulties encountered in using other methods. Delphi is a programme of sequential interrogations, interspersed with information and opinion feedback.[3] It is generally used to promote communication to enhance the prospects of obtaining group consensus regarding possible future developments.

Effective communication is often inhibited in a conventional conference by psychological factors, oratorical salesmanship, an inability to assure that all points of view are heard, specious arguments, and, perhaps most important, lack of concise documented statements of what has transpired. The Delphi technique attempts to maximise the focus and quality of the communication within the group by systematically exploring—in an objective environment—factors relevant to a given issue.

The Delphi process can be viewed as a series of controlled conferences. As such, it has two main characteristics:

- Individual contributions are requested from each participant simultaneously at each step, without knowledge of the inputs being submitted by the others for that step.
- Anonymity of the inputs (and, if possible, also of the participants) is maintained throughout the entire conference.

A Delphi conference typically sets aside areas on which the panel agrees and focuses upon areas of disagreement during subsequent rounds. Because Delphi conferences are typically conducted in writing, they produce concise

---

[3]N. C. Dalkey and O. Helmer, "An Experimental Application of the Delphi Method to the Use of Experts," *Management Science* 9, No. 3 (April, 1963).

written summaries of areas of consensus and dissensus, and the arguments supporting alternative view points. This product is often of value long after the conference is completed. However, a Delphi conference often compromises the desirable features of a conventional conference, such as speed, ability to perform a large number of iterations, and intellectual stimulation.

Concern over these limitations has given rise to Delphi research in which open discussions, or personal interviews take the place of written questionnaires in one or more rounds of the inquiry. It is too early, however, to judge the value of this research to make firm recommendations regarding desirable combinations or sequences of the possible types of interrogation.

While considerable research has been devoted to understanding the theory and mechanics of the Delphi technique in order to improve its accuracy,[4] it appears from actual practice that the most important advantages of the technique are those that stem from the improved communication that results from anonymity. It is anonymity which enables the Delphi technique to overcome many psychological barriers to communication, such as a reluctance to state unpopular views, to disagree with one's superiors or associates, or to modify previously stated positions. On the other hand, anonymity sacrifices individual recognition as a motive for contributing freely to the inquiry. Therefore, it is highly unlikely that participants in a Delphi conference will disclose, for example, the results of their latest (unpublished) research. It is equally unlikely that they will disclose proprietary information. However, the Delphi technique can be used effectively to bring together many points of view on complex issues to produce a group position that may otherwise be undetectable. Anonymity provides the necessary ingredient for accomplishing this objective, not just in theory, but in practice.

The Case Study

Cross-impact and Delphi techniques were used in a case study performed in September 1969 for the Seminar on Public Administration at the College of Europe in Bruges, Belgium. In this study 33 government officials from more than 10 countries explored a number of events they considered important to the economic, social, and political environment of Europe, for the 1970–80 decade.

In the course of the experiment ten events were selected which were likely to be important for the future of Europe if they occurred. Numerical estimates of their likelihood of occurrence was estimated, using the Delphi technique. The group then estimated the interdependence among the events, and the spread of opinion regarding these factors was presented in a table.

The spread of opinion regarding these factors is presented in Figure 2.

[4]N. C. Dalkey, "An Experimental Study of Group Opinion," *Futures* 1, No. 5 (September, 1969), and N. C. Dalkey, "Analyses From A Group Opinion Study," *Futures* 1, No. 6 (December, 1969).

Because these data are obtained from a Delphi analysis, the range of opinion regarding the cross-impacts is also available.

In addition to their use in the cross-impact analysis, the data presented in Figure 2 can be used in many other ways to determine factors related to potential decisions and actions. For example, the sum of the absolute values of a horizontal row is a measure of the magnitude of the impact that the occurrence of one event might have on the likelihood of occurrence of the other events in the set. This is an indicator of the sensitivity of the likelihood of occurrence of the other events in the set to the occurrence of that event, or to a change in sequence which accelerates or delays the occurrence of that

FIGURE 2: RANGE OF OPINIONS REGARDING CROSS-IMPACT FACTORS

If this event were to occur	The effect on these events would be*										
	1	3	4	6	27	33	35	37	39	42	**
		0	+1	+2	+3	+2	0	+1	+1	+2	UQ
		0	+1	+1	+2	+1	0	−1	+1	+1	M
1. British entry . . .		−1	+1	−2	+1	−1	0	−1	+1	+1	LQ
	+1		+2	+2	+1	+1	0	0	+1	+1	UQ
	0		+2	0	0	0	0	0	+1	+1	M
3. Peaceful re-unification . . .	−1		+1	−2	0	−1	0	−1	0	0	LQ
	+1	+2		0	+2	+1	0	0	+2	+1	UQ
	0	+1		0	+1	0	0	0	+1	+1	M
4. Worldwide open trade . . .	−1	+1		−1	+1	0	−1	−1	+1	0	LQ
	+2	+1	+1		+3	+3	0	+1	+2	+2	UQ
	+1	−1	0		+2	+2	0	0	+1	+1	M
6. Formulation of federations . . .	−1	−2	−1		+1	+2	0	−2	+1	+1	LQ
	+2	0	+2	+2		+3	0	+1	+2	+2	UQ
	+1	0	+1	+1		+2	0	0	+1	+1	M
27. Introduction of an inter . . .	−1	0	+0	+1		+2	0	−2	+1	+1	LQ
	+1	0	+1	+3	+2		0	+1	+1	+1	UQ
	−1	−1	0	+3	+2		0	+1	+1	+1	M
33. Social and economic . . .	−1	−1	0	+2	+1		0	0	+1	0	LQ
	0	+1	+2	+2	0	0		+1	0	+1	UQ
	0	+1	+1	0	0	0		+1	−1	0	M
35. Major warfare between . . .	0	−2	−2	0	0	0		0	−2	0	LQ
	+1	0	+1	+1	+1	+1	0		+1	+2	UQ
	−1	−1	0	−1	+1	−1	0		+1	+1	M
37. Closer relations between . . .	−2	−2	−1	−2	0	−2	0		0	+1	LQ
	0	0	+1	+1	+1	0	0	+1		+1	UQ
	0	0	+1	0	+1	0	0	0		0	M
39. Four-fold increase in . . .	0	0	0	0	0	0	0	0		0	LQ
	+1	0	+1	+2	+1	+2	0	+2	+2		UQ
	+1	0	+1	+1	0	+1	0	+1	+1		M
42. Ten-fold increase in . . .	0	0	0	0	0	0	0	0	+1		LQ

*A positive sign (+) indicates the effect of the occurrence of the development will be to increase the likelihood of occurrence of the subsequent development, and a negative sign (−) indicates the converse. The strength of the impact is indicated by the following code: 0 = No impact; 1 = Minor impact; 2 = Strong impact; and 3 = Very strong impact.
**UQ = Upper quartile; M = Median; LQ = Lower quartile.

event. Similarly, the algebraic sum of a vertical column of cross-impact factors is a measure of the sensitivity of the likelihood of occurrence of that event to the occurrence of the others in the set. Events which are most sensitive offer the greatest potential for changing outcomes, and hence may be of great interest to a decision-maker.

In addition, the spread of opinion (the difference between the upper and lower quartile estimates) regarding each of the cross-impact factors may be an indication of the uncertainty of the cross-impact. The sum of the spreads of opinion in the rows of the matrix is indicative of the uncertainty of the group as to the impact of the occurrence of any one event upon the likelihoods of occurrence of the others in the set. The sum of this quantity for the columns is, therefore, a measure of the group's uncertainty that the likelihood of one event will be affected by the occurrence of others in the set.

These measures (derived from Figure 2) are presented in Figure 3. Each cell of the matrix in Figure 3 contains two numbers. The upper number is the median value of the cross-impact factor. The lower number is the interquartile range for each cross-impact factor (the algebraic difference between the UQ and LQ values). The appropriate sum of each column and each row are given in the shaded column and row. From these it can be seen that the events whose occurrence would have the greatest effect on the others in the set are events 33, 1, 6, 27, 37, and 42. The events that are most strongly affected by the others in the set are 27, 4, 39, 42, 6 and 33. On the other hand, the events whose effect on the others is most certain are 39, 33, 4, 42, and 27. The events on which the effect of the other events is most certain are 35, 39, 42, 27, and 3.

While the significance of these quantities cannot be evaluated exactly, some conclusions are obvious. For example, the likelihood of occurrence of event 35 is unaffected by the occurrence of all of the other events in the set (the sum of the median cross-impact factors as shown in the upper half of column 35 being zero) and there appears to be a high degree of confidence in this zero impact (the sum of the interquartile ranges as shown in the lower half of this column being 1). Conversely, event 35 appears to have relatively little effect on the likelihood of occurrence of the other events in the set (the absolute sum of the median cross-impact factors in the upper half of row 35 being 4); however, there is considerable uncertainty about this low impact (the sum of the interquartile ranges in the lower half of this row being 13). Other events can be similarly evaluated, although with far less conclusiveness.

These data, in conjunction with importance ratings for each event, can strongly aid the decision-maker in identifying desirable actions and areas warranting further investigation. Important events which are insensitive to the others in the set would appear to necessitate direct action if they are to be strongly modified, whereas sensitive events may benefit from indirect action. Events that exhibit a wide uncertainty would appear to merit a closer evaluation before decisions are taken.

FIGURE 3: STRENGTH AND UNCERTAINTY AMONG CROSS-IMPACT FACTORS

The effect on these events would be

(Each cell shows the strength value over the number of responses. The two figures following the event title are the leading row figures.)

If this event were to occur		1	3	4	6	27	33	35	37	39	42
1. British entry into the Common Market	13 / 8	+1 / 16	+1 / 11	+7 / 14	+5 / 19	+9 / 10	+5 / 13	0 / 1	+2 / 15	+7 / 8	+7 / 9
3. Peaceful re-unification of Germany	13 / 4	0 / 2	+1 / 1	0 / 1	+1 / 4	+2 / 2	+1 / 3	0 / 0	−1 / 2	+1 / 0	+1 / 1
4. Worldwide open trade with Communist bloc nations	10 / 4	0 / 2	+1 / 1	+2 / 1	0 / 4	0 / 1	0 / 2	0 / 0	0 / 1	0 / 1	+1 / 1
6. Formulation of federations of European nations (consisting of groups of present nations)	16 / 8	+1 / 3	−1 / 3	0 / 2	0 / 1	+2 / 2	+2 / 1	0 / 1	0 / 3	+1 / 1	+1 / 1
27. Introduction of an international monetary system (non-gold) guaranteed by international monetary authority	12 / 7	+1 / 3	0 / 2	+1 / 2	+1 / 1	0 / 1	+2 / 1	0 / 0	0 / 3	+1 / 1	+1 / 1
33. Social and economic homogeneity among Common Market nations	8 / 10	−1 / 2	−1 / 1	0 / 1	+3 / 1	+2 / 1	0 / 0	0 / 0	+1 / 1	+1 / 0	+1 / 1
35. Major warfare between Russia and Red China	13 / 4	0 / 0	+1 / 3	+1 / 4	0 / 2	0 / 0	0 / 0	0 / 0	+1 / 1	−1 / 2	0 / 1
37. Closer relations between European countries and the USA in international enterprise and research fields, resulting in stronger ties with the USA than with each other	16 / 7	−1 / 3	−1 / 2	0 / 2	−1 / 3	+1 / 1	−1 / 3	0 / 0	+1 / 1	+1 / 1	+1 / 1
39. Four-fold increase in aid (with regard to 1969) to under-developed countries by East and West	5 / 2	0 / 0	0 / 0	+1 / 1	0 / 1	+1 / 1	0 / 0	0 / 1	0 / 1	0 / 1	0 / 1
42. Ten-fold increase in research capacities (people plus apparatus and techniques) in Europe and the USA	10 / 6	+1 / 1	0 / 0	+1 / 1	+1 / 2	0 / 1	+1 / 2	0 / 0	+1 / 2	−1 / 1	0 / 1

In this case study the group was asked to consider candidate events whose likelihood of occurrence they felt could be changed by social actions and to indicate the direction of change which they believed would be most desirable. Four such events were chosen and their initial likelihoods of occurrence perturbed in accordance with the group's desires. These changed events were included as pairs in two successive cross-impact analyses. Because of time constraints, it was not possible to repeat the analysis of the cross-impact matrix as often as would ordinarily be done or even to analyze the variances in the columns and rows of the matrix prior to making the selection of the four events. Had such information been available, these selections may have been considerably different.

Examining the candidate actions in retrospect and in light of the information presented in Figure 3 is quite revealing. The events the group felt they could and would like to perturb were (in order of preference) 39, 27, 6, and 42. It can be seen from the data in Figure 3 that their first choice, event 39, has the least impact on the likelihood of occurrence of the other events, but is highly affected by their occurrences. It is clearly a good candidate for indirect support. Event 42 has similar characteristics and may also be regarded as a poor candidate for direct intervention. Events 27 and 6, on the other hand, appear to be more effective candidates, although the occurrence of event 27 is also very strongly affected by the other events.

The most interesting candidate for action appears to be event 1. This event has a very strong effect on the others in the set, and is virtually unaffected by any of them. This event, however, was not chosen for the cross-impact analysis, perhaps because of the group's uncertainty regarding these interactions. This uncertainty is indicated by the high interquartile ranges in both the column and the row of event 1. It should be noted that none of these observations could have been made if the cross-impact factors had not been obtained through the use of the Delphi technique.

The results of the cross-impact analysis are presented in Figure 4. Shown are the initial and final probabilities of each event for the case without social intervention and the two cases with interventions.

It can be seen from these results that the effect of the cross-impact factors in general is very large, whereas the actions taken had relatively little across-the-board impact on the other events. However, only the initial probabilities were perturbed in this analysis and, as mentioned earlier, several of these events are not powerful. They may have exhibited greater sensitivity to sequence than to initial probabilities, or other combinations may have revealed their impacts. Further analyses would have clarified these matters.

The analytic procedure used in the case study provided the group with many new insights into future prospects with which they were highly concerned and to which they had given considerable thought. Because it was performed primarily as a demonstration, detail and completeness were neglected. This compromised the substantive results strongly. The most serious limitation of the demonstration was that the analysis was not repeated many times. Even so, the value of the technique in promoting an appreciation of complex social issues, and its potential for evaluating outcomes, were apparent to most members of the group.

In light of these and other results, research has continued to make the cross-impact technique more effective. Certain promising innovations are currently being programmed for operation on digital computers at the Institute for the Future. These changes address several of the difficulties mentioned earlier, which were apparent in the procedure used in the case study.

For example, as indicated earlier, the initial likelihood of occurrence of an event considered an environment which might have evolved normally from present circumstances. This could conceivably have included the anticipation of the occurrence of events included in the set being analysed.

Consequently, the analysis that is made, which adjusts the initial probabilities in light of the occurrence of an event, may be adding to what has already been partially included by the participants. In any event, it does not account for non-occurrence in assessing the inter-relationships. Therefore, the analysis

FIGURE 4: CHANGE IN PROBABILITIES OF OCCURRENCE RESULTING FROM THE CROSS-IMPACT ANALYSIS

Events	Without intervention Future A; Initial/Final probabilities	With interventions noted* Future B; Initial/Final probabilities	Future C; Initial/Final probabilities
1. British entry into the Common Market	0·8/0·8	0·8/0·8	0·8/0·75
3. Peaceful re-unification of Germany	0·1/0·15	0·1/0·1	0·1/0
4. Worldwide open trade with Communist bloc nations	0·5/0·8	0·5/0·85	0·5/0·75
6. Formulation of federations of European nations (consisting of groups of present nations)	0·5/0·7	**0·7/0·75**	0·5/0·65
27. Introduction of an international monetary system (non-gold) guaranteed by international monetary authority	0·6/0·8	**0·8/0·95**	0·6/0·9
33. Social and economic homogeneity among Common Market nations	0·6/0·85	0·6/0·85	0·6/0·85
35. Major warfare between Russia and Red China	0·23/0·3	0·23/0·25	0·23/0·2
37. Closer relations between European countries and the USA in international enterprise and research fields resulting in stronger ties with the USA than with each other	0·5/0·5	0·5/0·6	0·5/0·7
39. Four-fold increase in aid (with regard to 1969) to under-developed countries by East and West	0·3/0·6	0·3/0·7	**0·5/0·75**
42. Ten-fold increase in research capacities (people plus apparatus and techniques) in Europe and the USA	0·25/0·35	0·25/0·5	**0·45/0·45**

*Items in bold had their initial probabilities raised as a result of societal actions.

does not remove any cross-impact effects which may have been implicitly included in originally estimating the initial likelihoods of occurrence. Finally, the use of a mathematical analog (quadratic equation) to quantify the subjective inputs received from the participants may be questioned.

The changes being explored are as follows: 1. the criteria for determining the initial likelihoods of occurrence for the events being evaluated will be changed to assume the non-occurrence of all of the other events in the set, and a 'normal' evolution for other environmental factors; 2. the cross-impact factors will be elicited quantitatively in terms of how much more or less likely each subsequent event will be if preceded by the occurrence of any other single event; and 3. the cross-impact matrix will be analysed directly without the quadratic equation transformation.

The changes in criteria regarding what is to be considered and neglected in estimating the initial likelihood of occurrence and the manner of estimating the cross-impact factors—in terms of quantitative changes in likelihood rather than by some qualitative statement—are both intended to make the analysis more specific. The use of changes in likelihood also expands the domain of possible change, as will be discussed later. It is not maintained, however, that these modifications of the technique make the task of eliciting accurate information easier. On the contrary, it may be argued that in several ways it makes that task more difficult. For example, an expert may find it impossible to assume the non-occurrence of many important events simultaneously. Similarly, he may find it quite burdensome to judge changes in likelihood on a scale which ranges from near-zero to near-infinity. Nevertheless, these changes in methodology do overcome other shortcomings that appear to represent greater constraints.

Should the judgmental process involved in assuming the non-occurrence of all of the other events in the set prove too difficult, it is possible to revert to eliciting individual probabilities assuming a normal evolution and to include two cross-impact factors in each cell—one for the occurrence and one for the non-occurrence of each event. This would, of course, double the data requirements for the cross-impact matrix.

The result of using the quadratic equation is to confine the effect of one impact to the domain presented in Figure 5, which shows the initial and final probabilities for cross-impact factors. These factors may range only from $+ 1$ to $- 1$. The effect of the occurrence of one event on another can be determined by entering the Figure with the initial probability of the event being impacted, reading up to the value of S that represents the cross-impact factor between the two events, and reading across to obtain the new probability.

From Figure 5, it can be seen that when the cross-impact factor, S, is zero, the impacted probability is the same as the initial probability. For values of S other than zero, the impacted probability is increased or decreased according to the magnitude and sign ($+$ or $-$) of S and the initial probability of the event being impacted. In order for the quadratic equation to satisfy the con-

FIGURE 5: EFFECT OF CROSS-IMPACT FACTORS WHEN USING QUADRATIC EQUATION

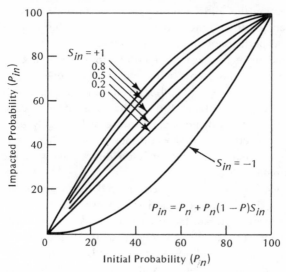

FIGURE 6: EFFECT OF CROSS-IMPACT FACTORS WHEN USING CHANGES IN LIKELI-HOOD

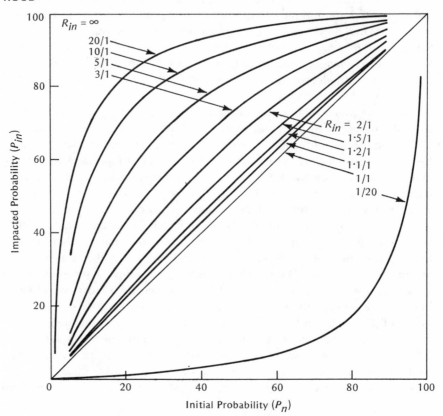

R_{in} = Change in likelihood of event E_n produced by occurrence of event E_i

straint that the probability can never exceed unity or become negative, the domain has to be constrained to values of S ranging from $+1$ to -1. Such a limitation is not intuitively clear in that it does not permit the occurrence of one event to have a large positive absolute impact on an event whose initial probability is very low, or a large negative absolute impact on an event whose initial probability is very high.

Changes in probability in the form of quantitative ratios opens the domain to the widest range of possibilities. Several of these are presented in Figure 6 in a form comparable with the previous Figure. From Figure 6 it can be seen that an event whose initial probability was 20% could, if impacted by an event that increased its likelihood by a factor of 20, be raised to 83%. When the quadratic is used, the maximum positive impact for an event with an initial probability of 20% is to raise it to 36%.

Conclusions

The approaches described in this programme are still highly experimental and far from their final form. Nevertheless, their contribution can be important, particularly since many techniques currently being used to plan and make decisions in complex situations seem unsystematic and appear to admit actions that may be inefficient or work at cross purposes.

Indeed, there is still much to be accomplished before futures analysis can be regarded, not as a science, but even a respectable art. The key problems of organising and understanding the issues and assessing the desirability of alternative outcomes, which are crucial to such an analysis, have been discussed only incidentally here, and hence a complete analysis has been impossible. The task of this paper has simply been to suggest several ways in which the Delphi technique and cross-impact analysis provide an appreciation of the interplay of individual problems and of opportunities that can be foreseen. Moreover, these methods do so in a highly comfortable manner, in the sense that they do not change basic thought processes or logic, but rather use these processes systematically, amplifying their implications in a retraceable manner. Because an opportunity is provided to trace ideas back to their origins, these techniques can be especially valuable in gaining the broad acceptance of proposed actions that is often essential where decisions will affect large segments of society.

COMPARISON OF DELPHI FORECASTING STUDIES IN 1964 AND 1969

● *robert h. ament*

The Institute for the Future recently completed a Delphi study that considered prospective developments in physical and biological technologies.[1] Because many of the forecasts were made for events and developments that were considered in a study five years earlier,[2] a comparison of the two studies provides an opportunity to observe the effect of the passage of time on forecasts. Such a review also makes it possible to develop data on the consistency and performance of different panels.

The primary goal of Delphi projects has been to establish probable dates of occurrence for potential scientific and technological developments. The method employs a series of carefully prepared questionnaires and controlled information feedback to determine group consensus among individually anonymous experts. The method has also been used to elicit expert opinion about the likely consequences of technological events and the potential social value of the predicted consequences. While predicted dates for technological achievements may be useful, the consideration of social consequences and values seems somewhat more speculative. Nevertheless, such opinion-seeking projects are beneficial if the study leads its participants to ponder their roles in creating the future, and if the published report stimulates reviewers to compare the world they desire with the alternatives suggested by expert consensus.

The first major application of the Delphi method was in the 1964 *Report on a Long-Range Forecasting Study*, which was concerned with six topics:

- scientific breakthroughs in physical and biological technologies
- world population growth
- innovations in automation
- progress in space
- new weapon systems
- causes and prevention of wars.

The near-term forecasts of the 1964 study were reviewed to determine which ones have already occurred. Some of the forecasts were too diffuse to establish whether they had taken place, and these were omitted from consideration.

[1] T. J. Gordon and R. H. Ament, *Forecasts of Some Technological and Scientific Developments and their Societal Consequences*, IFF Report R.6, September, 1969.
[2] T. J. Gordon and Olaf Helmer, *Report on a Long-range Forecasting Study*, The RAND Corporation, Paper P2982, September, 1964.

TABLE 1: Near Term Forecasts of 1964 Rand Report

	50% occurrence probability			Has the development occurred?		
	LQ	median	UQ	yes	no	partly
Scientific breakthroughs						
Economically useful de-salination of sea water	1964	1970	1980			0
Feasibility of effective large-scale fertility control by oral contraceptive or other simple and inexpensive means	1970	1970	1983	0		
Development of new synthetic materials for ultra-light construction	1970	1971	1978			0
Automated language translators	1968	1972	1976		0	
Reliable weather forecasts	1972	1975	1988			0
Operation of a central data storage facility with wide access for general or specialised information retrieval	1971	1979	1991		0	
Innovations in automation						
Increase by a factor of ten in capital investments in computers used for automated process control	1970	1973	1975			0
Air traffic control—positive and predictive track on all aircraft	1970	1973	1977		0	
Direct link from stores to banks to check credit and to record transactions	1972	1974	1980			0
Widespread use of simple teaching machines	1971	1975	1977			0
Automation of office work and services, leading to displacement of 25% of current work force	1970	1975	1975		0	
Automatic libraries, looking up and reproducing copy	1971	1976	1982		0	
Automated looking up of legal information	1971	1978	1988	0		
Automated rapid transit	1973	1978	1985			0
Progress in space						
USSR orbital rendezvous	1964	1964	1966	0		
USA orbital rendezvous	1965	1967	1967	0		
Increased use of near-Earth satellites for weather prediction and control	1967	1967	1970	0		
Unmanned inspection and capability for destruction of satellites	1967	1967	1970		0	
USSR manned lunar fly-by	1967	1967	1970		0	
Establishment of global communications system	1967	1968	1970	0		
USA manned lunar fly-by	1967	1970	1970	0		
Manned lunar landing and return	1969	1969	1970	0		
Rescue of astronauts stranded in orbit	1968	1970	1975		0	
Operational readiness of laser for space communications	1968	1970	1975			0
Manned co-orbital inspection of satellites	1970	1970	1974		0	
Manned scientific orbital station—ten men	1970	1970	1975		0	
Development of re-usable booster launch vehicle	1970	1975	1975		0	
Solid-core nuclear reactor propulsion	1970	1975	1975		0	
Ionic (nuclear-generator powered) propulsion	1972	1975	1975		0	

	50% occurrence probability			Has the development occurred?		
	LQ	median	UQ	yes	no	partly
Development of re-usable manoeuverable orbiting space craft	1972	1975	1979	0		
Future weapon systems						
Tactical kiloton nuclear weapons for use by ground troops	1964	1965	1967	0		
Extensive uses of devices that persuade without killing (water cannons, tear gas, etc.)	1968	1968	1970	0		
Miniature improved sensors and transmitters for snooping, reconnaissance, arms control	1968	1968	1970	0		
Rapid mobility of men and light weapons to any point on Earth for police action	1966	1969	1973	0		
Incapacitating chemical (as opposed to biological) agents	1965	1970	1975	0		
Use of lasers for radar-type sensors, illuminators, communications	1968	1970	1975	0		
Incapacitating biological agents	1968	1970	1976	0		
Cheap light-weight rocket-type personnel armament (silent, plastic, match-lit projectiles, capable of single or gang firing)	1966	1970	1980			
Lethal biological agents	1967	1970	1980	0		
Perishable counter-insurgent arms	1970	1971	1991		0	
Orbiting space reconnaissance station	1970	1972	1974		0	
Advanced techniques of propaganda, thought control, opinion manipulation	1970	1972	1980			0
Accurate intelligence correlation through use of computers	1970	1972	1985			0
Effective anti-submarine capability, at least against contemporary submarines	1970	1974	1975			0
Longer-endurance aircraft, perhaps nuclear-powered, for logistics supply or bombardment	1972	1975	1979	0		
Automated tactical capability (battlefield computers, robot sentries, tv surveillance)	1973	1975	1980	0		
ICBM's with other than nuclear warheads (such as snipers)	1973	1976	1980		0	

In the study, about a third of the developments were judged by at least a quarter of the respondents to have a 50% probability of occurrence by 1975. Table 1 lists these items along with the date of forecast. Different reviewers will offer conflicting opinions as to which events have already occurred, in part because of definitional imprecision. For example, 'economically useful de-salination of sea water' may or may not have occurred, depending on one's view of 'economical'. Except for a few very specific events, such as the lunar landing, dissent is likely about the progress which has been actually achieved toward each forecasted item. Consequently, the items listed in Table 1 were divided into three categories, describing whether the item had

TABLE 2: Comparison of Forecasts, 1964 and 1969 Developments

1964	1969	Possible bias from phrasing	1964			1969			Correlation
			LQ	median	UQ	LQ	median	UQ	
Availability of a machine which comprehends standard IQ tests and scores above 150 (where comprehend is to be understood as the ability to respond to questions printed in English and possibly accompanied by diagrams)	Availability of a computer which comprehends standard IQ tests and scores above 150 (where comprehend is to be understood as the ability to respond to questions printed in English and possibly accompanied by diagrams)	none	1984	1990	1996	1980	1992	2012	about the same, later upper quartile
Permanent base established on the moon (ten men, indefinite stay)	Establishment of a permanent base on the moon (say ten men, indefinite stay)	none	1981	1982	1983	1992	1992	1992	later, a less optimistic forecast
Widespread use of robot services for refuse collection, as household slaves, sewer inspectors, etc.	Availability of complex robots which are programmable and self-adaptive and capable of performing most household chores, such as independently preparing meals and cleaning or otherwise disposing of dishes	none	1980	1987	1996	1992	1992	2000	later, a less optimistic forecast
Economic feasibility of commercial manufacture of many chemical elements from sub-atomic building blocks	Economic feasibility of commercial manufacture of many chemical elements from sub-atomic building blocks	none	2007	2100	never	1992	2012	2012	earlier, a more optimistic forecast
Two-way communication with extra-terrestrials	Discovery of information that proves the existence of intelligent beings beyond the Earth	earlier, since discovery could come without communication	2000	2075	never	1985	2025	later	earlier as expected

1964	1969	Possible bias from phrasing	1964			1969			Correlation
			LQ	median	UQ	LQ	median	UQ	
Commercial global ballistic transport (including boost-glide techniques)	Routine use of re-usable ballistic sub-orbital transports for military or commercial passenger and cargo transportation	none	1985	2000	never	1992	2030	later	later, though more likely in the long run
Control of gravity through some form of modification of the gravitational field	Revision of gravitational theories leading to the possibility of new modes of space travel	revision of theories could come before control	2035	2050	never	1985	later	never	earlier possibility, more optimistic forecast
Non-rocket space drive: anti-gravity			2050	2400	never				
Reliable weather forecasts	Demonstration of regular and reliable weather forecasts 14 days in advance for areas as small as 260 km² (100 sq miles)	more limiting definition should bring later forecast	1972	1975	1988	1980	1980	2012	later
Controlled thermo-nuclear power	Laboratory demonstration of continuously controlled thermo-nuclear power	none	1980	1986	2000	1980	1985	1992	about the same; quartile range narrowed
Economically useful exploitation of the ocean bottom through mining (other than offshore petroleum drilling)	Invention of devices to permit economically useful exploitation of the ocean bottom through mining (other than offshore drilling)	none	1980	1989	2000	1980	1992	2000	same
Economically useful exploitation of ocean through farming, with the effect of	Availability of techniques that permit useful exploitation of ocean through aquacul-	none	2000	2000	2017	1985	1992	2000	earlier, a more optimistic forecast

1964	1969	Possible bias from phrasing	1964			1969			Correlation
			LQ	median	UQ	LQ	median	UQ	
producing at least 20% of the world's food	ture farming (including expanded fishing and ocean fishing cultivation) with the effect of producing at least 20% of the world's calories								
Feasibility of limited weather control, in the sense of substantially affecting regional weather at acceptable cost	Feasibility of limited weather control, in the sense of predictably affecting regional weather at acceptable cost	second formulation is more demand-ing	1987	1990	2000	1980	1992	2012	as expected
Earth weather control, in the sense of having the highly reliable capability of causing precipitation from certain types of clouds			1978	1982	2002				
Economically useful de-salination of sea water	Demonstration of large-scale de-salination plants capable of economically producing useful water for agricul-tural purposes (5·3 cents/1 000 l (20 cents per 1000 US galls))	more specific, hence perhaps later	1964	1970	1980	1973	1980	1985	later, as suggested
Operation of a central data storage facility with wide access, for general or specialized information retrieval	Establishment of a central data storage facility (or several regional or dis-ciplinary facilities) with wide public access (perhaps in the home), for general or specialised information retrieval primarily in the areas of library, medical,	none	1971	1980	1991				
Automated libraries, looking up and reproducing copy			1971	1976	1982				
Automated looking up of legal information			1971	1978	1988				

1964	1969	Possible bias from phrasing	1964			1969			Correlation
			LQ	median	UQ	LQ	median	UQ	
Development of new synthetic materials for ultra-light construction	and legal data A large number of new materials (for example, filament-re-inforced composites) for ultra-light construction (density of aluminium, strength and toughness of steel) commercially available for private use at competitive prices	later, since question ponders commercial availability of development	1970	1971	1978	1975	1980	1992	later, as suggested
Automated language translators	Laboratory operation of automated language translators capable of coping with idiomatic syntactical complexities	later	1968	1972	1976	1980	1980	2012	later
Automated language translators—correct grammar			1971	1978	1996				
Widespread use of sophisticated teaching machines	Development of sophisticated teaching machines utilising adaptive programmes which respond not only to the students' answers but also to certain physiological responses of the students, for example tension	more specific, hence perhaps later, likely the same	1975	1975	1990	1980	1980	1992	slightly later
Manned scientific orbital space station—ten men	Launch of continuously-manned scientific Earth orbital space station, say ten men with 90-day crew rotation	probably none	1970	1970	1975	1980	1980	1992	later, more distant forecast
Creation of a primitive form	Laboratory creation of a	none	1979	1989	2000	1980	1980	1980	earlier, with

1964	1969	Possible bias from phrasing	1964 LQ	median	UQ	1969 LQ	median	UQ	Correlation
of artificial life (at least in the form of self-replicating molecules)	primitive form of artificial life (at least in the form of self-replicating molecules)								precise consensus
Economic feasibility of commercial generation of synthetic protein for food	Laboratory demonstration of artificial generation of protein for food through in vitro cellular processes	earlier, since only laboratory development is described	1985	1990	2003	1980	1980	1980	earlier, as called for
New organs through transplanting or prosthesis	Laboratory demonstration of biochemical processes	none	1979	1989	2000	1980	1980	1980	earlier, with precise consensus
Biochemicals to stimulate growth of new organs and limbs	which stimulate growth of new organs and limbs		1995	2007	2040				
Implantable artificial organs made of plastic and electronic components	Demonstration of implantable artificial hearts with very long-duration power source	second formulation is narrower	1975	1982	1988	1980	1980	1992	
Feasibility (not necessarily acceptance) of chemical control over some human hereditary defects by modification on genes through molecular engineering		none	1984	2012	2050	1980	2000	2012	
Feasibility of using drugs to raise intelligence level (other than as dietary supplements and not in the sense of only temporarily raising the level of apperception)	Feasibility of raising the level of intelligence in some persons (other than as dietary supplements and not in the sense of only temporarily raising the level of apperception) allowing adults to solve	none	1984	2012	2050	1980	2000	2012	earlier, a more optimistic forecast

1964	1969	Possible bias from phrasing	1964			1969			Correlation
			LQ	median	UQ	LQ	median	UQ	
	problems previously unsolvable								
Chemical control of the age-ing process, permitting extension of the life span by 50 years	Demonstration of chemical control of the human age-ing process, permitting extension of the life span by 50 years with commensurate increase in years of vigour	possibly later because of qualification	1995	2075	2075	1980	2012	later	substantially earlier, a more optimistic forecast
Use of telepathy and ESP in communications	Laboratory demonstration of electronically amplified or augmented communication between brains (controlled ESP) Reliable use of ESP (such as telepathy in communications)	none	2040	never	never	later 2025	later later	never never	no substantial change, median from never to later
Effective widespread fertility control by oral contraceptive or other simple and inexpensive means	Development of economical mass-administered contraceptive agents	none	1970	1970	1983	1973	1980	1985	later, a less optimistic forecast
Widespread and socially widely accepted use of non-narcotic drugs (other than alcohol) for the purpose of producing specific changes in personality characteristics	Availability of cheap, non-narcotic drugs (other than alcohol) for the purpose of producing specific changes in personality characteristics, such as euphoria, anti-anxiety, anti-aggression, increased perception and increased attention	second formulation is more specific	1980	1983	2000	1973	1980	1980	later for changes in life style and attitude, earlier for temporary changes
	Public availability of cheap, non-narcotic drugs (other					1992	2012	2025	

1964	1969	Possible bias from phrasing	1964			1969			Correlation
			LQ	median	UQ	LQ	median	UQ	
than alcohol) for the purpose of producing specific changes in personality characteristics such as alterations in attitudes and life styles									
Biochemical general immunisation against bacterial and viral diseases	Development of immunising agent which can protect against most bacterial and viral diseases	more limiting definition	1983	1994	2000	1973	1980	1985	earlier, as was slightly expected
Long-duration coma to permit a form of time travel	Demonstration of long-duration coma or hibernation to permit a form of time travel	none	2006	never	never	1985	2012	later	much earlier, a more optimistic forecast
Man-machine symbiosis, enabling man to extend his intelligence by direct electro-mechanical interaction between his brain and a computing machine	Demonstration of man-machine symbiosis, enabling man to extend his intelligence by direct electro-mechanical interaction between his brain and a computing machine	none	1990	2020	never	2012	2012	later	about the same
Feasibility of education by direct information recording on the brain	Feasibility of education by direct information recording on the brain	none	1997	2600	never	2012	later	never	same

occurred, had not occurred, or had only partially occurred. An informal opinion sampling at IFF placed each relevant forecast into one of these categories.

Table 2 compares items that appeared in both the 1964 and 1969 studies. It shows that the more recent forecasts describe a probable future slightly different from the 1964 preview. Some developments now appear to be closer than forecast previously, while others seem more distant. In some cases slight changes in wording may have led to these changes, and these potential biases have been noted in Table 2. The 1964 and 1969 forecasts are shown in Figure 1. As a whole, the opinions collected in 1969 are very similar to the predictions of 1964.

Significantly, however, many of the biological items are now forecast earlier, while most items concerning the exploration of space are forecast later. This observation may reflect increased interest in biological research and development, and doubtless reflects a change in attitude toward the urgency of the space programme. Within this context, it is interesting to note the narrow range of forecasts pertaining to space exploration efforts already in progress. Future events such as a manned lunar landing, which has now occurred as projected in the second half of 1969, construction of temporary and permanent lunar bases, and launch of a scientific orbital space station, were remarked on thus in the 1964 report: "The quartile ranges are remarkably narrow, reflecting no doubt the rather firm timetable of near-future space achievements to which our space specialists expect to adhere."[3] Table 2 indicates that the 1969 forecasts about space are also quite precise, but have moved later in time.

Finally, Figure 1 compares the precision of the 1964 and 1969 forecasts. Although the respondents were different, their forecasting behaviour was remarkably similar. In both cases the length of the quartile range was about equal to the distance into the future of the median forecast.

It is true that speculation is limited by the certainty that the future will be determined at least in part by developments impossible to foresee today. But long-range projection is no less valuable just because the number of alternative futures is infinite and a comprehensive catalogue impossible. Forecasting studies such as these cannot narrow the breadth of potential and unexpected developments, and they almost surely prepare us for what would otherwise be surprises. Significantly, this 'early warning' advantage opens up the possibility of preventing or modifying developments.

In summary, a comparison of similar items in two forecasts that were made five years apart using different panels of respondents has shown:

- Relative consistency of the forecasts.
- A shift to earlier median dates of many biological forecasts and to later dates of several space forecasts.
- Similar forecasting behaviour, at least in terms of the spread of opinion, as a function of median time in the future.

[3] Ibid., p. 23.

FIGURE 1. COMPARISON OF PREDICTIONS FOR REPEATED DEVELOPMENTS.

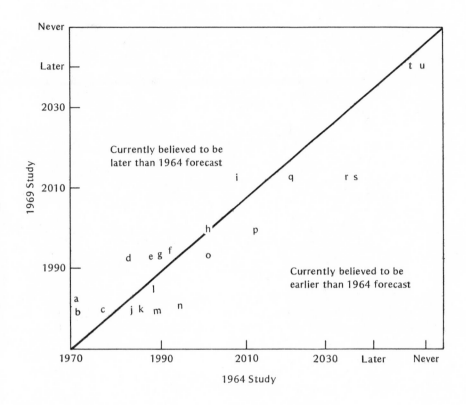

a Economically useful de-salination of sea water
b Continuously manned scientific earth orbital space station
c Automated language translators—correct grammar
d Permanent base on the moon
e Economically useful ocean mining
f Computer that comprehends standard IQ tests and scores above 150
g Feasibility of limited weather control at acceptable cost
h Feasibility of gene modification through molecular engineering
i Biochemicals to stimulate growth of new organs and limbs
j Implantable artificial organs
k Widespread use of non-narcotic personality-changing drugs
l Controlled thermonuclear power
m Creation of a primitive form of artificial life
n Biochemical general immunisation against bacterial and viral diseases
o Economically useful ocean farming producing 20% of the world's food
p Feasibility of using drugs to raise intelligence level
q Man-machine symbiosis; electro-mechanical interaction between brain and computer
r Chemical control of the human aging process
s Economic feasibility of commercial manufacture of chemical elements
t Feasibility of education by direct information recording on the brain
u Use of telepathy and extra-sensory perception in communications

6

Participatory Future Studies

LOOKING FORWARD: 1999

● *arthur i. waskow*

This paper will argue that one of the major tasks of intellectuals today is to assist the many publics in their countries to imagine the future, so that the future may be created more democratically than now looks likely. Nor should this mean simply the conventional process of "planning" or writing political programs. Rather, it should mean the much riskier process of building in the present institutions one has imagined for the future: a process that is risky because such institutions partake of the "law and order" that has not been enacted, and may well be illegal or disorderly under the existing rules. We suggest that one of the most powerful ways of achieving social change is to imagine in vivid detail a desirable and achievable future, and then *build* a part of that future in the present—rather than merely pleading for it to be built. Let us examine what that process of imagination and creation would mean for members of the world public standing in 1967 and addressing themselves to 1999: one generation hence, the last year before the new millennium. Let us do so remembering that George Orwell warned us, "Who controls the past controls the future; who controls the present controls the past." Our effort must be to show that *whoever frees the future frees the present*, and thus to make his warning come full circle in the service of liberty.

To begin with, why is it important that members of the public do future studies? First of all, because others are doing so. During the last two years in America, for example, there has begun to emerge a "profession" of the study of the future. The American Academy of Arts and Sciences created a Commission on the Year 2000, headed by Daniel Bell of Columbia University. The Commission very much regarded itself as a panel of the priesthood, to whom the mysteries were revealed and who could guide the people but would not open those mysteries to the people. In the RAND Corporation, there was grown out of its concern with the future of military strategy a more general interest in the future of official American policy, again oriented to the group of people that run the U.S. government, and again based on the assumption that this need not, could not, ought not, be in any sense the property of the American public. The new futurologists of course deny this is a problem at all, saying that just as astronomy is a matter for the professional, so the study of the future has to be. And very few of them respond to a challenge in terms of who the future belongs to, and whether it indeed is a subject like astronomy, or something quite different—in that the future of the world presumably belongs to all the people of the world, who should therefore understand and decide it.

For men who believe in the processes of democracy one possible response to the emergence of this highly professionalized, elitist study of the future is to shrug it off, saying that this makes little difference; that politics comes from quite different sources—not from intellectual analysis of what might be done and should be done, either on the part of the haves or the have-nots, but from much more visceral responses of people to the place they hold in society and the way that society is treating them: in short, that change comes from revulsion and anger at the present, so far as the excluded are concerned, and from an urgent desire to protect their holdings on the part of the powerful.

That may well be true; but it does not gainsay the old fact that knowledge is power, and that in a super-industrial (some people have even said a "post-industrial"), society, knowledge of the future is enormous power, and ignorance of the future may prevent one from feeling revulsion and anger until it is too late. Decisions on research and development of weapon systems made today will affect what the world looks like 20 years from now. They will affect, for example, whether it is even *possible* to achieve a disarmed world then. Decisions on seemingly less crucial matters, like supersonic transport, will affect the way our cities develop ten years hence. And very few people know this—only the experts with an "interest" in the matter, with an established political or economic interest which they already know about. The rest of the public is not ready to worry, not trained to worry; it won't get angry about sonic booms till the planes are already there, and that will be too late. In an era of very swift technological change, it has to be possible for the world public to understand the possible futures confronting their society 20, 25, 30 years from now, so that they may insist on the decisions to be made now that would enable the kind of society to emerge 20–30 years from now that they want.

All this, one might say, is the issue of democratic process, the issue of the actual workings of the democratic society in shaping its own future. There is a second issue: the issue of a democratic result. For of course there needs to be a democratic reconstruction in many countries. Decisions made or acquiesced in during the technological and organizational boom of the last half century have sapped the actuality of a democratic society, both at the top in national government, and in the various smaller institutions in the society: the schools, the health system, the legal system, housing, etc. So one of the major issues of the next half century will be whether it will be possible, and if so, how, to reconstruct the democratic society under the conditions of high technology. That is exactly what that political wave in America called "the movement" has been grappling with since 1960. I want to draw upon one future-oriented technique "the movement" has used but has not been fully conscious of using.

Indeed, "the movement" has been very unwilling to develop an image of the future of what the decent society might look like: to develop anything beyond the immediate present, or very, very near future a year hence, let's say. And yet as I look at what the "movement" did do, it seemed it had begun to do this in a very narrow and *ad hoc* way, in a way that we should recognize, mull over, and deliberately turn into a conscious method. The neatest case is the sit-ins, where the civil rights movement said, "Our desirable-achievable future is that we want to be able to eat in integrated restaurants. We will not petition legislatures to require integration, we will not petition the owners of the restaurants to integrate, *we will simply create the future.* That is, *we* will integrate the restaurants, and it will rest upon those who have the power of law and the power of ownership in their hands, to decide how to respond to that creation. So we will build *now* what it is we want to exist in the future, and society will have to react to that. It will have to let us build it, or it will have to punish us for building it. If it punishes us for building it, we believe we can build support around that vision of the future, and can, therefore, mobilize people into action to achieve that future."

Let me take another example: the creation of the Institute for Policy Studies. The Institute is not just an ordinary research center, because it is committed to the idea that to develop social theory one must be involved in social action and in social experiment. And therefore, the Institute stands on the bare edge of custom in the United States as to what an educational research institution is. By standing on that bare edge, it creates tension within the American legal and social system. What it says is that we want there to be many institutions in the United States in which social theory is learned from social action, and social action is derived from social theory. And since we wanted that to exist, rather than going to universities and arguing for it, rather than going into foundations and suggesting that they set up study committees to create it, we *did* it. And by doing it, created the strain, the tension, which requires the rest of American academia to attend to what we were doing, to decide whether it believed that was a good idea, to move in that direction, or to move against it.

That strain is enormously important to producing the change desired. The alternative possibilities (if one doesn't do well at estimating and creating strain) are these: one might create something so utterly out of relation with the present, and so challenging to it, that it is smashed immediately beyond repair, in which case one is unlikely to have created much change. In other words, if one imports into the present an image of the future so threateningly alien that it is not allowed to persist more than a week and a half, then one is not likely to have done much to change the future. On the other hand, one can import into the present something so irrelevant to the present that it is simply encapsulated and allowed to go its own way without creating any tension, and therefore any change at all. Both those poles have to be avoided if possible, and one way to avoid them is to simply keep experimenting and to discover at what point one is neither smashed nor ignored, but creates enough change to move the society. *That* is creative disorder; disorder because it obeys the "law and order" of some more or less distant future, and is therefore likely to be "unlawful" or "disorderly" by the standards of the present.

One who uses this approach should not expect that his picture of the future will be achieved. Sitting in 1967, one cannot expect to draw a 1999 which world society will, in fact, be like in 1999. We must expect exactly the opposite: that along the way the processes of imagination and creation will lead one to change his imagination. Hopefully, the process will engage wholly new people in imagining the future who do not now imagine it, and by doing that will engage them in creation of a kind of future which was not imagined by the ones who began the process. That's one of the major goals. And therefore, one should never expect to achieve that image, one should expect to move in the direction of it; one should expect perhaps to move in some quite different direction after moving part of the way, but never *to* it. And indeed, it might be wise to set a deadline, a five to ten year deadline, at the end of which we throw the old image away and start over again. In a sense this is like the process of science at its best: hypothesis, experiment, new hypothesis—always knowing that no theory is "the truth," but only a useful and beautiful way of understanding and reshaping the complex reality. And that this process never ends; not only is the process itself always open-ended, but so is the result.

Thus one starts with a mythical vision, a provisional vision, of the future as an open-ended future: a future which is free to decide on *its* own future: a society in which politics can happen, in which different groups of people are able to press toward change in the society.

This procedure offers one way of coping with the traditional problem of means and ends. In effect, it says that the means *are* the ends or that the ends become the means. In a sense it *is* the ends that justify the means, but only by becoming merged with them. If one has identified an end goal which one considers desirable, then if one translates that goal bodily into the present as a means to the achievement of the end, one has avoided the problem of judging whether certain means are legitimate to achieve certain ends.

Of course, there are other ways of dealing with the ends-means problem. One way has been insisting upon a transcendental ethic of the means—for example, the Gandhian ethic: under no conditions may one use violence as a means. Those who deal with the problem this way make the transcendental commitment that if one follows that ethic of the means, it will be *impossible* to end up with bad ends; if one is pursuing means which are good in themselves, they will *always* produce good ends. There seem to be two problems in this approach. *First,* it avoids the notion that the real moral judgment of the means is in its consequences; that is, in whether it produces results that seem desirable to the people that live with them. In short, it rejects the skeptical test, the test of both democracy and science, for a religious certitude. And *second*, it carries the danger that by simply pursuing means considered moral, it is fairly easy to be surrounded by the society and ignored by it, while the major thrust of the society keeps on in a totally different direction.

The American movement's "solution" to the problem of means and ends has been, I think, a different one; because although there has been an under-tone of Gandhian thought in the movement, most of it is not committed to a Gandhian or Christian or any other transcendental ethic of means. The move-ment has tried to get along with little ethic of means or ends. And that, while I think it could work from day to day precariously, seems to me to have in it the great danger of descent into anything from terror to meaninglessness. That is, if one has no clear vision of an end, and I think the "movement" has none; and if one has no clear commitment as to what means are legitimate and what means are not, and I think the "movement" as a whole has none; then one is likely, with neither of those, to descend into action out of pure revulsion. Action out of pure revulsion is not, in the long run, likely to build a decent society. There are too many things that one can do out of revulsion, if one has no clear picture of a decent future goal and no commitment to a present decent means—things that would build an indecent society.

There is of course the "typically American," the allegedly pragmatic (but not John Dewey's) solution to the means/ends problem, the one which Lyn-don Johnson quoted from Thomas Jefferson: that is, performing a lesser evil to avoid the greater. And it is not only liberals, real or phony, who cite the solution of the lesser evil. It is also, of course, the ethic of some parts of the "old left." So from some liberals and some leftists we are posed a question: could the two ethics, that of the lesser evil and that of the merging of ends and means, be used simultaneously by different people in de facto alliance to bring about change in the society? Is the ethic of the lesser evil a necessary one or not, if the creative disorder strategy is being pursued effectively? Is it possible to achieve all desirable social change by using the technique of creative disorder and eschewing the technique of performing a lesser evil—using violence for example—in the present in order to create something different in the future? If you imagine that it's necessary to have both, then of course you are forced back on the issue of how you measure the lesser evil as against the greater.

It is absolutely necessary in this process to be aware that one is making a practicable estimate as well as a desirable one about the image of the future. And "practicable" means within a certain length of time. With an indefinite length of time, perhaps any desirable society would be practicable. But 1999 is one generation hence. The legitimate length of a projection of this sort for any society is the one-generation length. As Jefferson said, "the earth belongs in usufruct to the living." It is both unreasonable and undesirable to attempt to project beyond one generation into the future. Undesirable because one is then governing the lives of those who are not yet living, or not yet in any position to make judgment, and unreasonable because the kind of social change available today, the kind of technological change especially, is of such a nature that one had better deliberately decide to make cutoff points because beyond them anything is possible and anything might be impossible.

If we keep in mind the practicable desirable future, then we are much more likely to be able to deal with the problem of the "correct" tension; the problem of the tension that is creative, enforcing change, and does not get either ignored or smashed. For if we try inventing only the desirable future, it is likely to be much too "far out" for effective pressure on the present society. Either it will not be relevant in the sense that it will be shrugged off, or it will not be relevant in the sense that it will be destroyed. So the political problem of achieving the correct tension is very closely related to the intellectual problem of projecting the practicable desirable future.

In order to distinguish this approach from the imagination of the merely desirable future on the one hand or the merely practicable future on the other hand, perhaps we should explore for a moment the deeper political differences between the kind of analysis of the future involved in "creative disorder" and the two most important more traditional ways of looking at the future.

One of these is the Utopia/Dystopia model: that is, imagining the perfect society or the upside-down or inside-out version of the perfect society, the disaster society, *1984* or *Brave New World*, the cautionary tale. Both of those tend to be done by people who are utterly out of power and have no hope within themselves either of achieving the results they are dreaming of, in the case of Utopia, or averting the results they are nightmaring about, in the case of Dystopia. Frequently the Utopians and Dystopians are people who represent the previous power-holders, thrust out and desperate by their exclusion from power; sometimes they are people from the bottom, people who have no sense that they can ever achieve power. But frequently the Utopia in fact is a backward look, the dream of the former aristocrat of the someday reestablishment of the kind of society he misremembers there was when he was running it; and frequently the Dystopia is a better attack upon how bad things already are and how much worse they will certainly get because the author had been replaced in power by a new and contemptible or horrifying class. Sometimes the Utopian can attach his reverie to the imagining of a really major social change, and sometimes the Dystopian can connect with a real revulsion of many of the powerless in society, so real that it might create major social change. But the imagery and feel of both Utopia and Dystopia is usually that there is no way for the man working on it to really affect what happens.

The other crucial way of imagining the future is the direct opposite of that: *planning;* which is the way for those who presently hold power to project their continuation in power over the period of years ahead. Planning is the way in which the Commission on the Year 2000 or the RAND Corporation serves those who hold power now, explaining to them how 30 years from now or 50 years from now they will be able to continue running the society, having changed those things which are necessary to change in order to be able to do that.

Imagery of the future as a tool for creating change is distinguishable from both of those (Utopia/Dystopia and Planning) because it addresses those who could have power but do not. Not those who are utterly out of power and see no hope of ever gaining it; not those who presently hold it; but those who can seriously imagine that they might be able to change the way the society operates. For that reason, of course, it is not neutral. Out of a number of "seriously possible" futures, it has selected one direction to develop—and that almost certainly depends on what direction the author thinks is desirable, even if he thinks it impossible for the society to move as far in that direction as he would like in the given time.

Just as this kind of future-building looks for the possible rather than either a replica of the present or an impossible though desirable future (impossible within the given time span) so it is an examination of the seriously *possible* rather than the most likely. Instead of being a prediction—that is, the author's best judgment as to what present trends are likely to produce—it is what might be called a *possidiction*—that is, the author's projection of how certain seeds of change that exist already might be made to flourish, given certain kinds of political action. The possidiction describes worlds that are, say 30% likely—as against either worlds that are only 1% likely or those that are 60% likely. There is a serious chance they can be brought into being, but it will take a lot of doing. And the possidiction acts as an incitement to the necessary action.

In order to examine that which is practicable for the society to create in the length of time one allots, one probably has to examine two major areas: what are the major social trends of the immediate past that could be expected to generate major changes, and what values do parts of the society hold—what are their desirabilities, not just the author's—that could be expected to set goals for change.

Naturally, an analysis of the possible impact of recent major trends does not mean that all one does is project those trends in a straight line. If the military budget has increased continuously over the last 25 years, one need not simply project that that increase goes on. That increase might, in a demonstration of what used to be called the dialectic, turn itself inside out—create its own opposite. That is, people might decide to disarm *because* the military machine had grown so large. Or they might not: the military budget might keep growing in a straight line. One has to have a serious analysis of how it would either create its own opposite or continue in its own pattern or create something quite different. In addition, one has to be able to take several independent or partially independent factors of this kind and knit together the possible changes in each in order to see the way a whole society might develop. One would have, for example, to knit together the direction in which the various military machines might go with the way the under-class might develop, to see how they might interact with each other, and what the results in the world will be. In short, one must do what can be called either a systems analysis or a social history.

In order to do the second job—to examine what various parts of society are likely to consider desirable and therefore to strive for, given the power to do so—there are two major methodologies to use. One of them is essentially a sociology of ideas. That is, one examines what the social roots of ideologies are, the social institutions they grow out of, and the social institutions that are created to fulfill them. Are those values in fact being fulfilled by the institutions that explain themselves by citing those values? If the Defense Department cites the value of liberty, does it in fact achieve that value or not? And, once having dug into the sociology of values, turn those findings on their head: having learned what values the society seems committed to but now finds unfulfilled in fact, analyze or project what real-life events, what real-life uses of institutions would in fact achieve those values which the society believes it holds. In short, turn the rhetoric of its values back upon the society to examine reality by the light of that rhetoric.

And secondly, there is the use of the participant-observation technique which illuminates both practicability and desirability. If the participant-observer acts out of what he believes people believe is desirable, he gets a chance to see how people respond to that, and so can reexamine from that response both what people seriously think is desirable and what is practicable as a way of change. Putting together these methodologies—analytical history, historical synthesis or systems analysis, the sociology of ideas, and participant-observation—the whole process of work looks like this: one develops a notion of possible social change and from that a vision of a desirable practicable future. One works out as vividly and in as much detail as possible, the way in which that practicable desirable future would work and would look. And then one works backward from that, in a kind of retroprojection, to see what kinds of change in *detail* would be necessary in order to get to that stage. In a sense this is a method of successive approximations, in which one could move from analysis of change to image of the future and back again, back and forth as many times as you like, getting more and more detailed each time.

7

Speculative Scenarios

ECO-CATASTROPHE

● *paul ehrlich*

I.

The end of the ocean came late in the summer of 1979, and it came even more rapidly than the biologists had expected. There had been signs for more than a decade, commencing with the discovery in 1968 that DDT slows down photosynthesis in marine plant life. It was announced in a short paper in the technical journal, *Science*, but to ecologists it smacked of doomsday. They knew that all life in the sea depends on photosynthesis, the chemical process by which green plants bind the sun's energy and make it available to living things. And they knew that DDT and similar chlorinated hydrocarbons had polluted the entire surface of the earth, including the sea.

But that was only the first of many signs. There had been the final gasp of the whaling industry in 1973, and the end of the Peruvian anchovy fishery in 1975. Indeed, a score of other fisheries had disappeared quietly from over-exploitation and various eco-catastrophies by 1977. The term "eco-catastrophe" was coined by a California ecologist in 1969 to describe the most spectacular of man's attacks on the systems which sustain his life. He drew his inspiration from the Santa Barbara offshore oil disaster of that year, and from the news which spread among naturalists that virtually all of the Golden State's sea-shore bird life was doomed because of chlorinated hydrocarbon interference with its reproduction. Eco-catastrophes in the sea became increasingly common in the early 1970's. Mysterious "blooms" of previously rare microorganisms began to appear in offshore waters. Red tides—killer outbreaks of a minute single-celled plant—returned to the Florida Gulf coast and were sometimes accompanied by tides of other exotic hues.

It was clear by 1975 that the entire ecology of the ocean was changing. A few types of phytoplankton were becoming resistant to chlorinated hydro-carbons and were gaining the upper hand. Changes in the phytoplankton community led inevitably to changes in the community of zooplankton, the tiny animals which eat the phytoplankton. These changes were passed on up the chains of life in the ocean to the herring, plaice, cod and tuna. As the diversity of life in the ocean diminished, its stability also decreased.

Other changes had taken place by 1975. Most ocean fishes that returned to fresh water to breed, like the salmon, had become extinct, their breeding streams so dammed up and polluted that their powerful homing instinct only resulted in suicide. Many fishes and shellfishes that bred in restricted areas along the coasts followed them as onshore pollution escalated.

By 1977 the annual yield of fish from the sea was down to 30 million metric tons, less than one-half the per capita catch of a decade earlier. This helped malnutrition to escalate sharply in a world where an estimated 50 million people per year were already dying of starvation. The United Nations attempted to get all chlorinated hydrocarbon insecticides banned on a worldwide basis, but the move was defeated by the United States. This opposition was generated primarily by the American petrochemical industry, operating hand in glove with its subsidiary, the United States Department of Agriculture. Together they persuaded the government to oppose the U.N. move—which was not difficult since most Americans believed that Russia and China were more in need of fish products than was the United States. The United Nations also attempted to get fishing nations to adopt strict and enforced catch limits to preserve dwindling stocks. This move was blocked by Russia, who, with the most modern electronic equipment, was in the best position to glean what was left in the sea. It was, curiously, on the very day in 1977 when the Soviet Union announced its refusal that another ominous article appeared in Science. It announced that incident solar radiation had been so reduced by worldwide air pollution that serious effects on the world's vegetation could be expected.

II.

Apparently it was a combination of ecosystem destabilization, sunlight reduction, and a rapid escalation of chlorinated hydrocarbon pollution from massive Thanodrin applications which triggered the ultimate catastrophe. Seventeen huge Soviet-financed Thanodrin plants were operating in underdeveloped countries by 1978. They had been part of a massive Russian "aid offensive" designed to fill the gap caused by the collapse of America's ballyhooed "Green Revolution."

It became apparent in the early '70's that the "Green Revolution" was more talk than substance. Distribution of high yield "miracle" grain seeds had caused temporary local spurts in agricultural production. Simultaneously, excellent weather had produced record harvests. The combination permitted bureaucrats, especially in the United States Department of Agriculture and the Agency for International Development (AID), to reverse their previous pessimism and indulge in an outburst of optimistic propaganda about staving off famine. They raved about the approaching transformation of agriculture in the underdeveloped countries (UDCs). The reason for the propaganda reversal was never made clear. Most historians agree that a combination of utter ignorance of ecology, a desire to justify past errors, and pressure from agroindustry (which was eager to sell pesticides, fertilizers, and farm machinery to the UDCs and agencies helping the UDCs) was behind the campaign. Whatever the motivation, the results were clear. Many concerned people, lacking the expertise to see through the Green Revolution drivel, relaxed. The population-food crisis was "solved."

But reality was not long in showing itself. Local famine persisted in northern India even after good weather brought an end to the ghastly Bihar famine of the mid-'60's. East Pakistan was next, followed by a resurgence of general famine in northern India. Other foci of famine rapidly developed in Indonesia, the Philippines, Malawi, the Congo, Egypt, Colombia, Ecuador, Honduras, the Dominican Republic, and Mexico.

Everywhere hard realities destroyed the illusion of the Green Revolution. Yields dropped as the progressive farmers who had first accepted the new seeds found that their higher yields brought lower prices—effective demand (hunger plus cash) was not sufficient in poor countries to keep prices up. Less progressive farmers, observing this, refused to make the extra effort required to cultivate the "miracle" grains. Transport systems proved inadequate to bring the necessary fertilizer to the fields where the new and extremely fertilizer-sensitive grains were being grown. The same systems were also inadequate to move produce to markets. Fertilizer plants were not built fast enough, and most of the underdeveloped countries could not scrape together funds to purchase supplies, even on concessional terms. Finally, the inevitable happened, and pests began to reduce yields in even the most carefully cultivated fields. Among the first were the famous "miracle rats" which invaded Philippine "miracle rice" fields early in 1969. They were quickly followed by many insects and viruses, thriving on the relatively pest-susceptible new grains, encouraged by the vast and dense plantings, and rapidly acquiring resistance to the chemicals used against them. As chaos spread until even the most obtuse agriculturists and economists realized that the Green Revolution had turned brown, the Russians stepped in.

In retrospect it seems incredible that the Russians, with the American mistakes known to them, could launch an even more incompetent program of aid to the underdeveloped world. Indeed, in the early 1970's there were cynics in the United States who claimed that outdoing the stupidity of American foreign aid would be physically impossible. Those critics were, however, obviously unaware that the Russians had been busily destroying their own environment for many years. The virtual disappearance of sturgeon from Russian rivers caused a great shortage of caviar by 1970. A standard joke among Russian scientists at that time was that they had created an artificial caviar which was indistinguishable from the real thing—except by taste. At any rate the Soviet Union, observing with interest the progressive deterioration of relations between the UDCs and the United States, came up with a solution. It had recently developed what it claimed was the ideal insecticide, a highly lethal chlorinated hydrocarbon complexed with a special agent for penetrating the external skeletal armor of insects. Announcing that the new pesticide, called Thanodrin, would truly produce a Green Revolution, the Soviets entered into negotiations with various UDCs for the construction of massive Thanodrin factories. The USSR would bear all the costs; all it wanted in return were certain trade and military concessions.

It is interesting now, with the perspective of years, to examine in some detail the reasons why the UDCs welcomed the Thanodrin plan with such open arms. Government officials in these countries ignored the protests of their own scientists that Thanodrin would not solve the problems which plagued them. The governments now knew that the basic cause of their problems was overpopulation, and that these problems had been exacerbated by the dullness, daydreaming, and cupidity endemic to all governments. They knew that only population control and limited development aimed primarily at agriculture could have spared them the horrors they now faced. They knew it, but they were not about to admit it. How much easier it was simply to accuse the Americans of failing to give them proper aid; how much simpler to accept the Russian panacea.

And then there was the general worsening of relations between the United States and the UDCs. Many things had contributed to this. The situation in America in the first half of the 1970's deserves our close scrutiny. Being more dependent on imports for raw materials than the Soviet Union, the United States had, in the early 1970's, adopted more and more heavy-handed policies in order to insure continuing supplies. Military adventures in Asia and Latin America had further lessened the international credibility of the United States as a great defender of freedom—an image which had begun to deteriorate rapidly during the pointless and fruitless Viet-Nam conflict. At home, acceptance of the carefully manufactured image lessened dramatically, as even the more romantic and chauvinistic citizens began to understand the role of the military and the industrial system in what John Kenneth Galbraith had aptly named "The New Industrial State."

At home in the USA the early '70's were traumatic times. Racial violence grew and the habitability of the cities diminished, as nothing substantial was done to ameliorate either racial inequities or urban blight. Welfare rolls grew as automation and general technological progress forced more and more people into the category of "unemployable." Simultaneously a taxpayers' revolt occurred. Although there was not enough money to build the schools, roads, water systems, sewage systems, jails, hospitals, urban transit lines, and all the other amenities needed to support a burgeoning population, Americans refused to tax themselves more heavily. Starting in Youngstown, Ohio in 1969 and followed closely by Richmond, California, community after community was forced to close its schools or curtail educational operations for lack of funds. Water supplies, already marginal in quality and quantity in many places by 1970, deteriorated quickly. Water rationing occurred in 1723 municipalities in the summer of 1974, and hepatitis and epidemic dysentery rates climbed about 500 percent between 1970–1974.

III.

Air pollution continued to be the most obvious manifestation of environmental deterioration. It was, by 1972, quite literally in the eyes of all Americans. The year 1973 saw not only the New York and Los Angeles smog disasters, but also the publication of the Surgeon General's massive report on air pollution and health. The public had been partially prepared for the worst by the publicity given to the U.N. pollution conference held in 1972. Deaths in the late '60's caused by smog were well known to scientists, but the public had ignored them because they mostly involved the early demise of the old and sick rather than people dropping dead on the freeways. But suddenly our citizens were faced with nearly 200,000 corpses and massive documentation that they could be the next to die from respiratory disease. They were not ready for that scale of disaster. After all, the U.N. conference had not predicted that accumulated air pollution would make the planet uninhabitable until almost 1990. The population was terrorized as TV screens became filled with scenes of horror from the disaster areas. Especially vivid was NBC's coverage of hundreds of unattended people choking out their lives outside of New York's hospitals. Terms like nitrogen oxide, acute bronchitis and cardiac arrest began to have real meaning for most Americans.

The ultimate horror was the announcement that chlorinated hydrocarbons were now a major constituent of air pollution in all American cities. Autopsies of smog disaster victims revealed an average chlorinated hydrocarbon load in fatty tissue equivalent to 26 parts per million of DDT. In October, 1973, the Department of Health, Education and Welfare announced studies which showed unequivocally that increasing death rates from hypertension, cirrhosis of the liver, liver cancer and a series of other diseases had resulted from the chlorinated hydrocarbon load. They estimated that Americans born since 1946 (when DDT usage began) now had a life expectancy of only 49 years, and predicted that if current patterns continued, this expectancy would reach 42 years by 1980, when it might level out. Plunging insurance stocks triggered a stock market panic. The president of Velsicol, Inc., a major pesticide producer, went on television to "publicly eat a teaspoonful of DDT" (it was really powdered milk) and announce that HEW had been infiltrated by Communists. Other giants of the petrochemical industry, attempting to dispute the indisputable evidence, launched a massive pressure campaign on Congress to force HEW to "get out of agriculture's business." They were aided by the agro-chemical journals, which had decades of experience in misleading the public about the benefits and dangers of pesticides. But by now the public realized that it had been duped. The Nobel Prize for medicine and physiology was given to Drs. J. L. Radomski and W. B. Deichmann, who in the late 1960's had pioneered in the documentation of the long-term lethal effects of chlorinated hydrocarbons. A Presidential Commission with unimpeachable credentials directly accused the agro-chemical complex of "condemning many millions of Americans to an early death." The year 1973 was the year in which Americans finally came to understand the direct threat to their existence posed by environmental deterioration.

And 1973 was also the year in which most people finally comprehended the indirect threat. Even the president of Union Oil Company and several other industrialists publicly stated their concern over the reduction of bird populations which had resulted from pollution by DDT and other chlorinated hydrocarbons. Insect populations boomed because they were resistant to most pesticides and had been freed, by the incompetent use of those pesticides, from most of their natural enemies. Rodents swarmed over crops, multiplying rapidly in the absence of predatory birds. The effect of pests on the wheat crop was especially disastrous in the summer of 1973, since that was also the year of the great drought. Most of us can remember the shock which greeted the announcement by atmospheric physicists that the shift of the jet stream which had caused the draught was probably permanent. It signalled the birth of the Midwestern desert. Man's air-polluting activities had by then caused gross changes in climatic patterns. The news, of course, played hell with commodity and stock markets. Food prices skyrocketed, as savings were poured into hoarded canned goods. Official assurances that food supplies would remain ample fell on deaf ears, and even the government showed signs of nervousness when California migrant field workers went out on strike again in protest against the continued use of pesticides by growers. The strike burgeoned into farm burning and riots. The workers, calling themselves "The Walking Dead," demanded immediate compensation for their shortened lives, and crash research programs to attempt to lengthen them.

It was in the same speech in which President Edward Kennedy, after much delay, finally declared a national emergency and called out the National Guard to harvest California's crops, that the first mention of population control was made. Kennedy pointed out that the United States would no longer be able to offer any food aid to other nations and was likely to suffer food shortages herself. He suggested that, in view of the manifest failure of the Green Revolution, the only hope of the UDCs lay in population control. His statement, you will recall, created an uproar in the underdeveloped countries. Newspaper editorials accused the United States of wishing to prevent small countries from becoming large nations and thus threatening American hegemony. Politicians asserted that President Kennedy was a "creature of the giant drug combine" that wished to shove its pills down every woman's throat.

Among Americans, religious opposition to population control was very slight. Industry in general also backed the idea. Increasing poverty in the UDCs was both destroying markets and threatening supplies of raw materials. The seriousness of the raw material situation had been brought home during the Congressional Hard Resources hearings in 1971. The exposure of the ignorance of the cornucopian economists had been quite a spectacle—a spectacle brought into virtually every American's home in living color. Few would forget the distinguished geologist from the University of California who suggested that economists be legally required to learn at least the most elementary facts of geology. Fewer still would forget that an equally distinguished Harvard economist added that they might be required to learn some economics, too. The overall message was clear: America's resource situation was bad and bound to get worse. The hearings had led to a bill requiring the

Departments of State, Interior, and Commerce to set up a joint resource procurement council with the express purpose of "insuring that proper consideration of American resource needs be an integral part of American foreign policy."

Suddenly the United States discovered that it had a national consensus: population control was the only possible salvation of the underdeveloped world. But that same consensus led to heated debate. How could the UDCs be persuaded to limit their populations, and should not the United States lead the way by limiting its own? Members of the intellectual community wanted America to set an example. They pointed out that the United States was in the midst of a new baby boom: her birth rate, well over 20 per thousand per year, and her growth rate of over one percent per annum were among the very highest of the developed countries. They detailed the deterioration of the American physical and psychic environments, the growing health threats, the impending food shortages, and the insufficiency of funds for desperately needed public works. They contended that the nation was clearly unable or unwilling to properly care for the people it already had. What possible reason could there be, they queried, for adding any more? Besides, who would listen to requests by the United States for population control when that nation did not control her own profligate reproduction?

Those who opposed population controls for the U.S. were equally vociferous. The military-industrial complex, with its all-too-human mixture of ignorance and avarice, still saw strength and prosperity in numbers. Baby food magnates, already worried by the growing nitrate pollution of their products, saw their market disappearing. Steel manufacturers saw a decrease in aggregate demand and slippage for that holy of holies, the Gross National Product. And military men saw, in the growing population-food-environment crisis, a serious threat to their carefully nurtured Cold War. In the end, of course, economic arguments held sway, and the "inalienable right of every American couple to determine the size of its family," a freedom invented for the occasion in the early '70's, was not compromised.

The population control bill, which was passed by Congress early in 1974, was quite a document, nevertheless. On the domestic front, it authorized an increase from 100 to 150 million dollars in funds for "family planning" activities. This was made possible by a general feeling in the country that the growing army on welfare needed family planning. But the gist of the bill was a series of measures designed to impress the need for population control on the UDCs. All American aid to countries with overpopulation problems was required by law to consist in part of population control assistance. In order to receive any assistance each nation was required not only to accept the population control aid, but also to match it according to a complex formula. "Overpopulation" itself was defined by a formula based on U.N. statistics, and the UDCs were required not only to accept aid, but also to show progress in reducing birth rates. Every five years the status of the aid program for each nation was to be re-evaluated.

The reaction to the announcement of this program dwarfed the response to President Kennedy's speech. A coalition of UDCs attempted to get the U.N. General Assembly to condemn the United States as a "genetic aggressor." Most damaging of all to the American cause was the famous "25 Indians and a dog" speech by Mr. Shankarnarayan, Indian Ambassador to the U.N. Shankarnarayan pointed out that for several decades the United States, with less than six percent of the people of the world had consumed roughly 50 percent of the raw materials used every year. He described vividly America's contribution to worldwide environmental deterioration, and he scathingly denounced the miserly record of the United States foreign aid as "unworthy of a fourth-rate power, let alone the most powerful nation on earth."

It was the climax of his speech, however, which most historians claim once and for all destroyed the image of the United States. Shankarnarayan informed the assembly that the average American family dog was fed more animal protein per week than the average Indian got in a month. "How do you justify taking fish from protein-starved Peruvians and feeding them to your animals?" he asked. "I contend," he concluded, "that the birth of an American baby is a greater disaster for the world than that of 25 Indian babies." When the applause had died away, Mr. Sorensen, the American representative, made a speech which said essentially that "other countries look after their own self-interest, too." When the vote came, the United States was condemned.

IV.

This condemnation set the tone of U.S.-UDC relations at the time the Russian Thanodrin proposal was made. The proposal seemed to offer the masses in the UDCs an opportunity to save themselves and humiliate the United States at the same time; and in human affairs, as we all know, biological realities could never interfere with such an opportunity. The scientists were silenced, the politicians said yes, the Thanodrin plants were built, and the results were what any beginning ecology student could have predicted. At first Thanodrin seemed to offer excellent control of many pests. True, there was a rash of human fatalities from improper use of the lethal chemical, but, as Russian technical advisors were prone to note, these were more than compensated for by increased yields. Thanodrin use skyrocketed throughout the under-developed world. The Mikoyan design group developed a dependable, cheap agricultural aircraft which the Soviets donated to the effort in large numbers. MIG sprayers became even more common in UDCs than MIG interceptors.

Then the troubles began. Insect strains with cuticles resistant to Thanodrin penetration began to appear. And as streams, rivers, fish culture ponds and onshore waters became rich in Thanodrin, more fisheries began to disappear. Bird populations were decimated. The sequence of events was standard for broadcast use of a synthetic pesticide: great success at first, followed by removal of natural enemies and development of resistance by the pest. Populations of crop-eating insects in areas treated with Thanodrin made steady comebacks and soon became more abundant than ever. Yields plunged, while farmers in their desperation increased the Thanodrin dose and shortened the time between treatments. Death from Thanodrin poisoning became common. The first violent incident occurred in the Canete Valley of Peru, where farmers had suffered a similar chlorinated hydrocarbon disaster in the mid-50's. A Russian advisor serving as an agricultural pilot was assaulted and killed by a mob of enraged farmers in January, 1978. Trouble spread rapidly during 1978, especially after the word got out that two years earlier Russia herself had banned the use of Thanodrin at home because of its serious effects on ecological systems. Suddenly Russia, and not the United States, was the *bête noir* in the UDCs. "Thanodrin parties" became epidemic, with farmers, in their ignorance, dumping carloads of Thanodrin concentrate into the sea. Russian advisors fled, and four of the Thanodrin plants were leveled to the ground. Destruction of the plants in Rio and Calcutta led to hundreds of thousands of gallons of Thanodrin concentrate being dumped directly into the sea.

Mr. Shankarnarayan again rose to address the U.N., but this time it was Mr. Potemkin, representative of the Soviet Union, who was on the hot seat. Mr. Potemkin heard his nation described as the greatest mass killer of all time as Shankarnarayan predicted at least 30 million deaths from crop failures due to overdependence on Thanodrin. Russia was accused of "chemical aggression," and the General Assembly, after a weak reply by Potemkin, passed a vote of censure.

It was in January, 1979, that huge blooms of a previously unknown variety of diatom were reported off the coast of Peru. The blooms were accompanied by a massive die-off of sea life and of the pathetic remainder of the birds which had once feasted on the anchovies of the area. Almost immediately another huge bloom was reported in the Indian ocean, centering around the Seychelles, and then a third in the South Atlantic off the African coast. Both of these were accompanied by spectacular die-offs of marine animals. Even more ominous were growing reports of fish and bird kills at oceanic points where there were no spectacular blooms. Biologists were soon able to explain the phenomena: the diatom had evolved an enzyme which broke down Thanodrin; that enzyme also produced a breakdown product which interfered with the transmission of nerve impulses, and was therefore lethal to animals. Unfortunately, the biologists could suggest no way of repressing the poisonous diatom bloom in time. By September, 1979, all important animal life in the sea was extinct. Large areas of coastline had to be evacuated, as windrows of dead fish created a monumental stench.

But stench was the least of man's problems. Japan and China were faced with almost instant starvation from a total loss of the seafood on which they were so dependent. Both blamed Russia for their situation and demanded immediate mass shipments of food. Russia had none to send. On October 13, Chinese armies attacked Russia on a broad front. . . .

V.

A pretty grim scenario. Unfortunately, we're a long way into it already. Everything mentioned as happening before 1970 has actually occurred; much of the rest is based on projections of trends already appearing. Evidence that pesticides have long-term lethal effects on human beings has started to accumulate, and recently Robert Finch, Secretary of the Department of Health, Education and Welfare expressed his extreme apprehension about the pesticide situation. Simultaneously the petrochemical industry continues its unconscionable poison-peddling. For instance, Shell Chemical has been carrying on a high-pressure campaign to sell the insecticide Azodrin to farmers as a killer of cotton pests. They continue their program even though they know that Azodrin is not only ineffective, but often *increases* the pest density. They've covered themselves nicely in an advertisement which states, "Even if an overpowering migration [sic] develops, the flexibility of Azodrin lets you regain control fast. Just increase the dosage according to label recommendations." It's a great game—get people to apply the poison and kill the natural enemies of the pests. Then blame the increased pests on "migration" and sell even more pesticide!

Right now fisheries are being wiped out by over-exploitation, made easy by modern electronic equipment. The companies producing the equipment know this. They even boast in advertising that only their equipment will keep fishermen in business until the final kill. Profits must obviously be maximized in the short run. Indeed, Western society is in the process of completing the rape and murder of the planet for economic gain. And, sadly, most of the rest of the world is eager for the opportunity to emulate our behavior. But the underdeveloped peoples will be denied that opportunity—the days of plunder are drawing inexorably to a close.

Most of the people who are going to die in the greatest cataclysm in the history of man have already been born. More than three and a half billion people already populate our moribund globe, and about half of them are hungry. Some 10 to 20 million will starve to death *this year*. In spite of this, the population of the earth will increase by 70 million souls in 1969. For mankind has artificially lowered the death rate of the human population, while in general birth rates have remained high. With the input side of the population system in high gear and the output side slowed down, our fragile planet has filled with people at an incredible rate. It took several million years for the population to reach a total of two billion people in 1930, while a *second two billion will have been added by 1975!* By that time some experts feel that food shortages will have escalated the present level of world hunger and starvation into famines of unbelievable proportions. Other experts, more optimistic, think the ultimate food-population collision will not occur until the decade of the 1980's. Of course more massive famine may be avoided if other events cause a prior rise in the human death rate.

Both worldwide plague and thermonuclear war are made more probable as population growth continues. These, along with famine, make up the trio of potential "death rate solutions" to the population problem—solutions in which the birth rate-death rate imbalance is redressed by a rise in the death rate rather than by a lowering of the birth rate. Make no mistake about it, *the imbalance will be redressed*. The shape of the population growth curve is one familiar to the biologist. It is the outbreak part of an outbreak-crash sequence. A population grows rapidly in the presence of abundant resources, finally runs out of food or some other necessity, and crashes to a low level or extinction. Man is not only running out of food, he is also destroying the life support systems of the Spaceship Earth. The situation was recently summarized very succinctly: "It is the top of the ninth inning. Man, always a threat at the plate, has been hitting Nature hard. It is important to remember, however, that NATURE BATS LAST."

8

Models And Cybernetic
Anticipations

COUNTERINTUITIVE BEHAVIOR OF SOCIAL SYSTEMS

● *jay w. forrester*

This paper addresses several issues of broad concern in the United States: population trends; the quality of urban life; national policy for urban growth; and the unexpected, ineffective, or detrimental results often generated by government programs in these areas.

The nation exhibits a growing sense of futility as it repeatedly attacks deficiencies in our social system while the symptoms continue to worsen. Legislation is debated and passed with great promise and hope. But many programs prove to be ineffective. Results often seem unrelated to those expected when the programs were planned. At times programs cause exactly the reverse of desired results.

It is now possible to explain how such contrary results can happen. There are fundamental reasons why people misjudge the behavior of social systems. There are orderly processes at work in the creation of human judgment and intuition that frequently lead people to wrong decisions when faced with complex and highly interacting systems. Until we come to a much better understanding of social systems, we should expect that attempts to develop corrective programs will continue to disappoint us.

The purpose of this paper is to leave with its readers a sense of caution about continuing to depend on the same past approaches that have led to our present feeling of frustration and to suggest an approach which can eventually lead to a better understanding of our social systems and thereby to more effective policies for guiding the future.

A New Approach to Social Systems

It is my basic theme that the human mind is not adapted to interpreting how social systems behave. Our social systems belong to the class called multiloop nonlinear feedback systems. In the long history of evolution it has not been necessary for man to understand these systems until very recent historical times. Evolutionary processes have not given us the mental skill needed to properly interpret the dynamic behavior of the systems of which we have now become a part.

In addition, the social sciences have fallen into some mistaken "scientific" practices which compound man's natural shortcomings. Computers are often being used for what the computer does poorly and the human mind does well. At the same time the human mind is being used for what the human mind does poorly and the computer does well. Even worse, impossible tasks are attempted while achievable and important goals are ignored.

Until recently there has been no way to estimate the behavior of social systems except by contemplation, discussion, argument, and guesswork. To point a way out of our present dilemma about social systems, I will sketch an approach that combines the strength of the human mind and the strength of today's computers. The approach is an outgrowth of developments over the last 40 years, in which much of the research has been at the Massachusetts Institute of Technology. The concepts of feedback system behavior apply sweepingly from physical systems through social systems. The ideas were first developed and applied to engineering systems. They have now reached practical usefulness in major aspects of our social systems.

I am speaking of what has come to be called industrial dynamics. The name is a misnomer because the methods apply to complex systems regardless of the field in which they are located. A more appropriate name would be *system dynamics*. In our own work, applications have been made to corporate policy, to the dynamics of diabetes as a medical system, to the growth and stagnation of an urban area, and most recently to world dynamics representing the interactions of population, pollution, industrialization, natural resources, and food. System dynamics, as an extension of the earlier design of physical systems, has been under development at M.I.T. since 1956. The approach is easy to understand but difficult to practice. Few people have a high level of skill; but preliminary work is developing all over the world. Some European countries and especially Japan have begun centers of education and research.

Computer Models of Social Systems

People would never attempt to send a space ship to the moon without first testing the equipment by constructing prototype models and by computer simulation of the anticipated space trajectories. No company would put a new kind of household appliance or electronic computer into production without first making laboratory tests. Such models and laboratory tests do not guarantee against failure, but they do identify many weaknesses which can then be corrected before they cause full-scale disasters.

Our social systems are far more complex and harder to understand than our technological systems. Why, then, do we not use the same approach of making models of social systems and conducting laboratory experiments on those models before we try new laws and government programs in real life? The answer is often stated that our knowledge of social systems is insufficient for constructing useful models. But what justification can there be for the apparent assumption that we do not know enough to construct models but believe we do know enough to directly design new social systems by passing laws and starting new social programs? I am suggesting that we now do know enough to make useful models of social systems. Conversely, we do not know enough to design the most effective social systems directly without first going through a model-building experimental phase. But I am confident, and substantial supporting evidence is beginning to accumulate, that the proper use of models of social systems can lead to far better systems, laws, and programs.

It is now possible to construct in the laboratory realistic models of social systems. Such models are simplifications of the actual social system but can be far more comprehensive than the mental models that we otherwise use as the basis of debating governmental action.

Before going further, I should emphasize that there is nothing new in the use of models to represent social systems. Each of us uses models constantly. Every person in his private life and in his business life instinctively uses models for decision-making. The mental image of the world around you which you carry in your head is a model. One does not have a city or a government or a country in his head. He has only selected concepts and relationships which he uses to represent the real system. A mental image is a model. All of our decisions are taken on the basis of models. All of our laws are passed on the basis of models. All executive actions are taken on the basis of models. The question is not to use or ignore models. The question is only a choice among alternative models.

The mental model is fuzzy. It is incomplete. It is imprecisely stated. Furthermore, within one individual, a mental model changes with time and even during the flow of a single conversation. The human mind assembles a few relationships to fit the context of a discussion. As the subject shifts so does the model. When only a single topic is being discussed, each participant in a conversation employs a different mental model to interpret the subject. Fundamental assumptions differ but are never brought into the open. Goals are different and are left unstated. It is little wonder that compromise takes so long. And it is not surprising that consensus leads to laws and programs that fail in their objectives or produce new difficulties greater than those that have been relieved.

For these reasons we stress the importance of being explicit about assumptions and interrelating them in a computer model. Any concept or assumption that can be clearly described in words can be incorporated in a computer model. When done, the ideas become clear. Assumptions are exposed so they may be discussed and debated.

But the most important difference between the properly conceived computer model and the mental model is in the ability to determine the dynamic consequences when the assumptions within the model interact with one another. The human mind is not adapted to sensing correctly the consequences of a mental model. The mental model may be correct in structure and assumptions but, even so, the human mind—either individually or as a group consensus—is most apt to draw the wrong conclusions. There is no doubt about the digital computer routinely and accurately tracing through the sequences of actions that result from following the statements of behavior for individual points in the model system. This inability of the human mind to use its own mental models is clearly shown when a computer model is constructed to reproduce the assumptions held by a single person. In other words, the model is refined until it is fully agreeable in all its assumptions to the perceptions and ideas of a particular person. Then, it usually happens that the system that has been described does not act the way the person anticipated. Usually there is an internal contradiction in mental models between the assumed structure and the assumed future consequences. Ordinarily the assumptions about structure and internal motivations are more nearly correct than are the assumptions about the implied behavior.

The kind of computer models that I am discussing are strikingly similar to mental models. They are derived from the same sources. They may be discussed in the same terms. But computer models differ from mental models in important ways. The computer models are stated explicitly. The "mathematical" notation that is used for describing the model is unambiguous. It is a language that is clearer, simpler, and more precise than such spoken languages as English or French. Its advantage is in the clarity of meaning and the simplicity of the language syntax. The language of a computer model can be understood by almost anyone, regardless of educational background. Furthermore, any concept and relationship that can be clearly stated in ordinary language can be translated into computer model language.

There are many approaches to computer models. Some are naive. Some are conceptually and structurally inconsistent with the nature of actual systems. Some are based on methodologies for obtaining input data that commit the models to omitting major concepts and relationships in the psychological and human reaction areas that we all know to be crucial. With so much activity in computer models and with the same terminology having different meanings in the different approaches, the situation must be confusing to the casual observer. The key to success is not in having a computer; the important thing is how the computer is used. With respect to models, the key is not to computerize a model, but instead to have a model structure and relationships which properly represent the system that is being considered.

I am speaking here of a kind of computer model that is very different from the models that are now most common in the social sciences. Such a computer model is not derived statistically from time-series data. Instead, the kind of computer model I am discussing is a statement of system structure. It contains the assumptions being made about the system. The model is only as good as the expertise which lies behind its formulation. Great and correct theories in physics or in economics are few and far between. A great computer model is distinguished from a poor one by the degree to which it captures more of the essence of the social system that it presumes to represent. Many mathematical models are limited because they are formulated by techniques and according to a conceptual structure that will not accept the multiple-feedback-loop and nonlinear nature of real systems. Other models are defective because of lack of knowledge or deficiencies of perception on the part of the persons who have formulated them.

But a recently developed kind of computer modeling is now beginning to show the characteristics of behavior of actual systems. These models explain why we are having the present difficulties with our actual social systems and furthermore explain why so many efforts to improve social systems have failed. In spite of their shortcomings, models can now be constructed that are far superior to the intuitive models in our heads on which we are now basing national social programs.

This approach to the dynamics of social systems differs in two important ways from common practice in social sciences and government. There seems to be a common attitude that the major difficulty is shortage of information and data. Once data is collected, people then feel confident in interpreting the implications. I differ on both of these attitudes. The problem is not shortage of data but rather our inability to perceive the consequences of the information we already possess. The system dynamics approach starts with the concepts and information on which people are already acting. Generally these are sufficient. The available perceptions are then assembled in a computer model which can show the consequences of the well-known and properly perceived parts of the system. Generally, the consequences are unexpected.

Counterintuitive Nature of Social Systems

Our first insights into complex social systems came from our corporate work. Time after time we have gone into a corporation which is having severe and well-known difficulties. The difficulties can be major and obvious such as a falling market share, low profitability, or instability of employment. Such difficulties are known throughout the company and by anyone outside who reads the management press. One can enter such a company and discuss with people in key decision points what they are doing to solve the problem. Generally speaking we find that people perceive correctly their immediate environment. They know what they are trying to accomplish. They know the crises which will force certain actions. They are sensitive to the power structure of the organization, to traditions, and to their own personal goals and welfare. In general, when circumstances are conducive to frank disclosure, people can state what they are doing and can give rational reasons for their actions. In a troubled company, people are usually trying in good conscience and to the best of their abilities to solve the major difficulties. Policies are being followed at the various points in the organization on the presumption that they will alleviate the difficulties. One can combine these policies into a computer model to show the consequences of how the policies interact with one another. In many instances it then emerges that the known policies describe a system which actually causes the troubles. In other words, the known and intended practices of the organization are fully sufficient to create the difficulty, regardless of what happens outside the company or in the marketplace. In fact, a downward spiral develops in which the presumed solution makes the difficulty worse and thereby causes redoubling of the presumed solution.

The same downward spiral frequently develops in government. Judgment and debate lead to a program that appears to be sound. Commitment increases to the apparent solution. If the presumed solution actually makes matters worse, the process by which this happens is not evident. So, when the troubles increase, the efforts are intensified that are actually worsening the problem.

Dynamics of Urban Systems

Our first major excursion outside of corporate policy began in February, 1968, when John F. Collins, former mayor of Boston, became Professor of Urban Affairs at M.I.T. He and I discussed my work in industrial dynamics and his experience with urban difficulties. A close collaboration led to applying to the dynamics of the city the same methods that had been created for understanding the social and policy structure of the corporation. A model structure was developed to represent the fundamental urban processes. The proposed structure shows how industry, housing, and people interact with each other as a city grows and decays. The results are described in my book *Urban Dynamics*, and some were summarized in *Technology Review* (April, 1969, pp. 21–31).

I had not previously been involved with urban behavior or urban policies. But the emerging story was strikingly similar to what we had seen in the corporation. Actions taken to alleviate the difficulties of a city can actually make matters worse. We examined four common programs for improving the depressed nature of the central city. One is the creation of jobs as by bussing the unemployed to the suburbs or through governmental jobs as employer of last resort. Second was a training program to increase the skills of the lowest-income group. Third was financial aid to the depressed city as by federal subsidy. Fourth was the construction of low-cost housing. All of these are shown to lie between neutral and detrimental almost irrespective of the criteria used for judgment. They range from ineffective to harmful judged either by their effect on the economic health of the city or by their long-range effect on the low-income population of the city.

The results both confirm and explain much of what has been happening over the last several decades in our cities.

In fact, it emerges that the fundamental cause of depressed areas in the cities comes from *excess* housing in the low-income category rather than the commonly presumed housing shortage. The legal and tax structures have combined to give incentives for keeping old buildings in place. As industrial buildings age, the employment opportunities decline. As residential buildings age, they are used by lower-income groups who are forced to use them at a higher population density. Therefore, jobs decline and population rises while buildings age. Housing, at the higher population densities, accommodates more low-income urban population than can find jobs. A social trap is created where excess low-cost housing beckons low-income people inward because of the available housing. They continue coming to the city until their numbers so far exceed the available income opportunities that the standard of living declines far enough to stop further inflow. Income to the area is then too low to maintain all of the housing. Excess housing falls into disrepair and is abandoned. One can simultaneously have extreme crowding in those buildings that are occupied, while other buildings become excess and are abandoned because the economy of the area cannot support all of the residential structures. But the excess residential buildings threaten the area in two ways—they occupy the land so that it cannot be used for job-creating buildings, and they stand ready to accept a rise in population if the area should start to improve economically.

Any change which would otherwise raise the standard of living only takes off the economic pressure momentarily and causes the population to rise enough that the standard of living again falls to the barely tolerable level. A self-regulating system is thereby at work which drives the condition of the depressed area down far enough to stop the increase in people.

At any time, a near-equilibrium exists affecting population mobility between the different areas of the country. To the extent that there is disequilibrium, it means that some area is slightly more attractive than others and population begins to move in the direction of the more attractive area. This movement continues until the rising population drives the more attractive area down in attractiveness until the area is again in equilibrium with its surroundings. Other things being equal, an increase in population of a city crowds housing, overloads job opportunities, causes congestion, increases pollution, encourages crime, and reduces almost every component of the quality of life.

This powerful dynamic force to re-establish an equilibrium in total attractiveness means that any social program must take into account the eventual shifts that will occur in the many components of *attractiveness*. As used here, attractiveness is the composite effect of all factors that cause population movement toward or away from an area. Most areas in a country have nearly equal attractiveness most of the time, with only sufficient disequilibrium in attractiveness to account for the shifts in population. But areas can have the same composite attractiveness with different mixes in the components of attractiveness. In one area component A could be high and B low, while the reverse could be true in another area that nevertheless had the same total composite attractiveness. If a program makes some aspect of an area more attractive than its neighbor's, and thereby makes total attractiveness higher momentarily, population of that area rises until other components of attractiveness are driven down far enough to again establish an equilibrium. This means that efforts to improve the condition of our cities will result primarily in increasing the population of the cities and causing the population of the country to concentrate in the cities. The overall condition of urban life, for any particular economic class of population, cannot be appreciably better or worse than that of the remainder of the country to and from which people may come. Programs aimed at improving the city can succeed only if they result in eventually raising the average quality of life for the country as a whole.

On Raising the Quality of Life

But there is substantial doubt that our urban programs have been contributing to the national quality of life. By concentrating total population, and especially low-income population, in urban locations, undermining the strength and cohesiveness of the community, and making government and bureaucracy so big that the individual feels powerless to influence the system within which he is increasingly constrained, the quality of life is being reduced. In fact, if they have any effect, our efforts to improve our urban areas will in the long run tend to delay the concern about rising total population and thereby contribute directly to the eventual overcrowding of the country and the world.

Any proposed program must deal with both the quality of life and the factors affecting population. "Raising the quality of life" means releasing stress and pressures, reducing crowding, reducing pollution, alleviating hunger, and treating ill health. But these pressures are exactly the sources of concern and action aimed at controlling total population to keep it within the bounds of the fixed world within which we live. If the pressures are relaxed, so is the concern about how we impinge on the environment. Population will then rise further until the pressures reappear with an intensity that can no longer be relieved. To try to raise quality of life without intentionally creating compensating pressures to prevent a rise in population density will be self-defeating.

Consider the meaning of these interacting attractiveness components as they affect a depressed ghetto area of a city. First we must be clear on the way population density is, in fact, now being controlled. There is some set of forces determining that the density is not far higher or lower than it is. But there are many possible combinations of forces that an urban area can exert. The particular combination will determine the population mix of the area and the economic health of the city. I suggest that the depressed areas of most American cities are created by a combination of forces in which there is a job shortage and a housing excess. The availability of housing draws the lowest-income group until they so far exceed the opportunities of the area that the low standard of living, the frustration, and the crime rate counterbalance the housing availability. Until the pool of excess housing is reduced, little can be done to improve the economic condition of the city. A low-cost housing program alone moves exactly in the wrong direction. It draws more low-income people. It makes the area differentially more attractive to the poor who need jobs and less attractive to those who create jobs. In the new population equilibrium that develops, some characteristic of the social system must compensate for the additional attractiveness created by the low-cost housing. The counterbalance is a further decline of the economic condition for the area. But as the area becomes more destitute, pressures rise for more low-cost housing. The consequence is a downward spiral that draws in the low-income population, depresses their condition, prevents escape, and reduces hope. All of this is done with the best of intentions.

My paper, "Systems Analysis as a Tool for Urban Planning" from a symposium in October, 1969, at the National Academy of Engineering, suggests a reversal of present practice in order to simultaneously reduce the aging housing in our cities and allocate land to income-earning opportunities. The land shifted to industry permits the "balance of trade" of the area to be corrected by allowing labor to create and export a product to generate an income stream with which to buy the necessities of modern life from the outside. But the concurrent reduction of excess housing is absolutely essential. It supplies the land for new jobs. Equally important, the resulting housing shortage creates the population-stabilizing pressure that allows economic revival to proceed without being inundated by rising population. This can all be done without driving the present low-income residents out of the area. It can create *upward economic mobility* to convert the low-income population to a self-supporting basis.

The first reaction of many people to these ideas is to believe that they will never be accepted by elected officials or by residents of depressed urban areas. But some of our strongest support and encouragement is coming from those very groups who are closest to the problems, who see the symptoms first-hand, who have lived through the failures of the past, and who must live with the present conditions until enduring solutions are found.

Over the last several decades the country has slipped into a set of attitudes about our cities that are leading to actions that have become an integral part of the system that is generating greater troubles. If we were malicious and wanted to create urban slums, trap low-income people in ghetto areas, and increase the number of people on welfare, we could do little better than follow the present policies. The trend toward stressing income and sales taxes and away from the real estate tax encourages old buildings to remain in place and block self-renewal. The concessions in the income tax laws to encourage low-income housing will in the long run actually increase the total low-income population of the country. The highway expenditures and the government loans for suburban housing have made it easier for higher-income groups to abandon urban areas than to revive them. The pressures to expand the areas incorporated by urban government, in an effort to expand the revenue base, have been more than offset by lowered administrative efficiency, more citizen frustration, and the accelerated decline that is triggered in the annexed areas. The belief that more money will solve urban problems has taken attention away from correcting the underlying causes and has instead allowed the problems to grow to the limit of the available money, whatever that amount might be.

Characteristics of Social Systems

I turn now to some characteristics of social systems that mislead people. These have been identified in our work with corporate and urban systems and in more recent work that I will describe concerning the worldwide pressures that are now enveloping our planet.

First, social systems are inherently insensitive to most policy changes that people select in an effort to alter the behavior of the system. In fact, a social system tends to draw our attention to the very points at which an attempt to intervene will fail. Our experience, which has been developed from contact with simple systems, leads us to look close to the symptoms of trouble for a cause. When we look, we discover that the social system presents us with an apparent cause that is plausible according to what we have learned from simple systems. But this apparent cause is usually a coincident occurrence that, like the trouble symptom itself, is being produced by the feedback-loop dynamics of a larger system. For example, as already discussed, we see human suffering in the cities; we observe that it is accompanied (some think caused) by inadequate housing. We increase the housing and the population rises to compensate for the effort. More people are drawn into and trapped in the depressed social system. As another example, the symptoms of excess population are beginning to overshadow the country. These symptoms appear as urban crowding and social pressure. Rather than face the population problem squarely we try to relieve the immediate pressure by planning industry in rural areas and by discussing new towns. If additional urban area is provided it will temporarily reduce the pressures and defer the need to face the underlying population question. The consequence, as it will be seen 25 years hence, will have been to contribute to increasing the population so much that even today's quality of life will be impossible.

A second characteristic of social systems is that all of them seem to have a few sensitive influence points through which the behavior of the system can be changed. These influence points are not in the locations where most people expect. Furthermore, if one identifies in a model of a social system a sensitive point where influence can be exerted, the chances are still that a person guided by intuition and judgment will alter the system in the wrong direction. For example in the urban system, housing is a sensitive control point but, if one wishes to revive the economy of a city and make it a better place for low-income as well as other people, it appears that the amount of low-income housing must be reduced rather than increased. Another example is the world-wide problem of rising population and the disparity between the standards of living in the developed and the underdeveloped countries, an issue arising in the world system to be discussed in the following paragraphs. But it is beginning to appear that a sensitive control point is the rate of generation of capital investment.

And how should one change the rate of capital accumulation? The common answer has been to increase industrialization, but recent examination suggests that hope lies only in reducing the rate of industrialization. This may actually help raise quality of life and contribute to stabilizing population.

As a third characteristic of social systems, there is usually a fundamental conflict between the short-term and long-term consequences of a policy change. A policy which produces improvements in the short run within five to ten years, is usually one which degrades the system in the long run, beyond ten years. Likewise, those policies and programs which produce long-run improvement may initially depress the behavior of the system. This is especially treacherous. The short run is more visible and more compelling. It speaks loudly for immediate attention. But a series of actions all aimed at short-run improvement can eventually burden a system with long-run depressants so severe that even heroic short-run measures no longer suffice. Many of the problems which we face today are the eventual result of short-run measures taken as long as two or three decades ago.

A Global Perspective

I have mentioned social organizations at the corporate level and then touched on work which has been done on the dynamics of the city. Now we are beginning to examine issues of even broader scope.

In July, 1970, we held a two-week international conference on world dynamics. It was a meeting organized for the Club of Rome, a private group of about 50 individuals drawn from many countries who have joined together to attempt a better understanding of social systems at the world level. Their interest lies in the same problems of population, resources, industrialization, pollution, and world-wide disparities of standard of living on which many groups now focus. But the Club of Rome is devoted to taking actions that will lead to a better understanding of world trends and to influencing world leaders and governments. The July meeting at M.I.T. included the general theory and behavior of complex systems and talks on the behavior of specific social systems ranging from corporations through commodity markets to biological systems, drug addiction in the community, and growth and decline of a city. Especially prepared for this conference was a dynamic model of the interactions between world population, industrialization, depletion of natural resources, agriculture, and pollution. A detailed discussion of this world system will soon appear in my book *World Dynamics*, and its further development is the purpose of the "Project on the Predicament of Mankind" being sponsored by the Club of Rome at M.I.T. for a year under the guidance of Professor Dennis Meadows. The plan is to develop a research group of men from many countries who will eventually base their continuing efforts in a neutral country such as Switzerland. The immediate project will reexamine, verify, alter, and extend the preliminary dynamic study of the world system and will relate it to the present world-wide concern about trends in civilization.

The simple model of world interactions as thus far developed shows several different alternative futures depending on whether population growth is eventually suppressed by shortage of natural resources, by pollution, by crowding and consequent social strife, or by insufficient food. Malthus dealt only with the latter, but it is possible for civilization to encounter other controlling pressures before a food shortage occurs.

It is certain that resource shortage, pollution, crowding, food failure, or some other equally powerful force will limit population and industrialization if persuasion and psychological factors do not. Exponential growth cannot continue forever. Our greatest immediate challenge is how we guide the transition from growth to equilibrium. There are many possible mechanisms of growth suppression. That some one or combination will occur is inevitable. Unless we come to understand and to choose, the social system by its internal processes will choose for us. The natural mechanisms for terminating exponential growth appear to be the least desirable. Unless we understand and begin to act soon, we may be overwhelmed by a social and economic system we have created but can't control.

Figure 1 shows the structure that has been assumed. It interrelates the mutual effects of population, capital investment, natural resources, pollution, and the fraction of capital devoted to agriculture. These five system "levels" are shown in the rectangles. Each level is caused to change by the rates of flow in and out, such as the birth rate and death rate that increase and decrease population. As shown by the dotted lines, the five system levels, through intermediate concepts shown at the circles, control the rates of flow. As an example, the death rate at Symbol 10 depends on population P and the "normal" lifetime as stated by death rate normal DRN. But death rate depends also on conditions in other parts of the system. From Circle 12 comes the influence of pollution that here assumes death rate to double if pollution becomes 20 times as severe as in 1970; and, progressively, that death rate would increase by a factor of 10 if pollution became 60 times as much as now. Likewise from Circle 13 the effect of food per capita is to increase death rate as food becomes less available. The detailed definition of the model states how each rate of flow is assumed to depend on the levels of population, natural resources, capital investment, capital devoted to food, and pollution.

Individually the assumptions in the model are plausible, create little disagreement, and reflect common discussions and assertions about the individual responses within the world system. But each is explicit and can be subjected to scrutiny. From one viewpoint, the system of Figure 1 is very simplified. It focuses on a few major factors and omits most of the substructure of world social and economic activity. But from another viewpoint, Figure 1 is comprehensive and complex. The system is far more complete and the theory described by the accompanying computer model is much more explicit than the mental models that are now being used as a basis for world and governmental planning. It incorporates dozens of nonlinear relationships. The world system shown here exhibits provocative and even frightening possibilities.

FIGURE 1: UPON THIS WORLD MODEL ARE BASED THE AUTHOR'S ANALYSES OF THE EFFECTS OF CHANGING POPULATION AND ECONOMIC GROWTH FACTORS IN THE NEXT 50 YEARS. IT SHOWS THE INTERRELATION OF POPULATION, CAPITAL INVESTMENT, NATURAL RESOURCES, POLLUTION, AND THE FRACTION OF CAPITAL DEVOTED TO AGRICULTURE ON WHICH IS BASED THE FOLLOWING DISCUSSION.

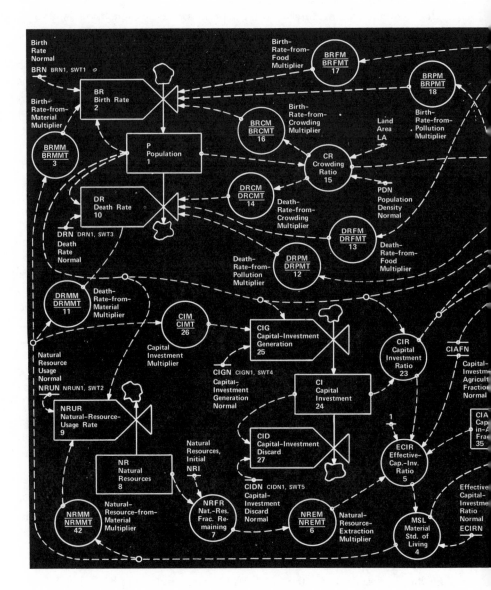

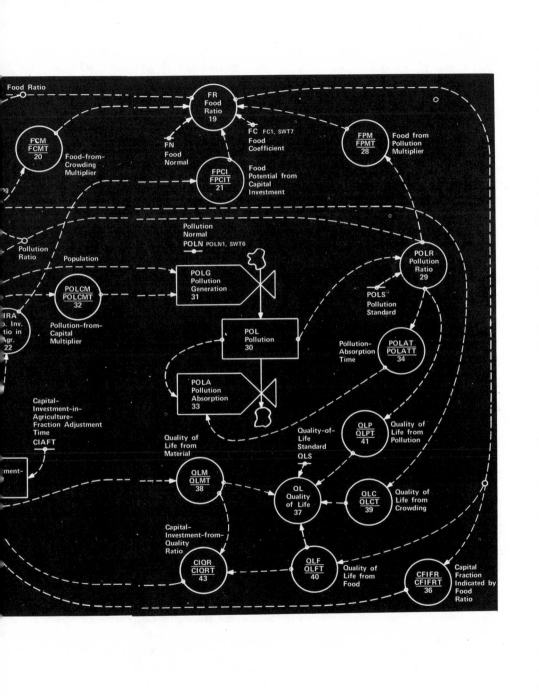

Transition from Growth to Equilibrium

With the model specified, a computer can be used to show how the system, as described for each of its parts, would behave. Given a set of beginning conditions, the computer can calculate and plot the results that unfold through time.

The world today seems to be entering a condition in which pressures are rising simultaneously from every one of the influences that can suppress growth—depleted resources, pollution, crowding, and insufficient food. It is still unclear which will dominate if mankind continues along the present path. Figure 2 shows the mode of behavior of this world system given the assumption that population reaches a peak and then declines because industrialization is suppressed by falling natural resources. The model system starts with estimates of conditions in 1900. Adjustments have been made so that the generated paths pass through the conditions of 1970.

In Figure 2 the quality of life peaks in the 1950's and by 2020 has fallen far enough to halt further rise in population. Declining resources and the consequent fall in capital investment then exert further pressure to gradually reduce world population.

But we may not be fortunate enough to run gradually out of natural resources. Science and technology may very well find ways to use the more plentiful metals and atomic energy so that resource depletion does not intervene. If so, the way then remains open for some other pressure to arise within the system. Figure 3 shows what happens within this system if the resource shortage is foreseen and avoided. Here the only change from Figure 2 is in the usage rate of natural resources after the year 1970. In Figure 3, resources are used after 1970 at a rate 75 percent less than assumed in Figure 2. In other words, the standard of living is sustained with a lower drain on the expendable and irreplaceable resources. But the picture is even less attractive! By not running out of resources, population and capital investment are allowed to rise until a pollution crisis is created. Pollution then acts directly to reduce birth rate, increase death rate, and to depress food production. Population which, according to this simple model, peaks at the year 2030 has fallen to one-sixth of the peak population within an interval of 20 years—a world-wide catastrophe of a magnitude never before experienced. Should it occur, one can speculate on which sectors of the world population will suffer most. It is quite possible that the more industrialized countries (which are the ones which have caused such a disaster) would be the least able to survive such a disruption to environment and food supply. They might be the ones to take the brunt of the collapse.

Figure 3 shows how a technological success (reducing our dependence on natural resources) can merely save us from one fate only to fall victim to something worse (a pollution catastrophe). There is now developing throughout the world a strong undercurrent of doubt about technology as the savior of mankind. There is a basis for such doubt. Of course, the source of trouble

FIGURE 2: BASIC WORLD MODEL BEHAVIOR SHOWING THE MODE IN WHICH IN-DUSTRIALIZATION AND POPULATION ARE SUPPRESSED BY FALLING NATURAL RE-SOURCES.

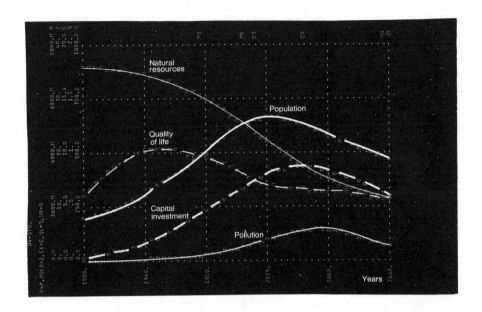

FIGURE 3: POLLUTION CRISIS PRECIPITATED BY LOWER USAGE RATE OF NATURAL RESOURCES. IN 1970 NATURAL RESOURCE USAGE IS REDUCED 75 PERCENT BY MORE EFFECTIVE TECHNOLOGY WITHOUT AFFECTING MATERIAL STANDARD OF LIVING.

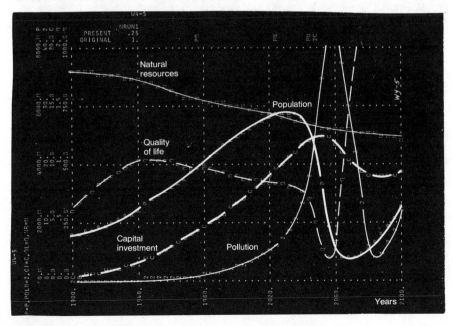

is not technology as such but is instead the management of the entire technological-human-political-economic-natural complex.

Figure 3 is a dramatic example of the general process discussed earlier wherein a program aimed at one trouble symptom results in creating a new set of troubles in some other part of the system. Here the success in alleviating a natural resource shortage throws the system over into the mode of stopping population caused by industrialization which has been freed from natural resource restraint. This process of a solution creating a new problem has defeated many of our past governmental programs and will continue to do so unless we devote more effort to understanding the dynamic behavior of our social systems.

Alternatives to Decline or Catastrophe

Suppose in the basic world system of Figures 1 and 2 we ask how to sustain the quality of life which is beginning to decline after 1950. One way to attempt this, and it is the way the world is now choosing, might be to increase the rate of industrialization by raising the rate of capital investment. Models of the kind we are here using make such hypothetical questions answerable in a few minutes and at negligible cost. Figure 4 shows what happens if the "normal" rate of capital accumulation is increased by 20 percent in 1970. The pollution crisis reappears. This time the cause is not the more efficient use of natural resources but the upsurge of industrialization which overtaxes

FIGURE 4: IN 1970 THE RATE OF CAPITAL ACCUMULATION IS INCREASED 20 PERCENT IN AN EFFORT TO REVERSE THE BEGINNING DECLINE IN QUALITY OF LIFE. THE POLLUTION CRISIS OCCURS BEFORE NATURAL RESOURCES ARE DEPLETED.

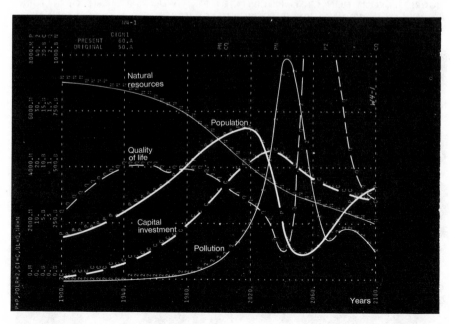

the environment before resource depletion has a chance to depress industrialization. Again, an "obvious" desirable change in policy has caused troubles worse than the ones that were originally being corrected.

This is important, not only for its own message but because it demonstrates how an apparently desirable change in a social system can have unexpected and even disastrous results.

Figure 4 should make us cautious about rushing into programs on the basis of short-term humanitarian impulses. The eventual result can be anti-humanitarian. Emotionally inspired efforts often fall into one of three traps set for us by the nature of social systems: The programs are apt to address symptoms rather than causes and attempt to operate through points in the system that have little leverage for change; the characteristic of systems whereby a policy change has the opposite effect in the short run from the effect in the long run can eventually cause deepening difficulties after a sequence of short-term actions; and the effect of a program can be along an entirely different direction than was originally expected, so that suppressing one symptom only causes trouble to burst forth at another point.

Figure 5 retains the 20 percent additional capital investment rate after 1970 from Figure 4 but in addition explores birth reduction as a way of avoiding crisis. Here the "normal" birth rate has been cut in half in 1970. (Changes in normal rates refer to coefficients which have the specified effect if all other things remain the same. But other things in the system change and also exert their effect on the actual system rates.) The result shows interesting behavior. Quality of life surges upward for 30 years for the reasons that are customarily asserted. Food-per-capita grows, material standard of living rises, and crowding does not become as great. But the more affluent world population continues to use natural resources and to accumulate capital plant at about the same rate as in Figure 4. Load on the environment is more closely related to industrialization than to population and the pollution crisis occurs at about the same point in time as in Figure 4.

Figure 5 shows that the 50 percent reduction in "normal" birth rate in 1970 was sufficient to start a decline in total population. But the rising quality of life and the reduction of pressures act to start the population curve upward again. This is especially evident in other computer runs where the reduction in "normal" birth rate is not so drastic. Serious questions are raised by this investigation about the effectiveness of birth control as a means of controlling population. The secondary consequence of starting a birth control program will be to increase the influences that raise birth rate and reduce the apparent pressures that require population control. A birth control program which would be effective, all other things being equal, may largely fail because other things will not remain equal. Its very incipient success can set in motion forces to defeat the program.

Figure 6 combines the reduced resource usage rate and the increased capital investment rate of Figures 3 and 4. The result is to make the population collapse occur slightly sooner and more severely. Based on the modified

FIGURE 5: IN 1970 THE 20 PERCENT INCREASE IN CAPITAL ACCUMULATION OF FIG-URE 4 IS RETAINED AND "NORMAL" BIRTH RATE IS REDUCED 50 PERCENT. CAPITAL INVESTMENT CONTINUES TO GROW UNTIL THE POLLUTION CRISIS DEVELOPS. AFTER AN INITIAL DECLINE, POPULATION IS AGAIN PUSHED UP BY THE RAPID RISE IN QUALITY OF LIFE THAT PRECEDES THE COLLAPSE.

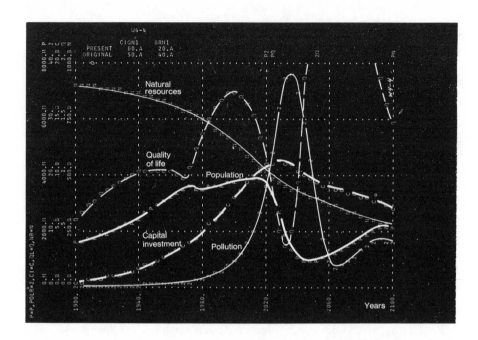

FIGURE 6: THE 20 PERCENT INCREASE OF CAPITAL INVESTMENT FROM FIGURE 4 AND THE 75 PERCENT REDUCTION OF NATURAL RESOURCE USAGE FROM FIGURE 3 ARE COMBINED.

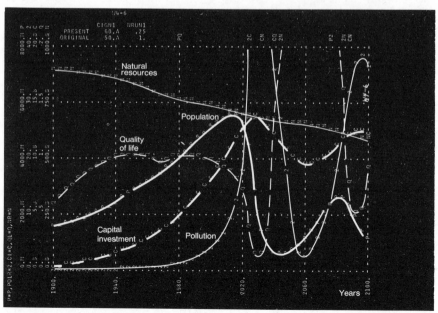

system of Figure 6, Figure 7 then examines the result if technology finds ways to reduce the pollution generated by a given degree of industrialization. Here in Figure 7, the pollution rate, other things being the same, is reduced by 50 percent from that in Figure 6. The result is to postpone the day of reckoning by 20 years and to allow the world population to grow 25 percent greater before the population collapse occurs. The "solution" of reduced pollution has, in effect, caused more people to suffer the eventual consequences. Again we see the dangers of partial solutions. Actions at one point in a system that attempt to relieve one kind of distress produce an unexpected result in some other part of the system. If the interactions are not sufficiently understood, the consequences can be as bad as or worse than those that led to the initial action.

There are no utopias in our social systems. There appear to be no sustainable modes of behavior that are free of pressures and stresses. But there are many possible modes and some are more desirable than others. Usually, the more attractive kinds of behavior in our social systems seem to be possible only if we have a good understanding of the system dynamics and are willing to endure the self-discipline and pressures that must accompany the desirable mode. The world system of Figure 1 can exhibit modes that are more hopeful than the crises of Figures 2 through 7. But to develop the more promising modes will require restraint and dedication to a long-range future that man may not be capable of sustaining.

Figure 8 shows the world system if several policy changes are adopted together in the year 1970. Population is stabilized. Quality of life rises about 50 percent. Pollution remains at about the 1970 level. Would such a world be accepted? It implies an end to population and economic growth.

In Figure 8 the normal rate of capital accumulation is *reduced* 40 percent from its previous value. The "normal" birth rate is reduced 50 percent from its earlier value. The "normal" pollution generation is reduced 50 percent from the value before 1970. The "normal" rate of food production is *reduced* 20 percent from its previous value. (These changes in "normal" values are the changes for a specific set of system conditions. Actual system rates continue to be affected by the varying conditions of the system.) But reduction in investment rate and reduction in agricultural emphasis are counterintuitive and not likely to be discovered or accepted without extensive system studies and years of argument—perhaps more years than are available. The changes in pollution generation and natural resource usage may be easier to understand and to achieve. The severe reduction in world-wide birth rate is the most doubtful. Even if technical and biological methods existed, the improved condition of the world might remove the incentive for sustaining the birth reduction emphasis and discipline.

Future Policy Issues

The dynamics of world behavior bear directly on the future of the United States. American urbanization and industrialization are a major part of the

**FIGURE 7: INCREASED CAPITAL INVESTMENT RATE AND REDUCED NATURAL RE-
SOURCE USAGE FROM FIGURE 6 ARE RETAINED. IN ADDITION IN 1970 THE "NORMAL"
RATE OF POLLUTION GENERATION IS REDUCED 50 PERCENT. THE EFFECT OF POLLU-
TION CONTROL IS TO ALLOW POPULATION TO GROW 25 PERCENT FURTHER AND TO
DELAY THE POLLUTION CRISIS BY 20 YEARS.**

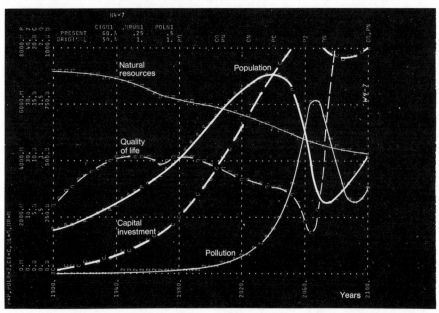

**FIGURE 8: ONE SET OF CONDITIONS THAT ESTABLISHES A WORLD EQUILIBRIUM. IN
1970 CAPITAL INVESTMENT RATE IS REDUCED 40 PERCENT, BIRTH RATE IS REDUCED
50 PERCENT, POLLUTION GENERATION IS REDUCED 50 PERCENT, NATURAL RESOURCE
USAGE RATE IS REDUCED 75 PERCENT, AND FOOD PRODUCTION IS REDUCED 20
PERCENT.**

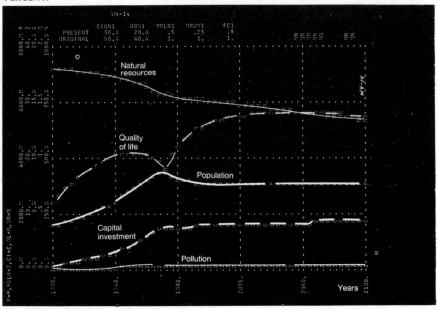

world scene. The United States is setting a pattern that other parts of the world are trying to follow. That pattern is not sustainable. Our foreign policy and our overseas commercial activity seem to be running contrary to overwhelming forces that are developing in the world system. The following issues are raised by the preliminary investigations to date. They must, of course, be examined more deeply and confirmed by more thorough research into the assumptions about structure and detail of the world system.

Industrialization may be a more fundamentally disturbing force in world ecology than is population. In fact, the population explosion is perhaps best viewed as a result of technology and industrialization. I include medicine and public health as a part of industrialization.

Within the next century, man may be facing choices from a four-pronged dilemma—suppression of modern industrial society by a natural resource shortage, collapse of world population from changes wrought by pollution, population limitation by food shortage, or population control by war, disease, and social stresses caused by physical and psychological crowding.

We may now be living in a "golden age" where, in spite of the world-wide feeling of malaise, the quality of life is, on the average, higher than ever before in history and higher now than the future offers.

Efforts for direct population control may be inherently self-defeating. If population control begins to result as hoped in higher per capita food supply and material standard of living, these very improvements can generate forces to trigger a resurgence of population growth.

The high standard of living of modern industrial societies seems to result from a production of food and material goods that has been able to outrun the rising population. But, as agriculture reaches a space limit, as industrialization reaches a natural-resource limit, and as both reach a pollution limit, population tends to catch up. Population then grows until the "quality of life" falls far enough to generate sufficiently large pressures to stabilize population.

There may be no realistic hope for the present underdeveloped countries reaching the standard of living demonstrated by the present industrialized nations. The pollution and natural resource load placed on the world environmental system by each person in an advanced country is probably 20 to 50 times greater than the load now generated by a person in an underdeveloped country. With four times as much population in underdeveloped countries as in the present developed countries, their rising to the economic level of the United States could mean an increase of 200 times in the natural resource and pollution load on the world environment. Noting the destruction that has already occurred on land, in the air, and especially in the oceans, no capability appears to exist for handling such a rise in standard of living for the present total population of the world.

A society with a high level of industrialization may be nonsustainable. It may be self-extinguishing if it exhausts the natural resources on which it depends. Or, if unending substitution for declining natural resources is possible, the international strife over "pollution and environmental rights" may pull the average world-wide standard of living back to the level of a century ago.

From the long view of a hundred years hence, the present efforts of under-developed countries to industrialize along Western patterns may be unwise. They may now be closer to the ultimate equilibrium with the environment than are the industrialized nations. The present underdeveloped countries may be in a better condition for surviving the forthcoming world-wide environmental and economic pressures than are the advanced countries. When one of the several forces materializes that is strong enough to cause a collapse in world population, the advanced countries may suffer far more than their share of the decline.

A New Frontier

It is now possible to take hypotheses about the separate parts of a social system, to combine them in a computer model, and to learn the consequences. The hypotheses may at first be no more correct than the one we are using in our intuitive thinking. But the process of computer modeling and model testing requires these hypotheses to be stated more explicitly. The model comes out of the hazy realm of the mental model into an unambiguous model or statement to which all have access. Assumptions can then be checked against all available information and can be rapidly improved. The great uncertainty with mental models is the inability to anticipate the consequences of interactions between the parts of a system. This uncertainty is totally eliminated in computer models. Given a stated set of assumptions, the computer traces the resulting consequences without doubt or error. This is a powerful procedure for clarifying issues. It is not easy. Results will not be immediate.

We are on the threshold of a great new era in human pioneering. In the past there have been periods characterized by geographical exploration. Other periods have dealt with the formation of national governments. At other times the focus was on the creation of great literature. Most recently we have been through the pioneering frontier of science and technology. But science and technology are now a routine part of our life. Science is no longer a frontier. The process of scientific discovery is orderly and organized.

I suggest that the next frontier for human endeavor is to pioneer a better understanding of the nature of our social systems. The means are visible. The task will be no easier than the development of science and technology. For the next 30 years we can expect rapid advance in understanding the complex dynamics of our social systems. To do so will require research, the development of teaching methods and materials, and the creation of appropriate educational programs. The research results of today will in one or two decades find their way into the secondary schools just as concepts of basic physics moved from research to general education over the past three decades.

What we do today fundamentally affects our future two or three decades hence. If we follow intuition, the trends of the past will continue into deepening difficulty. If we set up research and educational programs, which are now possible but which have not yet been developed, we can expect a far sounder basis for action.

The Nation's Real Alternatives

The record to date implies that our people accept the future growth of United States population as preordained, beyond the purview and influence of legislative control, and as a ground rule which determines the nation's task as finding cities in which the future population can live. But I have been describing the circular processes of our social systems in which there is no unidirectional cause and effect but instead a ring of actions and consequences that close back on themselves. One could say, incompletely, that the population will grow and that cities, space, and food must be provided. But one can likewise say, also incompletely, that the provision of cities, space, and food will cause the population to grow. Population generates pressure for urban growth, but urban pressures help to limit population.

Population grows until stresses rise far enough, which is to say that the quality of life falls far enough, to stop further increase. Everything we do to reduce those pressures causes the population to rise farther and faster and hastens the day when expediencies will not longer suffice. The United States is in the position of a wild animal running from its pursuers. We still have some space, natural resources, and agricultural land left. We can avoid the question of rising population as long as we can flee into this bountiful reservoir that nature provided. But it is obvious that the reservoirs are limited. The wild animal usually flees until he is cornered, until he has no more space. Then he turns to fight, but he no longer has room to maneuver. He is less able to forestall disaster than if he had fought in the open while there was still room to yield and to dodge. The United States is running away from its long-term threats by trying to relieve social pressures as they arise. But if we persist in treating only the symptoms and not the causes, the result will be to increase the magnitude of the ultimate threat and reduce our capability to respond when we no longer have space to flee.

What does this mean? Instead of automatically accepting the need for new towns and the desirability of locating industry in rural areas, we should consider confining our cities. If it were possible to prohibit the encroachment by housing and industry onto even a single additional acre of farm and forest, the resulting social pressures would hasten the day when we stabilize population. Some European countries are closer to realizing the necessity of curtailing urban growth than we are. As I understand it, farm land surrounding Copenhagen cannot be used for either residence or industry until the severest of pressures forces the government to rezone small additional parcels. When land is rezoned, the corresponding rise in land price is heavily taxed to remove the incentive for land speculation. The waiting time for an empty apartment in Copenhagen may be years. Such pressures certainly cause the Danes to face the population problem more squarely than do we.

Our greatest challenge now is how to handle the transition from growth into equilibrium. Our society has behind it a thousand years of tradition that has encouraged and rewarded growth. The folklore and the success stories praise growth and expansion. But that is not the path of the future. Many of the present stresses in our society are from the pressures that always accompany the conversion from growth into equilibrium.

In our studies of social systems, we have made a number of investigations of life cycle that start with growth and merge into equilibrium. There are always severe stresses in the transition. Pressures must rise far enough to suppress the forces that produced growth. Not only do we face the pressure that will stop the population growth; we also encounter pressures that will stop the rise of industrialization and standard of living. The social stresses will rise. The economic forces will be ones for which we have no precedent. The psychological forces will be beyond those for which we are prepared. Our studies of urban systems demonstrated how the pressures from shortage of land and rising unemployment accompany the usual transition from urban growth to equilibrium. But the pressures we have seen in our cities are minor compared to those which the nation is approaching. The population pressures and the economic forces in a city that was reaching equilibrium have in the past been able to escape to new land areas.

But that escape is becoming less possible. Until now we have had, in effect, an inexhaustible supply of farm land and food-growing potential. But now we are reaching the critical point where, all at the same time, population is overrunning productive land, agricultural land is almost fully employed for the first time, the rise in population is putting more demand on the food supplies, and urbanization is pushing agriculture out of the fertile areas into the marginal lands. For the first time demand is rising into a condition where supply will begin to fall while need increases. The crossover from plenty to shortage can occur abruptly.

The fiscal and monetary system of the country is a complex social-economic-financial system of the kind we have been discussing. It is clear the country is not agreed on behavior of the interactions between government policy, growth, unemployment, and inflation. An article by a writer for *Finance* magazine in July, 1970, suggests that the approach I have been discussing be applied in fiscal and monetary policy and their relationships to the economy. I estimate that such a task would be only a few times more difficult than was the investigation of urban growth and stagnation. The need to accomplish it becomes more urgent as the economy begins to move for the first time from a history of growth into the turbulent pressures that will accompany the transition from growth to one of the many possible kinds of equilibrium. We need to choose the kind of equilibrium before we arrive.

In a hierarchy of systems, there is usually a conflict between the goals of a subsystem and the welfare of the broader system. We see this in the urban system. The goal of the city is to expand and to raise its quality of life. But this increases population, industrialization, pollution, and demands on food supply. The broader social system of the country and the world requires that the goals of the urban areas be curtailed and that the pressures of such curtailment become high enough to keep the urban areas and population within the bounds that are satisfactory to the larger system of which the city is a part. If this nation chooses to continue to work for some of the traditional urban goals, and if it succeeds, as it may well do, the result will be to deepen the distress of the country as a whole and eventually to deepen the crisis in the cities themselves. We may be at the point where higher pressures in the present are necessary if insurmountable pressures are to be avoided in the future.

I have tried to give you a glimpse of the nature of multi-loop feedback systems, a class to which our social systems belong. I have attempted to indicate how these systems mislead us because our intuition and judgment have been formed to expect behavior different from that actually possessed by such systems. I believe that we are still pursuing national programs that will be at least as frustrating and futile as many of the past. But there is hope. We can now begin to understand the dynamic behavior of our social systems. Progress will be slow. There are many cross-currents in the social sciences which will cause confusion and delay. The approach that I have been describing is very different from the emphasis on data gathering and statistical analysis that occupies much of the time of social research. But there have been breakthroughs in several areas. If we proceed expeditiously but thoughtfully, there is a basis for optimism.

Suggested Readings

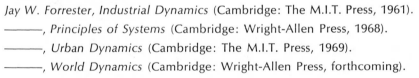

Jay W. Forrester, Industrial Dynamics (Cambridge: The M.I.T. Press, 1961).

————, *Principles of Systems* (Cambridge: Wright-Allen Press, 1968).

————, *Urban Dynamics* (Cambridge: The M.I.T. Press, 1969).

————, *World Dynamics* (Cambridge: Wright-Allen Press, forthcoming).

part two

ON THE SHAPE OF THE FUTURE: INSTITUTIONS AND POLICY SYSTEMS

9

The International System

ON THE FUTURE OF THE INTERNATIONAL SYSTEM

● *johan galtung*

1. Introduction

Our image of the international system is incomplete, subjective and uncertain, and the future is filled with possibilities none of which is certain—so the effort to indicate trajectories the international system may follow into the future must be a relatively hazardous enterprise. Some would claim it is not even meaningful,[1] but we feel good meaning can be given to future-oriented research on the international system,[2] as well as on any domestic system, if we split the task into three components:

1. *Value research*—the effort to establish not only basic values of the system, but also the conditions under which they are most likely to be realized.
2. *Trend research*—the effort to establish trends in the system, based on data from the past, and theories as to how extrapolations should be made.
3. *Exploration of relations between trends and values*—in other words, efforts to find out whether the trends do or do not lead the system into the "promised land": and in case they do, how to reinforce and stabilize them; in case they do not, how to change them.

Thus, future research has essentially three components or aspects, all of them well known in other connections. What is, perhaps, new in future research (but not new in planning) is the idea of rejecting the traditional division of

---

[1]A claim of this kind cannot be based on lack of data from the future, since that also applies to the natural scientist whose predictions have usually been regarded as legitimate. Rather, the claim must be based on the idea that a prediction becomes an element in the predicted system, and that this may create the well known self-fulfilling and self-denying mechanisms. Although this often is a highly exaggerated picture of what the publication of future oriented studies of social affairs may entail, it is difficult to see it as an objection against such studies. Rather, it should predispose one for the term *prevision* rather than *prediction*, as most authors in the field of futurology seem to agree. That such prevision may highlight attractive and objectionable points in the map of the future is obvious, just as obvious as it is that the researcher who wants to predict rather than to preview should lock up his findings rather than publish them.

[2]For some statements on this, see articles in the excellent *Daedalus* issue "Toward the Year 2000: Work in Progress" (summer, 1967) by Herman Kahn and Anthony J. Wiener (particularly pp. 705f), and by Ithiel de Sola Pool (particularly pp. 930f). Another article with some valuable ideas is Bruce Russett: "The Ecology of Future International Politics," *International Studies Quarterly* (1967), pp. 12–31.

226

labor between *ideologists* who establish the values, *scientists* who establish the trends, and *politicians* who try to adjust means to ends, by a more unified approach to the three fields. A consequence of this rejection is the rejection of any strict dividing line between values and trends, or "facts." Values are no longer seen as exogenous to the system, as given; but more as a part of the total system that also may emerge from the discovery of new, possible, trends —just as much as trends are seen as something that should be adjusted to existing values. In other words, a more symmetric relation between values and trends will probably emerge from this type of approach.[3]

As the matter stands today, particularly with regard to the international system, where the planning approach is highly undeveloped, the *ideologists* are likely to argue against the trend-makers' or prognosticians' saying that they make the future a prisoner of the past by their explorations, which are usually based on the assumption of continuity.[4] The *scientists* will argue against the ideologists' saying that they posit values that 1) are mutually inconsistent, so that they ask for non-viable social orders; 2) are so detached from trends that it becomes impossible to "reach them from here" (to which the ideologist may answer: true, except by a discontinuous jump, e. g., a revolution[5]). Both scientists and ideologists will turn against the *politicians*, claiming that the latter pay attention neither to values nor to trends but are merely enmeshed in a jungle of details, intrigues, petty conflict, and bureaucratic embroidery. The politicians will answer that this may be true, but such are the intricacies of the social order—very different from the views from the ivory towers of ideologists and scientists alike.

This debate is well-known and is only dissolved, it seems, when politics becomes sufficiently technified. The conditions for this, in turn, seem to be 1) that the values become highly consensual; 2) that applied science develops sufficiently to offer a supply of acceptable means whereby the values may be obtained with fair certainty; and 3) this level of development is generally

[3]Thus, one would and should expect social scientists to be able to map out viable worlds nobody else has thought of, discuss from the point of view of current values, but also to introduce new values that these constructs may realize.

[4]In general, the social sciences are remarkably inept in dealing with discontinuities, probably because they are engaged in by predominantly gradualistically oriented people who are sufficiently in opposition to want change, yet not so alienated from their society that they want absolute change, i.e. discontinuity. Marxist and neo-Marxist thinking have discontinuities built into their schemes, but are on the other hand usually not empirical enough in their approaches. A synthesis here should bring interesting insights, and is bound to come about with the current growth in cooperation between the Marxist and positivist camps.

[5]Because pure ideologists are more likely to be located so far from the decision-making nucleus that they do not feel the urge or the challenge to work out more continuous trajectories and feel that scientists who try to do so only try to reduce the degree of freedom in order to protect the *status quo*. For some efforts to analyze this relation, see Johan Galtung, "Foreign Policy Opinion as a Function of Social Position," *Journal of Peace Research* (1964), particularly pp. 207–216.

recognized. The argument in favor of a unified approach to the three components mentioned above is precisely that the unified approach is more likely to promote this kind of technification. We should, perhaps, add that this in no sense means "the end of ideology": only that technification takes some issues out of the ideological sphere, which then can move on to absorb new issues.[6]

Our task in this connection, then, is precisely to view all three components in that order, asking what are the basic values, what are the basic trends, and ending up with an exploration of the relation between them. To this we now turn.

2. Basic Values of the International System

The world consists of 3.3 billion human beings organized in a complex network of criss-crossing groups, some of which are called nation-states; and there is no reason to assume that the values of such groups should be essentially different from values found within the groups, e.g., within nation-states. But that also means that the values are far from consensual. They may include such elements as *cooperation* (as opposed to isolation), *freedom from fear*, *freedom from want*, values of *growth* and *development*, *absence of exploitation*, and concomitant values of *equality* and *justice*, *freedom of action*, *pluralism* and *dynamism*. But for all such values it is easy to list important cleavages that we shall not enter into here; they are very likely to be values that divide mankind and mobilize groups against each other—at least at present, and depending on how they are made more precise. They should be contrasted with the basic value of (negative) *peace*, which we define simply as "absence of organized, collective violence," where violence is defined in terms of bodily destruction as immediate consequences of action by human beings against others. We assume that this value at present is relatively consensual, that it unites mankind rather than dividing it—although the unification is lost in the divisive split in the search for appropriate means.[7]

Since peace research as a discipline tries to understand better how this value can be realized, and particularly how it can be realized if the system also tries to realize any combination of the other values mentioned above, we should require of a peace researcher that he be able to say something about the conditions under which negative peace is most likely to obtain. A highly abbreviated version of the present author's attempt to answer would run something like this:[8]

---

[6]Thus, an issue leaves Ideology and becomes Technology as soon as these conditions are fulfilled, much as a problem leaves Philosophy and becomes Science as soon as consensual criteria of validation (formal or empirical) are found—*and* there is consensus that the problem is still worth pursuing.

[7]This theme is developed further in Johan Galtung, *Theories of Peace* (forthcoming), section 1.3.

[8]*Ibid.*, sections 4.3 and 4.4.

There are two basic approaches to peace, the *dissociative* and the *associative*. The former consists in keeping groups apart, e. g., by balance of power principles or any kind of polarizing or isolating measures. The latter consists in making peace by getting groups closer to each other, e. g., by various ways of integrating them by any kind of depolarizing and unifying measures. In other words, to get peace you must either keep groups (such as nations) well apart or well together—in between there is a very dangerous zone where the parties are neither mutually isolated nor sufficiently close.

There are two reasons why today we would gamble much more on the associative approaches. First, the general communication revolution works against all kinds of dissociative policies, making them look rather artificial and counterproductive. Second, most of the other values mentioned above can be better realized in an associative than in a dissociative world, provided a number of other conditions are fulfilled.[9]

The associative conditions of peace we are thinking of can now be expressed under three basic headings:

1. *Symbiotic and symmetric cooperation between groups.*[10] Groups must stand in cooperative relations to each other, i.e., not be too self-sufficient. The mutual interdependence must be such that group A knows that to hurt and harm group B is also to hurt and harm itself. But this is only necessary, not sufficient; for such has also been the relation between masters and slaves during some periods. Hence, a maximum of egalitarianism must be worked into the cooperation, whether is it is between nations, between groups in the productivity system of any nation, between INGOs or IGOs (international non-governmental and governmental organizations, respectively).

2. *High entropy between actors and in the system of interaction.*[11] In a very approximate way we may say that the major idea behind this condition is that there be no clear fronts in the total system. Members of two races should mix completely in terms of occupations they have, or districts where they reside. Or more precisely: since human beings have different

[9]A crucial example is balance of power politics, one of the classical, dissociative formulas for peace-making. It presupposes a certain polarization and distance in general, and should, hence, work better for low levels of communication than for high levels. But it also presupposes communication of intentions and a certain measure of tacit agreement; which means that it should work relatively well when the international system has a well integrated elite. But when popular and populist forces press for other values as well and constrain the delicate maneuvers of the diplomats in maintaining balance of power, at the same time as the communication potential doubles and trebles, this mechanism will be of decreasing utility.

[10]For more details about this, see Johan Galtung, "Cooperation in Europe, A Report to the Political Commission, Council of Europe."

[11]For more details about this, see Johan Galtung, "Entropy and the General Theory of Peace," *Proceedings*, Second IPRA General Conference; and Ch. 5. in *Theories of Peace*.

capacities for the tolerance of ambiguity and storage and processing of information we may assume pockets of low entropy (e.g., where there is homogeneity with regard to race), but that these pockets should be mixed and stirred in such a way that the total system has very high entropy (low degree of order, high level of disorder, of "messiness"). The same applies to the system of interaction: we should avoid systems with very clear, unique, paths of interaction, and support systems where the interaction patterns are less clear, in many different directions.

3. *A high number of supra-group organizations.* For nations these are known as IGOs, but we are thinking in general terms that there should be a maximum of organizations bridging and facilitating communication between groups. Thus, INGOs should come together and form super-INGOs; IGOs should form super-IGOs; super-INGOs and super-IGOs may come together; and so on. This formation of increasingly complex systems should take place under the two conditions above, i.e., the members should enter on an egalitarian basis and there should be high entropy—at all levels in the decision-structure members of all member groups should be mixed together.

Without going into any detail, there seem to be excellent reasons to say that systems organized along such lines have high conflict-absorbing and conflict-solving capacites. The analytical point now is simply that these seem to be the conditions under which peace is most likely to be obtained. These conditions are phrased in system terms so that they can be compared with trends in the system; they are expressed in the same language, so to speak. Thus, if we merely looked at trends in system properties, then we could not read the chances of peace or war out of them, without any theory as to how system properties can be related to the chances of peace and war. To this it may be objected that we could have looked at the trends in peace and war as such, to see whether they are increasing or decreasing, and then tried to extrapolate. But such an approach will easily make us blind to the underlying dynamics; no social phenomena can be viewed independently of their structural correlates.

We then turn to the trends, to see how they relate to the three system properties mentioned above.

3. Trends in the International System

3.1. THE STATE-SOCIETY INCOMPATIBILITY THESIS

When we say "trends in the international system," what we really mean are trends in the *global* system, for we do not assume that this system is to remain, essentially, an inter*national* system. But nations are going to remain dominant actors still for some time to come, so we will also have to discuss trends in the relation between them on the basis of trends in what happens

TABLE 1: Stages of socioeconomic development

Term for the stage	Primitive (P)		Traditional (T)		Modern (M)		Neomodern (N)	
	Primary		Primary / Tertiary		Primary / Sec-on-dary / Terti-ary		Tertiary (Primary / Secondary / Tertiary / Post-tertiary education)	
	High	Low	High	Low	High	Low		
Term for the transition	Urban revolution		Industrial revolution		Automation revolution			
Population profiles								
primary sector	100	90	80	75	50	20	5	0
secondary sector	0	5	5	10	20	30	5	0
tertiary sector	0	5	15	15	30	50	90	100
GNP/capita Agricultural productivity	1 : 1 and less		1 : 1.25 1 : 1.33		1 : 2 1 : 5		1 : 20 and higher	
Communication goods, persons	walking, running rowing		animals, wheels sailing		steam engine combustion engine		jet rockets	
information	eye and ear		dispatches		post, telegraph, telephone		tele-satellite	
Economic system	subsistence economy		barter economy		money economy		credit economy	
Domain	group, clan, tribe		village, city-state		nation-state		region, world-state	
Magnitude	10^0–10^2		10^2–10^5		10^5–10^8		10^8–10^{10}	

inside these nations of relevance to the interaction between nation states.[12]

To do this, it is obvious that *nations* cannot be discussed under one heading. They have to be subdivided into groups of nations; and for a suitable discussion of this a point of departure is the concept of a *society*, which we take to mean a self-sufficient social structure in the sense that it will remain essentially the same if the rest of the world is removed. Thus, for any given person in the world we could in principle find his "circle of interdependence" by examining how much of the world could be removed before his life-situation changed—and here we might distinguish between the *maximum* circle needed for complete maintenance of the satisfaction level, and the *minimum* circle needed for the satisfaction of basic values. We are rather thinking of the maximum circle.

In Table 1[13] four societal forms have been outlined, the primitive, the traditional, the modern, and the neomodern; respectively. The indications of magnitude are very approximate indeed; they are rules of thumb, but like most rules of thumb more often right than wrong. In general, sociologists do not know enough about the number of people and occupations needed to make a social order viable at all. Read horizontally the Table gives some of the basic factors in the general development of the human society; read vertically it gives some of the internal (socio-)logic of these societies. In this presentation agricultural productivity—i. e., the number of families one family doing farming can feed—and the general distribution of the population on the primary, secondary, and tertiary sectors of production have been taken as basic.[14] But behind these, in turn, are variables that have to do with technology, particularly the technology of production *and* of communication— the latter added to Marx' emphasis on "means of production" as a factor of primary importance.

From this nothing follows in terms of changes inside or between nations. But if we introduce the following two assumptions, many consequences follow more or less immediately:

1. *The assumption of development*—that primitive societies tend to develop into traditional ones, traditional societies into modern ones, and modern

[12]Thus, in this paper we locate the basic source of change inside nations. This does not mean that there is no feed-back from the international system to the domestic systems, or dynamism in the international system *sui generis*. We only use this as a way of organizing the theory.

[13]This Table is taken from "Socioeconomic Development: A bird's-eye view," section 1.2 in Johan Galtung, *Members of Two Worlds* (forthcoming).

[14]This is done in the Fisher-Clark-Fourastié tradition. However, we very much agree with Kahn (*op. cit.*, p. 720) when he, as do other authors in this field, starts splitting the tertiary sector into some of its components, such as "quaternary occupations [that] render services mostly to tertiary occupations or to one another." The crucial factor, as we see it, is the general tendency towards occupations where the work consists mainly in the manipulations of symbols—direct contact with matter for extraction or processing has been automated.

societies into neomodern ones. This development may also take place in jumps, i.e., 'from the stone age to the electronic age'. The general move in this direction is not strictly linear, but more linear and in general more rapid the higher the level of communication between societies at different levels of development.

2. *The nation-state as a general pattern*—that the surface of the world is divided into generally contiguous territories called nation-states (about 135 of them; in addition there are some 85 territories with about 50 million inhabitants that do not as yet live in nation-states), and that some nation-states are composed of societies at various levels of development, and thus have dual or triple economies; others may coincide with one social order at a particular level of development, whereas other nation-states are segments within one society comprising more nation-states. The division is never thought of as final, but major changes by means of war are seen as illegitimate especially if a nation at a higher level attacks lower level nations.

These two assumptions now lead to what we see as the basic structural condition for change in the international, or global, system: *the consequences of the incompatibilities between state and society, between the nation-state and the social orders that it contains or is contained in.*

Let us first spell out some conditions under which there would be no such incompatibility. There are two such sets of conditions, depending on which assumption above we would negate. First let us assume that each nation-state coincided with *one* society, so that each nation-state would be self-sufficient, independent of the rest (e. g., it would not engage in any significant amount of trade or other forms of exchange). Some of these nation-states would be primitive, some traditional, some modern, and some neomodern, although the neomodern social order, strictly speaking, has not yet crystallized completely.[15] Needless to say, they would differ greatly in size, e.g., as indicated by the orders of magnitude in Table 1.

To make for compatibility we would have to assume that there should be no change in this situation, in other words that the societies should not develop further. For in this type of international system the societies that really started developing would soon outgrow the limits set by the nation-

[15]Thus, in neomodern society, or post-industrial society as some authors refer to it, close to 100% would be in the tertiary sector, manipulating symbols (science, arts, education, computers, etc.); traditional occupations would be automated. The urban form of life would be shared by most. Education would be a form of life, shared by almost all throughout their life-span; not a preparation for an occupation. To make such a society run, many people are needed; the high level of symbolic activity and communication facilities will make the society global because inhabitants will often have to travel far to find partners for meaningful symbolic interaction (so far above all in arts and sciences, later on probably also in styles of life, in tastes and manners, etc.). The society would also be highly vulnerable because of the high level of automation and the proliferation of complex machinery—and the removal of one part will affect many people, since they cannot fall back on "simple life on the farm" or anything like that.

states, which means that they would have to interconnect somehow, and this would immediately create a different international system from minimum to increasing interdependence. But with stability there would be compatibility, possibly with interaction, but not with interdependence since all states would be self-sufficient.

There is also another way of obtaining compatibility. We could divide the world into a small number of nations, which might then be called empires, each of them self-sufficient and consisting of societies at highly different levels of development. Inside each nation there would be development in the sense that the primitive segment would be transformed into traditional segments, which would then be transformed into modern segments, and in turn develop into a neomodern society. The nation-states in this type of world would be highly heterogeneous and at the same time flexible and spacious (both geographically and socially) enough to permit the gradual transformation into neomodern social orders. This type of world was approximated by the system of colonial empires prior to the First World War—as the societies developed and grew, the nation-states expanded correspondingly by means of territorial acquisitions—as they had always done before—so as to obtain compatibility, even for future development. Nations like Brazil and the Soviet Union, even China and India, can also be seen in this perspective.

But neither of these two models of compatibility obtain in the present international system. Instead the two assumptions above seem to be generally valid: high value is attributed to development (almost) all over the world, with modern societies in general contributing to make traditional societies more modern, while they themselves are rapidly becoming neomodern.[16] At the same time the net of nation-states is thrown in such a way that most of them have segments representing societies in different stages of development, and some of these intra-national segments are tied to segments in other nations and constitute cross-national social orders.[17] In other words, a highly

---

[16]Kahn's distinctions (*op. cit.*, pp. 716f) are in our mind too much based on GNP/capita, which is an aggregate measure and hence one that obscures the qualitative differences between the segments inside a nation-state. But his post-industrial is our neomodern, his "massconsumption or advanced industrial" is a mixture of modern and neomodern; his industrial is our modern; and his partially industrial and preindustrial are modern with increasing ingredients of traditional or perhaps even primitive segments. When his typology is based on GNP/capita and ours to some extent on % *not* in primary sector, comparisons can only be made under the assumption that there is a high correlation between these two measures; and that is a rather well established fact: it is 0.84, based on 76 nations (Russett et al., *World Handbook of Political and Social Indicators*, p. 279). Kahn's projections as to which nations will be in which stage in Year 2000 are, hence, very useful for our purposes, although some of the dynamics are lost when GNP/capita measures are used.

[17]There are two kinds of these cross-national, social orders, viz., the egalitarian ones, where the segments are at the same level of development; and the inegalitarian ones. The latter easily become exploitative and oppressive. Cross-national links at the N-N level may take the form of international conferences organized around some value or profession; at

complex picture, the consequences of which we have to examine.

Some reasons why the world looks like this and not like the two models with built-in compatibility above should now be spelled out. We may say that the reasons are not so much structural as cultural, due to the nearly universal prevalence of ideologies about development and national independence. The latter throws out the second model of compatibility, whereby modern and neomodern segments inside a large political unit dominate traditional and primitive segments; for the traditional and primitive segments organize themselves, get rid of the colonization, and declare their national independence. Experience shows it is exceedingly difficult to achieve a form of cooperation between societies at different levels of development that is both symbiotic *and* symmetric. Instead, patterns of exploitation, whereby the more developed receive much more from the less developed than they pay back, easily develop—patterns referred to as *external* colonization if they are found between nations (not necessarily nation-states), and *internal* colonization ("colonización interna") if they are found inside a nation (typically in the form for the modern urbanized sector exploiting the lagging, traditional rural economy[18]). Whether this leads to wars of independence and liberation probably depends on the second peace factor in the preceding section: the level of entropy. Inside nations, entropy is usually higher than between nations, providing less clear fronts than between the peoples in the colonizing and colonized nations. In addition, the amount and nature of supra-group organizations play an important role. One gets anti-colonial movements and wars, but domestic protests from the countryside are usually absorbed in the national machinery for conflict resolution—only rarely does it lead to revolutions.

---

the M-N level it may take the form of exchange of manufactured goods and expertise; at the T-T level, the exchange of manufactured goods form of traditional trade; at the P-P level, the form of cross-national tribalism. But then there are the M-T forms (manufactured goods against raw materials), the T-P forms (primary products against slaves) and the N-M form yet to flower: highest level expertise against manufactured goods. "Imperialism" is a term often used for the T-P and M-T relations.

[18]One logical pattern here seems to be as follows: the organizers of industries want to make a profit, whether they are private or public, whether they want the profit for own consumption or for investment, whether they want to invest in more industries or in some other goods. The less they can pay their workers, the more profit can they make. One solution is to keep low wages by keeping workers' expenses low. One such expense would be transportation to the place of work: this is cut down by urbanization. Another expense is food: this is cut down by paying farmers badly for their products. The major reason why this works is that farmers are badly organized; unlike workers their form of production is still very often neolithic, i.e. one family, one farm—whereas work organization brings workers together and facilitates union-formation. The theory may be that this is justified because the country gets industrialized so that it can later on pay the farmers back—but in the meantime these may have escaped from the countryside and settled in slums outside the cities—as found all over the Third World today.

Thus, the net result is a collection of independent nation-states, all formed in principle according to the model appropriate for nations that are also societies, and particularly societies at the level of development characterized as "modern." Since these units, the nations, are in interaction, a certain amount of homology is impressed upon them. They have to be organized in a relatively equal manner at the top to respond to at least some of the demands made by international interaction, to participate in the international game. This will facilitate the emergence of modern and even neomodern segments at the top of many nations, which in turn has a consequence that the "internal development distance" between the least and most developed segments is higher, the less developed the nation is—in general—making the less developed nations less cohesive.

Since all nations, in order to participate in the international game, must have at least some modern segment, we shall translate our typology of four types of societies into two types of nation-states: type PTM, which has primitive, traditional, and modern segments and hence is *less* developed; and type TMN, which has traditional, modern, and neomodern segments, and hence is *more* developed. There are, of course, also societies like Brazil, which would be PTMN, and this would to some extent also apply to the United States and the Soviet Union, but we would nevertheless put the first one in type PTM and the second ones in type TMN. Essentially, this typology can be operationalized by using the percentage not working in the primary sector as one indicator; and since this is highly correlated with GNP/capita, we have essentially the often-used division into poor and rich, developing and developed nations.

But this is not sufficient for our purpose, since we are concerned with the degree of compatibility with developmental level and the space provided by the nation-state. One measure of the latter would be in terms of size of population, as an indicator of the magnitude of the society the nation-state could house within its borders. This yields the typology in Table 2. Certainly, the level of development is the more important of these two dimensions, but it should also be related to size. The incompatibilities are clearly found in types II and III in Table 2; in the first case the societal units are too big for the

TABLE 2: A typology of nation-states*

	Big	Small
More developed (TMN)	I (34)	II (27)
Less developed (PTM)	III (32)	IV (24)

*Nos. in parentheses are no. of nations in each category. The correlation is only −0.03 with development expressed in GNP/capita.

nation-state, in the second case too small for the nation-state. The consequences of this will now be commented on in detail, using for simplification the simple division in developmental levels.

3.2. TRENDS IN THE MORE DEVELOPED PART OF THE WORLD

Characteristic of this part of the world, now, is the manner in which the societies with increasing development are *growing out of* their nation-states which even become like strait-jackets for them. A consequence of this is a certain general erosion of the nation-state, since it is perceived as being of decreasing relevance for an increasing fraction of the members of the nation. But there is a double process taking place: on the one hand, some layers of the population become identified with neomodern societies and grow out of the nation-state; while at the same time, formerly traditional, peripheral segments become more modern, and hence arrive at a level of social identification compatible with the nation-state. But the net result will nevertheless be a decrease in loyalty, a decrease in nationalism, because the "leavers" are on the top and the "joiners" come from the bottom.

Specific consequences of this should then be observable at the level of very concrete participation on behalf of the nation-state: as members of parliament or government, and as soldiers "giving their lives" for the country. The prediction would be that both decision-makers[19] and people willing to act as soldiers[20] for their country will come increasingly from the periphery; or rather, that the strata and levels from which they come will look increasingly peripheral, since an increasing fraction of the population will be located in the segments typical of neomodern society which in turn will reject this type of participation: To participate in parliament or in government will look the way participation in the county council or administration today looks to many today—as slightly comical—even if the county is urban. This does not mean that they are disinterested in power, only that their orientation is towards other foci.

In other words, we predict an increasing gap between the neomodern makers of new civilizations and the people making decisions and fighting for the "national interests." But what then happens to the identification patterns of the disenchanted intellectuals?—for that is essentially what they are. There seem to be four basic types of substitute identification for the lost national identification; we shall refer to them as subnational, crossnational, transnational and supranational.

1. Subnational identification. Individuals disenchanted with the nation-state, yet less inclined or less able to identify outside the borders of their

---

[19]We are thinking here of the relatively low number of high-ranking intellectuals participating in national assemblies and governments in most developed nations—to some extent isolating the universities.

[20]We are thinking here of the concentration of resistance to the Vietnam war on the campus, in terms of opinion-formation as well as in terms of such active forms of resistance as draftcard burning, etc. Interviews and stories from the US soldiers actively fighting in the war give an impression of a very strong rural, even peripheral element. For an example of this, see the story of "The Anderson Company" in *Le Figaro*, January, 1967.

own nation-state, will find a variety of subnational foci of identification. This may coincide with a trend dealt with in domestic futurology: the tendency to feel that we now see the end of this long and painful transition from the 100–0–0 population profile to the 0–0–100 profile, from "all in the primary sector" to "all in the tertiary sector," and that what we see seems less than worth while. That is, there may be a tendency for negative feedback to prevail once the goal is in sight; in other words, for the establishment of primitive pockets within a modern-neomodern society, like the legendary hippie communities on the Pacific West Coast of the US.[21] But there are, of course, also more traditional foci of identification, such as *geographical units* (a city, a county) or *organizations*—of which the latter are much more likely, since the salience of the former will continue to decrease with increasing communication capacity.

One more drastic result of this would be rejection of national policies by such subunits; in other words, open expression of the feeling that national policies, even if arrived at by a process of majority vote, are not necessarily to be obeyed. We envisage a relatively near future where one state or county or professional organization in a predominantly neomodern nation will tell the nation's capital *fate la guerra, ma senza noi.* That a value-oriented organization should do so would not be strange, for the members might be organized around precisely that value; the new factor would be that such values could predominate in subunits and even prevail over traditional national loyalties. If the subunit is geographical, the result may be a separatist movement.[22] In a sense, this is not much stranger than the idea that workers should go on strike against "their" factory; both are based on the feeling that the demands from the rulers or owners have lost their legitimacy. But in this case the "enemy from within" would above all be the intellectuals, and the most loyal cooperation would come from the rural and more traditionally industrial or commercial segments. This structural division will hold *a fortiori* true for foreign policies, since they more than any other type of policy will concern the nation as a whole, all citizens equally.

2. Crossnational identification. Much more basic to the logic of our general scheme of analysis is the idea that the neomodern societies are outgrowing their borders, so that they become dependent on corresponding or complementary segments in other nations. There is a general process of inter-

---

[21]For one description, see *Time* Magazine, July 7, 1967, pp. 12–20.

[22]The recent example of the poll in San Francisco over a proposal calling for an immediate cease-fire and withdrawal of American troops from Vietnam without prior negotiation is very interesting as a case here. The proposal was rejected by a majority of nearly two to one (132,402 against, 76,632 in favor)–but a pattern has been indicated that will definitely be followed in other local communities around the world, not only in the US, but predominantly in the most neo-modern parts of TMN nations (we would have predicted California or somewhere in the Boston–Washington range in the US), and in low entropy segments of PTM nations. (More details in *The Guardian*, November 9, 1967.)

penetration. Invariably this will mean that individuals are brought into all kinds of crossnational contacts that are both functional, relatively symmetric, and long lasting (as opposed to the contact between the tourist and the shoe-shine boy, taxi-driver or others from the lower ranks of the tertiary sector that he is likely to encounter). Contacts of this kind will not necessarily lead to a decrease in loyalty to one's own nation, but almost certainly to increase in loyalty to the other nation; and this crossnational identification may be cemented by crossnational marriage, dual positions (characteristic of most professions in the neomodern segments is precisely that they do not know national borders, the skills are universally valid—i. e., valid in other neo-modern segments all over the world).

Extrapolating from this well-known trend, we would predict that the amount of mobility, both of persons and of their loyalties, will lead to a re-evaluation of the meaning of national citizenship, more in the direction of membership in an organization. This has two implications: that the transfer from one nation to another will become easier (the individual tears up his membership card if he dislikes the way the organization, the nation, is run—even if it is according to the expressed wishes of the majority) and that multiple member-ship and zero membership will become possible. Today much energy still goes into the idea that citizenship should be a classification. An individual should be member of one and only one nation: both stateless and multiple citizens are to be avoided. Well before year 2000 these problems will prob-ably be solved as indicated, more in accordance with differential capacity for membership among people, and the fact that loyalty is, after all, distribu-tive, even in the set of nations—and particularly under the assumption of increasing neomodern forms of social organization.

3. Transnational identification. For the person with crossnational identifi-cation, the unit of identification is still the nation-state—only that he takes in more than one of them (just as the person with subnational identification takes in less than one). For transnational identification the focus of identifi-cation is an organization which transcends national borders, without com-prising nations; it is subnational, yet international: in other words, the INGO. Clearly, the person with subnational identification in his professional organiza-tion or value-organization will find support in his rejection of pure national loyalty if his organization is a branch of an INGO that ties him to individuals, perspectives, values rooted in other nations.

Characteristic of the INGOs (at present about 1600 in number with about 10% growth rate) is a dynamism in the growth pattern without comparison in the system of nation-states.[23] Thus, whereas a combination of likely inde-

[23]INGOs are presently being studied in a joint project by the International Peace Research Institute, Oslo and the Peace Research Centre, London. For some preliminary results, see Paul Smoker, "A Preliminary Empirical Study of an International Integration Sub-system," *Proceedings of the IPRA Inaugural Conference,* (Assen: van Gorcum, 1966), pp. 38–51. Richard Meier has brought to our attention a report indicating an even higher growth rate

pendence movements, fission processes, and fusion processes will yield a maximum of around 200 nation-states (provided we do not get large-scale fission processes of the kind envisaged in connection with subnational identification above), there is no limit at all to the number of INGOs. There is nothing corresponding to a finite territory to be divided into units that somehow have to be viable, so the growth can continue in an exponential pattern for many years to come.

Since the minimum size for viability of a nation increases with increasing level of development, we predict that the number of fusion processes of existing nation-states will tend to prevail over the fission processes. Or more correctly, there will be many fission processes, but leading to (con)federations rather than to autonomous nation-states; just as the fusion processes also will take the form of (con)federations rather than superstates. *Similarly,* we shall certainly also have fissions and fusions of INGOs, resulting in a number of super-INGOs, or organizations of INGOs.[24] But this does not restrict the number in any way, since there is almost no minimum requirement to make an INGO viable. As first steps in that direction INGOs will start exchanging *observers* to meetings of the executive council or to the general conferences; the next step will be exchange of *members* of executive and council; then there will be exchange of *missions* to each others' headquarters; and the next step is a super-INGO and possibly complete fusion. Thus, we shall probably witness a repetition of some centuries of international diplomatic history in the field of inter-INGO relations.

Most interesting from our point of view is the compatibility between INGO rules of membership and the difference in individual capacity for participation: a person can in principle become member of almost as many INGOs as he wants, since only relatively few INGOs are mutually exclusive.[25] Three particular kinds of INGOs seem to have specific relevance for our general problem.

First, the *internationalization of political ideologies.* The socialist and communist internationals, and to some extent the universal religious movements are old examples; but the international anti-Vietnam war movement is a much better one. The characteristic feature is the more or less spontaneous,

---

among international business corporations (INGOs are by definition non-profit) of as much as 15%—according to a study reported in *Chemical Abstracts.*

[24]An example of the International Social Science Council, coordinating activities of international social science associations, with headquarters in Paris and supported by the UNESCO.

[25]INGOs can generally be divided according to focus in three groups: ideology-oriented, status-oriented, and profession-oriented. In a world where a person is seen as having only one profession, most professional INGOs would be mutually exclusive; but typical of neo-modern societies seems to be persons with more than one profession, at least, during their life-time. And who knows whether ideologies will not once be conceived of that way too—not only that a basic change during one's life-time will be seen as quite normal, but also simultaneous belief in contrary or even contradictory ideologies?

international character of demonstrations and of ideologies. In this perspective they become concretizations of what von Weiszäcker calls *Weltinnenpolitik*— world domestic policy. In other words, INGOs may be formed by people having the same or corresponding views on domestic problems—to exchange ideas and to support each other. But much more relevant are INGOs built around value-positions in international politics, where members fight not only parallel causes but a common cause. We predict that this phenomenon will show a rapid growth in the years to come, and tend to internationalize foreign policies, just as the formation of national parties gave a nation-wide scope to district and regional policies.

The second factor is the possible *internationalization of age-sets*. By this we mean the following: inside each nation whose dominant social segment is neomodern there will be a rapid increase in the conflict between generations. This is not due to the traditional factors behind such conflicts (such as different position in the lifecycle; different amount of available physical, intellectual, creative, and sexual energy; different degree of experience; the fact that the younger generation is in search of positions and the older generation is defending their positions), but above all due to the speed with which social change takes place in neomodern societies. If the amount of time needed before any given social phenomenon—be it population, number of cars, number of scientists, number of organizations—has doubled,[26] becomes less than the average number of years separating generations, i. e., less than about 25 years, then parents will see their children grow up in a world quite different from that they grew up in. The rest is a question of adaptability rates for the older generation—and even if they can adapt themselves to short doubling times, they may not be able to adapt themselves to short trebling times. The net result will easily be that they are perceived as irrelevant to their own children, much like grandparents are today.

This will probably lead to increased solidarity among teen-agers against parents, teachers, professors; a rejection of leadership and tutelage from persons who are so old as to represent substantially different forms of social life. They will see teenagers in other societies at the same level of development as more comparable and compatible, associate with them and form a teenager-INGO, however loosely organized, much like today's hippie-INGO. This, in turn, will lead to a corresponding effort among the older generation to organize. Thus, just as traditional societies, by virtue of their stability essentially belonged to the old since they were superior in terms of experience; experience is less of an asset in neomodern societies which will belong to the young, because only they possess sufficient flexibility to adjust to the changes (or sufficiently unconditioned by irrelevant experience).

If these two bases of INGO-formation are combined, we would envisage some kind of world-wide generational conflict—the contours of which we get

[26] I am indebted to Herman Kahn for drawing my attention to this factor.

an idea of by observing the age of such political leaders as Fidel Castro, Che Guevara, and Stokely Carmichael. But world-shaking events of the type presented by the war in Vietnam (and many would see that as the only positive result so far) will perhaps also be needed in the future to crystallize these types of INGO and to fuse them sufficiently.

The third factor is the *internationalization of specialists in world welfare.* The world today faces two major problems, recognized as the two axes around which the UN system is built: the problems of *peace* and *development.* We predict the rapid emergence of *international peace specialists*[27] and *international development engineers,*[28] who look at these problems from a global point of view, not from the vantage point of any smaller unit. Such professionals will be exposed to heavy pressures from the environment, particularly if they reject national loyalties. They will have to seek protection somewhere, and this is likely to be some kind of professional organization built on the model of corresponding domestic organizations. In other words: two more INGOs—probably even to be started in the beginning of the 1970's.

But we also predict denationalization for a number of old professions, not only for new professions created with denationalization as a *raison d'être.* Physicians have in a sense been denationalized since Hippocrates—whether the oath is a myth or not—and all kinds of natural and physical scientists will probably be the next to come. Strong professional ties will control the use of innovations, much like composers' societies see to it that some revenue accrues to the composer upon public performances.

4. Supranational identification. We have mentioned fusion processes among nations and assume that they will continue to be very prominent features in the years to come. It is a serious analytical mistake to include only such dramatic examples as the EEC under this heading; any IGO will serve as an example of some level of fusion, with a consequent increase in supranational identification. That identification may be found among relatively few, for instance only among the secretariat members and staff in general: but people who somehow benefit from it or see the IGO as an expression of their own ideology will also easily identify.

The characteristic feature is that more and more functions will be taken care of by nations acting together; coordinating, harmonizing or even unifying their policies completely. And just as for INGOs, we predict that history will repeat itself: IGOs will become increasingly jealous of each other; they will be in conflict over functions belonging to none of them or claimed by several (just as big powers when their "spheres of influence" do not exhaust the surface of the world or are not mutually exclusive); and they will try to

---

[27]This is currently being studied under the auspices of the International Peace Research Association.

[28]This was suggested at the International Future Research Inaugural Congress by Richard Meier.

regulate their conflicts by inter-IGO and supra-IGO machineries. But there is almost no limit on these processes, for if we assume that an IGO has at least three members and that there are n nations in the world, then the total number of extensionally different IGOs is $2^n \div \frac{n^2}{2} \div \frac{n}{2} \div 1$, which could then be multiplied with the number of functions these IGOs could be concerned with. At present there are around 600 IGOs, with a very high growth rate.

Very important in this connection are the economic IGOs, the international corporations, the countless *coproduction* schemes that are rapidly becoming a normal form of neomodern economy. Another telling example of how much developed nations grow together is the tendency to form even military IGOs, called *alliances*. The intermeshing has then gone so far that the symbiotic relationship to a large extent is realized so that wars between these nations become virtually impossible. Alliances are usually formed only in the presence of a perceived common enemy, and justified in terms of this factor; but it is often forgotten that in order to share military secrets and integrate military units, a solid basis in the form of networks of cooperation in other fields may be a condition.

All these four processes (sub-, cross-, trans- and supra-national) are now seen as responses to the incompatibility between development level and size of the nation. Hence, we would assume these processes to take place in more developed nations much more than in less developed nations, and among the more developed nations much more in the small nations than in the big nations—since there will be a great fraction of neomoderns in small nations having to engage in extra-national interaction than in big nations. Big nations will be more self-sufficient even when it comes to providing a real neomodern with what he needs. Thus, we would expect small, developed nations to be particularly active and particularly well represented in IGOs and INGOs, and all relative to the size of the populations concerned. And we would expect to find the return to the subnational type of identification more frequently in the bigger nation, since only that nation will provide sufficient space and diversity. But we would also expect periods of increased nationalism in the biggest developed nations—on top of a generally downward trend —as new traditional strata grow into the nation-state, discover it, become identified with it, and fight for the national focus of identification—which maximizes their power and rank—to prevail. This is where the German NPD fits, not as neo-nazism: a revival of nationalism.

This said, our general prediction for the developed part of the world would be as follows. *We predict a steady growth in the mutual interpenetration and intermeshing of all developed, industrialized nations with neomodern segments with each other; using INGOs and IGOs as building structures and individuals with cross-, trans-, and supra-loyalties as building blocks.*

Small nations will be particularly important in this process. They have most to gain from the process, since their level of incompatibility is highest, so they will often deliver the best IGO/INGO personnel. They may serve as go-between for bigger nations that will still have a more purely national concept of "national interest" and hence tend to perceive each other in competitive terms. But also for them, i. e., particularly the United States and the Soviet Union, we predict that they will be caught in this generally integrative movement. This will eventually (i. e., at the very least by the year 2000, probably already around 1980) comprise the area from the Bering Strait to the Bering Strait; from Alaska via Canada, the United States, over the North-Atlantic Ocean into Western Europe and Eastern Europe (possibly with the exception of some Mediterranean countries), Soviet Union, Japan, and down to Australia and New Zealand: in other words, the OECD nations plus the socialist nations.[29] The Kennedy Grand Design vision of an Atlantic Community, the de Gaulle vision of a Europe from the Atlantic to the Urals, the visions expressed in the 1957 Treaty of Rome—all are partial visions, with clearly political constraints, of this total image based more on the logic of the socio-economic forces currently in operation.

In this area there will still be nations, maybe about the same as today, but most borders will play no more role than the border between Norway and Sweden or even between two counties (where, incidentally, change of membership is usually not so difficult, although the "one and only one" rule still obtains). As in marriage, nations will be tied; they will have less latitude; but, also as in marriage, most of them will decide that they gain more than they lose by the arrangement. There will also be regions with particularly strong supranational links: we will probably discern the EEC, the Comecon countries, etc. Some parts will call themselves socialist, others may call themselves capitalist—but that will be more like the difference between counties with socialist or with non-socialist majorities inside a nation: the logic of industrialized, highly educated societies will prevail over such ideological distinctions. The flow of persons (also as labor force: one works where one wants or is most needed), goods, and information across borders will be considerable and this permeability of borders will contribute tremendously to the erosion of the nation-state—as indicated above. Nations will look more like Armenians and Jews before Israel. This may also sometime in the 1970's facilitate the solution of the German problem in Central Europe.[30] *Peaceful coexistence* will be the general rule.

[29]This corresponds exactly to Kahn's list of 'visibly postindustrial' and 'early postindustrial' nations by Year 2000—but Kahn is more interested in their relative power positions whereas our position is that that question will have lost much of its meaning in the web of affiliations spun by neomodern societies growing into each other.

[30]In other words, that unification takes place not so much by a change in the legal and political order within and between the two Germanies, as by increasingly rapid diffusion across the border leaving the border issue uninteresting. Parallel with this development, towards higher entropy except in the early 1970's, there will probably also be a growth in the supra-German institutional network with increasingly symbiotic and symmetric patterns of cooperation, and, hence, good prospects for very peaceful relations.

Thus, the prediction is that East and West will rapidly disappear as meaningful contradictions, not because of any complete convergence in socio-economic system, but because of deideologization and technification of the economics and a relatively complete mutual interdependence—with the big two as the last to join (but they will be greatly stimulated to join when they see that the smaller nations on both sides and in the middle become gradually more integrated). This gigantic neomodern complex will not have a unified regional government, but rather be coordinated through a network of supra-national and supra-regional organizations that will have to work closely together with INGOs and super-INGOs. Thus, all three conditions of peaceful relations envisaged in section 2 above will be satisfied and increasingly so, and that will serve to absorb and solve conflicts bound to arise in a process of interpenetration.

As a crowning achievement there will even be integration of military forces in this area, starting with non-aggression treaties (partly bilateral between all pairs of nations, partly between sub-regions such as the NATO and Warsaw Pact countries), continuing with exchanges of observation teams and mutual inspection schemes, and ending up with some kind of unified command. Thus, we do not predict disarmament so much as arms control and a pooling of military resources, that will be less and less targeted on intra-region goals. Of course, for all this to take place a common enemy would be almost, but not quite, indispensable—and this will be discussed later.

In other words, the prediction would be that *in this region there will be no major war*, except, possibly, by technical failure or escalation in the first ten years. After that, even such factors will be under control. There may be some local conflagrations, but they will be absorbed quickly because of the high number of conflict-absorbing and conflict-solving organizations, the high entropy due to the high level of mobility, and the generally symbiotic pattern of cooperation. There is the uncertainty connected with the two big powers, not so much because of their power potential as because of their size. We may risk some kind of atavistic return to nationalistic rather than regional militarism, but this can be coped with by means of domestic opposition and the extent to which allies are able to control the superpowers and inform them that they cannot count on unconditional support. As mentioned above, it is felt that the smaller nations will increasingly feel that their interests are better served by general cooperation in the entire region than by subregional patterns of cooperation alone, and that East-West cooperation in general will have to be based on small-power interaction to a considerable extent, in the beginning.[31]

[31]One particular reason for this is the degree to which small nations even today depend on their environment much more than big nations. Thus, on the basis of *World Handbook of Political and Social Indicators* data we calculated the correlation (Yule's Q) between size (population) and foreign trade as a percentage of GNP, and found a correlation—.79. In other words, the bigger the nation, the less does it depend on trade for its GNP. Most spectacular in this connection is the position of the three biggest powers in the world:

3.3. TRENDS IN THE LESS DEVELOPED PART OF THE WORLD

Characteristic of this part of the world, now, is the manner in which the societies are *growing into* their nation-states, which are not like strait-jackets, but like jackets to be filled by a very lean person. A consequence of this is a certain general building-up of the nation-state, since it is perceived as being increasingly relevant for an increasing fraction of the members of the nation. But here too there is a double process taking place. On the one hand there is the general trend in this type of nation: primitive segments becoming traditional by tying themselves to urbanized sectors and market-economies; and traditional segments becoming modernized by means of industrialization and a growing tertiary sector of professionals. There are the "joiners"; they grow into the nation-state and are received by it. But there will also be some "leavers": people who were formerly the leaders and who never felt at home in their own nation, because the modern or neomodern segments surrounding them were too limited.

They were the Latin-American business elites and the Afro-Asian intellectual elites who felt that the environments provided for them in the more developed countries were more congenial; that only in such settings could they be sustained in the form of life they felt as theirs. The recent version of this is known as "brain-drain," where the typical cause seems to be that the returned fellowship-holders do not feel sufficiently sustained in their old environments; there are too few people with whom to have meaningful talks, no professional association, no milieu, very few people trained to receive and appreciate their products, and hence little influence potential.[32] These people may still, for some time, continue to be "leavers," and they may also feel repelled and rejected by the local stock of professionals, drawn from traditional and even primitive segments of their own less developed nation and then squeezed through a domestic educational system designed at keeping them in the country and providing them with a local environment. Thus, the generation of Oxbridge and Sorbonne graduates who wanted to do in their new nations what the English and the French had done before them, but do it themselves, will be replaced by a new stock with new ideas.

Specific consequences of this should then be observable at the level of very concrete participation on behalf of the nation-state; as members of parliament

---

USSR, USA, and China—at the bottom of the list, with their allies usually quite high, and higher the smaller they are.

Of both economic and political significance are the famous "Club of 9" initiatives, to try to find platforms for all-European cooperation. For an empirical and theoretical analysis of bilateral patterns of interaction in Europe, see Johan Galtung, "East-West Interaction Patterns," *Journal of Peace Research* (1966): 146–177.

[32]See studies by Ingrid Eide Galtung, "Student Scholars as Culture Carriers: A Study of Eastern Students Who Have Received Western University Training," "Brain Drain: An Attempt at Diagnosis and Therapy," both forthcoming.

or government,[33] and as soldiers "giving their lives" for their country.[34] We predict that both decision-makers and people willing to act as soldiers will come from the center of the society; or rather that the strata and levels from which they come will look central, since an increasing fraction of the population will be located in these segments—the modern and more developed traditional segments. Our assumption is that these segments identify with the nation-state in any nation; the point is merely that in the less developed nations there is a growth into these segments, whereas in the more developed there is a growth out of them. *Thus, just as the population as a whole will be in a process of decreasing nationalism in the more developed nations (particularly in the small ones), the populations as a whole in the less developed nations will be in a process of increasing nationalism (particularly the big ones).* Hence, the big nations of the world will increasingly understand each other's idiom.

This means that there is no question of finding alternative foci of identification, since the nation-state will provide a growing reservoir of such foci, as the internal segments become more connected to each other. On the other hand, all four alternative forms of identification will also be found, particularly the first one. However, subnational identification will not emerge as an alternative to and a rejection of national identification, but rather as an identification to be replaced with national identification when the circles of growing interdependence have grown large enough.

As to the other three, there are two reasons why there will be much slower growth in cross-, trans- and supra-national identification. The first reason is simply the lack of functional necessity: for the development levels concerned, the PTM states do not *have* to be in constant interaction with other states, as the TMN states must in order to sustain their social order. They do not have a high number of businessmen and professionals who depend for highly complex cooperation and communication on colleagues and partners in other nations. An apparent exception here is trade. Less developed nations, particularly the small ones, depend for a large fraction of their GNP on trade.[35] That does not mean that many people are involved, since such trade operations are usually handled by a low number of big export-import firms, often staffed more from the TMN nation to which they export. This is due to the concentration of the commodities; the states in question often have an economy based on mono-culture. Hence, few inhabitants of the PTM states will be

---

[33]We are thinking here of the legendary participation by teachers—the current intellectual elite—in many African parliaments and governments, of the participation of the "abogado" in Latin America, etc.

[34]Characteristic of the many movements currently known under the initials of NLF or FLN in various countries (Algeria, Vietnam, Venezuela, Aden, etc.) is that students always seem to play a dominant and positive role—compare this with the draftcard burners in the US.

[35]This does not mean that many of them have, in fact, high trade loadings in their GNP, because they may not have anything to trade with. See footnote 38 for further comments.

directly involved or exposed to a change of loyalties in the cross-national and trans-national directions.

The second reason has to do with the general structure of interaction in any system, or so it seems, that is stratified: interaction tends to concentrate on the top of the system, between the center nations, to be less developed between center and periphery nations, and to be at a far lower level between two periphery nations.[36] Interaction flows in the direction of high rank; and even though this will tend to link PTM nations to TMN nations, the tendency will be less pronounced than for relations between TMN nations, and particularly low between PTM nations. Thus, the growth rate of their participation will lag behind, particularly for inter-PTM IGOs: we would expect a very low growth rate in their formation, and that such IGOs will quickly and easily split up once they have been formed.[37] The supra-national identification most likely to be formed is in the direction of TMN nations, for it is in this general direction that the interpenetration takes place. More particularly, this is the direction in which military alliances are still likely to be formed, much more than TMN nations alone.

The difference between small and big PTM nations enters here. We would expect the peak of nationalism to be reached more quickly in the smaller nations, where the coincidence between society and state can be reached earlier, due to their often very small size. But at least as importantly: these nations are often far from self-sufficient, nor will they ever become self-sufficient because of their small size, which in turn also affects their growth rate negatively.[38] Thus they are less likely ever to develop substantial modern and neomodern fragments except on an IGO basis, as a spill-over from a

[36]For a general exposition of this theory, the feudality thesis, see Johan Galtung, "International Relations and International Conflicts: A Sociological Approach," *Transactions of the Sixth World Congress for Sociology*, pp. 121–161, particularly pp. 146–148. For a good test of this theory, see Smoker, *op. cit.*, pp. 46–49.

[37]For data on how slowly the poorer nations develop air communication between themselves, see Nils Petter Gleditsch, "Trends in International Air Communication," *Journal of Peace Research* (1967), pp. 366–408.

[38]We have already mentioned (footnote 31), that small nations depend much more on their environment for trade. But big nations also have a much higher growth-rate, on the average, as seen from Table A. To be big means to have internal markets, under central control at least to some extent, and hence possibilities of expansion and transformation of less developed segments into more developed ones. Industries can grow big without having to engage in complicated international transactions. But size is most important for the poor nations, leaving the small and poor very much behind. To the extent they do develop, however, they will outgrow themselves.

TABLE A: Relation between size, development level and growth rate

	Average growth rate		
	Big	Small	Difference
Rich	3.9	3.0	0.9
Poor	2.1	0.8	1.3

TMN nation, often with a commercial nucleus. This makes them particularly vulnerable to all kinds of TMN manipulation. The center of gravity for decisions affecting them will still for some time be outside themselves. We only say "less likely": there is also a chance that new forms of modern and neomodern societies requiring less in terms of size can be found, and that they can tie themselves to big PMT neighbors.

Concretely, what does all this mean for war and peace? There are three types of relations to predict: intra-PTM nations, inter-PTM nations, and the relations between less and more developed nations. We shall deal briefly with the first two here, and refer the third type to the following subsection.

Relations *within less developed nations* are likely to be increasingly characterized by all kinds of inter-group conflict, between tribes, classes, racial, and ethnic groups in general. The reason for this is generally that all three peace-making formulas seem to be unfulfilled: there is little symbiosis because of the self-sufficiency—although at a low level of development—of the many constituent units: where there is symbiosis it tends to be asymmetric and exploitative, because of the generally low level of entropy (e. g., with tribes to a large extent occupying specific areas) even though growing urbanization tends to increase the entropy considerably,[39] and because of the weakness and insufficiency of supra-group organizations. This is especially true for the bigger nations, and particularly because the "internal development distance"" will tend to make symbiotic relations particularly asymmetric.

In other words, we would predict the kind of internal antagonism that will almost call for foreign and domestic military intervention and for deposition of civilian regimes (the foreign version will be called a "peacekeeping force"). The present trend of military coups d'etat will probably continue, and the growth will continue;[40] to some extent because the military segment is often 1) the most efficient organization in the new nation; 2) the most achievement-oriented; 3) an organization with a broad national basis; and 4) with a high level of internal entropy (both officers and soldiers recruited from different groups)—the last two points because the organization has been colored by a strong nationalist ideology.[41]

But this is for the coming years, say till the end of the 1970's, when some of the imbalance between population growth and food resources has been engineered away.[42] The result will be consolidation of the regimes, concomitant

[39]Thus, one typical formula for national integration is the coexistence, in every ecological unit, of many different tribes and races, but not so many of any single group that they can run a viable society alone. Also to be avoided is the low entropy formula whereby tribes and races specialize in occupations or groups of occupations, so that tribes and races become stratified in accordance with the stratification of occupations.

[40]This coincides with the prediction made by Ithiel de Sola Pool, *op. cit.*, p. 932.

[41]For an important analysis of the conditions that favor military coups d'etat, see Egil Fossum, "Factors Influencing the Occurrence of Military Coups d'etat in Latin America," *JPR* (1967), pp. 228–251.

[42]To many this will sound too optimistic. They may point to pollution, growth curves for populations, and to dwindling food resources, e.g., caused by the circumstance that agri-

with the much more rapid growth of the modern and neomodern segment we predict for that period. In the process the geo-political map will have changed, there will have been both fissions and fusions, separatist and amalgamist movements, with the general consequence of increased homogeneity within nations and increased heterogeneity between nations. In other words, there will be a general loss of entropy in this part of the world, as against the predicted gain in entropy in the developed part of the world. Something called the "rectification of artificial borderlines created by imperialism" will take place, and that, then, is one basis for the prediction of *inter-PTM relations*.

We predict external warfare between them, much for the same reason as we predict internal warfare within them: lack of symbiotic relationship, lack of symmetry in relations between them, very low level of entropy, and weak supra-national institutions—all for reasons mentioned above. The lack of symbiosis is to a large extent due to the parallelism in the economies which directs trade in the direction of complementarity, i. e., upwards in the world ranking system. But this is also for the first decade or two; after that we would expect more possibilities of cooperative relationships. PTM nations with substantial modern sectors will expand trade relations. They will export to nations at the same level: after having exhausted the consumers' market at home they will turn to nations at the same level of development and the same demand profile. But this pattern is also likely to be asymmetric in the beginning; the smaller PTM nations will be exposed to the dominance and even exploitation stemming from the bigger ones until this to some extent can be alleviated by symmetrically designed supra-national organizations.[43]

---

cultural output of industrialized nations may decrease because migration to the cities offsets the effects of automation. That this will lead to some large-scale famines early in the 1970's is perhaps correct—and is in case a most telling indictment against professionals and politicians for not having engaged in sufficient future research when there was still time to remedy the evil. But after that, we would predict that we shall start reaping the benefits of what has been invested in propaganda for family planning and invention of contraceptive devices (probably more innovations in this field during the last 7 than in the preceding 7000 years); and that completely new methods of increasing food supply (ocean farming, three-dimensional agriculture, synthetic products) will start to pay off. Thus we are more in line with Colin Clark in his "Agricultural Productivity in Relation to Population" (Wolstenholme, ed., *Man and His Future*, London: Churchill, 1963) and Richard Meier in *Science and Economic Development: New Patterns of Living* (Cambridge: M.I.T. Press, 1966).

[43]The stage is already set for large-scale exploitation of small PTM nations by the larger ones by very feudal interaction patterns between nations in, say, Latin America. This theme is investigated in Johan Galtung, Manuel Mora and Simon Schwartzman, "El sistema latino-americana de naciones: Un analisis estructural," *America Latina* (1966), 59–94 and developed further, in a context of analysis of integration, in Per Olav Reinton, "International Structure and International Integration: The Case of Latin America," *Journal of Peace Research* (1967), pp. 334–365. In this context it is not strange if the smaller nations

In other words: the prediction for the PTM nations is a generally pessimistic one: revolutions, coups d'etat and separatism internally; competition rather than cooperation, mutual irrelevance, conflict and even exploitation and war between nations; all patterns that are likely to last far into the 1970's.

3.4. TRENDS IN THE RELATION BETWEEN MORE AND LESS DEVELOPED STATES

We then turn to the crucial type of relationship between more and less developed nations. If our general picture is correct, then there will be a high level of integration in the developed part of the world, and a low level of integration in the less developed part; with a low level of nationalism in the former, and a high level of nationalism in the latter—say, long into the 1970's. Thus, the stage is set in a way particularly advantageous for the developed nations, at least in a short time perspective.

To study these relations further we must introduce the value of equality. Nationalism and development are both seen as instrumental to equality, but not as identical with it. Thus, *nationalism* establishes representation in some IGOs, and *development* a move along the axis in Table 1—but neither guarantees equality. The less developed nations develop, usually by emulating some of the trajectories followed by the more developed nations—but at the same time there is a change of the more developed nations: they are gradually transformed into neomodern nations. Today there is much talk about increasing gaps (very true if one chooses indicators like GNP/capita, less true if one chooses indicators like literacy and health levels), and these are clear expressions of the lack of equality. We shall now relate these gaps to the gaps in nationalism and level of integration.

We should note here that equality between nations is *not* the same as equality between individuals. There may be much inequality between nations and yet some kind of equality between individuals, viz., if they are permitted to move around freely. Thus, the world will probably always have structural or ecological pockets that are low or high on some kind of dimension, but this is intolerable under an ideology of equality only if there is no freedom to move. A poor and/or predominantly primitive/traditional nation may change character completely if linked to a rich nation, provided free flow of persons both ways is permitted.

We can now imagine the typology of possibilities as to the relation between less developed and more developed nations as shown in Table 3.

In the first case in Table 3 there is a steady drift of individuals from PTM

---

look to their trade partners among the more developed nations for protection and recognition.

Table 3: Typology of relations between more and less developed nations

| | More developed deal with less developed at the | |
	Level of individuals	Level of nations
Low level of interunit solidarity; they are "taken one at a time"	I a. top level approach b. bottom level approach	III a. top level approach b. bottom level approach
High level of interunit solidarity; they organize	II a. bargaining approach b. international revolution	IV a. bargaining approach b. international revolution

into TMN nations, usually from (former) economic, political, and cultural colonies into the "mother-country." Equality is obtained at the level of individuals, i. e., for *some* individuals. The *top* of the PTM nations leave to find more congenial environments, whether in terms of political values (called "asylum"), in terms of economic values (called "absentee ownership"), in terms of cultural values (called "inspiration"), or scientific values (called "brain drain"). In general, this reduces the speed of development for the rest, but can be seen as an international expression of this very same process at the domestic level: development is seen in terms of improved chances for the individual (e. g., to go abroad), not in terms of improving the lot of society as a whole or of the underprivileged groups left behind. The perspective is individualistic.

But there is also the *bottom* level approach, whereby cheap labor is shunted into the lower echelons of the TMN society (as unskilled laborers, domestic servants, etc.) left empty by the general upward mobility in these societies.[44] Thus, the relation is highly symbiotic and generally useful for the PTM nation (in terms of accumulated cash and skills), but far from symmetric.

These processes may continue indefinitely if the diffusion rate is located well between "too high" (which leads to resentment, because it taps the PTM nation of too much of its skilled and unskilled manpower) and "too low" (which leads to resentment among those who are not let in, high or low). In both cases we would expect the reaction to take the form of solidification inside the PTM nation, increased loyalty, and efforts to develop local resources. In addition, automation will make cheap migrant labor less profitable, but the forces making for brain drain will increase rather than diminish. This will lead to increasingly tougher restraints on the free flow of intellectuals

---

[44]In societies in the Northern hemisphere there is a general drift of this kind from South to North, within nations (Italy) and between nations (Puerto Rico to the US; Italians, Spaniards, and Yugoslavs to Central and Northern European nations). In the Southern hemisphere this is reversed: there is migration into South Africa, into the southern part of Brazil, and so on. Inside nations this is probably one of the most important mechanisms in coping with accumulated frustration that may be converted into revolutions, but also a risky method since it is irreversible.

from less to more developed nations, in the name of the increased nationalism predicted.

This brings us to the second type in the typology in Table 3, where the PTM nation applies some kind of collective pressure on the TMN nation, usually a nation with which it has formerly had a symbiotic, but highly asymmetric, inegalitarian relationship. The nation may sell its cheap labor at a higher price, require many and very cheap experts in return for brain drainage,[45] etc. But the resentment may also go so far as to lead to more drastic measures against representatives and symbols of the TMN nation; supposedly above all when efforts to bargain do not lead to any result.

From the second type there is a straight line leading to the third type: the nation has a high level of internal solidarity, achieved through internal development and the rising tide of nationalism, but the level of solidarity between PTM nations is still low. In this situation the stage is set for "taking the nations one at a time."[46] The more developed nations are greatly helped here by their high level of both internal and external cohesion. This will lead to rapid growth in the tendency to deal with the less developed nations collectively, not necessarily through the UN, but typically through the EEC, the OECD, NATO (as coordinating agency), CEMA, etc. As the integration of the industrialized part of the world proceeds, there will be a certain unification in the approach to developing countries. Western nations will soon start helping more nations leaning to the East,[47] and the East will step up their assistance to nations leading to the West. There will be joint teams of technical assistance and especially capital-absorbing projects, and mixed East-West teams of volunteers (Peace Corps) to the less developed nations.[48] In other words, there will be a general regional and industrialized approach to PTM nations; and one goal of this approach would be precisely to get one nation at a time over the wall, so as to make it "developed." Japan would be the typical example of a nation that engaged in type II strategies, *in extremis*, and then became the leading exponent of type III strategies. Mexico, Venezuela, Tunis, Ghana and sometimes also India have been mentioned as examples of candidates for a joint investment, so as to have them cross the line.

But there is also a bottom level approach here, applied to very poor and very small nations that are, so to speak, "adopted" by a very rich and very big nation. We are thinking of the relation between the US and Puerto Rico, be-

---

[45]Herman Kahn on what this means to the neomodern nations: "This does not mean, as the Europeans think, that the United States is depending on this importation, but it does mean that we are benefitting; we are getting a subsidy from the rest of the world" (*Daedalus*, p. 962). This seems to be a fair assessment.

[46]I am indebted to Immanuel Wallerstein for this idea and expression.

[47]Thus, we predict that in the beginning of the 1970's, perhaps before, Western assistance in many forms will be forthcoming to Cuba, with the US reluctantly joining this effort, in the end.

[48]This has been a recurrent theme in all Pugwash conferences from the 12th conference January 1964 in Udaipur, India.

tween France and Senegal, between Britain and some Caribbean islands—
where the investment would matter little to the big nation but very much to
the small. This investment would also be particularly rewarding since it might
mean one supporting vote in the UN, regardless of the size of the nation
adopted.

The transition to type IV in the typology is now relatively clear: the process
of type III may go on indefinitely except if the diffusion rate is "too high," or
"too low." It can be so high that the PTM nations see that they lose an important chance to gain collectively by organized activity—particularly since
the "one at a time" approach is likely to deprive them of their best leaders
in a struggle of that type. Thus, there is complete isomorphism between the
transition from type I and II and the transition from types III to IV, although
with the important difference that it is more difficult to build up solidarity
at the international, less developed, level for the two reasons mentioned in
the preceding section.

But if integration takes place, and we predict that it will take place increasingly quickly, then this will change the picture completely. Bandoeng-, Beo-
grad-, Cairo-conferences; caucus groups of the Afro-Asians in the UN and *its*
agencies; the more or less concerted initiatives by the less developed nations
in UNCTAD; the Tri-Continental movement (OSPAAAL, Habana) are all clear
cases of attempts towards trade union formation among the underprivileged
nations of the world—with the latter as a trade union of groups engaged in
wars of liberation (second version, type II in the typology).

As mentioned under 3.3 above, such organizations work against the structural difficulty that they cannot, like the more developed nations, draw upon
a rich network of already existing IGOs and INGOs to cement the relationship. We nevertheless predict that effective trade union formation will be
forthcoming quite quickly, due to the resentment against types I, II, and III
strategies used by the TMN nations. The situation is too analogous to the
corresponding situation at the domestic level when trade union formation
took place, not to lead to relatively similar results.[49] But since the IGO/INGO
infra-structure is missing to a large extent, there must be something else to
keep the members closely together, e. g., a strong ideology, a charismatic
nation (not only a charismatic person), and some discontinuous event that
can be seen as a signal for effective organization. We would predict this
organization at least in the beginning of the 1970's—perhaps earlier.

However, it is likely that the first attempts will be in the general direction
of collective bargaining. The PTM nations will approach the TMN nations
collectively rather than singly, and this will also speed up the integration
between the TMN nations. When this is achieved, the North-South conflict,
as it is commonly called, will be well institutionalized, and since this is a class

---

[49]This argument is developed in Johan Galtung, "A Structural Theory of Integration,"
Journal of Peace Research, 1968.

conflict in the international system, the UN will probably play a role somewhat analogous to national parliament in serving as a medium, a mediator, and an arbiter of the conflict. The TMN bargaining position will be strengthened by the circumstance that there will be large groups in the PTM nations on their side—probably all three of the special INGOs mentioned under 3.2.c above.

In analogy with what has taken place within many nations, it seems reasonable to predict that the bargaining will be along two important lines:

1. *Trade union policies*: the PTM nations will put higher prices on what they have to sell, above all on raw materials. More particularly, they may set the price on oil so high that the petrol derived from it will cost just below the price of petrol derived from coal or in other 'artificial' ways. Similar policies can be adopted for many products, but just as for type I, strategies have to be carried out relatively quickly before the TMN nations become too clever at making synthetic substitutes.

2. *Welfare state policies*: typical of the welfare state are first, heavily progressive taxation, direct and indirect, so that the gap between top and bottom of the societies is decreased or at least so that a brake is put on it; second, the idea that the state shall distribute goods, services, welfare in a way both *anonymous* (no specific donor is mentioned, it is from everybody to everybody although a more authoritarian regime would like to add that it is from the state itself) and *universalistic* (according to objective criteria, not according to any particular relationship existing between donor and receiver). Translated to the international system, this would mean progressive taxation of nation-states (and possibly also of IGOs and even of INGOs) and individuals, the formation of a common pool under the leadership of the UN or some more complex international agency—and the redistribution of the resources in forms both anonymous and universalistic.[50] This might provide resources of the magnitude needed, and also put some brakes on the further development of the TMN nations into the neomodern types of civilization— probably the only realistic way short of war of bridging the gap in this century.

The alternative to this type of development, once effective organization formation has taken place on both sides of the class wall, would be organized

---

[50]This is brilliantly argued by Dudley Seers in "International Aid: the Next Steps," *Journal of Modern African Studies*, pp. 471–489. In practice this means that the amount of "aid" given will be decided by the rich nations alone only for some more years; we would be surprised if the point of gravity in the decision-making here would not be in the hands of the less developed nations as late as in 1975. Aid is already deeply resented as alimony and neo-colonialism, as a means in foreign policy strategies, much like domestic alimonies to "the poor" some generations ago. Thus, a taxation system is bound to emerge, and is actually less novel and utopian than many may think: it can be seen as an extrapolation of what nations may give to IGOs, particularly to UN specialized agencies and to the UN itself—e.g., to participate in UNDP programs.

warfare between the two groups, for it will take more time for non-violent techniques to be sufficiently developed. Since this would be a warfare engaged in by nations that perceive themselves as exploited, oppressed, betrayed, we should not believe that balance of power policies and deterrence will work well, for these policies presuppose a certain type of rationality, symmetry, and equality absent here. Throughout the entire human history, oppressed groups have taken to arms against odds, as an expressive outlet, to get revenge or simply because it appeared as the least evil when all other utilities were already so negative.[51]

Would nations or blocs be deterred from going to war by the possibly disastrous consequences? Not necessarily: they may believe they will be able to keep them limited, and they know that even though wars become more destructive, the recovery intervals become smaller. Besides, the PTM nations will know that the TMN nations by their social logic are more vulnerable, that the parts cannot function as before without the whole. They know that ten coordinated trucks with explosives in the tunnels and on the bridges leading to Manhattan will have a higher payoff than almost anywhere else in the world in terms of destruction, and accumulated hatred may be strong enough to translate this knowledge into action. Neither should we believe too much in arms control measures, since A, B, C weapons may relatively soon be available many places in the world due to discontinuous changes in production technologies—and there are countless ways in which they can be delivered.[52] Hence, the protection against this type of war must probably be along the lines of the more associative approaches to peace, indicated in section 2 above.

The problem, then, is to what extent it will be possible to set up patterns of symbiotic and symmetric cooperation with a high level of entropy and many supra-national organizations. We should note that organization-formation, types II and IV in Table 3, are in themselves entropy-reducing; but what is lost at one level may still be gained at the next, if one succeeds in setting up highly egalitarian and entropic supra-national organizations. This in turn depends on whether such organizations are really functional, which means that we are back at the general conclusion that type IV, subtype *violence*, will be the conclusion if type IV, subtype *bargaining* fails. The entropy is already low, as mentioned, and particularly so since the line drawn between

---

[51]This is an important line of argument in explaining why the Kaiser went to war in 1914 according to Robert North and his associates; and in explaining the Japanese attack on Pearl Harbor as done by Bruce Russett in "Pearl Harbor: Deterrence Theory and Decision Theory," *Journal of Peace Research* (1967), pp. 89–106.

[52]To believe that nuclear explosive devices will have to be delivered by rockets (and that the adequate defense, hence, is of the ABM variety) is to believe in the Maginot line once more. Much more likely is delivery in a suitcase, e.g., by using a dwarf submarine, and a strategically well-chosen site for the suitcase with an electronic long distance ignition mechanism combined with a trip-wire to avoid detection and dismantling. A 100% failsafe protection against this is not easily devised.

the PTM and the TMN nations is also to a considerable extent a geographical line (drawn along the tropics), *and* a color line.

However, these negative conditions for organized warfare are only (almost) necessary; they are not sufficient. Otherwise we would probably have the war already. Another necessary condition would usually be a leader nation, in this group a nation sufficiently identified with those less developed, yet sufficiently high on some dimensions of development to dare face the enemy —in other words, a nation with a strong *rank disequilibrium*.[53] Such a candidate is obviously present on the world scene in the form of the People's Republic of China, and predictions about its future power potential seem to indicate that it is also, in balance of power terms, a worthy candidate relative to the contenders: the USA and her allies, the Soviet Union and her allies, singly or combined.[54] But we would like to abstain from any kind of speculation as to China's inclinations in the future—and this is, of course, a crucial point.

Thus, we would expect increasingly coordinated efforts by all TMN nations to forestall such possibilities—and that these efforts will strongly color relations between less and more developed nations in the decades to come. This is a truism, but the forms these efforts will take are less trivial. More concretely, we predict the following:

1. *Strategies of types I, II and III will be increasingly given up*, partly because they create more resentment than gratitude, more enemies than friends. In some cases they may be pursued under confederate schemes, however. This means that bilateral technical assistance, as known from the 1950's and 1960's will be on its way out (the 1966 figure was already $400 million below 1965).

2. *There will be a heavily ideological, rather than organic and cooperative, organization of less developed nations early in the 1970's*, pressing forwards towards type IV relations. The developed nations will realize that their only hope of forestalling an international war lies in accepting even

---

[53]The theory of this is outlined in Johan Galtung, "A Structural Theory of Aggression," *Journal of Peace Research* (1964), pp. 95–119.

[54]One such prediction study is carried out in Wilhelm Fucks, "On the Future Development of Potentials of the Major and the Big Powers," Paper delivered to the International Political Science Association, Brussels, September, 1967. On the basis of production capacities (that can be converted into military power) Fucks concludes: "—the Soviet Union will never reach or exceed the power of the USA in the next decades—China should reach and exceed the virtual military-political power of the Soviet Union in the course of the seventies—the virtual military-political power of China will reach and exceed that of the USA in the eighties—in the nineties this virtual power should exceed that of the USA and her allies and in the next century even that of the Soviet Union added to these countries" (*ibid.*, p. 9). We have doubts about these predictions since they are not also based on assessments of the structure of the international system that will put a multiplier on any development figure for the strongly industrialized and integrated parts of the world. But they are interesting, particularly because many decision-makers are probably reflecting along such lines.

quite heavy demands made in bargaining, of the trade union and welfare state types—and some developed nations will accept this at an early stage as a part of their foreign policy, in order to build up friendly relations.

3. *A large-scale international class-war, between rich and poor nations is unlikely, but may come towards the end of the 1970's.* It is unlikely before because of the internal turmoil in the poor nations, because of their generally competitive relations and even exploitative relations, because it takes time to build up sufficient resources that can be converted into military power of any dimension, and because of the debilitation from famines, etc. Moreover, it is unlikely ever to come, because rich nations will use all strategies, I, II, III, and IVa to prevent it, because they have a tremendous organizational advantage, and because they probably will get the time they need to understand that they must yield to type IVa in order to avoid type IVb.

4. *The rich nations will also engage in preventive military and paramilitary operations to prevent an international class war.* As mentioned, we predict large-scale foreign military intervention in the poor nations when they are engaged in internal and external warfare, and this will increasingly take the form of peacekeeping forces (PKF), not necessarily under the United Nations. Each domestic upheaval, each border rivalry, will be one more pretext for stationing peace-keeping forces which will essentially also be used in the interests of the more developed nations—also in this type of long-term interest. Moreover, this will serve to bring about even some measure of military unification between East and West, thus providing them with the "common enemy" factor. Of course, all of this may be impeded by negative votes in the General Assembly, by refusals to accept PKF, by efforts to avoid the type of turmoil that will serve as a pretext for the more developed nations to intervene, etc. But again, at least in the first five-ten years to come, the rich nations will have greater resources in finding ways of getting around such hindrances. CIA type tactics to undermine Chinese influence, etc., will continue.

Thus, relations are bound to be uneasy to say the least, and there will probably be armed conflagrations somewhere along the perimeter of the modern-neomodern complex (such as the Amur and Rio Grande rivers). But whether the international class struggle is absorbed in a network of bargains of the type mentioned, or explodes in an international war depends on the relative growth rate of some of the major curves we have tried to trace—and their relative size would be a matter of pure guess, completely unguided by any theory.

4. Conclusion and Policy Implications

At this point we stop: we have tried to sketch some of the major structural forces shaping the landscape of the future—as we see it. It is an educated guess, intended as a base-line for discussion. The truism that non-structural factors—a technical error somewhere in a nuclear device, a particular personality type who gets power somewhere else—may completely upset this picture is no reason not to try to paint it, even if we have to use rather broad brushes.

The point is to try to see some of the implications of present-day trends and values, to guess where they might lead us if we did nothing about them. As indicated in section 3.4, this leads us inevitably to predictions about second and third order phenomena, not merely predictions about trends but about how actors will react to other actors' reactions to these trends, etc. Unnecessary to say, the speculations grow more and more tenuous, the higher the order of the trends, for actors may simply fail to do what we predict them to do.

What policy implications follow from such reflections, if we were to take the vantage point of the more globally identified decision-maker, not the vantage point of the nationally or regionally identified politician? In very brief terms, perhaps something like this:

Do not try to pursue neocolonialist policies of tying less developed nations to more developed nations in "regions" defined by affinity or vicinity; they will disrupt due to the social logic of the different levels of development. Rather, recognize the international class structure for what it is, and contribute to its institutionalization—at the top, at the bottom and above all at the global level. Engage in the trade union and welfare state policies on a global scale, with the less developed nations abstaining from extreme violence and the more developed nations abstaining from extreme exploitation; with large-scale redistribution of values and resources to reduce gaps, much like in modern welfare states. On top of this, build a maximum of egalitarian INGOs and IGOs, super-INGOs and super-IGOs, improve communications in all possible directions, facilitate at a maximum the free flow of persons, of goods, of information. If pockets of low entropy develop, let them be small and well encapsulated, so that there will be no escalation; if there is asymmetry in one relationship, try to balance it out in the next relationship; if there is a tendency for a (con-)federation to develop into a super-state, try to absorb it in a network of cooperation linking it to the rest of the world so as to soften the frontier effect.

By building on such elements as the above, some of the trends explored may be turned in a direction more conducive to the realization of peace. If they are engaged in with sufficient vigor, they may increase the growth rates of the more peace-productive curves and thus serve as a protection against major catastrophes. And this is not merely to telescope time, to use future research to make things happen more quickly; it would also be a way of controlling trends so as to decrease the likelihood of certain predictions. For just as we feel there is quite a lot of reason to be relatively optimistic about East-West relations, one may also feel that the factors operative in that context could be put to effective work in North-South relations. And if they were, a global system (it will surely not be a truly international system) where really large-scale wars and large-scale exploitation, would be extremely unlikely should be a possibility, even as early as sometime in the first half of the next century.

10

The Post-Industrial Society: A Prospectus

NOTES ON THE POST-INDUSTRIAL SOCIETY

● *daniel bell*

It was once exceedingly rare to be able to observe the formation of institutions *de novo*. Social change was crescive and moved slowly. Adaptations were piecemeal and contradictory, the process of diffusion halting. In his reflections on history, thirty-five years ago, Paul Valéry, the quintessential French man of letters, remarked that:

> There is nothing easier than to point out the absence, from history books, of major phenomena which were imperceptible owing to the slowness of their evolution. They escape the historian's notice because no document expressly mentions them. . . .
>
> An event which takes shape over a century will not be found in any document or collection of memoirs. . . .

Today, not only are we aware of, and trying to identify, processes of change, even when they cannot be "dated," but there has been a speeding-up of the "time-machine," so that the interval between the initial impetus to change and its realization has been radically reduced. A study by Frank Lynn of twenty major technological innovations that have had a substantial economic and/or social impact during the last sixty to seventy years indicates that every step in the process of technological development and diffusion has accelerated during this period. Specifically:

The average time span between the initial discovery of a new technological innovation and the recognition of its commercial potential decreased from 30 years (for technological innovations introduced during the early part of this century, 1880–1919) to 16 years (for innovations introduced during the post-World War I period) to 9 years (for the post-World War II period).

The time required to translate a basic technical discovery into a commercial product or process decreased from 7 to 5 years during the 60–70-year time period investigated.

The rate of diffusion (measured by economic growth) for technological innovations introduced during the post-World War II period was approximately *twice* the rate for post-World War I innovations and *four* times the rate for innovations introduced during the early part of this century.

Perhaps the most important social change of our time is the emergence of a process of direct and deliberate contrivance of change itself. Men now seek to anticipate change, measure the course of its direction and its impact, control it, and even shape it for predetermined ends.

261

The Prophet from the Past

More than a hundred and fifty years ago, the wildly brilliant, almost mono-maniacal technocrat, Claude-Henri de Rouvroy, le Comte de Saint-Simon ("the last gentleman and the first socialist" of France), popularized the word *indus-trialism* to designate the emergent society, wherein wealth would be created by mechanized production rather than be seized through plunder and war. Past society, said Saint-Simon, had been military society, in which the dom-inant figures were noblemen, soldiers, and priests, and the leading positions in the society were based either on control of the means of violence or on the manipulation of religious myth. In the new society, the "natural élite" that would organize society in a rational, "positive" fashion would be the industrialists (actually the engineers or technocrats), for the methods of in-dustry were methods of order, precision, and certainty, rather than of meta-physical thought. In this society, ordered by function and capacity, "the real noblemen would be industrial chiefs and the real priests would be scientists."

The revolution which ended feudal society—the French Revolution—could have ushered in the industrial society, said Saint-Simon, but it did not do so because it had been captured by metaphysicians, lawyers, and sophists, men with a predilection for abstract slogans. What was needed, Saint-Simon added, was a breed of "new men"—engineers, builders, planners—who would pro-vide the necessary leadership. And since such leaders require some inspiration, Saint-Simon, shortly before his death, commissioned Rouget de l'Isle, the composer of the "Marseillaise," to write a new "Industrial Marseillaise." This "Chant des Industriels," as it was called, was given its première in 1821 before Saint-Simon and his friend Ternaus, the textile manufacturer, at the opening of a new textile factory in Saint-Ouen.

The episode takes on a somewhat comic air, especially when we read that a number of the Count's followers established a new religious cult of Saint-Simonianism to canonize his teachings. (In the monastic castle to which the followers of Saint-Simon retreated, garments were buttoned down the back so that, in socialist fashion, each man would require the help of another in order to dress.) And yet many of these same followers of Saint-Simon were also the men who, in the middle of the 19th century, redrew the industrial map of Europe.[1]

---

[1] It is not too much to say, Professor F. H. Markham has written, "that the St. Simonians were the most important single force behind the great economic expansion of the second Empire, particularly in the development of banks and railways." Enfantin, the most bizarre of the St. Simonians, formed the society for planning the Suez Canal. The former St. Simonians constructed many of the European railways—in Austria, Russia, and Spain. The brothers Emile and Isaac Pereire, who promoted the first French railway from Paris to Saint-Germain, also founded the Crédit Mobilier, the first industrial investment bank in France, as well as the great shipping company, the Compagnie Générale Transatlantique which today sails the *Flandre* and the *France*, and which gave its first ships the names of St. Simonian followers, including the *Saint-Simon* (1,987 tons).

We may at this point leave the story of Saint-Simon and his followers to the *curiosa* of the history of ideas. But if, with the spirit rather than the method of Saint-Simon, one speculates on the shape of society forty or fifty years from now, it becomes clear that the "old" industrial order is passing and that a "new society" is indeed in the making. To speak rashly: if the dominant figures of the past hundred years have been the entrepreneur, the businessman, and the industrial executive, the "new men" are the scientists, the mathematicians, the economists, and the engineers of the new computer technology. And the dominant institutions of the new society—in the sense that they will provide the most creative challenges and enlist the richest talents—will be the intellectual institutions. The leadership of the new society will rest, not with businessmen or corporations as we know them (for a good deal of production will have been routinized), but with the research corporation, the industrial laboratories, the experimental stations, and the universities. In fact, the skeletal structure of the new society is already visible.

The Transformation of Society

We are now, one might say, in the first stages of a post-industrial society. A post-industrial society can be characterized in several ways. We can begin with the fact that ours is no longer primarily a manufacturing economy. The service sector (comprising trade; finance, insurance and real estate; personal, professional, business, and repair services; and general government) now accounts for more than half of the total employment and more than half of the gross national product. We are now, as Victor Fuchs pointed out in *The Public Interest*, No. 2, a "service economy"–i.e., the first nation in the history of the world in which more than half of the employed population is not involved in the production of food, clothing, houses, automobiles, and other tangible goods.

Or one can look at a society, not in terms of where people work, but of what kind of work they do—the occupational divisions. In a paper read to the Cambridge Reform Club in 1873, Alfred Marshall, the great figure of neo-classical economics, posed a question that was implicit in the title of his paper, "The Future of the Working Classes." "The question," he said, "is not whether all men will ultimately be equal—that they certainly will not be—but whether progress may not go on steadily, if slowly, till, by occupation at least, every man is a gentleman." And he answered his question thus: "I hold that it may, and that it will."

Marshall's criterion of a gentleman—in a broad, not in the traditional genteel, sense—was that heavy, excessive, and soul-destroying labor would vanish, and the worker would then begin to value education and leisure. Apart from any qualitative assessment of contemporary culture, it is clear that Marshall's question is well on the way to achieving the answer he predicted.

In one respect, 1956 may be taken as the symbolic turning point. For in that year—for the first time in American history, if not in the history of industrial civilization—the number of white-collar workers (professional, managerial, office and sales personnel) outnumbered the blue-collar workers (craftsmen, semi-skilled operatives, and laborers) in the occupational ranks of the American class structure. Since 1956 the ratio has been increasing: today white-collar workers outnumber the blue-collar workers by more than five to four.

Stated in these terms, the change is quite dramatic. Yet it is also somewhat deceptive, for until recently the overwhelming number of white-collar workers have been women, who held minor clerical or sales jobs; and in American society, as in most others, family status is still evaluated on the basis of the job that the man holds. But it is at this point, in the changing nature of the male labor force, that a status upheaval has been taking place. Where in 1900 only fifteen percent of American males wore white collars (and most of these were independent small businessmen), by 1940 the figure had risen to twenty-five percent, and by 1970, it is estimated, about forty percent of the male labor force, or about twenty million men, will be holding white-collar jobs. Out of this number, fourteen million will be in managerial, professional, or technical positions, and it is this group that forms the heart of the upper-middle-class in the United States.

What is most startling in these figures is the growth in professional and technical employment. In 1940, there were 3.9 million professional and technical persons in the society, making up 7.5% of the labor force; by 1962, the number had risen to 8 million, comprising 11.8% of the labor force; it is estimated that by 1975 there will be 12.4 million professional and technical persons, making up 14.2% of the labor force.

A New Principle

In identifying a new and emerging social system, however, it is not only in such portents as the move away from manufacturing (or the rise of "the new property" which Charles Reich has described) that one seeks to understand fundamental social change. It is in the defining characteristics that the nerves of a new system can be located. The ganglion of the post-industrial society is knowledge. But to put it this way is banal. Knowledge is at the basis of every society. But in the post-industrial society, what is crucial is not just a shift from property or political position to knowledge as the new base of power, but a change in the *character* of knowledge itself.

What has now become decisive for society is the new centrality of *theoretical* knowledge, the primacy of theory over empiricism, and the codification of knowledge into abstract systems of symbols that can be translated into many different and varied circumstances. Every society now lives by innovation and growth; and it is theoretical knowledge that has become the matrix of innovation.

One can see this, first, in the changing relations of science and technology, particularly in the matter of invention. In the 19th and early 20th centuries, the great inventions and the industries that derived from them—steel, electric light, telegraph, telephone, automobile—were the work of inspired and talented tinkerers, many of whom were indifferent to the fundamental laws which underlay their inventions. On the other hand, where principles and fundamental properties were discovered, the practical applications were made only decades later, largely by trial-and-error methods.

In one sense, chemistry is the first of the "modern" industries because its inventions—the chemically-created synthetics—were based on theoretical knowledge of the properties of macromolecules, which were "manipulated" to achieve the planned production of new materials. At the start of World War I, hardly any of the generals of the Western Allies anticipated a long war, for they assumed that the effective naval blockade of the Central powers, thus cutting off their supply of Chilean nitrates, would bring Germany to her knees. But under the pressure of isolation, Germany harnessed all her available scientific energy and resources to solving this problem. The result—the development of synthetic ammonia by Bosch and Haber—was a turning point, not only in Germany's capacity for waging war, but also in the connection of science to technology.[2]

In a less direct but equally important way, the changing association of theory and empiricism is reflected in the management of economies. The rise of macro-economics and of governmental interventions in economic matters is possible because new codifications in economic theory allow governments, by direct planning, monetary or fiscal policy, to seek economic growth, to redirect the allocation of resources, to maintain balances between different sectors, and even, as in the case of Great Britain today, to effect a controlled recession, in an effort to shape the direction of the economy by conscious policy.

And, with the growing sophistication of computer-based simulation procedures–simulations of economic systems, of social behavior, of decision problems—we have the possibility, for the first time, of large-scale "controlled experiments" in the social sciences. These, in turn, will allow us to plot

[2]In *Modern Science and Modern Man*, James Bryant Conant, who, before becoming a distinguished educator, was a prominent chemist, tells the story that when the United States entered World War I, a representative of the American Chemical Society called on Newton D. Baker, then Secretary of War, and offered the services of the chemists to the government. He was thanked and asked to come back the next day—when he was told that the offer was unnecessary since the War Department already had a chemist! When President Wilson appointed a consulting board to assist the Navy, it was chaired by Thomas Edison, and this appointment was widely hailed for bringing the best brains of science to the solution of naval problems. The solitary physicist on the board owed his appointment to the fact that Edison, in choosing his fellow members, had said to President Wilson, "We might have one mathematical fellow in case we have to calculate something out." In fact, as R. T. Birge reports, during World War I there was no such classification as "physicist;" when the armed forces felt the need of one, which was only occasionally, he was hired as a chemist.

"alternative futures," thus greatly increasing the extent to which we can choose and control matters that affect our lives.

In all this, the university, which is the place where theoretical knowledge is sought, tested, and codified in a disinterested way, becomes the primary institution of the new society. Perhaps it is not too much to say that if the business firm was the key institution of the past hundred years, because of its role in organizing production for the mass creation of products, the university will become the central institution of the next hundred years because of its role as the new source of innovation and knowledge.

To say that the primary institutions of the new age will be intellectual is not to say that the majority of persons will be scientists, engineers, technicians, or intellectuals. The majority of individuals in contemporary society are not businessmen, yet one can say that this has been a "business civilization." The basic values of society have been focused on business institutions, the largest rewards have been found in business, and the strongest power has been held by the business community, although today that power is to some extent shared within the factory by the trade union, and regulated within the society by the political order. In the most general ways, however, the major decisions affecting the day-to-day life of the citizen—the kinds of work available, the location of plants, investment decisions on new products, the distribution of tax burdens, occupational mobility—have been made by business, and latterly by government, which gives major priority to the welfare of business.

To say that the major institutions of the new society will be intellectual is to say that production and business decisions will be subordinated to, or will derive from, other forces in society; that the crucial decisions regarding the growth of the economy and its balance will come from government, but they will be based on the government's sponsorship of research and development, of cost-effectiveness and cost-benefit analysis; that the making of decisions, because of the intricately linked nature of their consequences, will have an increasingly technical character. The husbanding of talent and the spread of educational and intellectual institutions will become a prime concern for the society; not only the best talents, but eventually the entire complex of social prestige and social status, will be rooted in the intellectual and scientific communities.

Things Ride Men

Saint-Simon, the "father" of technocracy, had a vision of the future society that made him a utopian in the eyes of Marx. Society would be a scientific-industrial association whose goal would be the highest productive effort to conquer nature and to achieve the greatest possible benefits for all. Men would become happy in their work, as producers, and would fill a place in accordance with their natural abilities. The ideal industrial society would by no means be classless, for individuals were unequal in ability and in capacity. But social divisions would follow actual abilities, as opposed to the artificial divisions of previous societies, and individuals would find happiness and liberty in working at the job to which they were best suited. With every man in his natural place, each would obey his superior spontaneously, as one obeyed one's doctor, for a superior was defined by a higher technical capacity. In the industrial society, there would be three major divisions of work, corresponding, in the naive yet almost persuasive psychology of Saint-Simon, to three major psychological types. The majority of men were of the motor-capacity type, and they would become the laborers of the industrial society; within this class, the best would become the production leaders and administrators of society. The second type was the rational one, and men of this capacity would become the scientists, discovering new knowledge and writing the laws that were to guide men. The third type was the sensory, and these men would be the artists and religious leaders. This last class, Saint-Simon believed, would bring a new religion of collective worship to the people that would overcome individual egoism. It was in work and in carnival that men would find satisfaction; and in this positivist utopia, society would move from the governing of men to the administration of things.

But in the evolution of technocratic thinking,[3] things began to ride men. For Frederick W. Taylor, who—as the founder of scientific management—was perhaps most responsible for the translation of technocratic modes into the actual practices of industry, any notion of ends other than production and efficiency of output was almost nonexistent. Taylor believed strongly that "status must be based upon superior knowledge rather than nepotism and superior financial power," and in his idea of functional foremanship he asserted that influence and leadership should be based on technical competence rather than on any other skills. But in his view of work, man disappeared, and all that remained was "hands" and "things" arranged, on the basis of minute scientific examination, along the lines of a detailed division of labor wherein the smallest unit of motion and the smallest unit of time became the measure of a man's contribution to work.

In the technocratic mode, the ends have become simply efficiency and output. The technocratic mode has become established because it is the mode of efficiency—of production, of program, of "getting things done." For

[3]The word *technocracy* itself was first coined in 1919 by William Henry Smyth, an inventor and engineer in Berkeley, California, in three articles published in *Industrial Management* of February, March, and May in that year. These were reprinted in a pamphlet, and later included with nine more articles, written for the *Berkeley Gazette*, in a larger reprint. The word was taken over by Howard Scott, a one-time research director for the Industrial Workers of the World, and was popularized in 1933–34, when Technocracy flashed briefly as a social movement and a panacea for the depression. The word became associated with Scott, and through him with Thorstein Veblen, who, after writing *The Engineers and the Price System*, had been associated earlier with Scott in an educational venture at the New School for Social Research. Interestingly, when the word became nationally popular through Scott, it was repudiated by Smyth, who claimed that Scott's use of the word fused *technology and autocrat*, "rule by technicians responsible to no one;" whereas his original word implied "the rule of the people made effective through the agency of their servants, the scientists and technicians."

these reasons, the technocratic mode has spread in our society. But whether the technocrats themselves will become a dominant class, and in what ways the technocratic mode might be challenged are different questions.

Soldiers Ride Things

It was the root idea of Saint-Simon, August Comte, and Herbert Spencer, the 19th-century theorists of industrial society, that there was a radical opposition between the industrial and the military spirit. The one emphasized work, production, rationality; the other display, waste, and heroics. Out of technology, economizing, and investment would come productivity as the basis of an increasing wealth for all, rather than exploit and plunder as the means of seizing wealth from others. In ancient society, work was subordinated to war and the warrior ruled; in industrial society, the times would become pacific and the producer would rule.

The irony is that, while the economizing spirit—the deployment of limited resources to attain maximum results—has indeed spread throughout society, it has been war rather than peace that has been largely responsible for the acceptance of planning and technocratic modes in government.

Instead of peace, every industrial society has a *Wehrwirtschaft*, a "preparedness economy," or a mobilized society. A mobilized society is one in which the major resources of the country are concentrated on a relatively few specific objectives defined by the government. In these sectors, in effect, private needs are subordinated to social goals and the role of private decision is correspondingly reduced. The Soviet Union is a mobilized society *par excellence*. Most of the "new states," in their quest for modernization, have become mobilized: the basic resources of the society—capital and trained manpower—are geared to planned economic change.

In recent years, America has taken on the features of a mobilized polity in that one of the crucial scarce resources, that of "research and development"—and more specifically, the work of most of the scientists and engineers in research and development—is tied to the requirements of the military and of war preparedness. The United States has not done this by outright commandeering of talents, or by restricting the right of nongovernmental units to engage in R & D. But since R & D is always a risk, in that no immediate payoffs or profits are assured, and the costs of R & D have become astronomical, few institutions other than the government can underwrite such expenditures. And the government has been compelled to do so because of the extraordinary revolutions in the art of war that have occurred since 1945.

In one sense, as Herman Kahn has pointed out, military technology has supplanted the "mode of production," in Marx's use of the term, as a major determinant of social structure. Since the end of World War II there have been almost three total revolutions in military technology, with complete and across-the-board replacement of equipment, as older weapons systems were phased out without being used. Neither World War I nor World War II represented such complete breaks in continuity.

The source of these accelerated revolutions—changes in the character of atomic weapons, from manned bombers to missiles, from fixed missiles to roving missiles and from medium-range to intercontinental missiles—has been concentrated research and development, concerted planning for new systems of weaponry. And the technology of "custom-crafted" missile construction, as against bombers, was a chief element in changing the "production-mix" of the aerospace industry labor force, so much so that the Budget Bureau Report on Defense Contracting (The David Bell Report of 1962) estimated that the ratio of engineers and scientists to production workers in the aerospace industry was roughly one-to-one.

In the Economic Report of the President, presented to Congress in January 1963, President Kennedy declared: "The defense, space and atomic energy activities of the country absorb about two-thirds of the trained people available for exploring our scientific and technical frontiers. . . . In the course of meeting scientific challenges so brilliantly, we have paid a price by sharply limiting the scarce scientific and engineering resources available to the civilian sectors of the American economy." By now, it is likely that President Kennedy's estimates are too low.

Who Holds Power?

Decisions are a matter of power, and the crucial questions in any society are: who holds power, and how is power held? Forty-five years ago, as we have noted, Thorstein Veblen foresaw a new society based on technical organization and industrial management, a "soviet of technicians," as he put it in the striking language he loved to employ in order to scare and mystify the academic world. In making this prediction, Veblen shared the illusion of Saint-Simon that the complexity of the industrial system and the indispensability of the technicians made military and political revolutions a thing of the past. "Revolutions in the 18th century," Veblen wrote, "were military and political; and the Elder Statesmen who now believe themselves to be making history still believe that revolutions can be made and unmade by the same ways and means in the 20th century. But any substantial or effectual overturn in the 20th century will necessarily be an industrial overturn; and by the same token, any 20th-century revolution can be combatted or neutralized only by industrial ways and means."

This syndicalist idea that revolution in the 20th century could only be an "industrial overturn" exemplifies the rationalist fallacy in so much of Veblen's thought. For, as we have learned, though technological and social processes are crescive, the crucial turning points in a society are political events. It is not the technocrat who ultimately holds power, but the politician.

The major changes which have reshaped American society over the past thirty years—the creation of a managed economy, a welfare society, and a mobilized polity—grew out of political responses: in the first instances to accommodate the demands of economically insecure and disadvantaged groups—the farmers, workers, Negroes, and the poor—for protection against the hazards of the market; and, later, as a consequence of the concentration of resources and political objectives following the mobilized postures of the Cold War and the space race.

The result of all this is to enlarge the arena of power, and at the same time to complicate the modes of decision-making. The domestic political process initiated by the New Deal, which continues in the same form in the domestic program of the Johnson administration, was in effect a broadening of the "brokerage" system—the system of political "deals" between constituencies. But there is also a new dimension in the political process which has given the technocrats a new role. Matters of foreign policy are not a reflex of internal political forces, but a judgment about the national interest, involving strategy decisions based on the calculations of an opponent's strength and intentions. Once the fundamental policy decision was made to oppose the Communist power, many technical decisions, based on military technology and strategic assessments, took on the highest importance in the shaping of subsequent policy. And even the reworking of the economic map of the United States followed as well, with Texas and California gaining great importance because of the importance of the electronics and aerospace industries. In these instances, technology and strategy laid down the requirements, and only then could business and local political groups seek to modify, or take advantage of, these decisions so as to protect their own economic interests.

In all this, the technologists are in a double position. To the extent that they have interests in research, and positions in the universities, they become a new constituency—just as the military is a distinct new constituency, since we have never had a permanent military establishment in this country before —seeking money and support for science, for research and development. Thus the technical intelligentsia becomes a claimant, like other groups, for public support (though its influence is felt in the bureaucratic and administrative labyrinth, rather than in the electoral system and through mass pressure). At the same time, the technologists provide an indispensable administrative mechanism for the political office-holder with his public following. As the technical and professional sectors of society expand, the interests of this stratum, of this constituency, exert a greater pressure—in the demands not only for objectives of immediate interest but in the wider social ethos which tends to be associated with the more highly educated: the demands for more amenities, for a more urbane quality of life in our cities, for a more differentiated and better educational system, and an improvement in the character of our culture.

But while the weights of the class system may shift, the nature of the political system, as the arena where interests become mediated, will not. In the next few decades, the political arena will become more decisive, if anything, for three fundamental reasons: we have become, for the first time, a *national society* (though there has always been the idea of the nation) in which crucial decisions, affecting all parts of the society simultaneously (from foreign affairs to fiscal policy) are made by the government, rather than through the market; in addition, we have become a *communal society*, in which many more groups now seek to establish their social rights—their claims on society—through the political order; and third, with our increasing "future orientation," government will necessarily have to do more and more planning. But since all of these involve policy decisions, it cannot be the technocrat alone, but the political figures who can make them. And necessarily, the two roles are distinct, even though they come into complicated interplay with each other.

Social Choices and Individual Values

The irony is that the more planning there is in a society, the more there are open group conflicts. Planning sets up a specific locus of decision, which becomes a visible point at which pressures can be applied. Communal coordination—the effort to create a social choice out of a discordance of individual personal preferences—necessarily *sharpens* value conflicts.

Where a single policy (such as defense) constitutes, in the language of economic theory, a "single-peaked preference curve"—one on whose importance and priority the society, by and large, is agreed—there may be little conflict. But what about situations, such as social or welfare policy, where there may be less agreement: how then does one decide? Do we want compensatory education for Negroes at the expense, say, of places for other students when the number of positions is limited? Do we want to keep a redwood forest or provide a going industry to a local community? Will we accept the increased noise of jets in communities near the airports, or force the reduction of weight and payloads—with a consequent increased cost to the industry and the traveler? Should a new highway go through old pleasant sections of a community, or do we route around such sections with a higher cost to all? These, and thousands more, are issues which cannot be settled on the basis of technical criteria; inevitably they involve value and political choices.

In the "Great Society" more and more goods necessarily have to be purchased communally. The planning of cities and the rationalization of transit, the maintenance of open spaces and the extension of recreational areas, the elimination of air pollution and the cleaning up of the rivers, the underwriting of education and the organization of adequate medical care, all these are now necessarily the concern of "public institutions." Individuals have their own scale of values, which allow them to assess relative satisfactions against costs, and to make their purchases accordingly. But public life lacks such ready measures. We cannot ask for and individually buy in the market place our share of unpolluted air. Regulating the availability of higher education by the market alone would deny many families the possibility of such learning, and also deny the society some of the social benefits which a more educated, and therefore more productive, citizenry might create. But we have no effective social calculus which gives us a true sense of the entire costs and benefits of our public initiatives.

Moreover, *we are never likely to get any such perfected calculus.* For in recent years, while economists and mathematicians have been able to supply a "rational proof" of the individual utility preference model, they have become skeptical of the possibility of constructing a group welfare function model. When one turns from individual decision-making to that of groups, when one considers the problem of how best to amalgamate the discordant preference patterns of the members of a society so as to arrive at a compromise preference pattern for society as a whole, we seem to be at a theoretical impasse. In the first major effort to formulate the problem, Kenneth Arrow demonstrated, in his *Social Choice and Individual Values*, written in 1951, that the five requirements of "fairness" for social-welfare functions are inconsistent (i.e., no welfare function exists which satisfies all of them). Even the principle of majority rule which satisfies three, and possibly four, of the conditions is subject to the logical contradiction, first formulated by Condorcet, of the paradox of the cyclical majority.

The proof can be demonstrated simply. Supposing there are three voters, A, B, and C, whose preferences on issues x, y and z are ordered in the following pattern:

	Voters		
	A	B	C
Preferences			
First	x	z	y
Second	y	x	z
Third	z	y	x

Clearly, x is preferred to y by a majority (voters A and B); y is preferred to z by a majority (voters A and C); from the principle of transitivity (i.e., if an individual prefers x to y, and y to z, we assume he would also prefer x to z) we should predict that x is also preferred to z, and that x, therefore, is the choice of the majority of the voters; but in fact, z is preferred to x by voters B and C, so that no simple majority preference can be formulated on these three issues.[4]

---

[4]The most comprehensive effort to deal with the problem is that of Duncan Black, *The Theory of Committees and Elections.* (Cambridge University Press, 1958). Further discussion can be found in Buchanan and Tullock, *The Calculus of Consent* (University of Michigan, 1962). Some earlier discussions are in Dahl and Lindblom, *Politics, Economics and Welfare* (New York: Harper and Row, 1953), and Anthony Downs, *An Economic Theory of Democracy* (New York: Harper and Row, 1957).

There have been numerous attempts both to modify the original conditions which Arrow put forth as necessary to organize a group welfare-function and to resolve the voting paradox. But so far, at least to the extent that I can follow the technical literature, no satisfactory "solutions" have been forthcoming.[5]

This problem—of seeking to produce a single social ordering of alternative social choices which would correspond to individual orderings—is academic, in the best sense of the word. In the "real" world, the problem of social priorities, of what social utilities are to be maximized, of what communal enterprises are to be furthered, will be settled in the political arena by "political criteria"—i.e., the relative weights and pressures of different interest groups, balanced against some vague sense of the national need and the public interest. But it is precisely at this point that the problem becomes most irksome. For increasingly, one of the "issues" of a Great Society—which can be defined as a society that seeks to become conscious of its goals—is this relationship between "rationality" and "politics." The Great Society aims to rise above "mere" politics toward some kind of rational political behavior—but rigorous theoretical analysis leads us back to "mere" politics!

The New Prince

One other item of democratic theory would seem to be in trouble, too, empirically as well as theoretically. This is the theory of interest groups in a pluralistic society.

The theory of representative government reflected a picture of society as a "balance of forces." The legislature, in this conception, was supposed to contain representatives of the various social divisions and class interests in the country, for as Mill noted in appealing for the right of the working-class to be represented in Parliament, "in the absence of its natural defenders, the interest of the excluded is always in danger of being overlooked." Mill, in fact, was so intent on the idea of the representation of minorities, that he gave enthusiastic endorsement to the proposal of Thomas Hare for proportional representation, "a scheme which has the almost unparalleled merit of carrying out a great principle of government in a manner approaching to ideal perfection as regards the special object in view . . ."

This normative theory was refined by what might be called the "realist" school of political thought, from Arthur F. Bentley on. (Bentley's original formulations in 1908 were ignored for many years, but were restated three decades later by V. O. Key, David Truman, and Earl Latham.) If a "group

[5]Arrow, in an appendix to a new edition of his book (Cowles Foundation, Yale University, 1963) has sought to counter some discoveries of errors in his proofs by reformulating the conditions to show that the inconsistencies in the conditions still remain, and that no logical foundations for a complete social-welfare-function are possible. The most recent effort to prove the possibility of "collective rationality" is that of James Coleman, "The Possibility of a Social Welfare Function" (*American Economic Review*, December, 1966).

theory" was lacking in economics, it certainly made its appearance, in full flower, in American political thought in the last few decades. As V. O. Key put it most succinctly:

> At bottom, group interests are the animating forces in the political process. . . . Whatever the bases of group interest may be, the study of politics must rest on an analysis of the objectives and composition of the interest groups within a society. . . . The chief vehicles for the expression of group interest are political parties and pressure groups. Through these formal mechanisms groups of people with like interests make themselves felt in the balancing of political forces.[6]

And, in this conception, the role of the politician was to be a broker:

> The problem of the politician or the statesman in a democracy is to maintain a working balance between the demands of competing interests and values. . . . Within limits . . . special interests in a democracy are free to express their demands and their disagreements. . . . The politician in a democracy . . . must be able to hold together enough of these special interests to retain power; he must yield here, stand firm there, delay at the next point, and again act vigorously in a confusing complex of competing forces and interests. . . . The politician . . . must play the part of arbitrator and mediator, subject to the criticism of all. To avoid or mitigate conflict, he compromises.

Whatever the truth of this "model" as a description of the "nineteenth century inheritance,"[7] (or even as a superficial description of Lyndon Johnson), it is astonishingly out of date for an understanding of politics in the second half of the 20th century, for it fails to take into account the three most decisive characteristics, or shaping elements, of national policy today: the influence of foreign policy, the "future-orientation" of society, and the increasing role of "technical" decision-making.

1. Foreign policy is not formulated primarily in reaction to the needs and pressures of domestic pressure groups (though once decisions are taken, some modifications may be made in response to their demands, e.g., to build airplanes in the Southwest rather than in the Northwest). Foreign policy is shaped in accordance with great power and ideological interests, and as responses to perceived threats from other great powers or ideo-

---

[6]V. O. Key, *Politics, Parties and Pressure Groups* (New York: Alfred A. Knopf, 1942), pp. 23–24.

[7]The "group theory of politics," it should be noted, has been challenged on theoretical grounds by Mancur Olson, Jr., who, applying an "economic analysis" to the nature of aggregate choice, argues that interest groups do not best represent the interests of their members. See Mancur Olson, Jr., *The Logic of Collective Action: Public Goods and The Theory of Groups* (Cambridge: Harvard University Press, 1965).

logical forces. But its consequence, under conditions of a cold war, is to force a "mobilized posture" on the society as a whole, to create some sense of national unity, and to centralize decision-making and enormous resources in the hands of a national administration. (Of the $15 billion spent by the Federal government for research and development, ninety percent goes into three areas: defense, space, and atomic energy.) The social and economic map of the U.S. has been redrawn more in the past twenty years by the influence of defense and defense spending than by any other single factor.

2. The commitment to economic growth, and the new dimensions of social change—its more rapid shock effects on larger and larger sections of the society and the consequent need to anticipate social change and to a considerable extent to direct it—have brought with them a renewed emphasis on planning, on the need to become more conscious of national goals and of the "alternative futures" which a society with a steady increase in productivity (a constant 3 percent growth rate of productivity will double national output in 24 years) can provide.

3. The combination of these two elements brings into play the increasing role of technical decision-making. The shaping of conscious policy, be it in foreign policy, defense, or economics, calls to the fore the men with the skills necessary to outline the constraints ahead, to work out in detail the management and policy procedures, and to assess the consequences of choices. The revolutions in military technology (the introduction of nuclear power, the replacement of manned aircraft by missiles) were initiated by scientists. The development of systems analysis and cost-effectiveness techniques, which have revolutionized both the strategy process as well as the management structure of the Pentagon, was brought about by mathematicians and economists. The management of the national economy, with its close watch on the effects of government spending, requires the services of men skilled in the economic arts, and such crucial policy questions as when to have tax cuts or tax increases, how much to have, and what the wage-price guideposts should be, increasingly become technical decisions.[8]

But the most important political consequence of all this is the passing of effective power, in almost all political systems, from the legislative and parliamentary bodies to the executive, and the reemergence of what Bertrand de Jouvenel has called, in his elegant fashion, The Principate. How could it be otherwise when, in the nature of modern politics, foreign policy is no longer "diplomacy" but an unceasing round of strategic maneuver in which

---

[8]As one quondam bureaucrat has earnestly argued, "the development of public policy and of the methods of its administration owe less in the long run to processes of conflict among political parties and social or economic pressure groups than to the more objective processes of research and discussion among professional groups." Don K. Price, Government and Science—a statement written little more than ten years after V. O. Key, and reflecting the differences, perhaps, of the pre-war and post-war experiences of political analysts.

crucial decisions have to be taken speedily, and when, because of the new patterns of social change, the very need to plan policies, rather than lay down laws, gives the initiative to the Executive?

In the United States we have seen, in the past twenty-five years, the enormous transformation of the Presidency into the Executive Office of the President with the addition of new staff functions—such as the Bureau of the Budget, the Council of Economic Advisors, and the Office of the Science Adviser—directly within that office. For the long run, it is not the growth of the personal powers and prestige of the President that is important, but the *institutionalization* of such crucial control and directing functions.

Although these essential changes—the new role of the Executive, the conflict between technocratic rationality and political bargaining, and the orientation to the future—have been variously described, political theory has, so far, failed to absorb them into a new conceptual structure.

Number, Density, Interaction

While our eyes have been focused on the visible political changes, some underlying structural changes, of the kind that Paul Valéry alluded to, have in crescive fashion been transforming our society. Thus, the effects of the increase in number, interaction, and density of population are enormous. Here, I shall take the communication pattern as an instance.

a) The loss of insulating space. If one looks at American history, what strikes one immediately is the tremendous amount of violence, particularly labor violence, which took place over a period of 65 years (from 1877, beginning with the railroad strikes, and ending with the outbreak of war at the end of 1941). From any rough set of indicators that one chooses—the number of times troops were called out, the number of riots, the number of individuals killed, the amount of sabotage, the number of man-days of work lost, the amounts of money spent by corporations in fighting trade unions—it is highly likely that there was probably more violence here than in any country in Europe. Yet the U.S. did escape the political holocausts that wracked European society, and some basic accommodation between business and labor was reached.

One can identify many factors which account for this difference between American and European society, but surely one of the most important ones, particularly before World War I, was what one can call the factor of "insulated space." One of the distinguishing features of political violence in Europe is that most of it took place close to, or at, a political center. What would have happened to the French Revolution, for example, if the Constituent Assembly had met at Dijon, rather than at Versailles, twenty miles from Paris and subject to the pressures of the Paris crowds? Clearly all such *if* questions are unanswerable, but their formulation allows one to see the possibility of alternatives. In the United States, our early violence took place largely at the "perimeters" of the society (in isolated coal mining communities, in the Far West and Rocky Mountain areas) and the "shock effects" had small radial range.

The introduction of modern mass communication allows us, in many cases forces us, to respond directly and immediately to social issues. There is little question that the presence of the television cameras in Selma, Alabama, depicting the use of crude violence (snarling police dogs, electrified cattle prods) against the Negro marchers aroused an immediate national response which was reflected in the presence of thousands of persons who poured into Selma, the following week, from all over the country. Without television, it is likely that the shock effect, even if transmitted through news photos and newsreels, would have been dissipated (and, before the rise of the mass media, would have never had a national impact).

One can see this by a crude comparison of two incidents. In the winter of 1893–94, the growing economic distress and mass unemployment brought the formation of scattered groups of jobless into "armies" who declared for a "march on Washington" to demand relief. The best known of these was "Coxey's Army," led by the populist "general" Jacob S. Coxey. Although detachments of the armies started out from various parts of the country, and Coxey led his contingent from Massillon, Ohio, only 400 persons reached the national capital, and the "armies" were easily dispersed.

In the summer of 1963, Negro civil rights leaders called for a March on Washington to bring pressure upon the administration for the passage of a civil rights bill, and by plane, bus, rail and car, 250,000 persons descended onto the capital in an extraordinary demonstration of political purpose. Differences of issue apart, it is clear that one incident is a product of a regional society, the other of a mass society.

In effect, our society has become more "permeable" and open to plebiscitarian pressures. One may applaud the fact that the nature of the mass media increases the likelihood of a spectacular rise in "participatory" democracy, but these instances are also more likely to be on emotional issues, so that the loss of "insulating space" itself may permit the setting off of chain reactions which may be disruptive of civil politics and reasoned debate.

b) Communication overload. Whatever else may be said about the 20th century, it has produced the greatest bombardment of aural and visual materials that man has ever experienced in his history. To the linotype, camera, typewriter, telephone and telegraph, the 20th century has added radio (and radio telephone), teletype, television, microwaves, communication satellites, computers, xerography and the like. Transistors and miniaturization not only facilitate an incredible packaging of communication senders, receivers, and recorders in the small space of a space ship, they also allow automobile telephony, walkie-talkies, portable radios and television sets, and finally, on the agenda, person-to-person communication by "wrist-watch" radio anywhere in the country (and soon the world?). Radar and LORAN have taken over most of the air-sea guidance of transport, while an incredibly deployed watching system like SAGE (already, in part, obsolete) permits a national command-control system, using real-time computers, to patrol the continental defense from the distant early warning lines.

George Miller, the Harvard psychologist, once demonstrated, in a marvelous article, "The Magical Number Seven Plus or Minus Two," the finite limits to the number of different "bits" (or signals) that a human channel could encompass at one time.[9] But the problem is not the single instant, it is the total number of sensations that an individual is subject to. Some random sampling of the communication media illustrates, in a cursory way, the growth of the networks of interaction. In 1899, there were one million telephones in the United States, or 13.3 per 100,000 population; in 1963, there were 84,440,000 telephones or 442.5 per 100,000 population. (Over 350 million local calls are made daily in the U.S.) In 1899, 6,576,000 pieces of mail were moved in the U.S.; in 1963, 67,853,000,000 pieces of mail were sent (more than half of them first-class). In 1924, 1,250,000 families had radio sets, and 530 stations were on the air; in 1964, more than 90 percent of families had radio sets and 5,607 stations (AM and FM) were on the air. In 1949, 940,000 families had television sets, and 17 stations were sending pictures; in 1964, more than 90 percent of all families had television sets, and 564 television stations were broadcasting regularly.

The extension of the range of communication has brought the entire world into instant reach of any listener. Consider only the multiple geography lessons that each of us has had to learn in the last 25 years, from a knowledge of the strategic value of the Chagos Archipelago as an equatorial staging area halfway between Aden and Singapore, to the distinction between the Congo Republic (Leopoldville), formerly Belgian, and the Republic of the Congo (Brazzaville), formerly French. And consider, too, the number of different political figures and the bewildering number of political parties that we have to learn about to keep abreast of the news.

For the society and the political process, there are enormous problems which arise from this communications overload. At a time when, in our psychological values, we place a greater emphasis on individuation, where is the possibility of privacy, of a "psycho-social moratorium" (a term used by Erik Erikson to describe the need of sensitive adolescents to escape the pressures of schools, career choice, and the like), and a relief from the stresses created by these incessant "messages" out of the blue? Certainly, for the year 2000 this may be one of the most urgent of all social problems.

And for the political process, consider only one image: the number of problems, terrifying in number, which automatically flow today to Washington

[9]See George A. Miller, *The Psychology of Communication: Seven essays* (New York: Basic Books, 1966).

as a political center, and the multifarious issues which the President, therefore, has to confront, and often decide upon, in "real time." Can such a system continue, without breakdown?

Rates of Diffusion

The communications revolution, while accelerating many things, has most dramatically accelerated the rate of diffusion of social demands.

The point about diffusion is the critical one for any consideration of social change—and prediction about the future. For it is not the spectacular innovations (crucial as they may be as turning points) which are the important elements in changing the social map of a country, but the rate of diffusion of products and privileges. For diffusion is not automatic. In the case of products, it rests upon certain entrepreneurial talents, and the ability to break through the cake of custom or the barriers of entrenched interests. In the case of privileges, it rests upon the ability of disadvantaged groups to mobilize political pressures. And both of these are operative only within the framework of the value system of a society.

One of the reasons why the predictions of Tocqueville, made more than 130 years ago, are still so cogent, is that he had hit upon the great "master key" to American society—the desire for equality. What has been the property or privilege of the few is demanded, legitimately, by the many. The enormous change, for example, in the character of higher education, which affects us all, is not due to any sweeping technological innovations or even the post-World War II baby boom, but to the extension of higher education from the few to the many. In 1935, for example, 12.2 percent of the (9.2 million) 18–21 age group attended college, while in 1964, more than 40 percent of the (11.2 million) 18–21 age group was in college.

Out of this same impulse, there is a constant set of rising expectations about what the society can produce. It has been estimated, for example, that about twenty percent of our people live in poverty. But this is a definition of poverty by 1964 standards. If we applied, say, 1947 standards, only about fifteen percent of the people would be considered poor today. It is the nature of the American experience to "upgrade" constantly the notion of what constitutes a decent minimum, and correspondingly to upgrade the definition of poverty. As Herman Miller, the assistant to the director of the Census, points out in his book, *Rich Man, Poor Man*, according to the Bureau of Labor Statistics, a "modest but adequate living standard" in New York City in 1947 required a family income (in 1961 dollars) of $4000 a year. This criterion rose in 1961 to $5,200—a twenty-eight percent increase. At this rate, by 1975, the new decent minimum for a family will be (always in 1961 dollars) $7,000. As Mr. Miller concludes: our standards will be lifted a little higher, our belts will be opened another notch, and there will still be a large block of families living under new and higher substandard conditions.

In seeking for clues to social change, therefore, the important task is to be able to identify which aspects of privilege or advantage today will be demanded by the many tomorrow. (More travel, travel to more distant places, winter vacations, summer houses?) And it is the diffusion of these privileges to an increasing number that provides a key to the kinds of social and political demands we shall witness in the coming years.

But changes in number also mean a change in scale. Increases in size change the nature of organizations, give rise to multiple hierarchies, introduce new problems of coordination, and pose new questions of order and planning. Students at Berkeley, for example, complain of depersonalization because of the size of the University—yet decentralization (or the creation of more universities) is not a complete answer because of the scarcity of professional talent relative to the demand. The spread of medical care has prompted the introduction of more technological devices (e.g., multiphase diagnostic screens) which, many complain, "mechanize" the doctor-patient relationship. Yet this is a concomitant of a mass society. (The other answer, increase the number of doctors, is easy rhetorically, yet difficult both because of the problems of recruiting more doctors and the long time-lag in the training period.)

The question of the size and scope of all social units—the appropriate size of governmental units, the optimal size of various organizations, the decentralization of function and the creation of a "human scale" in a mass society —is the most crucial sociological problem that arises out of the influence of number, density and interaction, and the consequences of diffusion and change of scale.

The Public and the Private

The conventional model of the economy concentrates on the private, profit-seeking center. Yet what is public and what is private, and what is profit and what is not-for-profit, is no longer an easy distinction these days. The aerospace companies are private, yet the Federal government purchases 74 percent of their entire output. All profits above a negotiated sum are returned to the government; the government, rather than the competitive market, determines the firms' profitability, and even their survival. The New York Port Authority and Triborough Bridge Authority are non-profit public corporations, yet they make enormous profits, which are reinvested in new enterprises far beyond the original charter of these corporations. In practical effect, they differ little from private utilities who pay off a fixed sum of their indebtedness as interest charges and use profits for reinvestment. The Battelle Institute is a not-for-profit research foundation; the Arthur D. Little Company is profit seeking; yet the activities of the two are quite similar. (Battelle did the experimental and development work on xerography and now reaps large royalties; Arthur D. Little does a considerable amount of public service work at no fee.) Mutual insurance companies and mutual savings banks are not-for-profit, yet their dividends, interest rates, salaries, and practices are virtually identical with capital stock insurance companies and savings banks. The University of California at Berkeley is a state university, yet receives large amounts in corporate gifts and other private giving. Columbia University is a private school, yet more than half of its annual $100 million budget comes from Federal contracts and grants. The medical and health service field, the largest "growth industry" in the country, is a commingling of private, profit, non-profit, and government activities.

If one looks at the not-for-profit sector as a whole, taking into account the wide range of government, educational, and health services, the striking fact is that about one-fourth of G.N.P. and "not less than one-third and possibly almost two-fifths of all employment is accounted for by the activities of that sector"[10] In the 1950–1960 decade, in fact, nine of every ten *new* jobs added to the economy was generated in the not-for-profit sector—i.e., by the vastly enlarged role of the Federal government in connection with the cold war, the expanded activities of state and local governments in providing community services, and the growths of the education and health and welfare fields.

The growth of the not-for-profit sector brings into focus, as employers of significant amounts of manpower, a whole array of organizations whose structure and form differ to a considerable extent from the usual model of "bureaucracy." These are universities, research laboratories, hospitals, community welfare organizations and the like. The "received" doctrine, as drawn from Max Weber, and accepted by most students of stratification theory, posit a bureaucracy as having a division of labor based on functional specialization, a well-defined hierarchy of authority, impersonal, 'bureaucratic' rules of behavior, and the like. This is the "ideal type" model which is often best exemplified in business corporate structure. Yet the variety of new kinds of organizations that are emerging (particularly ones with a high component of technical and research personnel) indicate that the older models, patterned on pyramidal structures, may no longer be applicable, and that in the coming decades the "traditional" bureaucratic form will have given way to organizational modes more adaptive to the needs for initiative, free time, joint consultation and the like. The emergence of new structural forms of non-bureaucratic organization is one more item on the long agenda of new problems for the post-industrial society.

A System of Social Accounts

The development of national economic accounting provides us with an instructive picture of the workings of a modern economy. There are, at present, for example, four types of accounting systems which allow us to measure different kinds of economic phenomena and transactions: (a) National Income and Product Accounts sum up the total value of goods and services trans-

---

[10]These and subsequent figures are taken from Ginzberg, Hiestand and Reubens, *The Pluralistic Economy* (New York: McGraw-Hill, 1965).

acted in the economy and the allocation of net income among households, governments, business, and foreign units; (b) National Moneyflow Accounts trace the flow of funds between financial and non-financial units, including households and government; (c) National Interindustry Accounts set forth the value of purchases and sales of goods and services between variously "disaggregated" units of business, government, household and foreign sectors; (d) National Wealth Accounting, in effect a national assets inventory, evaluates the reproducible assets and resources of the nation.

Yet these and other economic concepts, particularly the now familiar Gross National Product, are limited in their use, and sometimes—more by popular opinion than by professional economists—give us a distorted picture of the social economy. GNP measures the sum total of goods and services transacted within the *market* economy. It is immediately apparent that services performed within a household—by a wife, for example—are not "valued." (The British economist A. C. Pigou, a pioneer of welfare economics, once remarked that if a widowed vicar paid his housekeeper a weekly wage, this was an addition to the national income; if he married her, it became a subtraction.) The point at stake is that "income" in rural areas (where a substantial amount of food may be produced at home) is often "under-valued" as against urban income—a fact neglected not only in some discussions about poverty in the U.S., but in the international comparisons between the U.S. and some well-to-do-agrarian countries, (e.g., Denmark, New Zealand) who, on the scale of GNP, rank lower than their real income would put them.

Moreover, if national income is understated by considering GNP alone, the sense of progress can be exaggerated by the "additive" nature of GNP accounting. Thus, when a factory is built, the new construction and the new payroll are an addition to the GNP. If, at the same time, the factory pollutes a stream and builds a filtration plant to divert the wastes, these expenditures, too, become an addition to the GNP.[11] True, more money has indeed been spent in the economy; but the gross addition simply masks an "offset cost," not a genuine contribution to economic progress. The definition of what is an addition and what is an offset clearly is a difficult task, but one insufficiently recognized in the popular discussion of national economic accounting, and in the widespread acceptance of GNP as a "welfare" or "growth" measuring device.

---

[11] In a similar vein, Victor Fuchs of the National Bureau of Economic Research, in writing of the expansion of the service sector of the economy, remarks: "There has been a presumption [among economists] that the more highly developed the economy the more useful the [real GNP as a] measure becomes. . . . But the trend may now be in the other direction, because at very high levels of GNP per capita, a large fraction of productive effort is devoted to the services (where real output is very difficult to measure) and to other activities (that are not measured at all)." Among the activities that are not measured today, in fact, are many government services, since these cannot be valued at market prices.

One can have a meaningful sense of progress only by knowing its costs, direct and indirect. A difficulty in national economic accounting today is that of assigning the costs generated by one group which often are borne by others (e.g., the costs to the community of strip mining, gouging out a countryside).[12] But the problem is not one that can be handled on an *ad hoc* basis. We need a broader cost matrix.

In effect, what we need is a System of Social Accounts which would broaden our concept of costs and benefits, and put economic accounting into a broader framework. The eventual purpose would be to create a "balance sheet" that would be useful in clarifying policy choices.

What would a system of social accounts allow us to do? The word "accounts," as it stands now, is perhaps a misnomer. Sociologists have been able to establish few completely consistent sets of relationships (such as the relationship, say, between unemployment and delinquency). Even where sophisticated social analysis can establish relationships, it is difficult to establish these in measurable terms. But we can begin by seeking to establish a conceptual framework.

A System of Social Accounts would begin with a series of social indicators that would give us a broader and more balanced reckoning of the meaning of economic progress as we know it. This effort to set up a System of Social Accounts would move us toward four goals:

a. the measurement of the social costs and net returns of innovations,
b. the measurement of social ills (e.g., crime, family disruption),
c. the creation of "performance budgets" in areas of defined social needs (e.g., housing, education),
d. indicators of economic opportunity and social mobility.

The following elaboration of the four problems referred to above is meant to be merely illustrative.

(a) Social Costs and Net Return: Technological advances create new investment opportunities. These investments are expected to be paid for by the enhanced earnings they produce. But clearly there are losses as well. The major loss is the unemployment created by technological change, particularly in those instances where the advanced age of the worker of the particular

---

[12]A "far-out," but still telling, example is that of New York City, which in order to reduce the "costs" of snow removal no longer hires additional private trucks to cart away the snow but has its sanitation department push the snow into the middle of the busy streets where passing taxis, buses and cars grind it into slush that is then hosed down the sewers. The city reduced its costs, but the amount of slush which splattered on the trousers, coats, and dresses of the passersby increased the cleaning and dyeing bills in the city by a substantial amount. From the point of view of the city and the cleaning industry there was a distinct gain; but this surely was an "irrational" way of distributing the extra costs involved.

skill that is displaced makes it difficult for him to find new employment. Or, a new plant in an area may create new employment opportunities, yet its by-products—water pollution and air pollution—may create additional costs for the community. Long ago, Professor A. C. Pigou demonstrated, in his *The Economics of Welfare*, that there is frequently a divergence between the private cost borne by an entrepreneur and the social costs. Into the cost account of the private entrepreneur goes only those items for which he has to pay, while such items as maintenance of the unemployed, provisions for the victims of industrial accidents or occupational diseases, costs of access roads, etc., are borne, in the old phrase of J. M. Clark, as "social overhead costs."

The question of which costs should be borne by the firm and which by the community is clearly a matter of public policy. Increasingly, for example, firms responsible for polluting the waters of a river are asked to bear the costs of filtration. The Ruhr, flowing through West Germany's most dense industrial region, is at present less polluted than it was twenty years ago. Swimming and boating are commonplace. This happy circumstance is the result of a cooperative arrangement between 259 municipalities and 2,200 industries along the river who have developed a system of effluent fees calculated to encourage the construction of waste disposal systems. In this case the entire cost of pollution is assigned to the source. On the other hand, certain costs of severance pay or maintenance of an older labor force on a firm's payroll may be so huge as to inhibit the introduction of useful technological devices, and such costs might more efficiently be borne by the community than by the firm itself. But these questions of public policy can only be decided when we have a clearer picture of the actual social costs and returns of particular innovations.[13]

(b) The Measurement of Social Ills: Every society pays a huge price for crime, juvenile delinquency, and disruption of the family. The costs of child care and mental health are also high. There are no simple causes, such as unemployment, of such social ills. Yet such ills and social tensions do, in a measurable way, have significant effects on the economy (from loss of able-bodied workers because of mental illness, to direct losses of property because of thefts and riots). Although data on crime, on health, dependent children and the like are collected by U.S. Government agencies, there is rarely any effort to link these problems to underlying conditions; nor is there a full

---

[13]Andrew Shonfield, in his book *Modern Capitalism*, points out that the construction of a new subway line in London was held up for over a decade on the premise that it couldn't pay its way—until someone demonstrated that the secondary benefits resulting for the people *not* using the line (in speeding taxi and private vehicular flow and the like) would result in a true return on investment which was 10 percent over the capital cost of the project. Andrew Shonfield, *Modern Capitalism* (Oxford University Press, 1965), pp. 227–229.

measure of the cost of these ills. Systematic analysis of such data might suggest possible courses of remedial action.

(c) *Performance Budgets*: The American commitment is not only to raise the standard of living, but to improve the quality of life. But we have few "yardsticks" to tell us how we are doing. A system of social accounts would contain "performance budgets" in various areas to serve as such yardsticks. A national "housing budget," for example, would indicate where we stand in regard to the goal of a "decent home for every American family." It would also enable us to locate, by city and region, the areas of greatest needs and so provide the basis for effective public policy. A series of community health indices would tell us how well we are meeting the needs of our people in regard to adequate medical care.

(d) *Indicators of Economic Opportunity and Social Mobility*: More than twenty-five years ago, in *An American Dilemma*, Gunnar Myrdal wrote: "We should . . . have liked to present in our study a general index, year by year or at least decade by decade, as a quantitative expression of the movement of the entire system we are studying: the status of the Negro in America. . . . But the work of constructing and analyzing a general index of Negro status in America amounts to a major investigation in itself, and we must leave the matter as a proposal for later research."

Two decades later, we still have no "general index" of the status of the Negro in America. In a strict methodological sense, no "comprehensive indexes" are perhaps possible; but we *can* assemble specific indicators. Thus, where once it seemed impossible to conceive of a "value" figure for "human assets," the creation of recent years of a "lifetime-earning power index" gives us a measure to reflect the improvements in income which come with increased education, improvement in health, and reduction of discrimination. And economists have a term, "opportunity costs," which allows us to calculate not only direct costs but also the gains foregone from the use of those resources elsewhere.

This approach derives from a proposition: American society would be in a better position to appraise its achievements, its needs, and its shortcomings by being able to specify broad national goals and national priorities. This proposition itself rests on the underlying assumption that we remain a democratic polity capable of peaceful bargaining and trade-off between groups, as well as being able to shape a political rationality which subordinates technique to consensual ends.

11

Political Futures

FRIENDLY FASCISM: A MODEL FOR AMERICA

● *bertram gross*

Today, in the 1970's, it is easy to talk about the dangers of repression in America. "Hard-hats," Birchers, police extremists, and George Wallace are viewed with alarm as the cutting edge of a new repression. Left-wingers and Black militants are solemnly warned that extremism in opposition to war or on behalf of justice will trigger repressive action. But it is much harder to analyze the nature of the repression we fear. It is extremely difficult to face up to the question, "*Could a new-style fascism happen here?*"

There are many reasons for this difficulty.

First, the media have focused much more on left-wing dissidents than on the more widespread activities of right-wing subversives, particularly those within the citadels of formal governmental authority.

Second, the terms "fascist" and "fascism" have at times been used by the Black Panthers and others as quick terms of abuse—without the conceptual foundations that might make the labels stick.

Above all, most of us have lost what Gunther Anders[1] calls the "courage to fear"! For a quarter of a century, under the threat of nuclear annihilation, we have been developing our ability to repress justified fear. If it seems there's nothing to be done, why think about the unthinkable—either the nuclear holocaust or the fascist horror?

Today, as Anders has suggested, we must strive not so much for the freedom from *fear* as for the freedom *to* fear. We need greater capacity to develop articulated fears that match the magnitude of tomorrow's dangers. We must accept *the possibility that in this decade our America—despite all that we may love or admire in it—may have a rendezvous with fascism.* And we must be aware that if fascism comes to the United States, as Huey Long suggested back in the 1930's, it will come under the slogans of democracy and 100 percent Americanism; it will come in the form of an advanced technological society, supported by its techniques—a techno-urban fascism, American style.

"Flabby" Futurism

"If repression is not yet as blatant or as flamboyant as it was during the McCarthy years," wrote Henry Steele Commager[2] in a recent article, "it is in many ways more pervasive and more formidable. For it comes to us now with official sanction and is imposed upon us by officials sworn to uphold

[1] Gunther Anders, "Theses for the Atomic Age," *The Massachusetts Review* (Spring 1962), pp. 493–505.

[2] Henry Steele Commager, "Is Freedom Dying in America?" *Look*, July 14, 1970.

the law: the Attorney General, the FBI, state and local officials, the police and even judges." Vice President Spiro Agnew's proposal to "separate [the protest leaders] from our society—with no more regret than we should feel over discarding rotten apples from a barrel" is described by Commager as "precisely the philosophy that animated the Nazis." He concluded that "it would be an exaggeration to say that the United States is a garrison state, but none to say that it is in danger of becoming one."

The idea of a "garrison state" has thus far been the most explicit model for examining future political developments in a grand style. First described in 1941 by Harold Lasswell, a garrison state is defined as a military-police society that differs from previous military dictatorships in three ways:

- It integrates militarism and modern technology.
- It continues to use the symbols of "mystic democracy" while promoting a deep and general sense of participation in the total enterprise of the state.
- It suppresses or controls legislative assemblies and opposition political parties.[3]

Reviewing the subject in 1965, Lasswell restated his earlier judgment that we are entering a world of garrison states, a "world of ruling castes (or a single caste) learning how to maintain ascendancy against internal challenge by the ruthless exploitation of hitherto unapplied instruments of modern science and technology."[4]

Most recent discussions of fascism, regrettably, lack Lasswellian vigor. William Ebenstein describes fascism as "the totalitarian way of resolving conflicts within an industrially advanced society."[5] He suggests that its principal elements are (1) a distrust of reason, (2) a denial of basic human equality, (3) a code of behavior based on lies and violence, (4) government by an elite, (5) totalitarianism, (6) racialism and imperialism, and (7) opposition to international law and order.[6] In his analysis of right-wing extremist attacks on church liberalism in America, Franklin H. Littell offers a longer list of elements and maintains that "fascism" is the most appropriate term to apply to the Radical Right.[7] But both Ebenstein and Littel derive their elements from other countries. The same is true of John Weiss, who—in contrast to Ebenstein —suggests that "the greatest potential for fascism lies not in the liberal West, but rather in the dialectical polarities even now increasing in non-Western or underdeveloped societies."[8]

[3]Harold Lasswell, "The Garrison State," *The American Journal of Sociology* (January 1941).
[4]Harold Lasswell, "The Garrison-State Hypothesis Today," in Samuel P. Huntington, ed., *Changing Patterns of Military Politics* (New York: Free Press, 1962).
[5]William Ebenstein, *Today's Isms* (Englewood Cliffs, N.J.: Prentice-Hall, 1954).
[6]William Ebenstein, *Totalitarianism: New Perspectives* (New York: Holt, Rinehart and Winston, 1962), p. 32.
[7]Franklin H. Littell, *Wild Tongues, a Handbook of Social Pathology* (New York: Macmillan, 1969).
[8]John Weiss, *The Fascist Tradition* (New York: Harper and Row, 1967).

If we look to explicit futurism, we get even less help. The bulk of "future-casting" is, of course, still in science fiction, in which scores of authors have developed endless variations on the theme of science-based dictatorships. Some are in the spirit of Huxley's *Brave New World* (1931), featuring the systematic reinforcement of desirable behavior. Others are modeled after Orwell's *1984* (1948), a society controlled almost exclusively by punishment.

By contrast, the official "future-casting" of Daniel Bell's Commission on the Year 2000 and *The Futurist* magazine is rather insipid. Both have concentrated on the gadgetry of technology and on the more trivial aspects of the social system. With but few exceptions, most of this work has represented escapism from contemporary political issues or even such "middle-range" questions as the quality of freedom in 1976 or 1984. Bell's own analysis of "postindustrialism," although opening up vital questions concerning current societal change, greatly exaggerates the power of the new "knowledge elites." Like Galbraith in his discussion of the "technostructure," he has developed a romantic fantasy that, though flattering to the egos of grateful colleagues, pushes into the background the unpleasant realities of militarism, repression, and neo-imperialism.

In my own work on postindustrialism I have thus far focused on current societal changes: from the production of goods to the provision of services, from big organizations to macrosystems, from white-collar work to extended professionalism, from metropolis to megalopolis, and the fragmentation resulting from all these trends.[9] In my work on social systems accounting, while tracing the transformations from agriculturalism, and industrialism to post-industrial service societies,[10] I have not yet explored the new "grand alternatives" facing service societies.

The "social indicator movement," unfortunately, has thus far avoided indicators of major institutional change. With support from both the White House and the Bureau of the Budget, the emphasis has been on routinized "management indicators," major attention being diverted away from "critical societal indicators" and the new concepts required to illustrate changing conditions. Wilbur Cohen and Mancur Olsen's *Toward a Social Report* (1969), submitted in the last days of the Johnson administration, dodged all important indicators of racism, injustice, police corruption, and the alienation of the young. Based mainly on outworn concepts, it studiously ignored future potentialities and goal alternatives.

Under Raymond A. Bauer, President Nixon's National Goals Research Staff aimed higher, but achieved still less. Its first goals report, *Toward Balanced Growth: Quantity with Quality* (July 4, 1970),[11] dealt directly with future

[9]Bertram M. Gross, "Some Questions for Presidents," in Bertram M. Gross, ed., *A Great Society?* (New York: Basic Books, 1968), Chapter 13.
[10]Bertram M. Gross, *The State of the Nation: Social Systems Accounting* (London: Tavistock, 1966).
[11]National Goals Research Staff, *Toward Balanced Growth: Quantity with Quality* (Washington, D.C., U.S. Government Printing Office, 1970).

potentialities, but confined itself to "safe and sane" subjects, avoiding any discussion of civil liberties, racism, urban decay, or war.

Probably the most significant hints for the study of future styles of fascism are contained in various forms of social and artistic criticism aimed at the present. For example, Jules Henry, in his *Culture Against Man*, has provided a passionate description of a culture of death, fear, and conformity. In his *One Dimensional Man* and other writings, Herbert Marcuse has identified new forms of control and repression in a "faceless," bureaucratized society moving toward new forms of totalitarianism. The "literature of the absurd"— e.g., Franz Kafka's *The Castle* and *The Trial*, or Beckett's *Waiting for Godot*— ushers us into a strange world in which groping individuals are at the mercy of all-powerful forces that cannot be seen or understood.

Techno-Urban Fascism, American Style

To do justice to the subject, we must realize that reactionary repression at home and expansion abroad, the essence of full-fledged fascism, cannot be identified by any single element or dimension. We need a model dealing with the many interrelated elements of a *fascist society* operating under the new conditions of cybernetic technology, electronic mass media, nationwide urbanism, and a new structure of world power. To emphasize the pervasive roles of modern technology and urban and suburban life-styles, I use the term "techno-urban fascism," a new form of garrison state, or totalitarianism, built by older elites to resolve the growing conflicts of postindustrialism. More specifically: *A managed society rules by a faceless and widely dispersed complex of warfare-welfare-industrial-communications-police bureaucracies caught up in developing a new-style empire based on a technocratic ideology, a culture of alienation, multiple scapegoats, and competing control networks.*

In examining these elements we can readily find similarities to the bureaucratic regimes of the ancient river valley empires of Mesopotamia, China, and Egypt and the later empires of Persia, Rome, and Byzantium. We can also find certain roots or antecedents in German and Japanese fascism, to a lesser extent in the Italian, Spanish, and Argentinian varieties, and in Soviet communism. On the other hand, the differences are rather striking. Under techno-urban fascism, certain elements previously regarded as inescapable earmarks of fascism would no longer be essential. Pluralistic in nature, techno-urban fascism would need no charismatic dictator, no one-party rule, no mass fascist party, no glorification of the state, no dissolution of legislatures, no discontinuation of elections, no distrust of reason. It would probably be a cancerous growth *within* and *around* the White House, the Pentagon, and the broader political establishment.

Let us now examine some of the major elements in the model.

A MANAGED SOCIETY

In industrial societies, the managed or planned economy was a conspicuous aspect of earlier fascism. Centralized management and control were invariably attempted—with varying degrees of success—through some system of "command economics."

In the postindustrial era, management practices (and, at a slower rate, management theory) have undergone fundamental changes:

1. Substantial decentralization, dispersion, and devolution have become the prerequisites of truly large-scale management.
2. Market-style rewards and punishments through the manipulation of prices, taxes, transfer payments, credit, and money supply have become indispensable accompaniments of direct control and regulation.
3. The Big Organization of the past has been encapsulated in the "complex": the macrosystem composed of overlapping networks of large private and public bureaucracies, trade associations, unions, friendly officials in all branches and levels of government, and specialized law firms, research groups, and consultants.
4. Macrosystem structure is characterized not only by formal hierarchy (which has received most attention in management theory) but also by multiple hierarchy and "polyarchic" forms of shared and diffused responsibility.
5. Macrosystem management, impossible through any single, central, planning agency, requires a "central guidance cluster" composed of partially competing elites performing overlapping roles in general leadership, financial management, general and special staff services, and the handling of critical problems.

Under techno-urban fascism, this style of management and planning would not be limited to the economy: it would deal with the political, social, cultural, and technological aspects of society as well. It would use the skills not only of economists but also of social and natural scientists, professionals, technicians, and assorted intellectuals. The focus of control would be not the economy, but the national society conceived of as a total system operating in the world environment. The key theme, therefore, would be not the managed economy, but rather, the *managed society*.

Obviously, this would be totalitarianism, but not in the older sense. Ebenstein, for example, distinguishes a totalitarian from an authoritarian regime on the ground that the latter (prevalent throughout history) "leaves the citizen a wide sphere of private life, in which he can still retain some of his dignity and self-respect." Totalitarianism, in contrast, means "all-encompassing control and unrestrained ruthlessness" as the "totalitarian ruler . . . seeks to dominate all aspects of life, nonpolitical as well as political."[12]

Even in the industrial era, this concept greatly exaggerated the extent of central omnipotence, an exaggeration that proved useful to both fascist propagandists and antifascist critics.[13] Under postindustrialist fascism, this

[12]Ebenstein, *Totalitarianism: New Perspectives*, p. 15.
[13]See discussion of "The Myth of Central Omnipotence," in Bertram M. Gross, *The Managing of Organizations* (New York: Free Press, 1964), pp. 65–72.

concept would no longer be operational. Efforts to control *all* aspects of life would be scotched—just as the managers of large, multiproduct corporations and holding companies long ago learned that detailed control would interfere with comprehensive control. The "total" in the new totalitarianism would refer to the totality of the society being managed rather than to the details of tight central control. Above all, the management system would be *faceless*—without a single dictator or a single party. With many rotating "faces," any one of them could be sacrificed when necessary without the system's losing face.

A WARFARE–WELFARE–INDUSTRIAL–COMMUNICATIONS–POLICE COMPLEX

Under techno-urban fascism the central guidance cluster would be a loose but enormously powerful, five-part complex extending far beyond the old-style military-industrial complex.

The warfare-business establishment, of course, would still be of central importance. A sizeable—and perhaps larger—proportion of the federal budget would still be automatically available to supply it with investment funds, working capital, pork-barrel contracts, and political slush funds. Sophisticated control systems—perceptively analyzed in Seymour Melman's *Pentagon Capitalism*—would continue the McNamara tradition of consolidating selective power over thousands of subcontractors in the name of alleged cost-cutting.[14] The symbiotic relationship between the White House and the Pentagon—which started slowly under Roosevelt and matured under Truman, Eisenhower, Kennedy, Johnson, and Nixon—would become still closer.

But the concept of a warfare-industrial complex is too limited to describe the commanding heights of postindustrialism's new modes of production and performance. Nor is it enough even to accept Melman's idea of the transformation of the military expenditure aspect of the complex into a more tightly managed "state administration." Indeed, to focus too much on the possibility of tighter expenditure management might be to detract attention from the possibility of a major enlargement of the complex itself from two to five components.

The first enlargement lies in the direction of Lasswell's original definition of the garrison state: the addition of *police*. But the police component of the complex would itself be far from unidimensional. It would involve far more than the expansion of the Pentagon's Directorate of Civil Disturbance Planning, set up in 1968, given a major role in Luttwak's *coup d'état* scenario.[15] It would include the Attorney General's office, the FBI, the CIA, the military intelligence agencies, federal-aid crime agencies, and new computer-based

[14]Seymour Melman, *Pentagon Capitalism: The Political Economy of War* (New York: McGraw-Hill, 1970).
[15]Edward Luttwak, "A Scenario for a Military *Coup d'Etat* in the United States," *Esquire*, July 1970.

dossier facilities tied in with the Internal Revenue Service, the Census Bureau, and credit-rating offices.

The second enlargement is equally terrifying, though less obvious: the addition of the major control elements in an expanding *welfare* establishment. In the industrial past, there has never been a successful empire or a successful fascist regime without a major program of domestic welfare. Under Hitler, for example, Bismarckian welfare measures were continued in new forms, accounting for a major part of the Nazis' appeal to rank-and-file workers and to the lower middle class. Under postindustrial neofascism, we might well expect guaranteed minimum subsistence programs, expanded social security, improved medical care, and enlarged housing and educational programs. Together, these programs would provide major forms of control and placation outside the area reachable through war contracts. Like William H. Whyte's organization men "imprisoned by brotherhood," millions of people would be imprisoned by the malign beneficence of an enlarged welfare state. Above all, under the combined blessings of HEW, HUD, OEO, and new coordinating agencies, ever-new and changing community participation games and carnivals would be staged to allow low-income and low-status leaders—from both white and Black ethnic groups—to work off their steam harmlessly without endangering the system.

The third enlargement—*communications*—would complete the five-part complex. This would include not only the central staffs of the major TV networks but also the wire services, the AT&T, and the FCC. A central role would be played by the new cable-based "narrowcasting" networks that will soon replace a major part of broadcasting and usher in the "wired society," with multichannels linked with almost every household and office in the country.

In toto, the warfare-welfare-industrial-communication-police complex would be the supramodern fascist form of what has hitherto been described as "oligopolistic state capitalism." Its products would be: (1) increasingly differentiated armaments (including more outer-space and under-sea instruments of destruction) that in the name of defense and security would contribute to world insecurity; (2) increasingly specialized medical, education, housing, and welfare programs that would have a declining relation to health, learning, community, or social justice; (3) industrial products to serve warfare-welfare purposes and provide consumer incentives for acceptance of the system; (4) communication services that would serve as instruments for the manipulation, surveillance, and suppression—or prettifying—of information on domestic and foreign terrorism; and (5) police activities designed to cope with the new "crime" of opposing the system, probably enlisting organized crime in the effort.

Unlike earlier forms of large-scale domination, the warfare-welfare-industrial-communications-police complex would have no single headquarters that could be seized, no central junta or executive committee that could be nationalized or liquidated, no set of orderly accounts that would keep track of all assets and activities, and no single, central, planning staff. Corporate profit-making and loss-avoidance would still be important objectives, but not within the framework of the old-fashioned balance sheet. Above all, they would be subordinated to more fundamental considerations of bureaucratic competition and system growth and maintenance as the basis for expanding power, prestige, and careerism.

As befits a complex, the social background of the key elites would be diverse. The hard core would doubtless be composed of middle-aged, male WASPs from both the older aristocracies of the social register and the new managerial "technopols." Tactical "mop-up" roles would be played by "knowledge elites," "hard-hat" storm troops, John Birchers, and "blockheads" or "know nothing" officials of the Lester Maddox or George Wallace variety. Each would have tactical missions to perform and would probably perform better if under the illusion of enjoying greater power and less subservience. Any effort to push too far or fast, however, would run the risk of quick liquidation.

Similarly, a selective sprinkling of "inferior" types would be conspicuous in middle-range positions: show-piece Blacks, Jews, Italians, Irish, and East Europeans, along with defeminized women and middle-aged "youth." It may also be confidently predicted that conspicuous advisory or public relations positions would be provided for former left-wingers of a previous generation —recanting Rudds, switching Savios, and penitent Panthers.

NEO-IMPERIALISM

Imperialism is an old phenomenon that has altered its form with changing social systems. In pastoral-nomadic societies, imperialist efforts were oriented mainly to hunting down and gathering in other people's wealth—in the form of land, slaves, women, tribute, and trophies. Under city-based agriculturalism, these efforts became consolidated in empires based on the forced import of capital. Under industrialism, imperialism concentrated on the export of capital to underdeveloped countries, the import of needed raw materials, the creation of new markets, and—above all—the consolidation of rival power blocs.

In postindustrial America, thus far, the course of empire has been more political, military, and ideological, with major emphasis on the development of anti-Soviet and anti-China blocs. The geographical orientation has been divided, some interests pressing mainly toward Europe, some mainly toward Asia or the Middle East, some mainly toward Latin America.

Under postindustrial American fascism, these cross-currents would probably be brought together in the *grand design of an Atlantic-Pacific anticommunist alliance* that would include the United States, the European Community, and

Japan—with support from the Organization of American States and assorted satellite and client states of Southeast Asia and the Middle East. Economic operations would be handled not only by the Pentagon and the largest private corporations but also by quasi-public corporations such as COMSAT. Above all, the huge American-dominated, multinational corporations and conglomerates would complete the process—the beginnings of which are vividly described in J. J. Servan-Schreiber's *The American Challenge*—of seizing economic power in Europe. With European satellites as bases and fronts, the American power complex could more easily control and exploit Third World countries in which a fully open American presence would be more forcefully resisted. Thus, the Atlantic-Pacific anticommunist alliance would become the dreaded form of imperialism long ago predicted by Rudolf Hilferding and systematically ridiculed by Russian Marxists: ultra-imperialism.

Under the banner of a *Pax Americana*, the new ultra-imperialism would seek full domination of the non-Soviet and non-Chinese world. This would probably involve successive deals with the Russians and the Chinese, in an effort to play one against the other. In the process, nuclear or biological confrontations would be risked.

MULTIPLE SCAPEGOATS

In Nazi Germany the Jews served as "societal scapegoats," as official objects of hatred and aggression. Organized anti-Semitism became a way of relieving the pent-up, hostile emotions of people in all classes and of channeling such emotions away from the harsh realities of the system. But the frenzy of Nazi anti-Semitism and the attempted "final solution" have partially obscured the fact that there were other scapegoats as well, namely, almost anyone who would not play ball with the Nazis and who could be tarred as "non-Aryan" or "bolshevik."

Under techno-urban fascism in America, the scapegoat role would be a double one: not only to divert aggressive energies and emotions but also to provide deterrents against the growth of effective opposition to the warfare-welfare state. But these deterrents, including the control networks to be discussed, could not be designed in the style of "those wonderful people who gave us Auschwitz and Belsen" (to paraphrase the title of a recent book on American advertising). Over-attention to one group in a heterogeneous society would hardly meet cost effectiveness standards. Even concentration on a few fixed groups would hardly comport with either principles of managerial flexibility or the necessity of building up an outward façade of a pluralistic, all-American, "friendly fascism."

Black people, of course, would be major scapegoats. But not *all*—as it was with *all* the Jews under the Nazis. Only Black traitors, Black criminals, Black deviants, and Black "effete snobs." Nor would there be any need whatever for costly concentration camps (despite current Black fears along these lines). Black ghettos in the central cities and in the older suburbs would serve apartheid purposes more cheaply and efficiently. Incursions across the lines into white areas would be met not only with suppression but also with retaliation.

In accordance with some of the worst of America's old traditions, there would also be a considerable amount of interethnic "scapegoatery." America's ethnic and religious diversity would be systematically exploited—the emphasis shifting back and forth between "melting pot" suppression of differences and the promotion of a seething cauldron of prejudice. Major roles would be played—particularly in the Black suburbs—by Black-Jewish conflicts, the inner-city cauldron being heated by Black-Puerto Rican and Black-East European conflicts.

Above all, a new invective would almost surely be invented—far sharper than that of Spiro Agnew recently, or of the "old" Richard Nixon and Joseph McCarthy—to stigmatize the traitors, foreign agents, criminals, and sniveling cowards among us: student rebels, intellectual protesters, and dropouts. From time to time, the official *Zeitgeist* would be revised to include additional targets. A menacing foreign enemy, it may be presumed, would figure centrally in this dramaturgy.

Old methods of pillorying scapegoats would not only be brought back but would be retooled and modernized. Security-risk blacklists would be both expanded and computerized, rating systems being introduced to calculate the extent to which each person had become a "rotten apple" and to provide opportunities for appropriate rehabilitation. Plots and conspiracies against the "public security" would be dramatically uncovered, usually just in the nick of time. Selected schools (or even specific courses or classes) would be closed down for considerable periods. Preventive detention would be extended to the "mentally unstable," who would be incarcerated in mental institutions. Finally, political assassinations would be used more widely, but with more frequent resort to presumably "accidental" means.

In its use of these methods, America's "friendly fascism" would strive for an efficient balance between the secrecy that allows large-scale action with minimum resistance and the public symbolism that can get a pound of terror from an ounce of violence. It may be presumed that a "revitalized" Rand Corporation would prepare special manuals on the staging of "optimal show trials" and on a minimax strategy for crucifying opponents without converting them, dead or alive, into martyrs.

At the crabgrass roots of various suburb-dominated states, we might also expect some state governments to assume their old role of serving as laboratories for "advanced" ideas in the arts of repression. State-supported universities would probably be among the first victims. In this way the older "creative federalism" and "new federalism" would be converted into a "fascist federalism."

A TECHNOCRATIC IDEOLOGY

Ebenstein[16] wrote, concerning the Hitler and Mussolini regimes:

> The distrust of reason is perhaps the most significant trait of fascism. The rational tradition of the West stems from Greece, and is one of the three basic components (the other two being Jewish monotheism and Christian love) that have given the West its characteristic culture and outlook. Fascism rejects this Greek root of Western civilization and is frankly *antirationalist*, distrusting reason in human affairs and stressing the irrational, sentimental, uncontrollable elements of man.

However, in this now commonly accepted analysis, Ebenstein fails to distinguish among various aspects of the rational tradition. In particular, he misses the distinction between what both Weber and Mannheim referred to as "substantive rationality" and "formal rationality." Substantive rationality is broad-gauged, transcends narrow means-ends distinctions, and deals more boldly and controversially with the good, and desirable, and the improbable. Formal rationality is narrowly instrumental and technocratic, emphasizing feasibilities and probabilities and disdaining basic human values or higher objectives.

In the formal sense, techno-urban fascism—particularly in America—would be frankly rationalist. Under it, nonsubstantive rationality would be raised to the level of a full-blown—if not authoritatively articulated—technocratic ideology. Stressing the controllable and nonsentimental, this essential component of new fascism would provide a continuing illusion of human progress in the form of new technological gadgets for killing people, controlling their behavior, eliminating mental and physical labor, and wasting natural resources. It would expand the principles of R-and-D-ology, i.e., the theory that any problem can be solved quickly, given enough investment of high-quality research-and-development hours with appropriate provisions for controlled testing and evaluation. Also, it would develop nationalistic rivalries in science and technology, with the continuing discovery of science-technology gaps that (as Russia's Sputnik once did) threaten the science-technology foundations of empire. Finally, it would provide elaborate rituals of certification, credentialism, and meritocracy. Huey Long's old slogan "Every man a king" would be converted into the more powerful "Every properly processed man or woman a technician or professional."

With such developments the two essential elements of rationality would be burst asunder. Emphasizing functions, roles, operationalism, and abstracted empiricism, the technocratic ideology would put aside rational analyses of human beings and personalities, of human groups as more than the sum or

[16]Ebenstein, *Today's Isms*, p. 105.

product of their parts, of totally new forms of social organization. With the accumulation of indigestible mountains of isolated facts, the proliferation of technical jargons and subspecializations, and declining interest in judgment, wisdom, and understanding, the new *Zeitgeist* would lead to a new *ignorance explosion*. Purportedly "value free," it would tend to be valueless apart from its vital role in buttressing a neo-imperialist warfare-welfare state. Above all, in encouraging new ways to waste resources on changing forms of overkill, technocratic ideology would carry instrumental rationality to the lowest depths of substantive irrationality: bureaucratized madness.

A CULTURE OF ALIENATION

In every period of confusing historical change and dislocation, older values and beliefs break down. In the Third Reich, an effort was made to develop a *Volkskultur* based on a mythical past, racial lies, and the social passions of a large, lower middle class. This fitted well into a situation in which millions of people were being prepared for active warfare.

Under techno-urban fascism, with different societal modes of behavior, a mass culture would be inappropriate. Active warfare would exist only on the fringes of the empire, with "coolie labor" used for most of the mass armies on the ground. At home, with huge populations concentrated in a few urban regions and huge numbers of young people in schools and universities, mass movements and mass culture would represent potentially uncontrollable elements. Under these conditions the appropriate milieu of neofascism would be a *culture of alienation*.

The major characteristics of a fascist culture of alienation would be social aphasis, loneliness, materialism, homogenized pluralism, and hopelessness. "Aphasis," writes Franklin H. Littell, in an effort to identify totalitarian movements in America, "is that condition either physical or psychological, which hampers or prevents a person from communicating with his fellows."[17] Fascist politics, he points out, would fatten on the breakdown of trust. Similarly, loneliness is better than shared feelings. The "lonely crowd" is safer than an organized crowd, unless the organization itself—as with both bureaucracies and labor unions—is designed to focus attention on career ambitions and individual grievances.

Materialist "goodies" in unending kinds and quantities would become the symbols of achievement, dissenters being subtly encouraged to fight for slightly larger slices rather than a new recipe for the pie. Every effort to develop a more humanist "counterculture" would itself be countered by profit-making or bureaucratic takeovers. The deviant drug culture of the 1960's could probably be taken over as a new instrument of conformity through "opium for part of the people." All this would contribute to a pluralistic

[17]Littell, *op. cit.*, p. 83.

variety of approved art forms—with no slowdown in the cycles of fad and fashion, but a greater homogeneity underlying the apparent differences.

The great majority of the people would be repressed isolates with very little to live for and nothing they would consciously be willing to die for. Nonetheless, death itself would be stripped of its human qualities, the victims of distant wars and domestic oppression being viewed as either nonhuman or subhuman. Large-scale violence in the hands of the Pentagon-police complex would be legitimated as a technical activity to be conducted by experts. Thus, to use the prescient words of Jules Henry's *Culture Against Man*, the new culture of alienation would lead to the "culture of death."

COMPETING CONTROL NETWORKS

Under previous forms of totalitarianism, behind the carefully promoted myths of central omnipotence and omniscience, competing systems of surveillance and espionage were invariably used to repress opposition, even to liquidate possible sources of future opposition.

Under techno-urban fascism, the range of competitive control systems would be much wider. There would be much more of what Herbert Marcuse, in *One Dimensional Man* and *Soviet Marxism*, refers to as ,"the pleasant forms of social control and cohesion," including what he calls "repressive tolerance" and "repressive desublimation."

Direct repression would, of course, be a major characteristic of the new managed society, as it is in all forms of totalitarianism. But it would be *selective repression operating through and around the established constitutional system*. It would destroy any confidence that the constitutional freedoms set forth in the U.S. Bill of Rights would be allowed to operate on behalf of any serious dissent or seriously organized opposition to the warfare-welfare-in-dustrial-communications-police complex, to neo-imperialism, to the technological ideology, or to the culture of alienation. Preventive detention, "no-knock" and "quick entry" practices, "martial law" lawlessness, and out-and-out domestic *Schrecklichkeit* would be used callously, but not indiscriminately.

The economizing on direct repression would be made possible only through the sophisticated development of indirect control and manipulation. The ordinary forms of indirect control, apart from ideology and culture, would be these:

1. *rationed welfare state benefits*, with categorical aid programs in health, housing, education, and subsistence contributions made conditional upon good behavior;
2. *accelerated consumerism*, with new services as well as new goods rewarding conformity;
3. *"credentialized" meritocracy*, with people moving from Marx's wage slavery to a post-Marxian form of status slavery; and

4. *market administration*, with incentive manipulation increasingly used to supplement the direct control of private corporations, mixed corporations, public authorities, and ordinary public bureaucracies.

But *co-optation* would be the most powerful form of indirect control. In Philip Selznick's older terms, co-optation was "the process of absorbing new elements into the leadership or policymaking structure of an organization as a means of averting threats to its stability or existence."[18] Under American-style techno-urban fascism, co-optation would be *the process of absorbing new elements into the interstices of the managed society as a means not only of averting threats but of strengthening the system.*

In the warfare-welfare components of the larger fascist complex, there would be many thousands of juicy, lower-level plums available for dissidents and rebels demanding "a piece of the action." Some of these would go preemptively in advance to those showing exceptional promise; others would be held out as prizes. In either case, choices would be available—as a well-organized vice ring allows star call girls to choose one city or another. Positions close to "the leadership or policymaking structure," however, would be available only after considerable effort and intra-system coalition-building and politicking. Often, entire organizations or subsystems would be co-opted. In what might be called "subsystem co-optation," liberal and purportedly radical organizations would be used to provide young people with opportunities to "work off their steam" harmlessly or to provide the backdrop for the system's normal compromising in the resolution of routine conflicts.

Still less conspicuously, "fifth column co-optation" would capitalize on the age-old policy strategy of the *agent provocateur*. But instead of relying on the individual undercover agent, this form of co-optation would involve the direct organization and financing of revolutionary groups that would trigger off whatever acts of violence might be needed as a pretext for quick and violent repression. A continuing task for the Hudson Institute, in friendly competition with the Rand Corporation, would be the simulation of revolutionary movements in the United States—as a guide to a variety of undercover ventures to take control of them at early stages.

Hydra-like System Maintenance

How long could mature techno-urban fascism be maintained in America?

Here, unfortunately, we have little choice but to look back at the record of mature fascism in Germany, Japan, and Italy. In each of these—with more primitive forms of domestic control—all serious internal resistance was liquidated. The only effective antifascism was defeat by external powers.

Looking at the future of a neofascist America, we find a picture that is both similar and different. One similarity is the *improbability of any effective internal resistance*. The new managed society would be like the mythical hydra

[18]Philip Selznick, *TVA and the Grass Roots* (Berkeley: University of California Press, 1949), p. 259.

of antiquity. Cut off one head, and another grows elsewhere. Strike here, and you will be struck from behind. Even organized disruption of water supply and power plants would not go very far. The system would heal itself quickly, and probably come back stronger than before.

One difference is the *impossibility of overthrowing fascism through war.* The only war that could defeat a fascist America would be a nuclear war, a holocaust from which no antifascist victors would emerge.

This brings us back to another similarity and another difference—the war-orientation of techno-urban fascism. The drive toward military conquest might not be so open as that of the German, Japanese, and Italian fascists. But the orientation toward worldwide destruction through the eventual use of nuclear weapons—whether "tactically" or "accidentally"—is unmistakable. Once neofascism arrives, the only choice would be *fascist or dead.*

In presenting his earlier model of the garrison state, Lasswell stated that he would "prefer it to be a self-disconfirming hypothesis"; I share this preference.

But in this new and more terrifying context, I cannot so readily adopt Lasswell's thought that "the master challenges of modern politics . . . is to civilianize a garrisoning world, thereby cultivating the conditions for its eventual dissolution."[19] Techno-urban fascism in America would already be largely civilianized. Indeed, as Lasswell himself foresaw in his original article, the neofascist form of the garrison state would in large part "abolish the distinction between civilian and military functions."[20]

The alternative to neofascism and nuclear annihilation, I am convinced, is far more exhilarating than minor ameliorism. It lies in the historic potentialities of human growth as mankind moves from the epoch of industrialism into an as-yet-uncharted postindustrial future, potentialities for a reconstructed world society based on more humanistic forms, ideologies, and cultures.

But any hope of such far-going social reconstruction depends, among other things, on increasing our capacity to fear. Thus, the purpose of this essay has been to frighten my neighbor as well as myself. I have tried to promote what Gunther Anders has called "a fearless fear, since it excludes fearing those who might deride us as cowards; a stirring fear, since it should drive us into the streets instead of under cover; and a loving fear, not fear *of* the danger ahead but *for* the generations to come."[21]

By itself, of course, fear would lead to inaction, spreading the intangible terror that would be the secret weapon of creeping fascism.

It is my hope that this article may contribute to a widespread discussion of neofascist tendencies in the United States, their societal roots, and their possible forms of expansion. Such a dialogue will unquestionably reveal that older styles of antifascism are obsolete and that we need new-style antifascist strategies, tactics, and coalitions.

[19]Lasswell, "The Garrison-State Hypothesis Today."
[20]Lasswell, "The Garrison State."
[21]Gunther Anders, *op. cit.*

12

Alternative Planning Systems

ON COPING WITH COMPLEXITY: URBAN
PLANNING AND POLITICS IN 1976

● *donald n. michael*

One forecast regarding the cities in 1976 can be made with considerable assurance: The requirements for urban improvement, perhaps even for urban
survival, will embroil city governments in extensive efforts at long-range
planning.[1]

It is becoming increasingly clear that no major social task can be realized
with less than a decade or more of sustained organized effort directed at the
realization of specific goals, whether they be pollution control, elimination of
ghettos, mass transit, adequate education, or building new cities. Because
human lives are what will be changed, the risks that can be taken in leap-
frogging to the attainment of hardware goals are not ethically acceptable.

Long-range planning will be an unprecedentedly complex activity because
the urban condition is complex and planning technology is increasingly using
sophisticated economic and social theory, applied through systems analysis,
program planning and budgeting, and the like. Since knowledge of this sort
will be the basis for city management, it will also be central to attaining and
maintaining political and bureaucratic power.

These circumstances presage new problems. In brief, long-range planning
requires continuity and some unknown degree of stability to reap its fruits,
but at the same time small percentages of the population will increasingly
have the ability or inclination to upset or to perturb the "system." Planners
and those responsible for managing the city will tend to do what they can to
prevent their long-range plans from being upset. More often than not, this
will involve partisan interpretations to the public of the purposes and prospects of the planning goals and their implementation. Given the complexity
of both the planning process and the urban situation, the citizen will probably be unable to find out the implications of pursuing one plan rather than
another. His option then will be disrupting protest, political withdrawal, or
ritual participation. None of these will be satisfactory if we want both democracy and long-range planning. A partial solution would be for the citizen to
be able to react to the plans in their full content and intent; he would
thereby appreciate what is going on and the possible consequences of the
changes. Such a process would not save plans from being changed, but plans

---

[1]The concept of long-range planning used here subsumes both the formulation of desired
end states and the design and implementation of the means for getting from here to
there. It thus includes procedures for revising the means and for re-evaluating the ends
as the program evolves over time. It is, thereby, responsive rather than rigid and, as such,
is much harder to formulate, but more likely to be socially justifiable and feasible.

should be designed to be altered as the pertinent context evolves. Nor would such knowledge eliminate politics or passion. It would, however, increase the chances of choosing and revising plans on the basis of truly shared knowledge and interpretations about urban realities. In addition to those conventionally anticipated uses of the computer for coping with urban complexity, it could provide prerequisites for such new forms of citizen participation in democratic governance.[2]

By 1976, the population of urban environments will be so large that even small percentages will represent politically and socially significant numbers of people. Moreover, the level of communications and physical mobility will be so great that even low-probability events will occur often enough to be politically and socially significant. Indeed, low-probability events will increase simply because the larger variety of collectives will provide a greater variety of actions and interactions.

The sit-in desegregation of the South, the Columbia demonstrations, the nationwide rioting in the ghettos, and the disruptiveness of protesting ad hoc groups in general all testify to the perturbing effects of very small percentages of the population. Small percentages have, of course, made big changes in the past, even when their numbers were also small. But high rates of communication and mobility and the greater numbers involved will mean that the consequences of particular actions will multiply and that these consequences will be felt in more diverse ways more quickly than in the past. Moreover, such actions will encourage further activity, thereby compounding the complications in responding to and coping with the urban scene in some coherent manner.

Meeting such demands, or simply cooling them, will become all the more complex (though perhaps more tractable, in some cases) because increased mobility and communications will facilitate their interaction and emphasize priority and resource conflicts and resolutions among them. Moreover, because the density of the human and physical environment will be so great, the number of low-probability events that do happen will increase. There will simply be more opportunities for such low-probability events to occur: power blackouts, tankers decimating shorelines with accidentally spilled cargo, assassinations, thalidomide-type tragedies, lethal atmospheric inversion layers, and so forth. In 1966, for example, only 1 percent of the baggage checked with the airlines in the United States was mishandled, but that represented 1.7 million pieces of luggage!

In almost every area of social planning, small percentages will also represent

---

[2]Let me immediately make clear I do not mean on-call, "push-button" voting. This simpleminded updating of the mythology of the golden age of the town meeting or the Greek forum could only limit the range of options and the time to deliberate needed by the policy-maker and planner, and restrict them to the inadequate understanding of the "voting" masses. In the absence of a truly sophisticated and enlightened citizenry—which absence will be amply evident in 1976—such voting would result in a tyranny of the masses, destructive of the very processes it was intended to preserve.

persisting large numbers of people needing—often demanding—specialized attention: job opportunities or training for the unemployed, even if they are only 4 percent (particularly if we ever give up Vietnam-type wars that skim off the marginally employable); education efforts like Head Start (for the affluent as well as the poor); more integrated and responsive local welfare services; airport noise and sonic boom protection; and so on.

When a city was run according to *ad hoc* or short-perspective considerations, the city government could respond to the action of small percentages of the population in the same spirit. But when long-range planning becomes both the style and the necessity, these perturbations may inadvertently jeopardize long-range plans that are being implemented, or they may indicate where changes are needed in the plan's implementation. Either way, the effects of these small percentages must be incorporated into long-range programs; thus, the planning and policy models must incorporate both information about these events and conceptual schemes that attempt to discover the relation of these perturbations to the destiny of the long-range programs. The computer is, therefore, all the more necessary for the management of the city—for processing data about the present in the present, as a primary basis for planning and revising plans.

It is commonplace today to recognize the necessity for moving in this direction in order to deal more adequately with the operating requirements of day-to-day government. Crime control, tax records, urban data banks, program planning and budgeting systems, and so forth all depend or are expected to depend on the computer's data-storing and data-processing capabilities. But using the computer for long-range planning in a context of social perturbations will demand a collaboration among planners, policy-makers, and politicians that will threaten the practice of democracy. This threat can, perhaps, be mitigated by using the computer in ways we shall examine later. First, however, we should be clearer about the nature of the threat.

Its source is twofold: the increasing dependence of those with political power or esoteric knowledge and the decreasing ability of the concerned citizen[3] to get the knowledge he needs to participate in matters of importance to him.

All decision-making related to a city government[4] or made by agencies of

---

[3]Throughout, "citizen" means concerned citizen: the citizen who is politically active and knowledgeable about the objects of his attention. Also, "citizen" is to be understood as shorthand for the citizen either as individual or as represented by a group (or a spokesman or newspaper), the latter being the likely mode of expression in the kind of situation to which this article attends. The purpose of the analysis and recommendation herein is not particularly to enlarge the portion of concerned citizens as such. Rather, it is to preserve and extend the capability of such citizens to be meaningfully concerned and usefully potent politically.

[4]By city government I mean all those offices, agencies, and activities empowered by the city to conduct its affairs. It includes the mayor or manager, the welfare agencies, the planning commission, and the port authority, to single out a few such entities. By 1976, there will probably be some new forms of urban government in response to the geo-

ON COPING WITH COMPLEXITY: URBAN PLANNING AND POLITICS IN 1976 • **305**

a government has a substantial political component, even those decisions based heavily on the kinds of information the computer and its human adjuncts provide. Any political decision is made with the intent of preserving or expanding the base of power, command, control, and influence of the organization or persons involved. Mayors, authorities, chiefs or commissioners of this and that do not choose to weaken their personal power, nor do their organizations deliberately act so as to lose control over their traditional mandates.

In the urban world of 1976 that control, that power, will increasingly be based on access to and control of information and the means for generating new knowledge out of it. Information will provide an increasingly potent basis for "adjusting" the outside world so that it is compatible with the survival and growth aims of the agency and for internally adjusting the agency so that it can respond to what it perceives as pertinent to it in the evolving complex environment. This is not a new situation; organizations have always acted to monopolize the knowledge they need for influence and for control of decisions and their implementation even when the knowledge served essentially a ritualistic or rationalizing purpose rather than as a realistic efficient basis for choosing options.[5]

But the situation takes on significant new aspects when the computer provides an improved basis for choosing among options. Then the politician (and I include the agency chief and the advocate planner), working in tandem with his technological advisers and program designers, is in a position to put forth interpretations of "urban reality," programs to deal with it, and evaluations of those programs as implemented based on knowledge either unavailable to those who might challenge him or unavailable at the time that a challenge might be most effective.

This situation characterizes the way military affairs and military policies are planned and operated (for example, the Vietnam war), but it is also true,

---

graphical and functional overlapping of some cities that now are still separate, and there will be new relationships with the federal government. But whatever forms these take, I assume political motivations will persist.

[5]Numerous studies attest to this. A recent study of the interaction between planning and politics concludes that "on the basis of these five [studies of the implementation of urban redevelopment plans] it seems reasonably clear that the realization of any of the democratic values incorporated in the procedural requirements of public law were fortuitous. The extent to which these values are reflected in the decision-making process will depend on the lineup of economic and political forces outside the legal system. This seems particularly true of the goal of disinterested planning. In all of the situations discussed, including the public housing of Chicago, the planning experts were sought and used as tactical support for the political decisions. The governmental planning units were distressingly ineffective in performing the role envisaged by the law. Planning was essential to achieve the redevelopment goals, but it was strictly partisan." J. Sheldon Plager, "The Politics of Planning for Urban Redevelopment: Strategies in the Manipulation of Public Law," Wisconsin Law Review (Summer, 1966), pp. 724–75.

and will be increasingly so, in more and more domestic areas. The partisan use of incomplete or selectively emphasized technological knowledge is already the case with regard to the justification offered for the supersonic transport or a man on the moon by 1970. It is beginning to be so with regard to methods advocated for pollution control, mass transport, educational technology, and social welfare. As these areas of planning and operations become more rationalized, the agencies and persons responsible for such plans and programs will try to protect their decisions and actions from effective criticism or impedance. We can expect this conventional organizational reflex to continue to operate, certainly over the next decade or more when bureaucracies will still be dominated by those who were trained in and rewarded by the traditionally successful operating styles. And given the nature and the basis for decision-making and operations—increased social complexity dealt with through increased conceptual complexity—it will be easier to obscure the organizations' situation than it was in a simpler day unless we specifically design means for keeping these reflexes from operating too well.

No computer-based, technology-based set of options will be exhaustive. Our knowledge about the nature of the urban present, although greatly improved, will be incomplete and our theories for interpreting that knowledge will be flawed. And since more and more of the urban tasks will be long-range ones, policy-planners and decision-makers will have to commit themselves on the basis of estimates of an essentially unpredictable future. (And citizens, choosing among the options offered, will be even more ignorant because a realistic estimate of the long-range consequences associated with an option requires an evaluation of the knowledge on which the option is based.) The politician, when choosing among any set of options, will face two facts of life he has customarily shared with the voter as little as possible. The first is the fallibility of the programs and plans to which he commits himself and his organization, the inherent uncertainty about the nature and distribution of costs and benefits. The second is that, given this state of uncertainty about the future, present political considerations pertaining to the preservation and extension of his power through time deeply influence his decisions. In the conventional situation, the politician and professional could cover up these two facts of life quite well most of the time. In the future, it will be even easier to cover them up because computer-based options will, by virtue of their source, carry great weight with many policy people and voters. The overwhelming complexity incorporated into the derivation of the options will make it excessively difficult to know in what ways the politician is covering up conceptual and data limitations in the computer program providing those options.

By 1976 not all agencies will be using computer aids to the extent they might. In many situations the changeover to such rationalized methods will be too threatening to those in power, too upsetting to their definitions of self, purpose, and status for them to move easily and quickly into the new arrangements, styles, and rewards appropriate when computer aids are used for planning. Given the mixed bag of autonomous, interlinking, semiduplicative, and competitive agencies and activities that characterize the urban condition of governance and control, foot-dragging will be difficult to overcome. These "foot draggers" will, however, feel that they must give their clients the impression that they indeed know where they are going and that, in the mode of the times, their knowledge somehow derives from the approved, sophisticated "systems" thinking. Thereby, they will have an additional reason for hiding their interpretative and programmatic fallibility, a fallibility appearing and in fact sometimes being greater for their dependence on "old-fashioned" non-computerized approaches.

These anticipated characteristics of urban governance suggest that we should be preoccupied with developing not only the means for making the political system manipulable by the poor, but also the new means that will enable affluent, concerned citizens to get at the political system in years to come. Unless we do so, the citizen of 1976 may find himself unable to judge whether he knows enough about a particular proposed policy or a proposed or ongoing program to discern where his and the community's interests lie. He probably will not be able to identify the set of options or the conceptual model used to transform the data. He will not even know what data were fed into the program or how adequate they were.[6] Nor will he be able to judge which costs and benefits of the secondary and tertiary impacts reverberating out through the urban environment have been taken into consideraation and by whom. (Given the autonomy of various agencies in the urban government, he will probably be safe in assuming that some of the "interface" issues have not been dealt with or even recognized by agencies indifferent to or ignorant of them—or by those avoiding them for political reasons.) Thus, even when he is offered a choice of programs, his ignorance about the assumptions made by the planners regarding the supposed future context in which the programs will operate and eventually "pay-off" will prevent him from choosing wisely, from committing himself to a long-range risk with an understanding of what the costs and benefits are thought to be.

[6]A sense of what is looming in pertinent urban issues is to be found in the controversy over the Moynihan report. The data, the conceptual model for interpreting them, and the program options following from the interpretation have all been subject to controversy and confusion. See Lee Rainwater and W. L. Yancey, The Moynihan Report and the Politics of Controversy (Cambridge, 1967). And see D. Schneider's review of the book in which he criticizes both the political and social science premises assumed by Rainwater and Yancey: Bulletin of the Atomic Scientists, Vol. 24, No. 3 (March, 1968), p. 20.

That the report produced controversy among experts is scant comfort when we look to the future. The controversy produced as much confusion as clarification, although it was based on relatively simple and accessible data and social-science models concerning the meaning of the data. What will the situation be when the data and models are as complex as we are anticipating them to become here?

If the concerned citizen felt ignorant or impotent in the past, he could take solace in the knowledge that the capacity of organizations to change things was usually small and potentially subject to some revision at the next election. That solace will disappear, however, when the requirement for long-range programs means that many programs will have to carry on through many elections if they are to have any chance of success.

This source of comfort will be gone, too, when the citizen comes to realize that computer-aided planning and operations allow programs to have a much greater impact on the urban environment, and that the intense and wide-ranging interaction within this environment encourages secondary and tertiary consequences of perhaps even greater impact than the primary ones. Obversely, the citizen will find no comfort in those cases where he wants some great impact on the environment, but where considerations—mostly unknown to him—result in choices that have little impact. The concerned citizen's discomfort will be increased in a new way: He will know he is unskilled in manipulating and evaluating the information from which the computer-based options are derived. Not only will he realize that he lacks some of the facts; he will know that he is unable to work with them, even when he has them.

These sources of discomfort suggest the direction in which we shall have to look for new arrangements allowing the citizen a meaningful role in influencing his urban destiny. The citizen must have as much access to the procedures of social planning and evaluating data as do those in the system who propose programs and evaluate their implementation. The citizen will need this access both during the period when the agencies and the politicians are developing the program and continuously once the program is in operation. The citizen would then be able to criticize more effectively a program's quality and relevancy, and he could be aided enormously in this process by the computer.

To do so, the citizen ought to be able to ask questions such as: What were the sampling procedures used to obtain the "raw data"? How accurate and how valid are they? How are they aggregated? What sensitivity to change or stasis is lost or gained by clustering the data demographically, temporally, economically, and so forth? Then he should know which conceptual models were used to relate various data so that interpretations could be made. These models may be mathematical or logical, based on economic theory or on social-psychological theories, perhaps supplemented in part by the decision-makers' hunches and wisdom. To the extent that the models provide a basis for sharing ideas and clarifying choices, they can be made explicit in words or mathematical statements. The citizen should also know how logic and data are related in the computing program. What are to be the measures of costs and benefits? What range of economic or social variation is to be considered and how are these variations related to one another? How does the computing program emphasize or alter the meanings of the data and the conceptual model for the sake of computing convenience? (For example, one way of averaging out variations in demand for a service may indicate no special need for an increase in that service; another way of averaging those variations may indicate very real needs in certain groups under certain variations in circumstances, but whose need-indicating behavior was "washed out" in the former averaging method.) What value assumptions are operating? What goals for the plan are revealed by the methods for ranking the options generated by the computer-manipulated data? Some of the options may be generated directly by computer analysis; others may use computer outputs supplemented by considerations outside the computer's option-generating program and introduced by politicians. One way or another, the variables attended to in creating the options will reveal underlying value preferences. Are economic savings to override other social gains? To what extent is the computerized option-generating model to operate within the constraints of the private enterprise value system? Is an assumption made that inequities for 4 percent of the target population are acceptable, but unacceptable for 5 percent? Will monitoring the plan in action require data about people presently considered private? Why is this "invasion of privacy" presumed to be worthwhile?

In principle, the citizen ought to be able to look over the shoulder of the planner and decision-maker as they prepare their plans and decisions. He ought to be able to ask all the questions of the computer that could be asked by the professionals working for the urban agencies—such questions as: "What happens to the ratio of costs to benefits when I use the same data the planners have used, but another definition of costs or benefits?" "If in *my* conceptual model the rate at which average personal income grows has consequences for the larger community that differ depending on the ethnic background of those whose income is changing, at what rate will the average personal income in district Y grow compared to district Z if the proposed industry is in location A rather than B?" Citizens with different perspectives and interests than the planners and politicians almost certainly will ask questions that the professionals forgot, thereby discovering significant implications the professionals overlooked. In this way, the professionals will have thrust on them a larger set of considerations to reconcile. Few professionals will embrace this additional decision-making burden or the challenge to their professional omniscience, but the advantages of this burden and challenge are too obvious to bear elucidation here. On the other hand, it is also obvious that the professionals could be immobilized by the effort involved in responding to the citizens; clearly, means for establishing a mutually useful balance have to be invented.

Again, in principle, the means for such citizen involvement exist today, operating in the form of multiple-access computer systems in which many people use the same computer and share one another's programs, data, thinking, and solutions. Each user has his own terminal equipment for instructing the computer and for receiving information from the computer. The terminal may be an especially adapted typewriter or a glass surface, like a television, that displays information and can receive instructions from the user via a pen that writes signals on it with a narrow beam of light to which the computer responds by a visual display on the screen or by printed symbols on paper. Thus whatever numerical data, charts, graphs, or designs are used, and whatever computer programs are used, the information can be stored in the computer and displayed through these terminals and the computer can be queried from them.

Imagine, then, similar terminals spotted around the urban area in the center cities, the suburbs, and the contiguous rural centers. Each of these could be linked to the same data banks and computers that the urban planning and governing agencies tie into. The laws could be so written that it would be illegal to deny these "citizen terminals" access to any of the data that the agencies use.[7] Since agencies cannot use data legally defined as private or privileged without special permission, misuse of such data may be discovered if the computational results the citizens obtain differ from those of the agencies, even though both are supposedly using the same data and computer programs. The law could further require that the computer programs for manipulating data and the conceptual schemes that the programs presumably reflect also be public information. And all ancillary information that the planners may not store in the computer, such as maps, must be displayable for the citizens' use. Thus, all the information and methods for manipulating information available to the planners and decision-makers would also be available to the citizen. If information was privileged or proprietary, this would have to be indicated when a citizen requested that information. Means would have to be established allowing the citizen to determine the significance of that information for the proposed plan or related project. Since such information is sometimes critical for choosing among options, confrontation procedures would have to be developed.

The hunches, biases, and political sense that usually influence the planner's preferences and the politician's choices probably could not be detected or evaluated by such means. The citizen *would* know, however, what there was to know about the data-based and theoretical relationships of the issue to the options. He could then apply his own hunches, preferences, and biases and push for one option or goal rather than another. Thus, this approach would not eliminate nor reduce the political or emotional factors in the pursuit of urban goals.

This approach seems to carry with it more than just a new means for maintaining an uneasy balance between the citizen and the urban government. Because we must cope with urban complexity by long-range planning, citizen

[7]The new "Freedom of Information Act" may set the precedent here. The persistent distrust of government—not a new response in American life, but one likely to remain exacerbated in this and the next generation of concerned citizens as a result of Vietnam—should add incentives too.

participation responsive to the same methods and types of data the planners use can help produce citizen attitudes oriented to the future and preferring the long-range planning approach to the *ad hoc* and spasmodic styles that have typified the American way of dealing with urban problems.[8] Because long-range planning must be flexible and responsive to changes in the human and material environment as the plan works its way out over the years, the government must be alert to and responsive to feedback about the general environment as well as the specific environment the plan is intended to effect. With access to all the data the government agencies will have about what is happening to their areas of responsibility, it can be expected that the citizens' various interests will result in one or another group scanning each pertinent situation, alert for new data revealing unexpected gains or losses that can be attributed to the working out of one or another plan. These continuing monitoring efforts could force the agencies not only to appropriate programmatic responses to what the citizens discover, but also to collect new types of data needed for improved evaluation of the programs.

Most important of all, the extraordinary degree of openness required to operate this way could mean that, over time, the political system, including the citizen, could come to recognize error and failure as natural products of trying to cope with a complex urban environment. No longer would the government have the need to cover up: The degree of ignorance about the feasibility and implications of any program would be evident to the recipients of the program at the time it was initiated as well as all along thereafter. Knowing that some error and failure are inevitable, both government and citizen would be able to accept social experiments more easily for what they are, making changes candidly and quickly when needed, without pretending or expecting that the initial plans were more certain to succeed than realistic estimates would suggest. And no one doubts that we will have to experiment socially if we are deliberately to invent a better urban world.

Even after one discounts the large majority of citizens who will be uninterested in such sophisticated participation in the conduct of the community, most of those who do want to take part will be unable to do so directly, being untrained in the statistical, social, and technological concepts involved in querying and interpreting the computer outputs. Specialists will be needed to do this, people who see the issue writ large, who can play with data, who see what is and is not in a computer program, who can invent alternative programs, who can sense the ethical and social problems and opportunities implicit in the planning options. Although the individual citizen can usefully contribute to the elucidation of some of these issues on the basis of his own

[8]While it is not obvious to all planners—and this is another reason for the approach proposed here—most of us would agree that there is much more to the human and urban condition than can be encompassed in computer-assisted long-range planning. But unless *this* planning activity succeeds, it is hard to see how the more ineffable and, quite possibly, more important aspects of living can be realized in the world of 1976.

circumstances, much of what he will need to transform his concerns into decisive queries to the information system will have to be provided by specialists. Analogous roles are filled today by lawyers, crusaders like Nader and Carson, some theologians, advocate planners, and even an occasional systems analyst, technologist, or scientist caught up in an urban issue that impinges directly on him. But the present roles are not refined enough to provide a readily accessible resource for linking citizens with computers.

A more specific delineation of specialties will be needed to implement the proposed system. These would provide the functional equivalent of the "shadow" planning, policy-making, and program-evaluation agencies of urban government. These specialists, retained by citizen groups, could be individuals or consulting firms that do not take government contracts and thus avoid conflicts of interest. The affluent ought to be able to pay for some services. As mobility and affluence increase, their interests in overlapping issues in non-overlapping geographic locales should also increase.[9]

The poor or the less affluent will need subsidization in this area much as we are beginning to provide them with legal services and other professional aid services. Perhaps foundations will help; the U.G.F., for example, might include such services among its worthy causes. Perhaps specialists could contribute their services part time as some do now in other activities. Universities might find some answers to their presently fumbling search for relevancy by providing such services on a nonpartisan basis. Their faculty members could raise the questions, pose alternative conceptual models and computer programs, and interpret findings in the light of their expertise. Just as universities encourage faculty members to consult in conventional ways, they might also encourage this sort of service, compensating their faculty members accordingly. Political parties might find ways of matching the interests of citizens and party by supporting particular efforts, publicizing the results, and using political leverage to get the alternatives attended to.

For those who want to participate in the political process, the opportunity to challenge the system or to support it on the basis of knowledge as the government develops its own position and then to monitor and criticize continuously the implementation of whatever policy prevails should be a heady incentive for extensive use of such computer facilities. But the approach proposed here involves no casual laying-on of minor modifications in the conduct of urban government. Opening up the information base of political decision-making would be one of the most painful wrenches conceivable for conventional styles of governing. Those now involved who have devised

---

[9]Consider the nationwide membership of the Sierra Club as a prototype response. The growing number of people who spend substantial time in more than one city may come to see proposals for pollution control and crime reduction as important for them to judge in one place as in another. They will not be able to vote in both places, but they may well be able to influence policy and programs—and votes—by helping to defray the costs of citizen computer terminal services.

over their political lifetimes elaborate strategies for maintaining operational power and a complimentary personal self-image would find themselves naked, having to armor themselves anew and in new ways. Many simply could not do this, and many will fight such an approach with the cunning and commitment elicited by threats to survival. As a result, the scheme proposed here would hardly be in fully effective use in any urban area by 1976. Political and dollar costs and the technical complexity of installing citizen terminals might be too great for more than a few experimental terminals to be operating. Moreover, the numbers and types of experts available to aid citizens might be too small to man more than a few terminals. Perhaps the most that can be done is to ensure that citizens have access to the computer in the offices of the planners so that they can query the computer there during periods when the planners are legally obligated to free it for citizen use.

Indeed, it is not at all clear that this scheme would, in fact, realize its goal: more vigorous and knowledgeable participation by even a small percentage of the population. Citizens doing the same sorts of professional-political thinking and feeling as those legally empowered to run the government full time may turn out to be as destructive of a workable democracy as citizens not participating meaningfully. We shall have to experiment over many years to discover if we can have *both* long-range planning and democracy—that is, if we can have a viable, complex, huge, and dignifying urban condition. Thus, an approach such as this to inventing mutual urban and democratic viability must be attempted, and we had better have made a good start in this direction by 1976. We really have no choice in the matter if we wish to maintain the reality of democracy. If one expects that the conventional political system will fight computer-based long-range planning or exploit it in order to preserve conventional political power, then one must expect that those who plan and decide for urban government will try to do so ever more protected behind impenetrable barriers of complexity. In that case, the citizen would be less and less able to assess the implications of what the government proposes in his best interest. Being unable to assess his interest, he would be forced either to abdicate political participation based on a knowledgeable assessment of the situation or to accept out of ignorance what the planners and politicians offer him. And in the urban world of 1976 these alternatives would, I hope, be unacceptable.

13

Beyond Bureaucracy:
Organizational Forms

THE COMING AD-HOCRACY

● *alvin toffler*

One of the most persistent myths about the future envisions man as a helpless cog in some vast organizational machine. In this nightmarish projection, each man is frozen into a narrow, unchanging niche in a rabbit-warren bureaucracy. The walls of this niche squeeze the individuality out of him, smash his personality, and compel him, in effect, to conform or die. Since organizations appear to be growing larger and more powerful all the time, the future, according to this view, threatens to turn us all into that most contemptible of creatures, spineless and faceless, the organization man.

It is difficult to overestimate the force with which this pessimistic prophecy grips the popular mind, especially among young people. Hammered into their heads by a stream of movies, plays and books, fed by a prestigious line of authors from Kafka and Orwell to Whyte, Marcuse and Ellul, the fear of bureaucracy permeates their thought. In the United States everyone "knows" that it is just such faceless bureaucrats who invent all-digit telephone numbers, who send out cards marked "do not fold, spindle or mutilate," who ruthlessly dehumanize students, and whom you cannot fight at City Hall. The fear of being swallowed up by this mechanized beast drives executives to orgies of self-examination and students to paroxysms of protest.

What makes the entire subject so emotional is the fact that organization is an inescapable part of all our lives. Like his links with things, places and people, man's organizational relationships are basic situational components. Just as every act in a man's life occurs in some definite geographical place, so does it also occur in an organizational place, a particular location in the invisible geography of human organization.

Thus, if the orthodox social critics are correct in predicting a regimented, super-bureaucratized future, we should already be mounting the barricades, punching random holes in our IBM cards, taking every opportunity to wreck the machinery of organization. If, however, we set our conceptual clichés aside and turn instead to the facts, we discover that bureaucracy, the very system that is supposed to crush us all under its weight, is itself groaning with change.

The kinds of organizations these critics project unthinkingly into the future are precisely those least likely to dominate tomorrow. For we are witnessing not the triumph, but the breakdown of bureaucracy. We are, in fact, witnessing the arrival of a new organizational system that will increasingly challenge, and ultimately supplant bureaucracy. This is the organization of the future. I call it "Ad-hocracy."

Man will encounter plenty of difficulty in adapting to this new style organization. But instead of being trapped in some unchanging, personality-smashing niche, man will find himself liberated, a stranger in a new free-form world of kinetic organizations. In this alien landscape, his position will be constantly changing, fluid, and varied. And his organizational ties, like his ties with things, places and people, will turn over at a frenetic and ever-accelerating rate.

Catholics, Cliques and Coffee Breaks

Before we can grasp the meaning of this odd term, Ad-hocracy, we need to recognize that not all organizations are bureaucracies. There are alternative ways of organizing people. Bureaucracy, as Max Weber pointed out, did not become the dominant mode of human organization in the West until the arrival of industrialism.

This is not the place for a detailed description of all the characteristics of bureaucracy, but it is important for us to note three basic facts. First, in this particular system of organization, the individual has traditionally occupied a sharply defined slot in a division of labor. Second, he fit into a vertical hierarchy, a chain of command running from the boss down to the lowliest menial. Third, his organizational relationships, as Weber emphasized, tended toward permanence.

Each individual, therefore, filled a precisely positioned slot, a fixed position in a more or less fixed environment. He knew exactly where his department ended and the next began; the lines between organizations and their substructures were anchored firmly in place. In joining an organization, the individual accepted a set of fixed obligations in return for a specified set of rewards. These obligations and rewards remained the same over relatively long spans of time. The individual thus stepped into a comparatively permanent web of relationships—not merely with other people (who also tended to remain in their slots for a long time)—but with the organizational framework, the structure, itself.

Some of these structures are more durable than others. The Catholic Church is a steel frame that has lasted for 2000 years, with some of its internal substructures virtually unchanged for centuries at a time. In contrast, the Nazi Party of Germany managed to bathe Europe in blood, yet it existed as a formal organization for less than a quarter of a century.

In turn, just as organizations endure for longer or shorter periods, so, too, does an individual's relationship with any specific organizational structure. Thus man's tie to a particular department, division, political party, regiment, club, or other such unit has a beginning and an end in time. The same is true of his membership in informal organizations—cliques, factions, coffee-break groups and the like. His tie begins when he assumes the obligations of membership by joining or being conscripted into an organization. His tie ends when he quits or is discharged from it—or when the organization, itself, ceases to be.

This is what happens, of course, when an organization disbands formally. It happens when the members simply lose interest and stop coming around. But the organization can "cease to be" in another sense, too. An organization, after all, is nothing more than a collection of human objectives, expectations, and obligations. It is, in other words, a structure of roles filled by humans. And when a reorganization sharply alters this structure by redefining or redistributing these roles, we can say that the old organization has died and a new one has sprung up to take its place. This is true even if it retains the old name and has the same members as before. The rearrangement of roles creates a new structure exactly as the rearrangement of mobile walls in a building converts *it* into a new structure.

A relationship between a person and an organization, therefore, is broken either by his departure from it, or by its dissolution, or by its transformation through reorganization. When the latter—reorganization—happens, the individual, in effect, severs his links with the old, familiar, but now no longer extant structure, and assumes a relationship to the new one that supersedes it.

Today there is mounting evidence that the duration of man's organizational relationships is shrinking, that these relationships are turning over at a faster and faster rate. And we shall see that several powerful forces, including this seemingly simple fact, doom bureaucracy to destruction.

The Organizational Upheaval

There was a time when a table of organization—sometimes familiarly known as a "T/O"—showed a neatly arrayed series of boxes, each indicating an officer and the organizational sub-units for which he was responsible. Every bureaucracy of any size, whether a corporation, a university of a government agency, had its own T/O, providing its managers with a detailed map of the organizational geography. Once drawn, such a map became a fixed part of the organization's rule book, remaining in use for years at a time. Today, organizational lines are changing so frequently that a three-month-old table is often regarded as an historic artifact, something like the Dead Sea Scrolls.

Organizations now change their internal shape with a frequency—and sometime a rashness—that makes the head swim. Titles change from week to week. Jobs are transformed. Responsibilities shift. Vast organizational structures are taken apart, bolted together again in new forms, then rearranged again. Department and divisions spring up overnight only to vanish in another, and yet another, reorganization.

In part, this frenzied reshuffling arises from the tide of mergers and "demergers" now sweeping through industry in the United States and Western Europe. The late sixties saw a tremendous rolling wave of acquisitions, the growth of giant conglomerates and diversified corporate monsters. The seventies may witness an equally powerful wave of divestitures and, later, reacquisitions, as companies attempt to consolidate and digest their new subsidiaries, then trade off troublesome components. Between 1967 and 1969 the

Questor Corporation (formerly Dunhill International, Incorporated) bought eight companies and sold off five. Scores of other corporations have similar stories to tell. According to management consultant Alan J. Zakon, "there will be a great deal more spinning off of pieces." As the consumer marketplace churns and changes, companies will be forced constantly to reposition themselves in it.

Internal reorganizations almost inevitably follow such corporate swaps, but they may arise for a variety of other reasons as well. Within a recent three-year period fully sixty-six of the 100 largest industrial companies in the United States publicly reported major organizational shake-ups. Actually, this was only the visible tip of the proverbial iceberg. Many more reorganizations occur than are ever reported. Most companies try to avoid publicity when overhauling their organization. Moreover, constant small and partial reorganizations occur at the departmental or divisional level or below, and are regarded as too small or unimportant to report.

"My own observation as a consultant," says D. R. Daniel, an official of McKinsey & Company, a large management consulting firm, "is that one major restructuring every two years is probably a conservative estimate of the current rate of organizational change among the largest industrial corporations. Our firm has conducted over 200 organization studies for domestic corporate clients in the past year, and organization problems are an even larger part of our practice outside the United States." What's more, he adds, there are no signs of a leveling off. If anything, the frequency of organizational upheavals is increasing.

These changes, moreover, are increasingly far-reaching in power and scope. Says Professor L. E. Greiner of the Harvard Graduate School of Business Administration: "Whereas only a few years ago the target of organization change was limited to a small work group or a single department . . . the focus is now converging on the organization as a whole, reaching out to include many divisions and levels at once, and even the top managers themselves." He refers to "revolutionary attempts" to transform organization "at all levels of management."

If the once-fixed table of organization won't hold still in industry, much the same is increasingly true of the great government agencies as well. There is scarcely an important department or ministry in the governments of the technological nations that has not undergone successive organizational change in recent years. In the United States during the forty-year span from 1913 to 1953, despite depression, war and other social upheavals, not a single new cabinet-level department was added to the government. Yet in 1953 Congress created the Department of Health, Education and Welfare. In 1965 it established the Department of Housing and Urban Development. In 1967 it set up the Department of Transportation (thus consolidating activities formerly carried out in thirty different agencies) and, at about the same time, the President called for a merger of the departments of Labor and Commerce.

Such changes within the structure of government are only the most conspicuous, for organizational tremors are similarly felt in all the agencies down below. Indeed, internal redesign has become a byword in Washington. In 1965 when John Gardner became Secretary of Health, Education and Welfare, a top-to-bottom reorganization shook that department. Agencies, bureaus and offices were realigned at a rate that left veteran employees in a state of mental exhaustion. (During the height of this reshuffling, one official, who happens to be a friend of mine, used to leave a note behind for her husband each morning when she left for work. The note consisted of her telephone number for *that* day. So rapid were the changes that she could not keep a telephone number long enough for it to be listed in the departmental directory.) Mr. Gardner's successors continued tinkering with organization, and by 1969, Robert Finch, after eleven months in office, was pressing for yet another major overhaul, having concluded in the meantime that the department was virtually unmanageable in the form in which he found it.

In *Self-Renewal*, an influential little book written before he entered the government, Gardner asserted that: "The farsighted administrator . . . reorganizes to break down calcified organizational lines. He shifts personnel . . . He redefines jobs to break them out of rigid categories." Elsewhere Gardner referred to the "crises of organization" in government and suggested that, in both the public and private sectors, "Most organizations have a structure that was designed to solve problems that no longer exist." The "self-renewing" organization he defined as one that constantly changes its structure in response to changing needs.

Gardner's message amounts to a call for permanent revolution in organizational life, and more and more sophisticated managers are recognizing that in a world of accelerating change reorganization is, and must be, an ongoing process, rather than a traumatic once-in-a-lifetime affair. This recognition is spreading outside the corporations and government agencies as well. Thus *The New York Times*, on the same day that it reports on proposed mergers in the plastics, plywood and paper industries, describes a major administrative upheaval at the British Broadcasting Corporation, a thorough renovation of the structure of Columbia University, and even a complete reorganization of that most conservative of institutions, the Metropolitan Museum of Art in New York. What is involved in all this activity is not a casual tendency but a historic movement. Organizational change—self-renewal, as Gardner puts it—is a necessary, an unavoidable response to the acceleration of change.

For the individual within these organizations, change creates a wholly new climate and a new set of problems. The turnover of organizational designs means that the individual's relationship to any one structure (with its implied set of obligations and rewards) is truncated, shortened in time. With each change, he must reorient himself. Today the average individual is frequently reassigned, shuffled about from one sub-structure to another. But even if he remains in the same department, he often finds that the department, itself, has been shifted on some fast-changing table of organization, so that his position in the overall maze is no longer the same.

The result is that man's organizational relationships today tend to change at a faster pace than ever before. The average relationship is less permanent, more temporary, than ever before.

The New Ad-hocracy

The high rate of turnover is most dramatically symbolized by the rapid rise of what executives call "project" or "task-force" management. Here teams are assembled to solve specific short-term problems. Then, exactly like the mobile playgrounds, they are disassembled and their human components reassigned. Sometimes these teams are thrown together to serve only for a few days. Sometimes they are intended to last a few years. But unlike the functional departments or divisions of a traditional bureaucratic organization, which are presumed to be permanent, the project or task-force team is temporary by design.

When Lockheed Aircraft Corporation won a controversial contract to build fifty-eight giant C-5A military air transports, it created a whole new 11,000-man organization specifically for that purpose. To complete the multi-billion-dollar job, Lockheed had to coordinate the work not only of its own people, but of hundreds of subcontracting firms. In all, 6000 companies are involved in producing the more than 120,000 parts needed for each of these enormous airplanes. The Lockheed project organization created for this purpose has its own management and its own complex internal structure.

The first of the C-5A's rolled out of the shop exactly on schedule in March, 1969, twenty-nine months after award of the contract. The last of the fifty-eight transports was due to be delivered two years later. This meant that the entire imposing organization created for this job had a planned life span of five years. What we see here is nothing less than the creation of a disposable division—the organizational equivalent of paper dresses or throw-away tissues.

Project organization is widespread in the aerospace industries. When a leading manufacturer set out to win a certain large contract from the National Aeronautics and Space Agency, it assembled a team of approximately one hundred people borrowed from various functional divisions of the company. The project team worked for about a year and a half to gather data and analyze the job even before the government formally requested bids. When the time came to prepare a formal bid—a "proposal," as it is known in the industry—the "pre-proposal project team" was dissolved and its members sent back to their functional divisions. A new team was brought into being to write the actual proposal.

Proposal-writing teams often work together for a few weeks. Once the proposal is submitted, however, the proposal team is also disbanded. When the contract is won (if it is), new teams are successively established for development, and, ultimately, production of the goods required. Some individuals may move along with the job, joining each successive project team. Typically, however, people are brought in to work on only one or a few stages of the job.

While this form of organization is widely identified with aerospace companies, it is increasingly employed in more traditional industries as well. It is used when the task to be accomplished is non-routine, when it is, in effect, a one-time proposition.

"In just a few years," says *Business Week*, "the project manager has become commonplace." Indeed, project management has, itself, become recognized as a specialized executive art, and there is a small, but growing band of managers, both in the United States and Europe, who move from project to project, company to company, never settling down to run routine or long-term operations. Books on project and task-force management are beginning to appear. And the United States Air Force Systems Command at Dayton, Ohio, runs a school to train executives for project management.

Task forces and other *ad hoc* groups are now proliferating throughout the government and business bureaucracies, both in the United States and abroad. Transient teams, whose members come together to solve a specific problem and then separate, are particularly characteristic of science and help account for the kinetic quality of the scientific community. Its members are constantly on the move, organizationally, if not geographically.

George Kozmetsky, co-founder of Teledyne, Incorporated, and now dean of the school of business at the University of Texas, distinguishes between "routine" and "non-routine" organizations. The latter grapple most frequently with one-of-a-kind problems. He cites statistics to show that the non-routine sector, in which he brackets government and many of the advanced technology companies, is growing so fast that it will employ 65 percent of the total United States work force by the year 2001. Organizations in this sector are precisely the ones that rely most heavily on transient teams and task forces.

Clearly, there is nothing new about the idea of assembling a group to work toward the solution of a specific problem, then dismantling it when the task is completed. What is new is the frequency with which organizations must resort to such temporary arrangements. The seemingly permanent structures of many large organizations, often *because* they resist change, are now heavily infiltrated with these transient cells.

On the surface, the rise of temporary organization may seem insignificant. Yet this mode of operation plays havoc with the traditional conception of organization as consisting of more or less permanent structures. Throw-away organizations, *ad hoc* teams or committees, do not necessarily replace permanent functional structures, but they change them beyond recognition, draining them of both people and power. Today while functional divisions continue to exist, more and more project teams, task forces and similar organizational structures spring up in their midst, then disappear. And people, instead of filling fixed slots in the functional organization, move back and forth at a high rate of speed. They often retain their functional "home base" but are detached repeatedly to serve as temporary team members.

We shall shortly see that this process, repeated often enough, alters the loyalties of the people involved; shakes up lines of authority; and accelerates the rate at which individuals are forced to adapt to organizational change. For the moment, however, it is important to recognize that the rise of *ad hoc* organization is a direct effect of the speed-up of change in society as a whole.

So long as a society is relatively stable and unchanging, the problems it presents to men tend to be routine and predictable. Organizations in such an environment can be relatively permanent. But when change is accelerated, more and more novel first-time problems arise, and traditional forms of organization prove inadequate to the new conditions. They can no longer cope. As long as this is so, says Dr. Donald A. Schon, president of the Organization for Social and Technical Innovation, we need to create "self-destroying organizations . . . lots of autonomous, semi-attached units which can be spun off, destroyed, sold bye-bye, when the need for them has disappeared."

Traditional functional organization structures, created to meet predictable, non-novel conditions, prove incapable of responding effectively to radical changes in the environment. Thus temporary role structures are created as the whole organization struggles to preserve itself and keep growing. The process is exactly analogous to the trend toward modularism in architecture. We earlier defined modularism as the attempt to lend greater durability to a whole structure by shortening the life span of its components. This applies to organization as well, and it helps explain the rise of short-lived, or throw-away, organization components.

As acceleration continues, organizational redesign becomes a continuing function. According to management consultant Bernard Muller-Thym, the new technology, combined with advanced management techniques, creates a totally new situation. "What is now within our grasp," he says, "is a kind of productive capability that is alive with intelligence, alive with information, so that at its maximum it is completely flexible; one could completely reorganize the plant from hour to hour if one wished to do so." And what is true of the plant is increasingly true of the organization as a whole.

In short, the organizational geography of super-industrial society can be expected to become increasingly kinetic, filled with turbulence and change. The more rapidly the environment changes, the shorter the life span of organization forms. In administrative structure, just as in architectural structure, we are moving from long-enduring to temporary forms, from permanence to transience. We are moving from bureaucracy to Ad-hocracy.

In this way, the accelerative thrust translates itself into organization. Permanence, one of the identifying characteristics of bureaucracy, is undermined, and we are driven to a relentless conclusion: man's ties with the invisible geography of organization turn over more and more rapidly, exactly as do his relationships with things, places, and the human beings who people these ever-changing organizational structures. Just as the new nomads migrate from place to place, man increasingly migrates from organizational structure to organizational structure.

The Collapse of Hierarchy

Something else is happening, too: a revolutionary shift in power relationships. Not only are large organizations forced both to change their internal structure and to create temporary units, but they are also finding it increasingly difficult to maintain their traditional chains-of-command.

It would be pollyannish to suggest that workers in industry or government today truly "participate" in the management of their enterprises—either in capitalist or, for that matter, in socialist and communist countries. Yet there is evidence that bureaucratic hierarchies, separating those who "make decisions" from those who merely carry them out, are being altered, sidestepped or broken.

This process is noticeable in industry where, according to Professor William H. Read of the Graduate School of Business at McGill University, "irresistible pressures" are battering hierarchical arrangements. "The central, crucial and important business of organizations," he declares, "is increasingly shifting from up and down to 'sideways.' " What is involved in such a shift is a virtual revolution in organizational structure—and human relations. For people communicating "sideways"—i.e., to others at approximately the same level of organization—behave differently, operate under very different pressures, than those who must communicate up and down a hierarchy.

To illustrate, let us look at a typical work setting in which a traditional bureaucratic hierarchy operates. While still a young man I worked for a couple of years as a millwright's helper in a foundry. Here, in a great dark cavern of a building, thousands of men labored to produce automobile crankcase castings. The scene was Dantesque—smoke and soot smeared our faces, black dirt covered the floors and filled the air, the pungent, choking smell of sulphur and burnt sand seared our nostrils. Overhead a creaking conveyor carried red hot castings and dripped hot sand on the men below. There were flashes of molten iron, the yellow flares of fires, and a lunatic cacophony of noises: men shouting, chains rattling, pug mills hammering, compressed air shrieking.

To a stranger the scene appeared chaotic. But those inside knew that everything was carefully organized. Bureaucratic order prevailed. Men did the same job over and over again. Rules governed every situation. And each man knew exactly where he stood in a vertical hierarchy that reached from the lowest-paid core paster up to the unseen "they" who populated the executive suites in another building.

In the immense shed where we worked, something was always going wrong. A bearing would burn out, a belt snap or a gear break. Whenever this happened in a section, work would screech to a halt, and frantic messages would begin to flow up and down the hierarchy. The worker nearest the breakdown would notify his foreman. He, in turn, would tell the production supervisor. The production supervisor would send word to the maintenance supervisor. The maintenance supervisor would dispatch a crew to repair the damage.

Information in this system is passed by the worker "upward" through the foreman to the production supervisor. The production supervisor carries it "sideways" to a man occupying a niche at approximately the same level in the hierarchy (the maintenance supervisor), who, in turn passes it "downward" to the millwrights who actually get things going again. The information thus must move a total of four steps up and down the vertical ladder plus one step sideways before repairs can begin.

This system is premised on the unspoken assumption that the dirty, sweaty men down below cannot make sound decisions. Only those higher in the hierarchy are to be trusted with judgment or discretion. Officials at the top make the decisions; men at the bottom carry them out. One group represents the brains of the organization; the other, the hands.

This typically bureaucratic arrangement is ideally suited to solving routine problems at a moderate pace. But when things speed up, or the problems cease to be routine, chaos often breaks loose. It is easy to see why.

First, the acceleration of the pace of life (and especially the speed-up of production brought about by automation) means that every minute of "down time" costs more in lost output than ever before. Delay is increasingly costly. Information must flow faster than ever before. At the same time, rapid change, by increasing the number of novel, unexpected problems, increases the amount of information needed. It takes more information to cope with a novel problem than one we have solved a dozen or a hundred times before. It is this combined demand for *more* information at *faster* speeds that is now undermining the great vertical hierarchies so typical of bureaucracy.

A radical speed-up could have been effected in the foundry described above simply by allowing the worker to report the breakdown directly to the maintenance supervisor or even to a maintenance crew, instead of passing the news along through his foreman and production supervisor. At least one and perhaps two steps could have been cut from the four-step communication process in this way—a saving of from 25 to 50 percent. Significantly, the steps that might be eliminated are the up-and-down steps, the vertical ones.

Today such savings are feverishly sought by managers fighting to keep up with change. Shortcuts that by-pass the hierarchy are increasingly employed in thousands of factories, offices, laboratories, even in the military. The cumulative result of such small changes is a massive shift from vertical to lateral communication systems. The intended result is speedier communication. This leveling process, however, represents a major blow to the once-sacred bureaucratic hierarchy, and it punches a jagged hole in the "brain and hand" analogy. For as the vertical chain of command is increasingly by-passed, we find "hands" beginning to make decisions, too. When the worker by-passes his foreman or supervisor and calls in a repair team, he makes a decision that in the past was reserved for these "higher ups."

This silent but significant deterioration of hierarchy, now occurring in the executive suite as well as at the ground level of the factory floor, is intensified by the arrival on the scene of hordes of experts—specialists in vital fields so narrow that often the men on top have difficulty understanding them. Increasingly, managers have to rely on the judgment of these experts. Solid state physicists, computer programmers, systems designers, operation researchers, engineering specialists—such men are assuming a new decision-making function. At one time, they merely consulted with executives who reserved unto themselves the right to make managerial decisions. Today, the managers are losing their monopoly on decision-making.

More and more, says Professor Read of McGill, the "specialists do not fit neatly together into a chain-of-command system" and "cannot wait for their expert advice to be approved at a higher level." With no time for decisions to wend their leisurely way up and down the hierarchy, "advisors" stop merely advising and begin to make decisions themselves. Often they do this in direct consultation with the workers and ground-level technicians.

As a result, says Frank Metzger, director of personnel planning for International Telephone and Telegraph Corporation, "You no longer have the strict allegiance to hierarchy. You may have five or six different levels of the hierarchy represented in one meeting. You try to forget about salary level and hierarchy, and organize to get the job done."

Such facts, according to Professor Read, "represent a staggering change in thinking, action, and decision-making in organizations." Quite possibly, he declares, "the only truly effective methods for preventing, or coping with, problems of coordination and communication in our changing technology will be found in new arrangements of people and tasks, in arrangements which sharply break with the bureaucratic tradition."

It will be a long time before the last bureaucratic hierarchy is obliterated. For bureaucracies are well suited to tasks that require masses of moderately educated men to perform routine operations, and, no doubt, some such operations will continue to be performed by men in the future. Yet it is precisely such tasks that the computer and automated equipment do far better than men. It is clear that in super-industrial society many such tasks will be performed by great self-regulating systems of machines, doing away with the need for bureaucratic organization. Far from fastening the grip of bureaucracy on civilization more tightly than before, automation leads to its overthrow.

As machines take over routine tasks and the accelerative thrust increases the amount of novelty in the environment, more and more of the energy of society (and its organizations) must turn toward the solution of non-routine problems. This requires a degree of imagination and creativity that bureaucracy, with its man-in-a-slot organization, its permanent structures, and its hierarchies, is not well equipped to provide. Thus it is not surprising to find that wherever organizations today are caught up in the stream of technological or social change, wherever research and development is important, wherever men must cope with first-time problems, the decline of bureaucratic forms is most pronounced. In these frontier organizations a new system of human relations is springing up.

To live, organizations must cast off those bureaucratic practices that immobilize them, making them less sensitive and less rapidly responsive to change. The result, according to Joseph A. Raffaele, Professor of Economics at Drexel Institute of Technology, is that we are moving toward a "working society of technical co-equals" in which the "line of demarcation between the leader and the led has become fuzzy."

Super-industrial Man, rather than occupying a permanent, cleanly-defined slot and performing mindless routine tasks in response to orders from above, finds increasingly that he must assume decision-making responsibility—and must do so within a kaleidoscopically changing organization structure built upon highly transient human relationships. Whatever else might be said, this is *not* the old, familiar Weberian bureaucracy at which so many of our novelists and social critics are still, belatedly, hurling their rusty javelins.

Beyond Bureaucracy

If it was Max Weber who first defined bureaucracy and predicted its triumph, Warren Bennis may go down in sociological textbooks as the man who first convincingly predicted its demise and sketched the outlines of the organizations that are springing up to replace it. At precisely the moment when the outcry against bureaucracy was reaching its peak of shrillness on American campuses and elsewhere, Bennis, a social psychologist and professor of industrial management, predicted flatly that "in the next twenty-five to fifty years" we will all "participate in the end of bureaucracy." He urged us to begin looking "beyond bureaucracy."

Thus Bennis argues that "while various proponents of 'good human relations' have been fighting bureaucracy on humanistic grounds and for Christian values, bureaucracy seems most likely to founder on its inability to adapt to rapid change . . .

"Bureaucracy," he says, "thrives in a highly competitive undifferentiated and stable environment, such as the climate of its youth, the Industrial Revolution. A pyramidal structure of authority, with power concentrated in the hands of a few . . . was, and is, an eminently suitable social arrangement for routinized tasks. However, the environment has changed in just those ways which make the mechanism most problematic. Stability has vanished."

Each age produces a form of organization appropriate to its own tempo. During the long epoch of agricultural civilization, societies were marked by low transience. Delays in communication and transportation slowed the rate at which information moved. The pace of individual life was comparatively slow. And organizations were seldom called upon to make what we would regard as high-speed decisions.

The age of industrialism brought a quickened tempo to both individual and organizational life. Indeed, it was precisely for this reason that bureaucratic forms were needed. For all that they seem lumbering and inefficient to us, they were, on the average, capable of making better decisions faster than the loose and ramshackle organizations that preceded them. With all the rules codified, with a set of fixed principles indicating how to deal with various work problems, the flow of decisions could be accelerated to keep up with the faster pace of life brought by industrialism.

Weber was keen enough to notice this, and he pointed out that "The extraordinary increase in the speed by which public announcements, as well as economic and political facts, are transmitted exerts a steady and sharp pressure in the direction of speeding up the tempo of administrative reaction . . ." He was mistaken, however, when he said "The optimum of such reaction time is normally attained only by a strictly bureaucratic organization." For it is now clear that the acceleration of change has reached so rapid a pace that even bureaucracy can no longer keep up. Information surges through society so rapidly, drastic changes in technology come so quickly that newer, even more instantly responsive forms of organization must characterize the future.

What, then, will be the characteristics of the organizations of super-industrial society? "The key word," says Bennis, "will be 'temporary'; there will be adaptive, rapidly changing *temporary systems.*" Problems will be solved by task forces composed of "relative strangers who represent a set of diverse professional skills."

Executives and managers in this system will function as coordinators between the various transient work teams. They will be skilled in understanding the jargon of different groups of specialists, and they will communicate across groups, translating and interpreting the language of one into the language of another. People in this system will, according to Bennis, "be differentiated not vertically, according to rank and role, but flexibly and functionally, according to skill and professional training."

Because of the high rate of movement back and forth from one transient team to another, he continues, "There will . . . be a reduced commitment to work groups . . . While skills in human interaction will become more important, due to the growing needs for collaboration in complex tasks, there will be a concomitant reduction in group cohesiveness . . . People will have to learn to develop quick and intense relationships on the job, and learn to bear the loss of more enduring work relationships."

This then is a picture of the coming Ad-hocracy, the fast-moving, information-rich, kinetic organization of the future, filled with transient cells and extremely mobile individuals. From this sketch, moreover, it is possible to deduce some of the characteristics of the human beings who will populate these new organizations—and who, to some extent, are already to be found in the prototype organizations of today. What emerges is dramatically different from the stereotype of the organization man. For just as the acceleration of change and increased novelty in the environment demand a new form of organization, they demand, too, a new kind of man.

Three of the outstanding characteristics of bureaucracy were, as we have seen, permanence, hierarchy, and a division of labor. These characteristics molded the human beings who manned the organizations.

Permanence—the recognition that the link between man and organization would endure through time—brought with it a commitment to the organization. The longer the man stayed within its embrace, the more he saw his past as an investment in the organization, the more he saw his personal future as dependent upon that of the organization. Longevity bred loyalty. In work organizations, this natural tendency was powerfully reinforced by the knowledge that termination of one's links with the organization very often meant a loss of the means of economic survival. In a world wracked by scarcity for the many, a job was precious. The bureaucrat was thus immobile and deeply oriented toward economic security. To keep his job, he willingly subordinated his own interests and convictions to those of the organization.

Power-laden hierarchies, through which authority flowed, wielded the whip by which the individual was held in line. Knowing that his relationship with the organization would be relatively permanent (or at least hoping that it would be) the organization man looked within for approval. Rewards and punishments came down the hierarchy to the individual, so that the individual, habitually looking upward at the next rung of the hierarchical ladder, became conditioned to subservience. Thus: the wishy-washy organization man—the man without personal convictions (or without the courage to make them evident). It paid to conform.

Finally, the organization man needed to understand his place in the scheme of things; he occupied a well-defined niche, performed actions that were also well-defined by the rules of the organization, and he was judged by the precision with which he followed the book. Faced by relatively routine problems, he was encouraged to seek routine answers. Unorthodoxy, creativity, venturesomeness were discouraged, for they interfered with the predictability required by the organization of its component parts.

The embryonic Ad-hocracies of today demand a radically different constellation of human characteristics. In place of permanence, we find transience —high mobility between organizations, never-ending reorganizations within them, and a constant generation and decay of temporary work groupings. Not surprisingly, we witness a decline in old fashioned "loyalty" to the organization and its sub-structures.

Writing about young executives in American industry today, Walter Guzzardi, Jr., declares: "The agreements between modern man and modern organization are not like the laws of the Medes and the Persians. They were not made to stand forever . . . The man periodically examines his own attitude toward the organization, and gauges its attitude toward him. If he doesn't like what he sees, he tries to change it. If he can't change it, he moves." Says executive recruiter George Peck: "The number of top executives with their résumés in their desk drawer is amazing."

The old loyalty felt by the organization man appears to be going up in smoke. In its place we are watching the rise of professional loyalty. In all of the techno-societies there is a relentless increase in the number of professional, technical and other specialists. In the United States between 1950 and 1969 alone, their number has more than doubled and this class continues to grow more rapidly than any other group in the work force. Instead of operating as individual, entrepreneurial free lancers, millions of engineers, scientists, psychologists, accountants and other professionals have entered the ranks of organization. What has happened as a result is a neat dialectical reversal. Veblen wrote about the industrialization of the professional. Today we are observing the professionalization of industry.

Thus John Gardner declares: "The loyalty of the professional man is to his profession and not to the organization that may house him at any given moment. Compare the chemist or electronics engineer in a local plant with the non-professional executives in the same plant. The men the chemist thinks of as his colleagues are not those who occupy neighboring offices, but his fellow professionals wherever they may be throughout the country, even throughout the world. Because of his fraternal ties with widely dispersed contemporaries, he himself is highly mobile. But even if he stays in one place his loyalty to the local organization is rarely of the same quality as that of the true organization man. He never quite believes in it.

"The rise of the professions means that modern large-scale organization has been heavily infiltrated by men who have an entirely different concept of what organization is about . . ." In effect, these men are "outsiders" working within the system.

At the same time, the term "profession" is itself taking on new meaning. Just as the vertical hierarchies of bureaucracy break down under the combined impact of new technology, new knowledge, and social change, so too, do the horizontal hierarchies that have until now divided human knowledge. The old boundaries between specialties are collapsing. Men increasingly find that the novel problems thrust at them can be solved only by reaching beyond narrow disciplines.

The traditional bureaucrat put electrical engineers in one compartment and psychologists in another. Indeed, engineers and psychologists in their own professional organizations assumed an airtight distinction between their spheres of knowledge and competence. Today, however, in the aerospace industry, in education, and in other fields, engineers and psychologists are frequently thrown together in transient teams. New organizations reflecting these sometimes exotic intellectual mergers are springing up all around the basic professions, so that we begin to find sub-groupings of bio-mathematicians, psycho-pharmacologists, engineer-librarians and computer-musicians. Distinctions between the disciplines do not disappear; but they become finer, more porous, and there is a constant reshuffling process.

In this situation, even professional loyalties turn into short-term commitments, and the work itself, the task to be done, the problem to be solved, begins to elicit the kind of commitment hitherto reserved for the organization. Professional specialists, according to Bennis, "seemingly derive their rewards from inward standards of excellence, from their professional societies, and from the intrinsic satisfaction of their task. In fact, they are committed to the task, not the job; to their standards, not their boss. And because they have degrees, they travel. They are not good 'company men'; they are uncommitted except to the challenging environments where they can 'play with problems.' "

These men of the future already man some of the Ad-hocracies that exist today. There is excitement and creativity in the computer industry, in educational technology, in the application of systems techniques to urban problems, in the new oceanography industry, in government agencies concerned with environmental health, and elsewhere. In each of these fields, more representative of the future than the past, there is a new venturesome spirit which stands in total contrast to the security-minded, orthodoxy and conformity associated with the organization man.

The new spirit in these transient organizations is closer to that of the entrepreneur than the organization man. The free-swinging entrepreneur who started up vast enterprises unafraid of defeat or adverse opinion, is a folk hero of industrialism, particularly in the United States. Pareto labeled the entrepreneurs "adventurous souls, hungry for novelty . . . not at all alarmed at change."

It is conventional wisdom to assert that the age of the entrepreneur is dead, and that in his place there now stand only organization men or bureaucrats. Yet what is happening today is a resurgence of entrepreneurialism within the heart of large organizations. The secret behind this reversal is the new transience and the death of economic insecurity for large masses of educated men. With the rise of affluence has come a new willingness to take risks. Men are willing to risk failure because they cannot believe they will ever starve. Thus says Charles Elwell, director of industrial relations for Hunt Foods: "Executives look at themselves as individual entrepreneurs who are selling their knowledge and skills." Indeed, as Max Ways has pointed out in *Fortune*: "The professional man in management has a powerful base of independence—perhaps a firmer base than the small businessman ever had in his property rights."

Thus we find the emergence of a new kind of organization man—a man who, despite his many affiliations, remains basically uncommitted to any organization. He is willing to employ his skills and creative energies to solve problems with equipment provided by the organization, and within temporary groups established by it. But he does so only so long as the problems interest *him*. He is committed to his own career, his own self-fulfillment.

It is no accident, in light of the above, that the term "associate" seems suddenly to have become extremely popular in large organizations. We now have "associate marketing directors" and "research associates," and even government agencies are filled with "associate directors" and "associate administrators." The word associate implies co-equal, rather than subordinate, and its spreading use accurately reflects the shift from vertical and hierarchical arrangements to the new, more lateral, communication patterns.

Where the organization man was subservient to the organization, Associative Man is almost insouciant toward it. Where the organization man was immobilized by concern for economic security, Associative Man increasingly takes it for granted. Where the organization man was fearful of risk, Associative Man welcomes it (knowing that in an affluent and fast-changing society even failure is transient). Where the organization man was hierarchy-conscious, seeking status and prestige within the organization, Associative Man seeks it without. Where the organization man filled a predetermined slot, Associative Man moves from slot to slot in a complex pattern that is largely self-motivated. Where the organization man dedicated himself to the solution of routine problems according to well-defined rules, avoiding any show of unorthodoxy or creativity, Associative Man, faced by novel problems, is encouraged to innovate. Where the organization man had to subordinate his own individuality to "play ball on the team," Associative Man recognizes that the team, itself, is transient. He may subordinate his individuality for a while, under conditions of his own choosing; but it is never a permanent submergence.

In all this, Associative Man bears with him a secret knowledge: the very temporariness of his relationships with organization frees him from many of the bonds that constricted his predecessor. Transience, in this sense, is liberating.

Yet there is another side of the coin, and he knows this, as well. For the turnover of relationships with formal organizational structures brings with it an increased turnover of informal organization and a faster through-put of people as well. Each change brings with it a need for new learning. He must learn the rules of the game. But the rules keep changing. The introduction of Ad-hocracy increases the adaptability of organizations; but it strains the adaptability of men. Thus Tom Burns, after a study of the British electronics industry, finds a disturbing contrast between managers in stable organizational structures and those who find themselves where change is most rapid. Frequent adaptation, he reports "happened at the cost of personal satisfaction and adjustment. The difference in the personal tension of people in the top management positions and those of the same age who had reached a similar position in a more stable situation was marked." And Bennis declares: "Coping with rapid change, living in the temporary work systems, setting up (in quick-step time) meaningful relations—and then breaking them—all augur social strains and psychological tensions."

It is possible that for many people, in their organizational relationships as in other spheres, the future is arriving too soon. For the individual, the move toward Ad-hocracy means a sharp acceleration in the turnover of organizational relationships in his life. Thus another piece falls into place in our study of high-transience society. It becomes clear that acceleration telescopes our ties with organization in much the same way that it truncates our relationships with things, places and people. The increased turnover of all these relationships places a heavy adaptive burden on individuals reared and educated for life in a slower-paced social system. . . .

FURTHER READING

For those seeking wider familiarity with policy-oriented futures research, a selection of books and articles that I have found most useful and stimulating is presented below. The literature on the future is so rich and diversified, however that for most readers of this collection the next step ought to be perusal of one of the many excellent available bibliographies in the field. Because of their broad scope and generous annotations, I recommend: 1) *Studies of the Future: A Selected and Annotated Bibliography*, by Bettina J. Huber, published as an appendix in James Mau and Wendell Bell, eds., *The Sociology of the Future* (New York: Russell Sage Foundation, 1971), pp. 339–454; and 2) *Alternative Futures for Learning: An Annotated Bibliography*, by Michael Marien, published by the Educational Policy Research Center at Syracuse, 1971.

I also recommend the following significant works:

Ayres, Robert U. *Technological Forecasting and Long-Range Planning.* New York: McGraw-Hill Book Company, 1969.

Bell, Daniel, ed. *Toward the Year 2000: Work in Progress.* Boston: Houghton Mifflin Company, 1968.

Bell, Wendell and Mau, James A., eds. *The Sociology of the Future.* New York: Russell Sage Foundation, 1971.

Boulding, Kenneth E. *The Meaning of the Twentieth Century: The Great Transition.* New York: Harper & Row Publishers, 1965.

Brown, Harrison. *The Challenge of Man's Future.* New York: Random House, Inc., 1971.

Brunner, John. *Stand on Zanzibar.* New York: Ballantine Books, Inc., 1968.

Brzezinski, Zbigniew. *Between Two Ages: America's Role in the Technetronic Era.* New York: The Viking Press, Inc., 1970.

Churchman, C. West. *The Systems Approach.* New York: Dell Publishing Company, 1968.

Commoner, Barry. *The Closing Circle: Nature, Man, and Technology.* New York: Alfred A. Knopf, Inc., 1971.

De Jouvenel, Bertrand. *The Art of Conjecture.* Translated from the French by Nikita Lary. New York: Basic Books, Inc., 1967.

Dror, Yehezkel. *Design for Policy Sciences.* New York, London, Amsterdam: Elsevier, 1971.

Dror, Yehezkel. *Public Policy-Making Reexamined.* San Francisco: Chandler Publishing Company, 1968.

Drucker, Peter F. *The Age of Discontinuity.* New York: Harper & Row, Publishers, 1969.

Etzioni, Amitai. *The Active Society.* New York: The Free Press, 1968.

Ferkiss, Victor C. *Technological Man: The Myth and the Reality.* New York: George Braziller, Inc., 1969.

Helmer, Olaf. *Social Technology*. New York: Basic Books, Inc., 1966.

Kahn, Herman. *Thinking About the Unthinkable*. New York: Avon Books, 1966.

Kahn, Herman and Wiener, Anthony J. *The Year 2000: A Framework for Speculation on the Next Thirty-Three Years*. New York: The Macmillan Company, 1967.

Kuhn, Thomas S. *The Structure of Scientific Revolutions*. Chicago: University of Chicago Press, 1962.

Lasswell, Harold. "The Political Science of Science," *American Political Science Review*, December 1956.

McHale, John. *The Future of the Future*. New York: George Braziller, Inc., 1969.

Mead, Margaret. *Culture and Commitment: A Study of the Generation Gap*. New York: Doubleday and Natural History Press, 1970.

Meadows, Donella H., Meadows, Dennis L., Randers, Jorgen, and Behrens, William W., III. *The Limits to Growth*. New York: Universe Books, 1972.

Michael, Donald N. *The Unprepared Society: Planning for a Precarious Future*. New York: Basic Books, Inc., 1968.

Mishan, E. J. "Making the Future Safe for Mankind," *The Public Interest*, No. 24, Summer 1971.

Schelling, Thomas C. "On the Ecology of Micromotives," *The Public Interest*, No. 25, Fall 1971.

Vickers, Geoffrey. *Value Systems and Social Process*. New York: Basic Books, Inc., 1968.

Ways, Max. "Don't We Know Enough to Make Better Public Policies?," *Fortune*, April 1971.

DATE DUE

OCT 7 76			
OCT 22 76			
NOV 8 76			
NOV 23 76			
DEC 7 76			
MY 4 '77			
MY 9 '77 AP 26 78			
DE 13 '78			
MR 26 '79			
OC 19 '80			
DE 13 '82			
GAYLORD			PRINTED IN U.S.A.